MUTINY

BLUE JACKET BOOKS

MUTINY

A HISTORY OF
NAVAL INSURRECTION

Leonard F. Guttridge

NAVAL INSTITUTE PRESS
Annapolis, Maryland

Naval Institute Press
291 Wood Road
Annapolis, MD 21402

First Bluejacket Books edition 2006
ISBN 1-59114-348-9

The Library of Congress has cataloged the hardcover edition as follows:
Guttridge, Leonard F.
    Mutiny: a history of naval insurrection/Leonard F. Guttridge.
 p. cm.
Includes bibliographical references and index.
ISBN 0-87021-281-8
1. Munity—History.   I. Title.
    VB860.G87   1992
    355.1'334'09—dc20   92-6616

Printed in the United States of America on acid-free paper ∞

12 11 10 09 08 07 06   9 8 7 6 5 4 3 2
First printing

Cover photo: Bettmann/Hulton. © Corbis Images

For Shaun, Shannon, Caleb, and Luke

Contents

◢

Acknowledgments

Thanks are due to many kind persons and organizations whose aid and cooperation made my task less formidable than it had appeared at the outset. They include research personnel at the Library of Congress, the Naval Historical Center, and the National Archives, all in Washington, D.C.; the Office of the Judge Advocate General, Department of the Navy, in Alexandria, Virginia; the U.S. Naval Academy Museum, Annapolis, Maryland, and, on that same hallowed campus, the Nimitz Library; the Mariners' Museum, Newport News, Virginia; and the Huntington Library, San Marino, California, to which I am indebted for permission to quote from the letters of Adm. Earl Howe. The staff of the Historical Society of Pennsylvania, Philadelphia, was courteous and helpful, as most certainly were, in the same city, Beth Carroll-Horrocks and Martin Levitt of the American Philosophical Society. In other countries the Finnish National Museum, Helsinki; the National Library of Australia, Canberra; and the Mitchell Library, State Library of New South Wales, Sydney, also gave me welcome assistance. On the British scene, my thanks go to the staff at the National Maritime Museum; the Imperial War Museum; and the Public Records Office, where naval historian N. A. M. Rodger kindly furnished guidance and useful comments.

My personal gratitude is also due the following people, who well know the measure of their help and inspiration without my stating it here: Bill Dunne, adjunct professor of history and literature, Long Island University, Southampton campus; Jan K. Herman, historian and editor, Naval Medical Command, Washington, D.C.; Douglas F. Greer, M.D., P.C.; Jack Towers; Mickey Questal; Marty Deblinger; and Mark Seidenberg. If I have omitted any whose names might have been mentioned, my apologies and assurance that their contributions were and are appreciated.

MUTINY

Introduction

The notion of mutiny, the very sound or appearance of the word, may stir the imagination in various ways and in some of us even strike a sympathetic chord. We all appear to have entered the world with an inborn readiness to flout authority, as harassed new parents, bracing for shrieks of defiance from the crib, can confirm. This instinct to rebel is only partly sublimated through successive stages of youth and adulthood, and even within the conservative souls of those quick to condemn proletarian dissent it can be aroused by such everyday annoyances as the bossiness of some local bureaucrat or the too-overbearing manner of a flight attendant. It is not surprising that in the Garden of Eden story the first utterance directed at humanity is a divine injunction and disobedience the almost immediate response.

That biblical act of insubordination is of additional significance because it occurred when the man had a mate. Down to our own time the tendency has been to concede that simple disobedience by one person alone may not properly be construed as mutinous conduct. Dating from the sixteenth century and first coined to describe open revolt against lawful authority, the word mutiny has usually implied collective action or conspiracy. Legal convention has retained this traditional concept of mutiny, especially where soldiers and sailors are involved. But the point is contestable. Even today there is by no means unanimous agreement that it takes two or more malcontents to make a mutiny.

Still more at issue is the question of intent. Mere refusal to obey a superior officer, even by a large number of subordinates, can be a far cry from conspiratorial determination to overthrow authority *and seize control*. Yet both have qualified as mutiny. Must there be violence to warrant such indictment? Can there be a passive mutiny? What if the dissidents simply do nothing? Is a sit-down strike a mutiny? Seldom has a term weighted with such gravity and threat so eluded consensus upon its true definition. In addition, accord cannot always be found as to who is the best judge of what is, or is not, a mutiny. One might expect it to be the ship's captain or army commander directly concerned. The former's dilemma is all the more acute when a breakdown in discipline occurs at sea, far from the scrutiny of impartial witnesses, for the captain alone has to judge whether or not mutiny is at hand, and cannot be sure that his or her judgment, whichever way it leans, will not be questioned when the ship makes port.

Sea captains once held the view, and doubtless many still do, that mutinous outbreaks reflect gross personal failure of officership. "Mutiny, sir!" the stern if fatherly Adm. Cuthbert Collingwood is said to have declared. "Mutiny in my ship! If it can have arrived at that it must be my fault, and the fault of every one of my officers." Another British naval notable of the Georgian era, Adm. the Earl St. Vincent, thought the suppression of mutiny "the most meritorious of all military services." Mutiny has its paradoxes, and here would appear to be one, that a failure of command contains a unique opportunity for glory. But it is that implication of failure that most burdens the officer faced by anything remotely smacking of mutiny, mindful as he or she must be of the possible disapprobation of superior officers and the damage to his or her career should it be necessary to report such incidents. And it ought to follow from this that officers in command will not use the word lightly, that a naval captain is, therefore, entitled to unreserved acknowledgment of his or her faculty, above that of anyone else, for identifying a mutiny on his or her ship. But Alexander Slidell Mackenzie of the United States brig of war *Somers* was not uniformly accorded that right when he returned home in late 1842 to report that he had hanged three men for plotting the crime. More than a century and a quarter later, neither was another controversial United States Navy officer, Lt. Comdr. Marcus Aurelius Arnheiter, when he denounced his junior lieutenants for allegedly conspiring against him. And even as the commander of a United States Navy aircraft carrier insisted before a congressional investigating panel that recent disturbances on his vessel constituted all-out mutiny, his superiors and the fleet's public affairs branch were running out of euphemisms in their urgency to steer clear of the very word.

It is an emotive one, an appellative said to carry its own exclamation mark. In the higher reaches of naval or military command there are few if any more dreaded expressions. The service establishments of major nations have gone to absurd lengths in their efforts to avoid using it in situations where officers on the scene of the trouble deemed it the only word applicable, even though such admission might jeopardize their careers. Few theories have arisen to explain this odd verbal abhorrence, the closest to truth probably that which suggests a fundamental and primarily political fear of eroding popular faith in the state's control over its fighting forces. Another reason could be the conviction, perhaps justified, among those in ultimate command that their lofty vantage point better equips them for balanced assessment. Whatever the explanation, the fact is that while mutiny has its place in formal service rules and regulations, the lexicon of top naval bureaucracy appears at times to have omitted it altogether.

The tendency is to regard mutiny as unspeakable if not unthinkable. And the instinctive strategy is to check or overrule too hasty a readiness within lower-echelon commands to pin the label of mutiny upon infractions more comfortingly recorded as trivial if not routine. Near the close of the First World War an ensign on the USS *Robert M. Thompson* ordered thirteen members of the crew to go below after they had gathered in protest against the ship's allegedly deplorable living conditions. The men refused to obey. Prompt reports to Washington cited "various mutinies" on the vessel. But by the time the case went to trial in the Brooklyn Navy Yard all references to mutiny had been expunged. Subsequent convictions were solely for disobedience, and Secretary of the Navy Josephus Daniels reduced or overturned the sentences; nevertheless, writing privately to a congressman in connection with one of the accused, he resorted to the forbidden word by calling the incident "practically a mutiny."

Two years later four inmates of the jailhouse at the Great Lakes (Illinois) Naval Training School attacked their guard with a pickax handle, stole his pistol, and fled. Recaptured, they were charged with, among other offenses, "uniting with a mutiny." But issuing directions for their court-martial, Secretary Daniels again brushed aside the allegation of "mutiny" and confined the charges to assault, unauthorized absence, and theft of government property. Not long afterward in August 1922 some of the crew of a torpedo-testing barge moored off Piney Point, Maryland, were staging a midnight party topside near the observation tower. Their refreshment, the official record states, was made up of liquor extracted from "alcohol regularly carried as part of authorized torpedo stores," and their homemade still was "a mechanical device [consisting] of one torpedo torch pot shell, some copper tubing, and an empty primer case, the property of the United States." The officer of the deck interrupted the party and confiscated a bottle. Three men tried to retrieve it, threatening if they did not to "clean out the C.P.O. quarters." They were in due course subdued. But the most aggressive of the group, locked below in a torpedo room, broke out through a hatchway onto the deck, roaring curses and brandishing a fire-ax. He was disarmed only when the barge commander, hastily summoned from business ashore, drew a pistol and aimed it at his head.

The officers on that barge felt themselves under no illusions. What had occurred was a mutiny. The wording of their report was "uniting with mutiny or mutinous assembly." As revised at the highest level, the charges remained grave enough—drunk on duty, conduct to the prejudice of good order, breaking arrest, threatening to assault a superior officer, and using abusive and obscene language. But with mutiny, once more, deleted.

Distaste for the word is not confined to the United States naval establishment. Prior to the First World War the British Admiralty, apprehensive of anything that might endanger the Royal Navy's reputation as the world's most powerful and proudest naval force, routinely dismissed mutinous stirrings or actual outbreaks within the fleet as "regrettable incidents." With the additional motive of soothing public fears at a particularly tense juncture in Britain's economic affairs, her naval bureaucracy in 1931 reported serious goings-on at Invergordon as "unrest," "disaffection," and "collective disturbance." But this episode also sharply revealed a parallel aversion to the word mutiny on the part of the mutineers themselves. It certainly appears that sailors in revolt do not, generally, like their conduct to be stigmatized as mutiny. The seamen at Invergordon described what they were doing as a "strike" and proclaimed their loyalty and patriotism with a verve reminiscent of that exhibited by their recusant predecessors at The Nore and Spithead more than a century earlier.

On the one hand, then, naval bureaucracy is seen to shrink from the use of the word mutiny, while on the other mutinous sailors self-righteously disavow it. Thus can be perceived an element of isolation in the plight of those who happen to be caught in the middle. These are the officers on the spot, who have not only to quell insubordinate outbreaks, should any develop, but court the professional risks of finding themselves alone in their unequivocal identification of such occurrences as mutinies and in their conscientious readiness to go on record accordingly. In the chapters that follow, as we chart a course through controversial if not always incontrovertibly mutinous waters, their experience will receive the same fair consideration as that of shore-based arbiters and the traditionally trusted yet forever unpredictable fellowship of the lower deck.

One

THE GEORGIAN YEARS

*T*here is no shortage of theories to explain why mutinies appear to occur most commonly at sea. A ship on the ocean is a world of its own—cramped, self-contained, and prone to a unique remoteness that modern forms of communication have by no means eliminated. Emotions born of collective discontent, which in a larger social context may become diffused, channeled, or otherwise rendered harmless, may within the close confines of a ship fester and turn explosive, especially during a long voyage. Charles Vidil, a French writer who made a study of naval mutiny, regarded shipboard life as the ideal environment "favoring the disturbance of minds, the spreading of false rumors, the growth of group suggestion." During off-duty hours men with grievances might furtively cluster on the gun deck or in the forecastle: "the many recesses on board ship make it easy for secret discussions to go on."

In this same nautical world, where command may imply a burdensome sense of parental responsibility, it is when the filial bond weakens and indiscipline threatens that another ingredient of sea command is most keenly felt, the consciousness of isolation. Capt. Thomas Truxtun's reaction to mutinous murmurs aboard his frigate *Constellation* in 1798 was to muster the crew and, "having the best disposition toward my People," read them the Articles of War— and very likely he cut the kind of friendless figure that David Porter, a midshipman on that vessel, had in mind when, reviewing his own career, he wrote that a commander of a man-of-war "stands alone . . . . a solitary being in the midst of the ocean." Somber words these, and they are applicable to the captain of another *Constellation,* twenty times larger a ship than Truxtun's and several generations later, who discovered that little more than his own inner resources were of any help in trying to quell what he if no one else would swear was a mutiny below his carrier's flight deck.

Mutinies in seafaring life have a long history. The sixteenth century produced a notable one that nearly destroyed Ferdinand Magellan's attempt to circumnavigate the globe. Stalled by doldrums off the Brazilian coast, hungry and homesick and with nothing like their commander's zeal for exploration, the crews of his five ships were ripe material for officers jealous of his command. Magellan suppressed their mutiny through a combination of force and cunning but at considerable cost in lives. One mutinous officer was stabbed to death, another was beheaded, and Magellan left his principal rival, Juan de Cartagena, marooned on land where survival or rescue was unlikely. The great explorer himself died in the Philippines, and it was a mutineer he had pardoned, Juan Sebastian del Cano, who completed the global voyage for him in the *Victoria,* which was by that homecoming year of 1522 the only vessel left of Magellan's little fleet.

The many fatalities that befell another celebrated voyage around the world, Adm. George Anson's in the years 1740–44, were not caused by scurvy alone. When one of his ships, the *Wager,* foundered off the Chilean coast, most of her crew turned on the captain. After he had shot a rebellious midshipman, the mutineers stole off with the best of the surviving ship's boats and left him stranded with a loyal handful. For Britain's navy, that episode alone might have served as a reminder that in a period of unprecedented naval expansion and activity, problems of morale and discipline were ever likely to grow in magnitude and complexity. But there had been other instances. At the close of the seventeenth century three ratings of the man-of-war *Speedwell* tried to take over the ship and turn pirates. They were seized, and the leader was hanged, the others flogged through the fleet. Some few years later a British captain, Francis Hosier, wrote, "The *Albemarle*'s and the *Oake*'s men are so extreme mutinous that we do not know what to do with them; my officers cannot go between decks without being abused or knocked down."

In 1758 fifteen men of HMS *Namur* attempted mutiny and were court-martialed and sentenced to hang. Perhaps because they had wished only to protest against their transfer from a ship they had grown fond of, a royal reprieve at the last minute saved all but one from the noose. But they had to draw lots to determine who should be the luckless among them. Their suspense was brief, fate selecting the second man who drew.

The British Admiralty's naval Articles of War had come into existence nine years earlier. There were thirty-six of them, and four dealt with mutiny or mutinous conduct. For any person convicted by court-martial of making or trying to make "any mutinous assembly upon any pretence whatsoever," the death sentence was mandatory. Death or "such other punishment as a court martial shall deem him to deserve" befell anyone found guilty of "uttering words of sedition or mutiny" or of concealing mutinous practice or design. Anyone who heard mutinous or traitorous talk and failed to report it should be punished as a court-martial saw fit. Men with just grievances concerning, for instance, "the unwholesomeness of the victual," must complain quietly to a superior. It was a court-martial offense to "stir up a disturbance." For a seaman convicted of striking a superior on duty or even threatening to do so, the only penalty was death. Disobedience could bring the same or such other punishment a court-martial determined, "according to the nature and degree of the offence."

Not that mutiny and related misdeeds were the only ones deemed deserving of capital punishment. Seamen in the navy of King George III could be put to death for murder, high treason, theft, cowardice, desertion, sabotage, and sodomy. But mutiny and disciplinary measures to prevent it preoccupied the thoughts of genuine reformers concerned about the efficiency and future of the service. Asserting, "The adage that idleness is the root of evil is with no people more strongly verified than with sailors and soldiers," the battle-hardened Rear Adm. Richard Kempenfelt proposed the formation of divisions, a system eventually adopted in fleets around the world. "The only way to keep large bodies of men in order is by dividing and subdividing them, with officers over each, to inspect into and regulate their conduct." Except for rest, meals, washing, and mending, they must be kept constantly employed. The purpose was to prevent their massing together in an uncontrolled and idle manner for any length of time. "Such a crew must remain a disorderly mob. . . . The officers know nothing of their proceedings; and the people, left to themselves, become sottish, slovenly and lazy, form cabals, and spirit each other up to insolence and mutiny."

Here was a choice of words betraying the sort of lofty prejudice that itself contained seeds for trouble. Kempenfelt was an experienced officer who probably knew better than his warning suggests he did. It took more than idleness and concourse below decks to ignite a mutiny. A sense of grievance had also to be present, supplying the action taken with a stated objective. Britain's sailors appear to have seldom rebelled against prevailing conditions, harsh as they were by today's standards, and never with any wildly dramatic goal of taking over the ship. The impression drawn from contemporary evidence is of outbreaks intended to redress real or imagined wrongs connected, for the most part, with pay, food, furlough, or the disciplinary attitudes of individual officers.

Eighteenth-century life in the British navy was in fact not nearly so horrendous as legend implies. Long months at sea in the cramped confines of a ship of war aggravated tensions and discontents, especially among the products of impressment that made up the majority of most crews. But shipboard interdependence and shared perils fostered a camaraderie that embraced the officers as well as the sailors, at least until the heightening of class consciousness during the century's final decades. In their own practical interests, conscientious captains strove to keep their people well nourished. Livestock carried to sea ensured as far as possible a supply of fresh meat, with large quantities of fresh bread and vegetables. The means to preserve food were limited, and once the fresh provisions were gone the men had to subsist on a daily intake of salt pork or beef, pease pudding, ship's biscuit (hardtack), beer or grog, and sometimes butter and cheese. But however monotonous the diet, lowly seamen tolerated it because they never expected to dine on anything like the roast beef and fine wines enjoyed by the privileged class they served, and only when maggots infested their biscuit, the cheese filled with worms, and the beer became rancid were sullen comparisons apt to be made with the superior fare of the wardroom.

Neither were disciplinary practices as barbarous as romantic litera-ture often suggests. On the face of it, this may sound far from accurate. One need only contemplate certain forms of punishment to wonder if their cruelty could possibly be exaggerated. Running the gauntlet, not abolished until 1806, meant to drive an offender stumbling between two lines of shipmates who flayed at him with knotted ropes. A variation had him hauled about the deck in a tub, again under a storm of blows. For sundry infractions a man might be ducked from the yardarm into the sea or towed half-drowning in the ship's wake. The dreaded keelhauling might be ordered, the hapless fellow dragged half-naked beneath the thickly barnacled ship's bottom from one side to the other. Yet there is no body of evidence to show that these were other than quite uncommon excesses. The lash was regular punishment for serious offenses. Usually wielded by the boatswain's mate, the cat-o'-nine-tails could tear the flesh from a man's torso or leave it resembling "roast meat burned nearly black before a scalding fire." But flogging was, at the time, not generally regarded as inhumane. Seamen themselves would have understood its rationale. A ship's safety depended upon their prompt and efficient compliance with orders. Slackness and incompetence endangered the welfare of all. When proven shirkers were flogged, overworked mess-mates might well have applauded. Flogging was traditional punishment, to be stoically borne so long as justly deserved, and about the only permissible rejoinder to such a sentence was a respectful request that it be executed on the installment plan.

This could be arranged. Sometimes the commander himself initiated it. Early in 1745 off Spithead five crew members of His Majesty's Ship *Captain* were awarded five hundred lashes each for mutiny. "As I thought they could not undergo the whole at one time," Adm. James Steuart informed the Admiralty lords in London, "I ordered the sentence to be put in execution at four different times." After the first flogging session of 125 lashes each, the men pleaded infirmity and begged for a fortnight's respite to recover their strength. The ship's surgeon con-firmed that to proceed too soon with the next bout would mean the offenders' "immediate death. I have therefore," the admiral continued, "ordered the [flogging] to be postponed for a time." Resigned to their punishment, the men wished only to be in good enough shape to get it over with. "They pray that when they are recovered of their illness they may receive the 375 lashes at one time."

From his flagship *Sandwich*, this same admiral found cause to report a troubling incident that occurred on the *Prince Frederick* after that ship's company complained of skipped meals. "To be sure, I have been continually pressing Captain Norris to use the utmost expedition in getting everything done, in order to comply with their Lordships' very urgent commands for sending [the ship] to sea without delay, so . . . the men were kept from their victuals longer than perhaps was necessary." In addition, however, the men were protesting alleged mistreatment at the hands of the boatswain and a lieutenant. They had brought all this to the attention of the sailing master, "but in so tumultuous a manner and with such an apppearance of mutiny that the master called out for his pistols (for near 150 or 200 of the men in a body left work and came down to the wardroom)." The sailing master told them they deserved to be shot. Admiral Steuart concluded that the crew of the *Prince Frederick* had no real cause for complaint. "There will always be found men in every ship of war uneasy and discontented be there ever so little occasion for it."

This was (and still is) true enough. But that sort or expression had become too ready an excuse within the British naval establishment for its failure to devise remedies and exact reforms. Complacent in their knowledge that conspiracy to usurp authority was not characteristic of the British seaman, too many admirals refused to heed the signs that it was becoming very much in his nature to protest vigorously against perceived unfairness. Substantially because of this purblindness in the halls of Britain's Admiralty and on the quarterdecks of certain flagships of the fleet, the nation was to find itself on the very brink of catastrophe before the century ended.

It was the captain's disregard or simple oversight that caused a mutiny on HMS *Egmont* early in 1779. He had gone ashore without signing an authority for the men to be paid. They thereupon disobeyed orders to muster and remained on the lower deck, chanting, "*Pay . . . Pay. . . .*" When the *Egmont*'s fourth lieutenant, Henry Pullen, went among them with a lighted candle and appealed for their patience, some of the rowdier types knocked the candle from his hand and pelted him with chalk. His brother officers dragged Pullen away for safety, and order on the *Egmont* was restored only when the squadron's flagship *Blenheim* sent over a troop of the Royal Marines. A court-martial convicted seven men of mutiny. John Carr, William Cook, and John Singleton were sentenced to death, the others given three hundred lashes each. In a petition for mercy the doomed trio proclaimed themselves "strangers to Mutiny and disaffection, always ready to obey but now led away through error."

Two years later a fatally erratic and fussy Captain Linzee of the English frigate *Santa Monica*, moored at Antigua, returned from a shore visit to find his crew gathered forward on the main deck, defying the first lieutenant's orders to go about their duties. Some had boldly retorted that while always prepared to fight for king and realm, they wanted a new captain or transfer to another ship. Linzee too was forced to call on the marines, the sight of whose uniforms had the same explosive effect upon already embittered emotions as was manifest in identical circumstances nearly two hundred years later on the hangar deck of the American aircraft carrier *Kitty Hawk*. The sailors broke into curses and bombarded the marines with whatever they could lay hands on. Captain Linzee shouted orders to fire. Muskets roared, and a mutineer died. The rest quickly surrendered. Again, following a court-martial, death sentences were passed on several of the accused.

In 1782 six men were hanged and fourteen flogged for mutiny on HMS *Narcissus*. And a year later it took the personal intervention of Earl Howe, newly appointed First Lord of the Admiralty, to prevent a mutiny on the 44-gun warship *Janus* from turning into a massacre.

In none of these events did the mutineers demand other than a redress of their grievances. This is not to say that the grievances were valid in every case or the eventual court-martial penalties excessive. The point is that what all mutinies of the lower deck appear to have had in common was a display of collective discontent, never approaching the slightest semblance of a desire to overthrow authority and seize the ship. That sort of mutiny, its only true expression in the opinion of some, was altogether rare in British naval service and when manifest at all seems invariably to have required an officer's leadership. One night in 1748 while the captain of HMS *Chesterfield* and most of his colleagues were dining ashore at Cape Coast Castle, on the coast of West Africa, the first lieutenant, Samuel Couchman, proclaimed himself commander and put to sea with the stated intention of turning pirate. He was abetted in the crime by a lieutenant of marines. After a few days the *Chesterfield*'s boatswain, backed by thirty of the ship's crew, recaptured the vessel, and in due course both officers were court-martialed and shot.

It was later speculated that drink and the hot African climate had driven those two out of their minds. Mental derangement of some kind was more likely an underlying cause when some four decades later another officer made bold to replace his captain and take over the ship, in what would become acknowledged as the classic example of mutiny, according to a narrow but most romantic definition.

The true causes of history's most celebrated and debated mutiny have little to do with poor food, sadistic punishment, or inadequate pay. They are unknown and doubtless will remain so. This accounts for its evergreen appeal and explains why so many people, upon discovering that motion-picture and other media portrayals of William Bligh and Fletcher Christian are not to be trusted, find their curiosity sharpened rather than quenched. For genuine votaries of sea lore, the impression of a maltreated crew led by a valiant master's mate in revolt against a tyrant of the quarterdeck has never been other than simplistic myth. But the evidence for what really took place is all too murky or fragmented for safe conclusion. While elements of lust, fear, and hatred may be tantalizingly glimpsed, the story of the *Bounty* is, after more than two hundred years, what it has been all along, an authentic mystery played out amid lonely seas and upon corruptive tropic shores.

The truth is hard to get at because so much testimony was composed in later decades and mostly dictated by self-interest. Facts were distorted into figments and reputations ravaged in the process of safeguarding one's own or that of a loved one. Once this is acknowledged, the search for answers becomes more of a hunt for clues. This may be all to the good, for if solved, the riddle of the *Bounty* would long ago have lost its attraction. Inquiry can be essayed with small risk of that coming

about, and the very dearth of reliable source material serves as an entice-
ment affording fair room for speculation on the drama's chief protagonists.

William Bligh was born on 9 September 1754 to a Plymouth customs
officer and his second wife. (Bligh's father would marry twice more.)
Their only child, he entered the Royal Navy at age fifteen, became a
midshipman six years later, and so acquitted himself in seamanship that
Capt. James Cook, preparing for his third voyage of exploration, selected
him over others, notwithstanding their seniority, to be his sailing master
on the *Resolution*. The expedition—Cook's flagship and her consort, the
Discovery—left England in the summer of 1776. By the close of the
following year, after navigating three oceans and making new discoveries, Cook took his ships north from the Pacific in the hope of finding
an Arctic passage that led eastward or westward into the Atlantic.

Ice halted them at Bering Strait. Cook returned to Hawaiian waters
for the winter. The voyage north and south, however, was one of major
accomplishment, the charting of North American and Asian coastlines,
an exercise that amply demonstrated the skills of Cook's sailing master.
February 1779 found the vessels anchored in Kealakekua Bay, where a
stay prolonged by storm damage to the *Resolution* had turned sour, the
usual friendliness of the natives giving way to hostility and thieving.

In the middle of the month some of them made off with the *Discovery*'s cutter. Cook decided to seize the local king and hold him hostage
for the boat's return. Because of the mood of the natives, this was hardly
the wisest course. But Cook had become something of a brooding
martinet, perhaps still mourning the loss of three of his children, whose
deaths had occurred while he was at sea on a previous voyage. Gastric
ailments combined with the physical and mental strain of endless voyag-
ing were enough to have impaired his judgment, but the hostage tactic
had worked for him in the past. So with ten armed marines he made for
the shore. He had stationed two ship's boats at the mouth of the bay in
case islanders tried to escape with the cutter or other stolen equipment.
One of these craft was in the charge of Sailing Master Bligh, who chased
and fired upon a canoe heading out to sea. The other patrol boat
followed suit, and its guns killed a native chief. When Cook landed
with his marines, he was allowed no chance to seize anybody. Thickly
concentrated along the shore and presumably enraged by the shooting,
the islanders fell upon his party with stones, knives, and clubs. The
captain and four marines died under their onslaught.

After Cook's body was recovered and given a sea burial, and with
Lt. Charles Clerke of the *Discovery* in command, the little expedition

struck north in another search for the elusive Arctic Passage. This attempt was also unsuccessful, and while still in northern waters Clerke died. Command passed to James King, one of Cook's second lieutenants, who had himself narrowly escaped death under native attack and who appeared to have blamed William Bligh's act of firing on the canoes for the ensuing bloodshed. The ships sailed for England by way of the coast of Japan, the China Sea, and the East Indies, thence across the Indian Ocean and around the Cape of Good Hope.

For some reason Bligh was excluded from the general promotion that greeted the expedition's return. Events during the long passage home might, if scrupulously recorded, have suggested why. Doubtless there was tension. If Lieutenant King held Bligh responsible for Cook's death, Bligh for his part thought Cook's marines had made a cowardly showing. And Bligh's detestation of King, eventually affirmed, may already have matured. But also evident, it is safe to assume, were the jealously arrogant manner and irascible tongue for which Bligh would become notorious. When promotions were decided at the Admiralty, criticism of his personality very likely weighed in the selection process.

Like most mariners since time immemorial, Bligh ashore could be a markedly different man from Bligh afloat. His unfavorable descriptions issue from men with whom he had sailed or their partisan kin. Land-based acquaintances seem not to have found much fault with him. Elizabeth Betham's family thought him agreeable. Two years his senior (he was then twenty-five), she was the daughter of a customs collector and local educator on the Isle of Man, where Bligh met her while on holiday. They married in 1781 and the following year produced the first of six children, all girls. Promoted to lieutenant—belatedly in his opinion— Bligh served briefly in the final stages of England's latest war against France. Then, with appropriate Admiralty clearance, he left naval service for a lucrative four years as shipmaster in the employ of Duncan Campbell, his wife's uncle, a shipowner and merchant for whose rich West Indian sugar plantations Bligh would also act as agent.

These were, in all likelihood, the happiest years of Bligh's adult life, marred only by the upsetting appearance in 1784 of *A Voyage To The Pacific Ocean*. The first two volumes of this "official" narrative were attributed to Cook but edited by James King, who completed the work and was designated the late commander's co-author. For all the mention made of the *Resolution*'s sailing master, especially his superb skills displayed during coastal charting, Bligh might as well have never served on her, and angrily reading the book, he filled some of its margins with corrections and acid comments. King died soon after the book's release, and what might have lurked behind those omissions of Bligh's important role in Cook's last voyage never came to light.

Duncan Campbell gave Bligh command of his newest ship, *Britannia*. Elizabeth's family asked if he had a berth for a young man wishing to broaden his sea experience. There was no immediate vacancy, and more than a year would pass before Fletcher Christian was able to sign on with William Bligh. Then eighteen (Bligh was ten years older), Christian did so as an insignificant foremastman but was soon quite plainly in the captain's good books.

The Christians were a Cumberland clan of once-considerable eminence. Fletcher's father had died when the boy was four. One of his brothers became a moderately successful lawyer. Fletcher was of more adventurous bent, but what most quickened his response to the call of the sea was probably his frustrated love for Isabella Curwen, a beautiful and wealthy near relative, and the financial misfortunes that overtook his widowed mother. Of their relationship during two voyages together on the *Britannia*, neither Christian nor Bligh would leave any direct clue. The testimony of Edward Christian, lawyer, presumably based on information from his brother Fletcher, suggests a master-pupil intimacy. It was characteristic of Bligh to school younger men on points of seamanship, and Christian would not have been the only youth to benefit thereby. But Christian does seem to have received preferential treatment on board the *Britannia*, to a degree not lost on others of the ship's company. Writing to Bligh long afterward, the first mate, Edward Lamb, recalled "your putting him in articles as a gunner, telling me at the same time you wished him to be thought an officer." Bligh had ordered that he wanted the crew so advised. He had Christian to dinner in his cabin two or three times a week, even allowing him free access to his liquor chest. The first mate concluded that "you were blind to his faults."

That Bligh never had a son, nor Christian a father since infancy, may explain something of this apparent affinity. There appears no significant evidence to support a theory some have voiced implying a homoerotic element. As for Christian's "faults," Bligh was to bitterly deem crass ingratitude as among the most glaring. But at least during their early acquaintance Christian, according to his brother, appreciated the older man's professional guidance and those shipboard favors, and although considering him "a very passionate man . . . I have learned how to humour him."

Two

◢

BLIGH AND CHRISTIAN

*W*hile this enigmatic mutuality developed between William Bligh and Fletcher Christian on the *Britannia* at sea, decisions were being made at home that would lead to its no-less-strange pitiless rupture. There grew in the Pacific a farinaceous fruit that when baked was so like bread in taste and consistency that British capitalists with West Indian holdings expected it would prove a cheap and staple diet for their slave labor on the sugar plantations. (James Cook had thought its taste "insipid, with a slight sweetness resembling that of the crumb of wheaten bread mixed with a Jerusalem artichoke.") Through Sir Joseph Banks, eminent botanist and president of the Royal Society, the plantation owners had secured government participation in a scheme to transplant quantities of breadfruit from Tahiti, where it grew in profusion, to the West Indies, and the Admiralty with some reluctance agreed to find a ship for the purpose. William Bligh's familiarity with both the West Indies and the islands of the South Pacific made him, in Sir Joseph's view, an excellent choice for command. The Admiralty agreed.

Bligh was at sea, unaware of the assignment for which his name was under consideration, when the Admiralty purchased a three-masted merchantman, the *Bethia*, 215 tons, and pronounced her "an Armed vessel by the name of the *Bounty*." Her arms were four short 4-pounders and ten swivel guns. She was hardly spacious enough for the kind of renovation prescribed by the botanist Banks, yet for the long voyage ahead, perhaps lasting two years, it was calculated that the ship's company dared not number less than forty-five officers and men. This certainly guaranteed an overcrowded vessel. The Admiralty had selected a small ship to save money. Even so, the *Bounty* soon proved no bargain, the cost of alterations more than doubling her purchase price. At the same time, judging from his communications with the Admiralty and others, Sir Joseph Banks had his mind fixed on the nurture and conservation of those breadfruit plants, with little thought paid to the physical comfort of the *Bounty*'s people. Cabin and berth space would have to be appropriated for a greenhouse that would contain rows of pots and an apparatus to maintain a constant flow of fresh water. On His Majesty's ship *Bounty*, breadfruit, not men, would claim priority. "The master and crew," wrote Sir Joseph, "must not think it a grievance to give up the best of her accomodation."

When Bligh returned home in the *Britannia*, the Admiralty and Sir Joseph Banks left to each other the necessity of briefing him on the mission. Bligh had little time for educating himself. Nor had he all that much incentive. Informed by the First Lord of the Admiralty that promotion to post-captain must await his return on the *Bounty*, he faced leaving "my poor little family" to subsist on a navy lieutenant's allotment, a pittance compared with the generous salary and benefits received while in Duncan Campbell's employ. The Blighs, now residing in London, had at this time three daughters—the youngest, Anne, an epileptic—and Elizabeth Bligh was again pregnant. To further Bligh's anxieties, the strict limitation imposed on the size of the ship's complement by its confined living space meant that he would be denied a marine contingent. Nor would there be any other commissioned officer with whom to share the concerns of command. Contemplating a long, hazardous voyage under such conditions was enough of a distraction. Little wonder that although he had formally thanked Sir Joseph for the "honour" of recommending him for command, the botanical objective got from Bligh only belated and marginal attention.

Calling upon him at the Deptford shipyard where the *Bounty* was fitting out, Banks was surprised by the lieutenant's apparent ignorance of details. "If it had not been for my visit, he should never have known anything about [the project]." Yet Bligh was nothing if not conscientious. Banks professed to find him so eager for an education that he "even begged to be assisted in studying the subject. He is become my pupil by accident. I will make him a botanist by choice."

There was not much time for that. With a total complement of forty-six, including a botanist from Kew Gardens and an assistant gardener, the *Bounty* left Deptford on 9 October 1787 and took three weeks in some of the English Channel's worst weather to reach Spithead. This

William Bligh in captain's uniform. From a portrait done two years after the mutiny. *(Library of Congress)*

initial experience confirmed Bligh's fears that the vessel was of the wrong size and class for the voyage ahead. It also gave him a chance to size up his people under stress. He had personally recruited a number of them—which did not mean that he had investigated every man's background—and he would soon regret the choice of ship's surgeon, Thomas Huggan, who was overweight and "a drunken sot . . . constantly in liquor." John Fryer, the master, was of Bligh's age and reassuringly experienced, but a master for seven years, he was thereby overdue for promotion and foreseeably prone to sulk. Bligh picked some because they had sailed with him before. In none of these did he place more trust than in the twenty-two-year-old Fletcher Christian, whom he appointed one of the *Bounty*'s two master's mates.

The mentor's unfulfilled expectations of excellence can make the life of a protégé unpleasant, and to this possibility some have assigned the eventual breach. But there were no signs of any such when Bligh assembled his crew for the *Bounty*. He and Christian were by this time proven shipmates. Had Christian any grievance against Bligh he need not have sailed with him again. None of Bligh's crews on the West Indiamen, as far as is known, had found him difficult to serve under. Were Bligh a poor skipper on the merchantmen, he is unlikely to have remained in Duncan Campbell's employ. Bligh's dislikable traits, the fault-finding and temperamental outbursts, would for some reason grow less tolerable only with his assumption of naval command.

Bureaucratic delay in the issuance of final sailing orders kept the *Bounty* at Spithead until almost midwinter. Bligh thought the Sea Lords deserved flogging for detaining him so late into the season while yet expecting him to reach the Pacific by way of Cape Horn. "I must do it if the ship will stand it at all or I suppose my character will be at stake." But once at sea he registered optimism. The ship was in good order and her company "happy under my direction." The overcrowded little vessel weathered gale after gale, and on 16 February 1788, in a letter he gave a passing whaler for home delivery, Bligh praised her as "fit to go round half a score of worlds" and her men as "all active good fellows . . . tractable and well-disposed."

After calling for supplies at Tenerife, in the Canary Islands, where Bligh honored Christian by sending him as his personal emissary to the Spanish governor, the *Bounty* bore southwest across the Atlantic for Cape Horn. Bligh mustered the crew and announced the purpose of the voyage, its destination and probable duration, at the same time promising promotion to all whose endeavors merited it. About then appeared the first symptoms of trouble. A quantity of cheese was missed. Bligh accused the crew of stealing it and ordered a cut in each man's allowance to make up for the deficiency. (Boatswain's Mate James Morrison wrote long afterward that Bligh himself had purloined the cheese before the ship left England.)

Bligh was not in the most secure position for enforcing discipline because he was the only commissioned officer on board, the others warrant or petty officers. This made him the more concerned with keeping up morale. Most ships employed the two-watch system, which meant that seamen were on duty four hours in eight. Bligh adopted the three-watch system, four hours in twelve, believing that "not being jaded by keeping on deck every four hours it adds much to [their] content and cheerfulness." His watch officers were Master John Fryer; William Peckover, the Gunner; and Midshipman Christian, Master's Mate. With an order read to all hands Bligh appointed Christian acting lieutenant. Any thought that he might have given to the corrosive effect such a step would surely have on Master Fryer had clearly succumbed to his professional regard or personal affection (or both) for the younger man.

Such acts of favoritism were bound to have subverted Bligh's good intentions, as certainly did his sudden fits of rage and his egocentric attitudes. At times he appeared consumed by intolerance and conceit, venting a professional jealousy that left subordinate officers confused or humiliated. Compounding Bligh's emotions at the start of the voyage were doubts about the ship, which he sought to mask, perhaps even from himself, with forced displays of sanguinity. Their purpose was to preserve that shipboard "cheerfulness" that along with "exercise and a sufficiency of rest" he believed was the most powerful weapon against scurvy and other scourges. This recourse of dogged optimism suffered a blow when Master Fryer, himself quick to take offense, reported Seaman Matthew Quintal for "insolence and contempt," leaving Bligh no choice but to order two dozen lashes. Until that March afternoon Bligh "had hopes I could have performed the voyage without punishment to anyone."

The following weeks were a battle for survival. Tempestuous seas broke over the cramped ship, and miles gained in days were lost within hours. So bad were hail and snow squalls that Bligh had sometimes to be lashed to the foremast to take observations. Scant rest was permitted him, and this he obtained only in that portion of the great cabin not taken over by five rows of double-tiered planks, holes cut in them to receive the breadfruit pots. The closer the *Bounty* approached Cape Horn, the fouler the weather. Snow and ice stiffened her sails and lines and numbed the men struggling to work them. Bligh made sure his sodden and shivering men had hot meals; "took care to nurse them," he would claim afterward, "with every comfort in my power." But the ship kept losing ground, the Horn seemingly beyond reach. With seas still running high, the *Bounty* sprang a leak. More of her crew fell sick, some frozen half-mute. "I cannot expect my men and officers to bear it much longer," Bligh wrote on 13 April 1788, but the ship took a beating for a further nine days before "I ordered the helm put around to the universal joy of all hands."

Not that the weather improved all that much. But the westerlies that Bligh's people had fought now sped them along their new course. Stamina revived, and to preserve it Bligh ordered evening dancing on the forehatch to the music of Michael Byrne, nearly blind but the only fiddler he could recruit. "Upon the whole," Bligh boasted, "no people could live better." He watched over them with zeal, courting the sort of resentment or ridicule invariably the lot of a too-fussy parent, the more so because of his sharp tongue and rough temper. Also, once the relief over Bligh's decision to retreat from the Horn had ebbed, the monotony of ship's routine and diet, the discomfort of the crowded living quarters, the compulsory dancing, and the regular inspections for cleanliness, not to mention the persistent bad weather, all combined to rekindle old discontents. Still, the lash was seldom used. And nothing recorded or later recalled would so much as hint at the emergence, at this stage, of any mutinous spirit. Nothing either to suggest any serious alteration in the feelings between Bligh and Christian except fragmentary references to a quarrel they might have had when the *Bounty* anchored off the Cape of Good Hope in June.

Two months later the *Bounty* had reached Adventure Bay, Tasmania, which was familiar to Bligh because he had called there with Cook eleven years earlier. He assigned a shore party to collect botanical specimens. Others were set to bringing on board fresh water. During these tasks William Purcell, the ship's carpenter, exploited his warrant officer's immunity from instant chastisement by dodging work and ignoring Bligh's commands. Purcell could have been sent below and confined pending court-martial. Instead, Bligh stopped his meals, a punishment that "immediately brought him to his senses." Bligh thought it for the good of the voyage that he refrain from making any man a prisoner. There was much to be done, and even the healthy were "but barely sufficient to conduct ship's duties."

The *Bounty* left Adventure Bay on 4 September. A month later, as she neared the end of her easterly voyage, the alcoholic incompetence of Surgeon Huggan caused the death of a Scots seaman named Valentine. Bligh had yet to read the burial service over Valentine's body before committing it to the deep when Master Fryer refused to perform his routine duty of signing the ship's expense books. First, he demanded, the captain must sign a paper certifying his, Fryer's, faultless conduct as the *Bounty*'s master. Short of gross perversity, the product of smoldering resentments, no clear reason would emerge for Fryer's behavior. Bligh already had him figured as "troublesome." Unrecorded clashes may have occurred. At any rate, here again was an instance when a warrant officer's imprisonment might have been justified. Instead, Bligh ordered all hands assembled and read them the Articles of War. At this, Fryer "saw his error" and in front of the crew signed the books. Bligh thought Fryer should consider himself lucky that "I forgave him." He had certainly humbled him, making the master more than ever a potential foe.

As the *Bounty* passed south of New Zealand, her commander, not for the first time, may well have regretted the absence of another commissioned officer on whom he could depend for support, or a marine unit whose presence alone might have deterred any tendency toward indiscipline. What help or cooperation Bligh got from Fletcher Christian

The *Bounty,* reconstructed for a 1962 motion picture, off Tahiti under full sail. *(Luis Marden, © National Geographic Society)*

in this regard is unknown, the nature of their relationship over this lengthy period more or less a blank. A surviving fragment of ship's document dated 2 June 1788 at the Cape of Good Hope, the scene of their unspecified quarrel, indicates that Christian was no longer "acting lieutenant." The scrap bears the signatures "Jn. Fryer, master, Wm. Cole, Boatswain, F. W. Christian, Master's Mate." For the preservation of discipline Bligh could properly have looked to the *Bounty*'s master-at-arms, Charles Churchill. But that man's capacity to intimidate was to be brutally misdirected.

With a Tahitian landfall imminent Bligh checked the health of his people. Huggan reported three cases of scurvy. Bligh discounted these because the surgeon had been drunk for days, utilizing a private stock of liquor Bligh unwisely allowed him to keep on board. "He may turn sober again," Bligh noted, falling back on optimism, and ordered a general inspection for venereal disease. "It could not be expected that the intercourse of my people with the natives should be of a very reserved nature." Bligh felt it his responsibility to prevent, as far as he was able, any defilement of the islanders by anyone under his command. Huggan reported all hands free of infection. He had treated a number of past cases, and a mulct charged against the patient and recorded undated in

The reconstructed *Bounty* anchored in Matavai Bay. She was a magnet for the native Tahitians, as was her original namesake. *(Luis Marden, © National Geographic Society)*

one of the ship's pay books attended each "cure." The names listed included Fletcher Christian's.

And now the *Bounty* was anchored in Matavai Bay. Tahitians swarmed out in boatloads, some to sit staring at the ship's feminine figurehead, which Bligh had "directed to be painted in colours." Others climbed excitedly on board. After twenty-seven thousand miles of sea voyage lasting ten months, Bligh's people were only too eager to relax and fraternize. The captain, meanwhile, using blandishments of his own, including the promise of gifts from the King of England, began negotiations with interested chiefs for the procurement of those breadfruit plants.

HMS *Bounty* lay in Tahitian waters from late October 1788 to the following April. Like much else, the reasons for so lengthy a stay became the stuff of guesswork. It took only two or three weeks for Bligh's collection parties to gather almost all the breadfruit required. Bad weather or adverse winds may have altered plans for a prompt departure. Or Bligh's conscientiousness held them there, a delay based on the advice of the Kew Gardens's botanist, David Nelson (a previous visitor to the Pacific with Bligh and Captain Cook), that the breadfruit cuttings not be borne away until firmly rooted in their pots. At any rate, the longer the *Bounty's* people tarried, the more enamored they became, Bligh included, of life in that carefree island paradise.

Death visited briefly. About six weeks after the *Bounty's* arrival Surgeon Huggan collapsed on deck in an alcoholic stupor and expired shortly afterward in his cabin. Lamenting the doctor's "drunkenness and indolence," Bligh had him buried at Point Venus, a peninsula east of Matavai Bay. And Tahiti was not all idyllic dalliance either. Work assignments were plentiful. Bligh gave only two men at a time a day's freedom to amuse themselves ashore. But this schedule had quickly dissolved. And inevitably, over the long period, intermingling led to steady liaisons. The sailors found Tahiti's women irresistibly generous with their bodies, while its young men, far from displaying jealousy on that account, attached themselves to the visitors as devoted friends, *taios*. Bligh, who had called at Tahiti in earlier years and knew something of the local tongue, ingratiated himself with the island's royalty, setting up trade deals and more often than not blaming his own men for the petty thievery to which, it soon transpired, the islanders were addicted. Charging Alexander Smith with negligence when the gudgeon of the *Bounty's* large cutter disappeared, he had the seaman flogged. But Bligh felt constrained when dealing with offending warrant officers. The carpenter Purcell, who had given trouble before, disobeyed his order to make a grinding stone for the Tahitian helpers. Bligh's recourse was to confine him only briefly: "I can but ill spare the loss of a single man."

He had begun to view his officers as a worthless set, habitually "remiss." He wrote of them with contempt and exasperation, but mostly as a group, never specifically naming Fletcher Christian, logging no clues to the approaching breach. Persistent winds forced Bligh to transfer his shore camp and about seven hundred potted plants to a more sheltered anchorage in Oparre Bay. The mishandling of the *Bounty's* launch, in service as a pilot boat, led the burdened ship aground, and kedging her free proved a study in further clumsiness. It was all particularly embarrassing to Bligh, for he had the native chief Tynah with his wife and entourage on board as guests. The officers most culpable would have been Master John Fryer and Master's Mate Christian, and Bligh may well have given each a personal dressing down. But he named neither one in the ship's log—which would show, however, that two days after Christmas he ordered twelve lashes across the bare hide of Steward William Musprat for "neglect of duty."

Early in the new year three men deserted. "Had the Mate of the Watch been awake no trouble of this kind would have happened." He was Midshipman Thomas Hayward, and Bligh disrated him on the spot.

He lost his temper with Hayward's close friend, Midshipman John Hallet, and slapped him. Bligh then barked repeatedly at Master Fryer for letting the spare sails mildew and for failing to arrest a native who had confessed to helping the trio of deserters. Bligh could not contain his disgust. "Such neglectful and worthless petty officers I believe was never in a ship as are in this. They have drove me to everything but corporal punishment and that must follow if they do not improve."

Bligh appears to have recorded no objection to alliances between the Polynesians and his people and may have all but given them his blessing. In his view, Tahitian women "are handsome and have sufficient delicacy to make them admired and loved." He himself had opportunity to indulge and perhaps at times yearned to do so. But he was faithfully committed to his "dear Betsy" and the family that, assuming her safe parturition, he supposed must by now have grown in number. Fletcher Christian, whose duties kept him mostly ashore, had acquired at least one *taio* and a woman, Mauatua, but there is little evidence of jealousy stirring within Bligh beyond vague stories that on at least one occasion he humiliated Christian in front of his native friends.

The three deserters returned and surrendered. One of them was the ship's master-at-arms, Charles Churchill. Perhaps in deference to his rank, Bligh ordered that he be given twelve lashes, while each of the others received twenty-four. They were then confined for a week in irons, and despite a penitent letter written from their imprisonment, he brought them back on deck for a second flogging. (For the crime of desertion this was by no means unduly severe justice.) At each of the punishment musters Bligh rebuked Thomas Hayward, also ironed and confined, for having aided the desertions by sleeping on watch. It frustrated the captain that he could not deal more rigorously with his errant subordinates. But Hayward's punishment was altogether too cruel in the eyes of the ex-midshipman's *taio*, and perhaps it was indeed he who swam out and with an axe all but severed the *Bounty*'s cable, Bligh afterward professing himself "at a loss to account for this malicious act."

More than a thousand young breadfruit plants rooted in pots, tubs, and boxes awaited loading. Other than adverse weather, there was no reason to linger any further amid Tahiti's forested slopes and golden shores. Bligh could count the weeks well spent. He had successfully conducted trade and diplomacy, even managed scientific observations and some coastal charting. At the same time, it was fixed in his mind that his officers were letting him down. If he had thus far singled out Fletcher Christian for special criticism (and there is no strong evidence that he had), it could have been because in the past he had so befriended him. But Bligh's rage fell upon all of his officers. Some were mere boys, and the relatively few instances of delinquency on record suggest that they were not all that sloppy a group. It made no difference. With a passion bordering on paranoia, Bligh had decided that they could do nothing right. "I have such a neglectful set about me that I believe nothing but a condign punishment can alter their conduct."

It was time to leave. Rainsqualls slowed the loading, but at last the plants were safely installed in their floating greenhouse. Livestock and provisions also taken on board included two dozen hogs and seventeen goats. The islanders gave Bligh's people a memorable send-off. Scores of *taios*, sweethearts, and others boarded the ship to feast, dance, weep, and embrace, above and below deck. Entertaining King Tynah and the royal party, Bligh noted "a vast excess of grief." Finally, the Tahitians rowed away in mournfully chanting canoeloads. Once ashore, most watched in silence as the *Bounty* hoisted anchor and turned out of Oparre Bay for the open sea. Then she was gone.

But Tahiti had not seen the last of her.

Three

■

"I AM IN HELL"

ligh had no warning of disaster. Nightly he slept with his door unlocked. He continued to excoriate his officers and by comparison mollycoddle the rest. (The log for this period shows a single flogging.) Three weeks had passed since the *Bounty*'s departure from Tahiti. Secure in the conviction of his own rectitude, Bligh failed to appreciate that life on the cramped vessel must be more dismal for all hands after Tahiti's freedom and sensual delights. But shipboard growling fell short of conspiracy. And while many would have leaped at the chance of returning to that island paradise, others, Fletcher Christian among them, had proud families awaiting them in England and naval careers to think of. Did such considerations mean nothing to the twenty-four-year-old Christian? Were they, on the other hand, elements in setting the strange course he was about to pursue? The woman Maua-tua—whom he had named (or would so name) Isabella after the girl he had loved and lost back in Cumberland—was his attachment to her among the psychological urgencies? And insofar as these questions bear on Fletcher Christian's mental state, they invite at least passing heed to the disease from which, knowing Surgeon Huggan as well as the therapeutic deficiencies of that day, one might fairly suspect the master's mate still suffered.

The ship paused at Nomuka, in the Friendly Islands (now Tonga). Watering parties went ashore under Christian and the elder master's mate, William Elphinston. Bligh had directed them to "keep themselves unconnected with the natives," also to leave their weapons in the boat, an unwise order that Fletcher Christian allegedly cited in indignant self-defense when Bligh cursed him for appearing afraid of the islanders. Tools were stolen. Bligh sent Master Fryer ashore to take proper charge, but the thefts continued, and it fell Fryer's turn to face the captain's wrath. Bligh allowed natives on board to trade, seized five chiefs as hostages for the return of the stolen tools, then paraded all hands and delivered a semihysterical lecture, during which he called them "a parcel of lubberly rascals" and threatened to shoot Seaman William McCoy for failing to pay attention.

So, at any rate, wrote Boatswain's Mate James Morrison years afterward. That same belated account portrays Fletcher Christian as the special target of an abusive volley when, two days out of Nomuka, Bligh wildly overreacted to the disappearance of some coconuts bought from the islanders with nails and stacked between the *Bounty's* guns. Another retrospective version painting Bligh as a commander gone suddenly haywire makes no mention at all of Fletcher Christian. Bligh eventually produced his own story. All but twenty coconuts had vanished. "Here was public theft, a contumacy and direct disobedience of orders." Again, no reference to Christian, but at that future date Bligh was, in any case, obliged to show that he had not systematically persecuted him. One point all accounts agree upon is that Bligh invited Fletcher Christian to his cabin for supper that same evening of 27 April 1789.

Had Captain Bligh indeed browbeaten Christian more than the others over those missing coconuts, perhaps he had quickly repented and wished to make amends in private. Mood swings came naturally to Bligh. The master's mate, "with whom, in particular, I was on the most friendly terms," was already engaged to dine with him the next day. But others too would then have been present. In all probability, Bligh had not singled out Christian for a special drubbing over the coconuts, and the affair was not, as myth has it, the ultimate in a series of provocations finally driving Christian over the edge. Still, Christian may have suffered Bligh's verbal lash once too often, having become abnormally sensitized by unfathomable pressures. At any rate, he no longer felt respect, much less affection, for the officer whose protégé he had formerly been. And on Bligh's part, what that curious invitation to a nightcap may have signaled was a certain desperation, the pathetic gesture of an essentially lonely commander hoping to salvage what remained of a once-cherished intimacy.

Christian excused himself as unwell. Brooding and depressed as he had become, this was hardly an untruth. Not that Bligh supped alone, evidently, for he next invited Thomas Hayward, the midshipman he had demoted, by no means one of Bligh's favorites but not ill-disposed toward the captain. And Hayward accepted.

"The secrecy of this mutiny is beyond all conception." Bligh's professed incredulity conformed with his version of a well-concealed plot hatched by scoundrels determined upon sailing back to Tahiti. He was never publicly to acknowledge otherwise, never to modify his self-portrayal as the most astonished man on earth when the outbreak occurred. "Had it been occasioned by any grievances, either real or imagined, I must have discovered symptoms of discontent." Certainly, as the *Bounty* bore steadily westward her people were well fed, good discipline appeared to prevail, and the cat-o'-nine-tails was seldom in use. However erratic and hot-tempered their commander, and painful their own repressed longings, all hands physically thrived under that command as healthily as did David Nelson's breadfruit plants. Thomas Ledward, Huggan's successor as the *Bounty*'s surgeon, attested to the "extreme care [Bligh] took of the ship's company." Bligh's own complexes may have blinded him to the genuine discontent lurking between decks. But there was no secret plot. No one conspired to a mutiny. Bligh's gravest misfortune was his failure to detect (or decision to ignore) the signs that a mental distress was afflicting the young man he had so closely befriended and schooled. Not that even Christian felt any compulsion to mutiny at first, and the night before actually committing it he seemed more bent upon ending his life under the guise of a reckless attempt at desertion.

Before going to bed, Bligh had made his customary round of the deck, giving Master Fryer, who had the first night watch, directions for the course he wished held. A thin moon hung in a clearing sky. Some of the crew studied a fitful glow on the horizon, perhaps caused by the eruption of a distant volcano. The *Bounty*'s approximate position was latitude 19° 45' south and longitude 175° 05' west. No one would report the sound of hammering, although Christian had asked William Purcell to get him nails, planks, and ropes with which to construct a raft. The carpenter had obliged, perhaps to humor him. It was already plain to some that the master's mate was undergoing an emotional anguish. Before another twelve hours had elapsed, his agitation would be obvious to everyone, yet by then it would also be unsafe not to take him seriously.

Christian told Purcell and no more than three or four others that he intended to go overboard with the raft and make for Tofua, bearing thirty miles northeast. Assembling a raft can be a prolonged and noisy business. There is no evidence that Christian got far with it. He is said to have prepared sustenance, portions of roast pig stuffed in a bag, and to have collected nails and beads for barter. But he seems not to have bothered with weapons, charts, or navigational instruments. The notion was clearly suicidal, its likely outcome death from sharks, starvation, drowning, or violence at the hands of hostile islanders. But then he thought better of it, or had actually been shamming, for he did not go over the side. Instead, Christian had turned in by 3:30 A.M. and half an hour later was aroused by Midshipman George Stewart to relieve the watch. Years afterward, when neither Stewart nor Christian was available to confirm or deny, it was said that the midshipman found Christian "very much out of order," that he begged him not to attempt swimming away, and that he planted for the first time in Christian's mind the idea of seizing the ship by describing the *Bounty*'s people as "ripe for anything."

Neither Thomas Hayward nor John Hallet, respectively mate and midshipman of the watch, had put in an appearance. Laggards both, they still slept, but since each was suspected of being a toady of Bligh's, this tended to suit Christian's new purpose. (Midshipman Peter Heywood, acquitting his by then deceased chum Stewart of responsibility for inciting Fletcher Christian to mutiny, would claim that Christian himself declared that taking the ship never entered his mind until he relieved the deck and found his two watch officers asleep.) Within minutes Christian had at his side probably the *Bounty*'s most recalcitrant pair, Master-at-Arms Churchill and Seaman Matthew Thompson. They joined Christian less out of sympathy for him than odium for their captain, along with the prospect of returning to Tahiti. Others shared their feelings, but not to the extent of seizing the ship on the say-so of an emotionally disturbed master's mate. It took such hard-bitten customers as Churchill and Thompson to quickly cow or confuse them. Christian commanded no particular loyalty, and without Churchill and others of that intimidating ilk the mutiny might have collapsed with the sanity of its leader. (Mr. Christian "looked like a madman," thought a scared Seaman Thomas Ellison.) Still, Christian had taken the first awesome step. He would be aided by the torpor of almost half the crew.

Having secured control of the upper deck, Christian raced below and shook Hallet awake. The midshipman had been sleeping on the arms chest at the foot of the main hatchway. The chest was opened, and arms were distributed. Christian posted sentinels about the ship, and with five mutineers, including Churchill, he next made aft for the captain's cabin.

Bligh's unlocked door swung open. He sat bolt upright in his nightshirt to face his former young friend, who wielded a cutlass and demanded silence. Three of the others grabbed him, "tied my hands,

threatening me with instant death if I spoke or made the least noise."
Bligh's cabin stood on the starboard side of the ship. The master's
quarters were opposite. Hearing the commotion, Fryer had sprung from
the locker on which he slept for coolness and peered through his door
window. He saw the captain, wrists bound behind him, bundled out
of his cabin. "Our eyes met," Bligh bitterly recalled. "He had a pair of
ship's pistols loaded. A firm resolution might have made good use of
them." Two versions claim to account for Fryer's inaction. Either he
had no ammunition for the weapons, or he was so flustered that he had
forgotten they were there. Not that Fryer could have done much at that
moment. Christian's men burst into his cabin as well, "told me to lay
down again, and hold my tongue or I was a dead man."

Dawn lit the scene: Bligh, permitted the dignity of trousers, was a
captive on his quarterdeck, abaft the mizzenmast, with hands tied and
an armed guard at either side, one of whom spoke nervously of "only
acting as the others do" in response to the captain's pleas for an explanation. Grasping the line attached to Bligh's wrists, Christian had, some
would say, a sounding plummet hanging from his neck so that, should
the mutiny fail, he would jump overboard and drown. Master Fryer,
certainly with no love for Bligh but no desire to hang for mutiny, was
allowed on deck, then driven below again at bayonet point after a sharp
exchange with Christian, who told him (according to Fryer), "I have
been in hell for weeks past. Captain Bligh has brought this on himself."
Boatswain Cole obeyed Christian's order to hoist out the large cutter,
in which the captain would be cast adrift with any who were permitted
to join him. The rest were milling about uneasily, responding in different
ways to the threatening bluster of Churchill, Thompson, and others
upon whom Fletcher Christian depended for the success of his mutiny.
Some of the men, including the botanist Nelson, remained below, the
armed guards Christian had stationed at each hatchway preventing their
emergence on deck.

Bligh did not receive any help from the young midshipmen whose
families he had pleased by gathering the boys under his wing. Peter
Heywood and Christian were "objects of my particular regard and
attention. I had taken great pains to instruct them." The seventeen-year-
old Heywood (whose name on the mulcts lists of venereal "cures"
indicated an occurrence at Tahiti) was to plead youthfulness as his excuse
for failing to stand by his captain. He did not awaken until after daybreak
and once on deck was bewildered by the sight of senior midshipmen
apparently siding with Fletcher Christian. "I remained for a while a
silent spectator." Then he decided on "the lesser of the two evils," to

stay with the mutineers, and "with this in mind I helped hoist out the boat." Bligh had a different impression of Heywood's role. Displaying "ingratitude of the blackest dye," the boy was in effect "one of the ringleaders. . . . It is incredible that these very young men I placed every confidence in . . . took the *Bounty* from me. I curse the day I ever knew a Christian or a Heywood."

Bligh exaggerated by calling Heywood a ringleader. But the midshipman had to all intents and purposes enlisted in the mutiny, as had his friend George Stewart, allegedly Christian's furtive instigator, who was said to have pranced happily about the deck once the mutiny was under way. A third "young gentleman," Edward Young, cooperated with Christian and may have egged him on. Master Fryer reappeared on deck in the hope (he later claimed) that the mutineers would get drunk, enabling him with others to disarm them, and this was why he begged Christian's permission to stay on the *Bounty*. Christian said no. Boatswain's Mate Morrison, who did remain with Christian, would profess to have had the same notion as Fryer, his beaming countenance as he helped hoist out the launch (the large cutter was found unseaworthy) craftily masking an intention, "at the first opportunity, of taking the ship."

Thus sundry explanations for acquiescing in a mutiny. Beyond argument, there was no concerted effort to nip it in the bud. No more than a dozen were actively engaged, but the rest of the men on deck had succumbed to a kind of neutral inertia. None of Bligh's officers stood up for him. Doubtless there were seaman who were inwardly pained but helpless to act, being unarmed, others who looked to their superiors for guidance and example. All they saw was complicity or impotence. What the success of Fletcher Christian's mutiny had come to hinge upon was how the *Bounty*'s people, her officers especially, regarded their commander. And there the scales were tipped against him. No one rushed to William Bligh's aid because proficiency, fatherly solicitude, and fair play in command had lost out to a thoroughly dislikable personality.

The sightless fiddler, Byrne, had climbed into the now-unwanted cutter and remained there alone, crying. John Samuel, the captain's clerk, helped load the launch, collecting Bligh's journal, commission, and certain ship's papers from his cabin, but he was "prohibited on pain of death" from bringing up the maps and a box of surveys and sketches, Bligh's fifteen years' navigational work. Astronomical instruments were forbidden at first, then a compass and sextant grudgingly allowed. The launch filled with men, including the botanist, Nelson, his breadfruit

Bligh cast adrift at Christian's orders. Note the cutlasses thrown into the boat and the breadfruit plants lashed to the stern of the *Bounty*. From a painting by Robert Dodd in 1790. *(National Library of Australia)*

garden sadly abandoned, and the carpenter, Purcell, permitted his tool chest only after an argument. Master Fryer, still pleading to stay, was ordered into the boat. Finally it was Bligh's turn. The knots at his wrists loosened, he was prodded to the ship's side. "The remembrance of past kindness produced some signs of remorse in Fletcher Christian. I asked him if this treatment was a proper return for my friendship. He appeared much disturbed at my question and answered with much emotion. 'That—Captain Bligh—that is the thing—I am in hell—I am in hell.'"

Bligh included, there were nineteen men in the undecked launch, four above its capacity. Measuring twenty-three feet long, less than seven feet wide, the boat had six seats athwartships for oarsmen and contained two masts to be stepped. The castaways' supplies consisted of 150 pounds of bread and some pork, 6 quarts of rum, 6 bottles of wine, and 28 gallons of water. A few more than half the *Bounty*'s complement remained on board with Christian, and some had broken out the ship's liquor, grinning drunkenly over the side and taunting the woebegone boatload veered astern by a rope. Others, probably Christian among them, watched in silence. The ship's armorer and two carpenter's mates called plaintively for Bligh to remember that they had stayed on the vessel against their will. Bligh shouted a request for arms. It was met with jeers, then four cutlasses were thrown into the launch. For tense moments it looked to Bligh's party as if some of the wilder drunks on board might open fire on them. Midshipman Hayward wept. Others in the launch were now only too anxious to unship oars and make away. Then it was done. "After having undergone a great deal of ridicule, and been kept for some time to make sport for these unfeeling wretches, we were at length cast adrift in the open ocean."

The *Bounty* had vanished below the horizon. Crouched in the stern of his overladen launch, Bligh wasted no time in fuming. He had more than three thousand miles of ocean to navigate. The piratical and humiliating theft of his ship, that ordeal at least lay behind him: "I felt an inward happiness." His first intended halt was Tofua. Under sail and oars, the party got there within four days. The first natives in view acted in friendly fashion, but after twenty-four hours more gathered and began rhythmically knocking stones together, a Polynesian danger signal to which Bligh reacted by ordering preparations for a quiet departure. "We walked down the beach, everyone in a silent kind of horror." Before they could reach the boat, "stones flew like a shot." John Norton, the *Bounty*'s quartermaster, died under the volley as, strenuously rowing, the rest of Bligh's party escaped in the falling dusk.

Their destination now was the Dutch colony at Timor, in the East Indies. "We bore away across the sea where the navigation is but little known." Nights were often pitch-black: "not a star could be seen to steer by." Yet in an astonishing feat of seamanship, Bligh would fill in some of those gaps in navigational knowledge. No less was it a feat of human endurance. While passing among the Fiji Islands the launch almost foundered in storms. Drenched and shivering, so densely packed their bones ached, the men groaned all the more from stomach cramps caused by a monotonous diet that was soon down to bread scraps and spoonfuls of rum. Landing on any island was ruled out, after that experience on Tofua. By the fourth week since the mutiny, Bligh was suffering gastric pains, "several of my people seemed half dead . . . and I could look no way without catching the eye of someone in distress." It was perhaps in part to avoid looking at his fellow sufferers that he strove to maintain some sort of log and record observations, his equipment limited to a ten-inch brass sextant, an old quadrant found in the boat, Gunner Peckover's compass, and a couple of navigation manuals. "I am prevented from doing as much as I wish," he wrote in his notebook, yet he managed to survey, chart, and usefully sketch as they drifted across the Fijian archipelago.

To pass the time and keep up morale, he told of early sea experiences

"Just before Sun Rise the People Mutinied." A page from Bligh's notebook log that he kept while in the open boat. *(National Library of Australia)* and occasionally offered up prayers: "Almighty God, relieve us from our extreme distress such as Man never felt." Halfway through the 1500-mile passage of the Coral Sea, bursts of sunshine "gave us as much pleasure as on a winter's day in England." And they caught and cut up an occasional bird, Bligh apportioning it fairly, "giving the blood to those most in want of food." On 21 May he proudly calculated from the long line heaved out at the end of each hour that they had accomplished 130 miles in a single day. But the next night "the sea flew over us with a great force and kept us bailing." At the close of the month they came through safely, under Bligh's formidable leadership, to within the welcome sounds of breakers pounding the New Holland (Australia) reefs. It only remained for them to find an opening, then they were in calmer waters, had scooped oysters from the shallows, and found a tinderbox in the boat, some brimstone, and a magnifying glass. And on a rocky islet, with a small fire going under a bubbling pot, William Bligh braced for yet another mutiny.

Master John Fryer wrote afterward that Bligh was "in a sad passion," cursing the people, telling them they owed their lives to him. Fryer thought some of the credit for their survival was his. In the boat he had more than once argued with Bligh, who questioned him on his failure to use the pistols on the *Bounty* and was unlikely to have believed his excuses. The trouble now began with Purcell who, rebuked by Bligh for grumbling, "told me with a mutinous aspect that he was as good a man as myself." Bligh seized a cutlass and challenged Purcell to prove it. Fryer broke in, calling on Boatswain William Cole to put their captain under arrest. At that, Bligh turned on Fryer. "I declared that if [he] interfered I would put him to death first. This had a proper effect on the man."

Discord had continued. Bligh gave Seaman Robert Lamb "a good beating" for greedily eating raw all nine birds that he had caught and again took Fryer to task, for building a fire big enough to be seen by possibly hostile natives. But the party had many sea miles to traverse. By 10 June all hands in the boat were too weak to move, much less mutiny. Boatswain Cole told Bligh he looked the worst. The next day when the emaciated and sore-covered men sighted land, none had the strength to croak a cheer—nor could believe their eyes. "It appeared scarcely credible to ourselves that in an open boat, and so poorly provided, we should have been able to reach the coast of Timor in forty-one days after leaving Tofua, having in that time run, by our log, a distance of 3618 nautical miles."

Once he had put Captain Bligh over the side, Fletcher Christian had

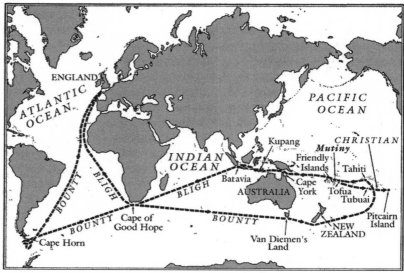

The voyage of the *Bounty* and of Captain Bligh's return to England. *(Bill Clipson)*

to think of a plan. With the impulsive madness of the mutiny behind him and he, like it or not, in supreme command, Christian recovered some degree of common sense and cool thinking. Given Bligh's seamanship and strength of will, he or others in the launch might well survive and carry their story of mutiny to England. Naval ships would put to sea in search of the mutineers, with Tahiti their first Pacific destination. Christian's people may not have thought that far ahead, and doubtless some were as intoxicated by the prospect of another Tahitian idyll as by the *Bounty*'s rum. But Christian reasoned that Tahiti was not a prudent choice for settlement. And as the boatload of castaways dwindled to a speck in the west, Christian had ordered topgallant sails loosened and course set for Tubuai, an island 450 miles south of Tahiti.

There a prolonged stay seemed impossible. Native hostility and a shortage of stock sent the *Bounty* indeed back to Tahiti. The ship anchored in Matavai Bay about a week before Bligh's half-dead party staggered ashore at Kupang on the western tip of Timor. Christian told enquiring Tahitians that Bligh had met Captain Cook, of whose death they were unaware, and gone off with him. Then Christian took from Tahiti nine women, including Mauatua (his Isabella), also some men and boys, and sailed again for Tubuai. The mood on the *Bounty* those weeks was one of simmering uncertainty. Of the two dozen who had remained on board with Christian, he could count on scarcely half as hard-core supporters, among them Charles Churchill, and each of these, like that ill-designated master-at-arms, of unstable and potentially treacherous character. But here again the aberration or emotional fit that had touched off Christian's mutiny was followed by a return in some degree of professional practicality. As exercised by his most brutal adherents, Christian's discipline was closer to tyranny than Bligh's had ever been, but it kept the men in a sort of organized thrall, even to the extent of their building a fort during two strife-torn months on Tubuai.

Most trouble came, eventually, from the natives, dozens of whom were slain by the *Bounty*'s guns. But the mutineers also fought among themselves, not in the course of any attempt to overthrow Christian and retake the ship, but because there were not enough desirable women to go around. Again the *Bounty* left Tubuai for Tahiti. There Peter Heywood and George Stewart "moved to a former friend's house, determined to remain as much apart from the mutineers as possible and wait patiently for the arrival of a ship." So Heywood would testify. Fourteen others of the *Bounty* had gone ashore with them. Christian was apparently in no mood to stop anybody. His resolve now, once he had taken on supplies and felt as confident as he dared of the loyalty of the men, and women, who chose to stay with him, was to cruise to some remote and uninhabited Pacific island and there, safe from retribution, spend the rest of his days.

It was on this final visit to Tahiti, if Midshipman Heywood can be believed, that Fletcher Christian unburdened himself of a private explanation for his mutiny. After telling Heywood that "you are innocent, no harm can come to you," he went on to disclose "for the satisfaction of his relatives, other circumstances connected with that unfortunate disaster which, after their deaths, may or may not be laid before the public. And although they can implicate none but himself, either living or dead, they may extenuate but will not contain a word of his in defence of the crime he committed." With this cryptic fragment the world would have to be content. Christian had confessed to some inner fault or weakness that his relatives must be told about but which, presumably to save them embarrassment, should not be made public during their lifetime. Neither Peter Heywood (who died a captain in 1835) not Christian's family shed any further light on the subject.

Also something of a puzzle is the abruptness of HMS *Bounty*'s next move. In the early hours of 23 September 1789, quite without warning to anyone ashore, Christian ordered the anchor cable cut, and with eight of the crew and their "wives," also six islanders and their women, he stole away from Tahiti, "God knows whither." And for twenty years nothing would be known of their fate.

Bligh's party recuperated at Kupang, except for David Nelson, the botanist, who caught fever and died. As strength returned to the others, so did a resurgence of feuds. Off Surabaja, to which Javanese harbor the survivors sailed in a schooner Bligh purchased at the British Admiralty's expense, Fryer and the carpenter, Purcell, turned openly mutinous. Bligh had them transferred to Dutch custody, where they were overheard to say that he would hang in England, and they accused him of falsifying expense claims. Bligh denied the charges and produced receipts and vouchers in defense of his honesty. Midshipman Thomas Hayward tearfully begged Bligh not to regard him as one of the malcontents. What the Dutch thought of it all may be titillating to muse upon. But the intriguing fact about this most serious breach between Bligh and the *Bounty*'s master is its almost overnight accommodation. Fryer wrote Bligh a letter. "I wish to make everything agreeable as far as lay in my power, that nothing might happen when we get home." Perhaps he did have something on Bligh, whose own story, however, was of a master pleading forgiveness, who "trembled . . . looked pale . . . declared he would make every concession and disavowal of those reports."

The men returned to England in two ships that sailed separately. Their number had shrunk to twelve, Bligh included. Besides Nelson, the cook, the quartermaster, and Master's Mate Elphinston had all died in the Dutch East Indies. There too Ledward, the ship's surgeon, had disappeared (one account has him lost at sea). Yet another of the boat's crew, Seaman Robert Lamb, died on the passage to England. Thus had Bligh's party dwindled. But he arrived home in March 1790 to find his family grown by twin girls, and he was delighted, his paternal compassion boundless as always. At the same time he never missed a chance to vent bitterness over the loss of his ship. To Midshipman Peter Heywood's mother, newly widowed and having last seen her son when he was fourteen, Bligh wrote, *"His baseness is beyond all description."* And to Heywood's uncle, "His ingratitude to me is of the blackest dye, for I was a father to him in every respect. It will give me much pleasure to hear that his friends can bear the loss of him without much concern."

Bligh's best-selling account of the *Bounty*'s voyage under his command appeared in late summer. Shortly afterward, on HMS *Royal William* at Spithead, he was tried by his peers for the vessel's loss, an

Another Claimant has ſtarted up for the long conteſted ANGEL ESTATE—the cauſe is to be tried at the enſuing aſſizes for Surry.

It is with much concern we relate the fate of Captain BLIGH, who had been cruſing in the South Seas, and particularly amongſt the Society Iſlands, to explore the Vegetable Syſtem, and to make a collection of the Bread Tree and other productions of nature, peculiar to that climate :— After a ſucceſsful voyage, he was on his return to England, with a valuable cargo of the produce of thoſe Iſlands, eſpecially of the Bread Tree, when on the 20th of April laſt, he was ſurprized in his cabbin by a party of his crew, who preſented piſtols to his head, threatening to blow out his brains, unleſs he would quietly ſubmit to be pinioned, and to make diſcoveries favourable to their purpoſe. The conſequences were ultimately, that the Captain, and ſeventeen of his truſty friends, were forced into the long-boat, and committed to the Ocean, with a ſcanty allowance of bread and water.

The mutineers poſſeſſed themſelves of the ſhip and her cargo, on the coaſt of the Friendly Iſlands.—The Captain and his unfortunate aſſociates, with the aſſiſtance of a ſmall compaſs with which they were furniſhed, gained one of the ſmall iſlands on the coaſt, the inhabitants of which proved unfriendly and hoſtile on their attempting to land ; being without ammunition and weapons of defence, the little crew were compelled to ſteer off, and encounter their fate once more, after the Captain had been wounded, and one of his men killed.—The ſurvivors at length providentially reached Batavia, where they met with humane and friendly treatment.—The Captain has arrived ſince at the Cape of Good Hope, from whence this intelligence has been received.

"He was surprised in his cabin." The *Times* of London, 17 March 1790, tells England of the mutiny. *(Library of Congress)* expected formality that acquitted him of blame. Asked if he had any complaints against those who had survived with him, he replied. "None but Purcell." His silence on Fryer's misconduct, and Fryer's on Bligh's alleged chicanery, would leave suspicions of a secret deal. But all hands, also the Admiralty, seemed disposed to tread lightly, and even Purcell, charged with insolence and disobedience, got off with only a reprimand.

On 23 March 1791 the 24-gun frigate *Pandora,* seeking the mutineers, anchored off Tahiti. The midshipmen Heywood and Stewart were soon aboard, to report the first in a series of atrocities Fletcher Christian's mutiny would bring upon those fragrant isles. Seaman Matthew Thompson had shot Master-at-Arms Churchill in the back. Churchill's *taios* had stoned Thompson to death. Several seamen had even joined in a Tahitian civil war. From Tahiti's standpoint the *Pandora*'s arrival was nothing less than merciful, ridding its shores of British mutineers. All fourteen surrendered or were rounded up. Capt. Edward Edwards, a martinet who had himself once weathered mutiny (on HMS *Narcissus* in 1782), ordered them chained within a small unventilated deckhouse inevitably dubbed Pandora's Box, and he turned a deaf ear to the sobbing entreaties of their women, mothers or mothers-to-be among them, left abandoned on shore.

The *Pandora* contributed her own chapter to the tragedy that had begun on another ship's decks. She left Tahiti in May and after a fruitless search for Christian headed into Torres Strait on a course for home. The night of 28 August she struck a submerged reef and by the next morning was sinking fast. Thirty-four men went to the bottom with her, including four prisoners, still manacled in the box, one of them Midshipman George Stewart. Like Bligh before him, Captain Edwards was confronted with the challenge of a prolonged voyage in an open boat—which he too met successfully, bringing the *Pandora*'s survivors ashore at Timor seventeen days after leaving the scene of the wreck.

By then Bligh, promoted post-captain, was again at sea, bound for the South Pacific. At Sir Joseph Banks's urging, King George had authorized a second breadfruit expedition. This time, on his own insistence, Bligh commanded a vessel, HMS *Providence,* twice as large as the *Bounty* and with a force of marines to support him. He also had as escort the *Assistant,* a smart little brig with a seasoned commander, Nathaniel Portlock. But past experiences had assuredly left their mark. Headaches plagued him for most of the cruise. "My illness is of the nervous kind," and it worsened his disposition. George Tobin, a lieutenant on the *Providence,* would recall his "violent tornadoes of temper." Yet after each outburst Bligh was ready with "something like an emollient plaster to heal the wound."

This time Bligh stayed at Tahiti for only three months while the *Providence* took on board more than two thousand breadfruit plants. His pleasure upon learning that the *Pandora* had nabbed a number of mutineers was diluted by the news that Fletcher Christian had not been among them. But at least Bligh could presume that the trial of those recaptured would be deferred until his return. Had he known that it was about to begin in his absence, his reaction might have provoked another mutiny. As things were, while the *Providence* meandered westward from the Pacific into the Indian Ocean, thence to the South Atlantic, her destination the West Indies, the captain's vanity and irascibility, as Francis Bond, the first lieutenant (a nephew), attested, were close to insufferable. Perhaps it was those headaches, or the acute homesickness Bligh expressed in letters to his beloved Betsy.

He finally got the breadfruit to Jamaica. (The slave laborers are said to have hated its taste, and in any event the days of profitable sugar production in that region were numbered.) A letter from the superintendent of Jamaica's botanic gardens hints of a "disagreement" with Bligh and asserts, without amplification, that "many plants were certainly lost by his obstinacy." But planters were for the most part effusive with praise for Sir Joseph Banks and his naval captain. As for Bligh, he now wanted only to get home. But the renewed war with France and the requirements for naval defense in the West Indies delayed his departure until late 1793. And long before then the *Bounty* courts-martial had run their course.

Four

◢

FLASH POINT
AT SPITHEAD

T he trial lasted six days and was conducted on board HMS *Duke* at Spithead before a court of eleven naval officers presided over by Admiral Lord Hood. Bligh's reports on the mutiny had exonerated the sightless fiddler, Byrne, and three others of complicity, and they were duly acquitted. Among the remaining six accused, Midshipman Peter Heywood was a central figure. His influential family pulled strings on his behalf, not too easy a task even though the principal witness against him was on the far side of the world. Senior naval officers felt that in a mutiny "the man who stands neuter is equally guilty with him who lifts his arms against the captain." Heywood had to fall back on pleading his extreme youth. Another of those charged, Boatswain's Mate Morrison, had stayed with Christian because (he said) the launch was overcrowded and Bligh himself objected to additional passengers. Heywood and Morrison were found guilty, in each case with a recommendation for mercy. The *Bounty*'s steward, William Musprat, was also convicted, but thanks to shrewd legal coaching he secured his freedom on a technicality. Able Seaman Thomas Burkitt, one of those who had burst into Bligh's cabin, received the death sentence. So did John Millward and Thomas Ellison. Hanged aboard HMS *Brunswick* on 29 October 1792, they were the only men put to death for the mutiny on the *Bounty*.

Five weeks of relentless lobbying by Heywood's family won him a royal pardon. During that same period Boatswain's Mate Morrison, his life also in the balance, composed a purported chronicle of events that was injurious to Bligh's character, and Morrison's advocates circulated it widely. Morrison, like Heywood, escaped hanging. But even in this so-called journal (a "memorandum" also surfaced, ascribed to the same author), replete as it is with stories of Bligh's unpopularity on the *Bounty*, his endless nagging, and his alleged cheating, there is, as Bligh properly observed when a copy came into his hands, "among all these charges not one of cruelty or oppression."

This proved small comfort. Those scribblings of an erudite boatswain's mate seeking desperately to save his neck were shortly coupled with a publication by Edward Christian assertedly based on confidential interviews with Bligh's companions in the open boat. Together they would become an insufficiently challenged staple of the lore of the *Bounty*, perpetuated well into the next century and beyond. When he returned home in 1793, Bligh found the damage already done. The crew of the *Providence* cheered him sympathetically when he left the ship. But his reception at the Admiralty was decidedly cool, and while unwilling to resign himself to a tarnished reputation, he could do little to refute the defamations by then in popular currency. Following a brief and ignoble exchange of pamphlets with Fletcher Christian's brother—"that sixpenny professor"—Bligh wearied of the controversy. At forty, with more than half his life spent in the Royal Navy and conscious of "enemies . . . full of so much wickedness they exceed the bounds of credibility," he wished now for years of quietude with his family.

They were denied him. In 1795, while in command of the *Calcutta* off Scotland, he found himself aiding the suppression of a mutiny on the *Defiance*, whose crew was demanding new officers, more shore leave, and less water in the daily grog. Some of the mutineers were seized and imprisoned, whereupon shipmates clamored for their release. Bligh took part in discussions among the fleet officers on "how to subdue this Mutiny, and I did not hesitate to declare that a party of troops [be] embarked and laid alongside." Bligh himself was selected to lead them. As they approached the *Defiance* in boats, the mutineers called for the guns to be cleared. Along with an army major, Bligh called upon the soldiers to ignore the rebels' threats and get up the ship's side. This they did, and the mutiny ended. "I trust," wrote Bligh, "that all the offenders may be brought to condign punishment." He still bore the taint of the *Bounty:* "A few fellows [had] pointed at me and said there *he* goes."

Bligh's next command was of the 64-gun *Director*, assigned to blockade the Dutch coast, a relatively uneventful wartime assignment. But forces in motion within the Royal Navy were about to precipitate a mutiny that would eclipse any heretofore by threatening the integrity of Britain's sea force and thereby her very existence as a sovereign power.

There were some in England who might have seen it coming. Admiral Lord Howe, widely respected even before his triumph at the battle known as The Glorious First of June, had lamented the crumbling of discipline on his own flagship. In 1795 another officer had handed First Lord of the Admiralty Earl Spencer a memorandum on sailors' grievances that raised the dread specter of a general mutiny among the King's ships. The following year Spencer received a warning that the low rate of an able seaman's pay had become a dangerous source of shipboard discontent. But a quickening tempo of events that allowed little time for the fair study of causes or the introduction of reforms had itself given impetus, in the closing years of the century, to an unrest on the lower decks that inevitably bred conspiracy.

The ingredients for trouble were varied, their degree of responsibility never to be satisfactorily determined. How much was Thomas Paine to blame? His inflammatory words, so bloodily effective in France, had also compelled Englishmen to reconsider their lot under the royal yoke, many of them excited to perceive for the first time that they had rights as men. And if the revolutionary zeal convulsing France and on display earlier in the American colonies had begun to flicker in British breasts as well, it was bound sooner or later to have crept aboard His Majesty's warships. A letter from below decks on HMS *Shannon* to the Lords of the Admiralty in 1796 complained of the "ill-treatment we received from the tiriant of a Captain which is more than the spirits and harts of true English Man can cleaverly bear for we are born free but now we are slaves." The letter concluded with an unconcealed threat, should the captain not be replaced, to sail the *Shannon* into a French port. Its significance lies in the choice of words that, even if the evidently less than literate writer had not actually read *The Rights of Man,* suggests that he was at least familiar with Paine's radical philosophy.

Naval discontent approached a flash point at one of the gravest hours in British history. Nelson had defeated the Franco-Spanish fleet off Cape St. Vincent, and memories of The Glorious First could still stir proud hearts. But naval victories seemed suddenly irrelevant. Bonaparte's military genius on land dictated the course of the war. Britain's armies were driven from the continent, and the allies she had so heavily subsidized against the French Republic left the field one after the other. A French expedition had even touched the shores of Ireland, and although storms scattered it, the foray presaged a full-scale landing in support of Ireland's separatist movement. Another enemy invasion force was believed assembling across the North Sea off the Dutch island of Texel. And Britain's Treasury slid closer to collapse under the weight of the war effort. Fear and war weariness governed the national mood by 1797, compounding the unrest that was already rife among the sailors on the inactive ships of the North Sea and English Channel fleets.

The navy had grown fourfold since the start of the war. It remained Britain's ultimate shield against foreign aggression and in defense of its far-flung trade routes, but what preoccupied the Whitehall hierarchy now was the necessity of keeping it up to numerical strength in the struggle with Revolutionary France. Impressment and a bounty system were the Admiralty's principal means of securing personnel. Of the approximately one hundred thousand men in the navy by 1797, only one-fifth were genuine volunteers. And while those helplessly swept up by roving press gangs were as always of crude and ill-educated stock, the supplemental wartime practice of recruiting a formal quota from each English county had brought into naval service many with some political sophistication. These men were certainly better able to articulate the perennial complaints against low pay scales, poor food, inadequate shore leave, and dislikable officers.

Systematic if furtive communication between the ships of the Channel Fleet, located at Spithead, off Portsmouth, was under way early in the year. One exchange provides evidence that keen and skillfully cautious minds were at work. During the preparation of a petition addressed to the Lords of the Admiralty through Lord Howe, commander of the fleet, for an increase in seamen's pay, a draft was sent from HMS *Queen Charlotte,* a focal point of the protest movement, to the *London* for comment. "One thing you have forgot," came the response. "You intreat his Lordship to intercede the Board of the Admiralty for augmentation of pay but that is not under their jurisdiction to do, it is a national affair and must be addressed to the House of Commons, the pursebearers of the Nation." The Charlottes were ready with an explanation. The Admiralty's attention was sought in preference to Parliament's because the Lords "are all professional men and might take umbrage at not having the compliment paid them first." But whatever course was adopted, "we have not the least doubt but by Unity among ourselves and a steady peaceable perseverance to carry our point."

Unsigned, bearing only the names of ships, the petition reached

"The Sailor's friend," war hero and mediator in the mutiny: Richard, Earl Howe (1726–1799). From a painting by J. S. Copley. *(National Maritime Museum, London)*

seventy-one-year-old Lord Howe at Bath, where he hoped the waters would cure his gout, just as his second-in-command, Lord Bridport, received orders to put the fleet to sea. Additional petitions followed. Low pay was the chief grievance. In a separate letter to Charles James Fox, the Whig opposition leader in Parliament, the Channel Fleet sailors insisted that "indigence and extreme penury alone is the cause of our complaint." The rates of pay for petty officers and the lower ranks in the British navy had not risen in more than a hundred years, and payments were seldom delivered on schedule. The army's pay scales had improved. Sailors had expected a similar benefit, "but alas no notice has been taken of them, not the smallest provision made for their wives and families." Yet their patriotism, the petition to London concluded, was equal to that of the soldiers, "as your Lordships can witness who so often led them to Victory and Glory."

But the army's pay raise was two years old, and this was now a bad time to seek higher wages because Britain was in the throes of a wartime money crisis. Although Howe was known as "the sailor's friend," he looked askance at anonymous petitions, perhaps "fabricated by some malicious individual," intending to create "a general discontent of the fleet." A perfunctory check at Portsmouth reassured him that all appeared tranquil on His Majesty's ships. Not until after he had received eleven petitions did Lord Howe journey to London and place them before the Lords of the Admiralty. By then it was late March. Following a short cruise, the Channel Fleet, under Bridport on his 100-gun flagship *Royal George,* returned to its anchorage, with the sailors expecting some favorable answer to their petitions. Instead, they seemed to have been ignored. So the secret plotting resumed, in an ever-hardening mood.

Within a fortnight, during which period Lord Bridport replaced the ailing Howe as fleet commander, the seamen agreed on a bold course of action. Officers ashore got wind that something was afoot and wig-wagged warning messages to London, sixty miles away, along the chain of hilltop signal stations that formed the Portsmouth line of the Admiralty's national telegraph system. (In good weather such transmission might take less than ten minutes.) A letter followed from Lord Bridport, reporting the formation of "some disagreeable combinations" on his ships, especially the *Queen Charlotte.* Lord Spencer wrote back that the Admiralty had decided to ignore those petitions, hoping the matter would die down, and Bridport in the meantime must keep Whitehall informed about "any individuals . . . pointed out as leaders in the business."

London society knew the second Earl Spencer, aged thirty-nine, as a wealthy and agreeably polished man with a comely wife. In the Admiralty's board room, Spencer cut a more serious and methodical figure. He was energetic and conscientious, with a sometimes overconfident air that had made more than one disgusted admiral contemplate premature retirement. But he knew nothing of life below decks in the naval force he presided over, and he was about to receive a lesson.

The day of Spencer's complacent letter to Bridport, the port admiral at Portsmouth, Sir Peter Parker, wrote to his London superiors that seamen on the *Queen Charlotte* and *Royal Sovereign* planned a refusal of duty as a means of winning better rates of pay. Bridport, meanwhile, would "keep a watchful eye to prevent ill consequences." The fleet commander had already testily concluded that only a prompt response

First Lord of the Admiralty Earl Spencer. His conscientiousness and compassion were no substitute for remedial action. From a painting by J. S. Copley.
(National Maritime Museum, London)

to the petitions could prevent "ill consequences." He had himself just received another petition signed (or otherwise marked) by two "delegates" from each of sixteen ships representing the entire Channel Fleet. Bridport sent it and the original eleven petitions (which had been tossed into his lap) back to London with a caustic comment: "I have very much to lament that some answer had not been given to the various letters transmitted to Earl Howe and the Admiralty." It would have headed off "the disappointment and ill-humour which at present prevails in the ships under my orders." He expected the Admiralty to promptly order the fleet to sea again, where mischief might be less likely to flourish. However, Bridport clearly feared that the crews might refuse to sail, and he had no doubt at whose direction: "*Queen Charlotte*'s people have taken the lead in this business.

As anticipated, Spencer sent fresh sailing orders. Crossing Bridport's sharp-toned letter, they reached Spithead on Saturday evening, 15 April. Throughout this chill Easter weekend officers carried despatches, and crew delegates drafts of petitions, from one ship to another. And accompanying the constant boat traffic was a tension felt at all levels, among admirals and ordinary seamen alike. Few shrank now from the only word applicable to what appeared imminent. Spencer ordered Sir Peter Parker to make sure that officers would remain in their ships "and upon any disposition to Mutiny amongst the crews . . . take immediately the most vigorous and effective means for checking its progress and securing the Ringleaders."

Again Lord Bridport sought what he considered the only means of preventing the paralysis of his fleet. From his cabin bed in the *Royal George* during the early hours of 16 April, he wrote to Lord Spencer that the men would go to sea "provided an answer is given to their petition." Bridport could scarcely have better sensed the gravity of the moment had he known of a message sent just then from the *Royal Sovereign* to the *Defence,* which said, "We flatter ourselves with hopes that we shall obtain our wishes for they had better go to War with the whole Globe than with their own Subjects." But Bridport was bound to pass along the Admiralty's instructions to sail, and in compliance Adm. Sir Alan Gardner, flying his flag on the *Royal Sovereign,* ordered her prepared for sea. Defiant jeers arose from his people. He soon notified Bridport that "to a man" they refused to sail until their complaints were redressed. Gardner was middle-aged, had served in the navy for forty-two years, and was known for his pugnacity. That Sunday morning it proved of little use. He employed "every argument in my power" to change their minds, including strenuous reminders that their conduct could only help the enemy. All to no avail: "The whole ship's company is in a state of mutiny."

The ringleaders of the movement set out in boats from the *Queen Charlotte* and Bridport's flagship *Royal George*. They toured the whole fleet, boarding each vessel in turn and directing the crews to appoint delegates. Valentine Joyce, a twenty-six-year-old quartermaster's mate from the *Royal George,* had the most to say and would emerge as a principal spokesman. That evening two delegates from every one of the sixteen line-of-battle ships at Spithead proceeded to the *Charlotte,* and before the presumably stupefied gaze of the ship's officers they installed themselves in the admiral's cabin for discussion. Among the delegates were five aging midshipmen who had, apparently, long abandoned hope of ever passing their lieutenancy examinations. Under Joyce's guidance, the delegates drew up rules. Normal ship's routine would continue, officers were to be treated with respect, and all orders were to be obeyed except those for sailing. On Tuesday, should there still be no news from Whitehall promising redress of grievances, "the whole of the officers are to be secured and sent ashore."

The Sea Lords at first refused to be rushed, informing Bridport that the matter required "mature deliberation." In the meantime, he was to exert "every means to restore the discipline of the fleet," and Admiral Gardner's squadron, as already ordered, must drop down to St. Helen's, an anchorage just south of Spithead. But the crisis gathered momentum. Over that Easter weekend every man in the Channel Fleet had taken an oath to support the mutiny. Several officers were given notice to quit their vessels. (Two on the *Glory* were banished for "beating, blacking, tarring and putting the people's heads in bags.") Only then did Whitehall finally act. After conferring with Prime Minister William Pitt and anxious members of his cabinet, the First Lord agreed to go and see for himself what was troubling the Channel Fleet.

With two other peers and sundry aides, enough to constitute a board, Spencer set out by coach on a rainy Monday night and unpacked the next morning at the Fountain Inn, Portsmouth. Bridport was relieved to see him. The Admiralty, he felt, had in its ignorance expected him to single-handedly tone things down. "Would to God I had influence sufficient," he told Spencer and listened to the proposals the First Lord had brought for a modest pay increase. On Tuesday afternoon three flag officers bore these proposals to the *Queen Charlotte* and read them aloud to the assembled delegates. There was no immediate acceptance. Higher pay remained a pivotal demand, but the delegates,

with strengthening confidence, were now emphasizing additional grievances as well—harsh discipline, poor food, neglect of the sick, and
inadequate shore leave. All that the flag officers could tell Spencer when
they returned to the Fountain Inn was that the seamen would study his
proposals and make their decision known the next morning.

The waiting period stretched all that day. While cooling his heels,
Lord Spencer made clear to Bridport and the ships' commanders that
the Admiralty's largesse could not extend beyond pay adjustment and a
pardon for refusing duty, and that continued disobedience must bring
severe punishment under the Articles of War. Zealous on this point,
Spencer suggested that the captains return to their ships while the
delegates still debated on board the *Queen Charlotte* and, except for that
vessel, slip cables and put to sea. This would isolate the delegates from
their following and enable them to be arrested, and their leaderless flock
could thereupon be talked back into proper conduct. Spencer quite
evidently did not realize how unified the mutiny had become. But the
captains did, and they so warmly opposed his idea that he withdrew it.

On board the rebellious ships some men whiled away the time by
venting personal grudges and complaints against specific officers. The
crew of *La Nymphe* charged excessive use of the lash, citing the case of
a man doubly flogged for showing "silent contempt"—he had smiled
during the first blows across his flesh—and of another flogged for too
slow an ascent into the rigging. Men of the *Glory* and *Duke* called for
the dismissal of the officers by whom they were "cruelly and unmercifully
beaten." The *Ramillies*'s surgeon maltreated his patients, and the midshipmen were "of a most cruel and vindictive disposition."

Adding a bizarre touch to the scene of general protest was the
appearance of the port commissioner's barge, colorfully bedecked, bearing the Prince of Württemburg, betrothed to England's Princess Royal
and just honored with the key to the city of Portsmouth. It having been
decided to give the distinguished foreign visitor a tour of the Spithead
fleet, he was taken around it with all due ceremony and lustily hurrahed
by its insubordinate crews.

The mood then darkened. "We none of us know the end of this most
awful affair," wrote the beauteous Lady Spencer, who appears to have
joined her husband in Portsmouth. "The quietness of the men, though
comfortable in some respects yet in others is most alarming—it proves
a steadiness in them to accomplish their object." She marveled that a
mutiny could have brewed three months without the officers' getting
wind of it. The mutineers' "prudence and decency" impressed one of
those officers, a lieutenant on the *Monarch,* and he commended them

for their solemn avowal that if the French came out they would suspend their struggle with the Admiralty and haul anchors to meet the nation's foe. But even prudence and patriotism have their breaking point, as Spencer may well have feared. When the delegates' terms for ending the mutiny finally lay before him, demanding higher pay rates than those already offered and assurances of a royal pardon, their lordships at the Fountain Inn gave grudging acquiescence.

That, however, was as far as Spencer was prepared to go. Inadequacies in victualing, pensions, medical treatment, and shore leave—all grievances that had taken shape along with the question of pay—would have to wait. Further concessions would only invite fresh demands. Of this Spencer felt convinced. The First Lord still underestimated the solidarity of the protest movement, and while his board's resolution, read to the crews on Thursday morning, 20 April, pleased them, it stirred no will to end the mutiny before word came to do so from their delegates conferring on the *Queen Charlotte*.

All that day boats clustered about the flagship, waiting. The suspense was too much for Sir Alan Gardner, who left the *Royal Sovereign*, gathered two fellow admirals, and boarded the *Queen Charlotte*, intending to harangue the delegates. He found that nothing was happening. Valentine Joyce and three other top leaders had gone ashore to see Lord Spencer, and when Joyce and his companions returned, Gardner was still holding forth on the forecastle, threatening "condign punishment . . . the utmost vengeance of the law." In the presence of a conceivably apoplectic Gardner the four leaders delivered some thoughts of their own, precisely those with which they had just dumbfounded the First Lord of the Admiralty at the Fountain Inn. Mere promise of a royal pardon was not good enough. Pledges had been broken before, and officers were not to be trusted. The delegates knew only too well that nothing but a pardon signed and sealed by King George was a sure shield against later retaliation. So until such a document existed, no deal would be made with the Admiralty's board.

The words of Quartermaster's Mate Joyce were too much for Gardner. He wheeled on the delegates and, according to an Irish newspaper, called them "a damned mutinous blackguard set who deserved hanging." Other accounts have him charging them with fear of the French—"cowardice alone had given birth to the mutiny"—and shaking a delegate by the collar, swearing to hang him and every fifth man in the fleet. But excoriation and bluster were no longer of avail. Chased, hustled, or respectfully escorted, depending on the version believed, Sir Alan was quickly off the *Queen Charlotte*. The temper on the Spithead ships was now one of no surrender. A red flag flew in place of Admiral Lord Bridport's on the *Royal George,* and Lord Spencer hurried back to London for a personal audience with the king.

The delegates drafted three letters. Of the two addressed to Bridport, one was conciliatory, apologizing for the affront of striking his flag. The other pointlessly attributed the continuance of the mutiny to Admiral Gardner's display on the *Queen Charlotte.* The third, to the Lords of the Admiralty, reaffirmed that without a settlement of grievances and the issue of a royal pardon, "the fleet will not lift an anchor, and this is the total and final answer." Bridport, ashore at Portsmouth, settled down to wait, in the weary conviction that he could do little else. Everything now depended on Spencer's judgment, the cabinet's attitude, and the sovereign's temperament.

After a meeting with William Pitt and the king at Windsor Castle on Saturday afternoon Spencer was able to authorize the printing of one hundred copies of a royal pardon. Before midnight they were on their way to Portsmouth. But this was the easy part. Getting parliamentary action on the demands for better pay and food proved a lengthier, more complicated process entailing the appointment of a subcommittee to survey the matter and make estimates, followed by further study and debate by the full legislature. A whole week would pass before Pitt received a favorable report from Parliament on the seamen's petitions. And at Portsmouth, meanwhile, the mood ashore and afloat fluctuated between anger and hope.

The pardons were read aboard each ship and loudly cheered. Bridport himself addressed the men on the *Royal George,* and they promptly rehoisted his flag. But many still suspected a double cross and thought they ought to see the original draft instead of printed copies. When this was arranged, tensions relaxed again. Once more cheers echoed. On the morning of 24 April Admiral Lord Bridport marshaled the Channel Fleet for sea. But only six sail of the line dropped down to St. Helen's. Men on the *Marlborough, Minotaur, Ramillies,* and *La Nymphe* were too fiercely at loggerheads with officers whom they did not like. Bridport left those ships lying at Spithead. Yet some degree of good order had returned, or so it seemed to Lord Spencer, who congratulated Bridport on the "termination of the mutiny" and was pleased to learn that "a part of the fleet [is] actually in motion this morning." His relief was short-lived. Within twenty-four hours, following intelligence reports of enemy preparedness across the English Channel, he was again writing Bridport, this time urging him to assemble as many ships as he could and "show yourself at sea."

Adverse winds prevented Bridport's ships from venturing beyond St. Helen's. At the same time, in London, politicians worried by the nation's financial crisis dragged their feet on the question of improved naval pay scales. Action was thus slowed or stalled both in Parliament and off Portsmouth, and the delay allowed more ominous clouds to gather.

A small squadron mutinied at Plymouth, partly out of sympathy with the Spithead sailors but also because seamen on the 74-gun *Leviathan*, newly arrived from prolonged duty in the West Indies, were owed two years' back pay and were complaining of bad food. The outbreak at Plymouth was more or less orderly and soon subsided. So, at first glance, had a rumpus in the North Sea Squadron, which was based at Great Yarmouth and was fitfully blockading the Dutch at Texel. The monotony of that duty was among the elements of discontent, as well as other causes more familiar—men of the 64-gun *Nassau* had not been paid for nineteen months, and their second lieutenant was allegedly a brute. No such epithet attached to the skipper of a sister ship, HMS *Director*, although from a growing number of insubordinations her captain, William Bligh, may well have sensed the imminence of that feared act of shipboard infamy that it was his misfortune to have already suffered. But the North Sea Squadron's commander, Adm. Viscount Adam Duncan, appeared to have aborted a mutiny of his sailors by dint of his intimidating personality and his armed marines.

Over six feet tall and considered one of the handsomest men in the fleet, Duncan had faced down a rebellion on his flagship *Venerable* the afternoon of 30 April. As he told the Admiralty the next day, he had called out his marines, then addressed a sullen gathering on the forecastle. Patience was necessary, grievances would be redressed, and all hands must understand "the enormity of the crime of mutiny." Thus "satisfied," the men had returned to duty. In London a troubled First Lord of the Admiralty had just written off the Channel Fleet as "absolutely lost to the country as if at the bottom of the sea." Feeling better after Duncan's report of mutiny quelled in the ships at Great Yarmouth, Spencer sent his compliments: "A little well-placed presence of mind on these occasions is everything, and I have no doubt that your people will not only obey you better but like you better for it." Spencer's wife added her own commendation, regretting "that we have not more Admiral Duncans."

Duncan's optimism was misleading. The admiral was prey to unspoken fears concerning the morale of his crews, and that report to Spencer had not told all. The mutineers on the *Venerable*'s deck had in fact so infuriated Duncan that it took the ship's chaplain to stop him from plunging his sword into one of them. Conditions at Great Yarmouth settled into the kind of uneasy peace prevailing to the south off Portsmouth. And it was the Admiralty itself, through a letter that officers in the troublous areas called "unfortunate . . . a masterpiece of folly," that well and truly shattered it.

The letter, dated 1 May 1797, was circulated to all commands and reflected an abrupt hardening of the Admiralty's attitude. Captains were to keep their marines alert, weapons ready for action, and "on the first appearance of mutiny to use the most vigourous means to suppress it." The imprudence of the order was in its timing. The seamen, who soon got wind of it, had felt that they were showing commendable patience while Parliament debated the issue of pay increases. Now they suspected the government of planning to reject their demands and to use force to crush any expression of dissatisfaction. Again boats shuttled between the ships at Spithead and St. Helen's. The surgeon's mate on HMS *Mars* told his captain that dissidents below decks were threatening to seize the ship and take it into Brest as a prize for the French. It was plain to Lord Bridport that another mutiny brewed. He knew too what had caused it: "I have always considered peevish words and hasty orders detrimental. . . . I think it wiser to soothe than irritate disturbed and agitated minds." But that hapless order had done its work, leaving Lord Bridport to control the damage, a task that was all the more critical in view of the incoming reports of stepped-up French activity across the Channel. Tirelessly, he communicated with his restless crews, striving to clear false impressions and to explain the delay in London.

In the capital's political circles there seemed indeed a deplorable lack of urgency. There was, after all, a war on, and fiscal restraints notwithstanding, few essentials could claim greater priority than the sustained morale of those the country expected to fight it. William Pitt might have done more to speed up the parliamentary process. The prime minister was, however, not only at grips with problems of state but emotionally shaken by the collapse of an intimate friendship. Those reports of an imminent French attack ought perhaps to have expedited matters, but it is clear that they were not always taken seriously. In all probability, what would have moved the pay proposals through Parliament faster was proof that the sailors meant business. That indeed they did could have been inferred from the secret messages then passing between Bridport's ships. From HMS *Ramillies* to the *Royal George:* "The Admiralty lords, by their promises, mean to lull us into a supposed sense of security." From the *Pompée* to the *Royal George:* "Our opinion is there is not the least reliance to be placed in their promises."

None can say to what extent radical agitators or even enemy agents within the service manipulated simple sailors and exploited their grievances. Some political subversives had doubtless infiltrated the fleet. Certain sea lords and other members of the naval hierarchy attributed the unrest to Jacobin ideologues and read sinister meaning in the sailors' manner of addressing themselves as brothers and their designation of representatives as "Delegates." The radical clubs or "corresponding societies" springing up in Britain's larger cities came in for much of the blame, and early in May a young London magistrate named Aaron Graham arrived in Portsmouth on a secret assignment to learn what he could of conspiratorial links and origins. He played the detective well, buttonholing seamen in taverns, spying on assumed ringleaders, even trying to ingratiate himself with the relatives of Valentine Joyce who lived in the neighborhood. But his reports during an investigation that lasted a fortnight suggest that either the Spithead sailors were wholly untainted by subversion or he had been hoodwinked (or won over) by them during his conscientious sleuthing. "There is not a man in the fleet," he wrote, "whose attachment to the King need be doubted." A little later, "Nothing like want of loyalty to the King or attachment to the government could be traced in the business."

Those conclusions were altogether too rosy. Evidence of secret societies and Jacobin instigation may have been slight or nonexistent. But had the agent donned disguise and spent a few days on one of His Majesty's ships he could not have missed the signs that within the hearts and minds of British sailors time-honored traditions of patriotism and loyalty to the Crown were perforce making room for novel concepts of fundamental human rights.

Five

MISCHIEF AT THE NORE

The men of Admiral Lord Bridport's ships were by this time convinced that while a pardon from the king was all very well, his parliament was seeking to avoid any action on the promise of indemnity and redress of grievances. On Sunday morning, 7 May 1797, the winds in the English Channel at last shifted. But when Bridport, in erroneous belief that the French were sailing from Brest, ordered Sir Alan Gardner's squadron out from St. Helen's to meet them, its crews instead jeered defiantly from the forecastles, tops, shrouds, and booms. Delegates from HMS *Pompée* went among the other ships, calling forth their comrades. The *Defence* hung back until the *Pompée* and *Glory* trained their 32-pounders on her. On HMS *Mars* a marine guard blocked the captain's path to his quarterdeck. A note handed to the captain of the *Duke* listed the officers that the crew wanted off the ship, "never to return again." Men on the *Glory* declared a work stoppage. On the flagship *Royal Sovereign* mutineers took over Sir Alan's cabin. Vessel after vessel ran up the red flag, traditional symbol of anarchy and rebellion.

Delegates' boats made for the *Queen Charlotte*. Capt. Walter Locke called on his marines to repel boarders. They refused, and he had helplessly to stand aside while the delegates conferred with his own ship's mutineers in the state cabin. The delegates returned to their boats and began to row across the three miles of water to Spithead, where lay four line-of-battle ships, the *Marlborough*, *La Nymphe*, *London*, and *Monarch*, with several frigates and smaller vessels. The purpose now was to unify the mutiny, then concentrate the entire Channel Fleet at St.

Helen's, at a safe distance from the Portsmouth shore batteries. (Valentine Joyce, foremost among the original mutineers, no doubt continued to have a role in the decision making, but in the absence of any subsequent inquiry, a clear identification of the ringleaders would be lost to history.) Word of the approach of the delegates' flotilla reached Admiral Lord Bridport on the *Royal George*. He wrote an emotional letter to the Admiralty. "I cannot command the fleet as all authority is taken from me. . . . My mind is too deeply wounded. . . . I am so unwell that I can scarcely hold my pen to write these sentiments of distress."

The squadron still at Spithead was under the direct command of Adm. Sir John Colpoys, who was flying his flag on HMS *London*. Colpoys intended no truck with mutineers. When informed of the situation at St. Helen's, he mustered his people, harangued them into sullen obedience, and sent them below, with hatches sealed and guarded. He also had the lower-deck guns drawn in and the portholes shut to prevent communication with anyone coming alongside. He stationed his officers and marines about the warship's upper deck, then waited. Soon the splash of oars could be heard as the delegates' flotilla drew closer. The sound was also audible to the men below, who began shoving at the hatches. Within minutes they had broken out and were swarming on deck. Colpoys told his officers to fire, but some of the men had muskets too. Shots clattered, and at least one seaman died. Another sprang to a forward gun, unlashed it, and slewed it around to sweep the quarterdeck. Lt. Peter Bover hailed at him to stop. When he refused, Bover shot him. But by then Colpoys's marines had edged from the scene or openly gone over to the mutineers. Acknowledging defeat, shaken by the bloodshed on his decks, Colpoys ordered a cease-fire.

He and Bover were promptly seized. Only the intervention of the ship's surgeon and Bover's moderately good standing with the crew saved the lieutenant from an instant hanging. During the heated discussions that followed the arrival of the delegates from St. Helen's, Bover's fate hung in the balance. Valentine Joyce threw his weight in favor of restraint. Admiral Colpoys, the captain, and Lieutenant Bover were confined in their separate cabins. And the delegates continued to the other ships in turn.

The expulsion of undesirable officers proceeded apace. Those selected were told to leave peaceably or be manhandled over the side. From eighteen different ships at Spithead and St. Helen's, scores of officers were sent ashore. Some were treated with the deference due their rank, others abused or jeered at. Those ousted included Adm. Sir Alan Gardner and three captains. Before the ships at Spithead dropped down to St. Helen's in accordance with the mutineers' plans, a fourth captain, commanding the frigate *Eurydice*, had left his ship. He did so voluntarily, amid mutual regret, his men sadly explaining that unless they took the ship to St. Helen's the *Marlborough* would fire into her. The *Eurydice* was back at her Portsmouth anchorage the next day, and the entire crew invited the beached capain to return: "We are men that loves the present cause as men ought to, yet we are not elevated that degree to neglect our duty to our country or our obedience to you." The mutiny, it appeared, was still short on unanimity.

But the mere petitioning for better pay and food had escalated into the wholesale eviction of officers from their ships. These latest tidings from Portsmouth reached London by overnight courier, weather having interrupted the shuttle telegraph. At about this time an American merchant captain just out of Brest described an invasion force assembled there, and still further dire intelligence told of an enemy armada preparing to leave Texel—Ireland, already seething with revolt, the likely destination of both fleets. The Admiralty sent grim word to Prime Minister Pitt: "Total destruction is near."

Some of the reports were magnified, perhaps intentionally to gain effect. But there was a nationwide impatience with the government's dilatory handling of the naval crisis, compounded now by a concern for the physical safety of Admiral Colpoys and the other officers imprisoned on their own ships. Westminister and Downing Street had to take notice. Pitt's bill for improving pay and victuals was passed in committee without a dissenting vote and laid before Commons, and there too it won unanimous approval. Its next stop was the House of Lords. Pitt kept his legislators in session until the process was completed. The new bill, Lord Spencer wrote Bridport with unconcealed relief, would "remove all the difficulties" and bring the sailors back to "their old habits of regularity and obedience." To secure this ideal state more promptly, it was decided that some forceful personage respected by the seamen should talk to them directly with a copy of the bill in his hands. This brought Lord Howe back into the picture. Having returned to his London residence, he had only partly recovered from gout, but when Spencer called upon him, he at once agreed to the First Lord's proposal.

The act of Parliament received the royal assent on 10 May. Lord Howe and his wife arrived in Portsmouth the next day. A boat took his lordship across The Solent to St. Helen's, where he first boarded the *Royal George* and proclaimed the mutineers' demands granted, with a royal pardon to follow. For the next two days Howe toured the Channel Fleet, addressing its crews with a blend of paternal solicitude and military sternness. Afterward he wrote that "the complaints in the ships under Lord Bridport . . . were of a nature that admitted of immediate gratification." What nevertheless surprised and probably disconcerted him was the stubbornness of the men's resolve not to permit any return of unpopular officers. Though aware as he must have been of the dangerous precedent it set, Howe felt that he had to yield even on this point. Otherwise, as he indicated to the Admiralty, "fresh difficulties" must be expected. And at a two-hour conference with delegates in the gun room of the *Royal William* at Spithead on the morning of 13 May he accepted their list of officers to be dismissed or superseded—forty-nine, including an admiral and four captains.

That was not all. Even as Howe proceeded with his mission of appeasement off Portsmouth, the Plymouth squadron showed up suddenly, eight ships in open mutiny with red flags aflutter. Howe at once had himself rowed over to the flagship *Prince* and turned jeers into cheers with an explanation of the new bill. But the Plymouth mutineers, like their Portsmouth brethren, were adamant in demanding the departure of obnoxious officers. They confronted Howe with an even longer blacklist, sixty-five names. Having already given in on the matter, Howe had to accede, yet not as tamely as might have been supposed, for he could anticipate the Admiralty's reaction. But it was, after all, their lordships who had saddled him with the assignment, and his judgment was that only through this risky course could it be discharged.

More than one hundred naval officers were ejected from their ships, among them Adm. Sir John Colpoys of the *London*. Peter Bover, Colpoys's lieutenant who had shot a mutineer on that vessel, was forgiven and welcomed back with cheers. Sir Alan Gardner's men appear to have had second thoughts about their irascible commander, and he reboarded the *Royal George*, grumbling but promising justice for all. The Spithead mutiny reached its formal conclusion in the great cabin of the *Royal William* on Sunday, 14 May, and the delegates proposed that they publicly thank Lord Howe and his lady at a ceremonial dinner in Portsmouth the next day. Howe agreed, still on his conciliatory tack and unlikely to have changed it even had he known that mutiny was flaring elsewhere in his beloved navy.

While Howe toured the Channel Fleet, some two hundred miles away off Great Yarmouth agitation among the crew of HMS *Adamant* had brought Admiral Duncan hurrying on board. His towering presence alone might have given the unruly men pause. He told them that while he would rather have them love than fear him, "I will with my own hand put to death the first man who shall display the slightest sign of rebellious conduct." Suiting action almost to the word, Duncan grasped a presumed miscreant by the collar, hauled him to the ship's rail, and dangled him over the side. "Look, my lads, at the fellow who dares depose me." Duncan's no-nonsense display had the desired effect, and writing the next day to the Admiralty, he reported conditions at Great Yarmouth "all orderly and quiet." If this was Duncan's true impression, events southward near the mouth of the Thames River, at the dual anchorage known as Great Nore and Little Nore, were about to disabuse him of it.

The Royal Navy's force in these waters bore little comparison with the Channel Fleet or even Duncan's modest squadron. It was a somewhat ragtag assortment of vessels used for conducting local patrols or for piloting merchantmen up the Thames Estuary and consisted of only three line-of-battle ships, eight frigates, and a scattering of sloops and smaller craft. Their crews had little sense of belonging to a unified and strategically motivated command and would have been difficult to organize for a royal review, much less a mutiny. Yet what they did culminated the navy's season of discontent and was all the more a phenomenon because it crested after the Admiralty had gone to extraordinary lengths to appease the mutineers at Portsmouth.

Regardless of events elsewhere, an outburst of some sort at the Nore was probably inevitable. The fuse had long sputtered on the *Sandwich*, a grossly overcrowded receiving ship, whose surgeon had weeks earlier warned that the men crammed on board were "unhappy sufferers." The breaking point occurred early on 12 May when the *Sandwich*'s people defied their captain and ordered Lt. Philip Justice off the ship. (One of the lieutenant's alleged sins had been the "insulting" removal of screens placed about the hammocks of seamen and their visiting wives or sweethearts.) Justice took the news to the 64-gun *Inflexible*, interrupting a court-martial and sending the assembled captains hurrying back to their ships.

One of the officers on the court-martial was Capt. William Bligh, whose ship the *Director* had recently put in at The Nore for repairs. Returning from the *Inflexible*, he was met with demands for the removal of two lieutenants and the master, all charged with "ill-usage." Bligh compromised by confining the officers to their quarters. The time was just ahead when Bligh must have felt his career inescapably dogged by mutiny, but right then he was not alone as tensions mounted on every vessel anchored at The Nore.

The interrupted court-martial resumed on the frigate *San Fiorenzo*, at The Nore under orders to convey the newlyweds Prince and Princess of Württemburg to Germany. A boatload of mutineers came alongside and told the crew to cheer when the *Inflexible*, with a captain of the foretop in command, stood out to sea. At first the men of the *San Fiorenzo* demurred, but the *Inflexible* herself drew abreast the frigate with ports open, guns manned, and tompions out. A single shot across the *San Fiorenzo*'s bow set the crew to vigorous cheering.

Several of the ships had each appointed not one or two delegates but a whole committee of twelve. On the *Sandwich*, whose officers had been ordered ashore under the threat of gunfire, squabbling among the delegates led them to seek a suitably commanding leader. By the third day of the uprising a newcomer working in the carpenter's mate's berth had captured their interest through his persuasive manner and superior education. The delegates invited him to take charge, and as he later asserted, given his compassion and awareness of the people's grievances, "how could I indifferently stand by?" In rapid time Richard Parker became the self-styled president of what newspapers soon called the Floating Republic.

Aged thirty, well built with black hair, Parker had had an earlier, spotty naval career. As a midshipman he had been court-martialed for some obscure infraction and in 1784 was discharged for either disobedi-ence or nervous disorder, perhaps both. He had married the daughter of a Scots farmer, and after a brief and unsuccessful term as schoolmaster in Leith, Scotland, he borrowed heavily from her family. Unable to repay, he landed in a debtor's jail. (His wife told a magistrate that he was deranged.) To gain his release Parker took the "quota bounty"—moneys paid by cities and counties to secure their quota of men for the king's service—and thus found himself back in the navy, aboard the *Sandwich* as one of many supernumeraries among the eleven hundred men crowded into a vessel built for one-third that number.

Once in place as ringleader of a mutiny, Parker strove for a show of discipline, solidarity, and organization. It was probably at his direction that delegates went about the Nore ships, getting the sailors to sign loyalty oaths. There was, however, some haziness about grievances and demands. News had percolated to the nearby garrison town of Sheerness and among the ships that the Spithead uprising had forced the Admiralty to make generous concessions. The Nore seamen, Parker included, were not certain that they had grounds upon which to justify any mutiny, a question that decided them to send four delegates to Portsmouth, who would report back precisely what went on there. The idea may have been that of one of the four, Matthew Hollister, a delegate from Bligh's ship *Director*. At any rate, he and the others arrived in the naval port on

Richard Parker, self-styled president of the "Floating Republic." *(National Maritime Museum, London)*

15 May as its townsfolk celebrated the settlement Lord Howe had just secured.

The Channel Fleet's delegates, yesterday's mutineers, had come ashore for breakfast, then toured the ships with Lord and Lady Howe. Not that everybody took delight in the way the mutiny had ended. "Much mischief has been done," wrote Adm. William Young privately, "by the mode in which the mutineers at Spithead were treated by Lord Howe." The celebration particularly angered Lord Bridport, to whom it smacked of a mutineers' victory fete, and when he received sailing orders two days later, he complained that it was Howe's fault that the ships were not prepared to put out right away. Lord Bridport could never have brought himself to acknowledge that he had Howe to thank that the Channel Fleet was in any shape to sail at all.

Howe was not the only hero of the hour. Valentine Joyce shared in the plaudits. The former mutineer and the revered admiral were cheered and toasted together at a dinner in the city governor's house that evening. And by then the delegates from The Nore had seen enough, having made contact with Joyce and accompanied him on board the *Royal George* to hear Lord Howe, seated on the quarterdeck, read the king's proclamation of pardon to the assembled crew. Howe had held the document aloft so that the sailors could see its royal seal. Meanwhile, the last red flag had come fluttering down, to be replaced by the royal standard. Hollister and his fellow delegates conveyed all of this to Richard Parker at The Nore, along with details of what else the Admiralty had conceded.

Upon hearing the news from Spithead, the Nore mutineers felt that the privilege of expelling unwanted officers belonged to them as well. Officers thereupon told to go included William Bligh, turned out of his ship for the second time in his career. But the report from Spithead seemed to take the wind out of Parker's sails, for it was difficult to see what he was left with to support a mutiny. This one developed a life of its own. Sailors who could scarcely have articulated grievances strutted about Sheerness with cutlasses or lounged on the decks of their ships, enjoying the sudden freedom. Others more conscious of the gravity of their conduct saw a need to formulate demands. The principal one was that already granted at Spithead, namely, a royal pardon. Once that was secured, the men might call off their mutiny in safety, without giving the appearance of caving in to the Admiralty.

Perhaps Parker was indeed somewhat mad. While continuing to exert a hold on the men through oratory at once pretentious and incoherent, he betrayed a recklessness that bordered on insanity. Belittling the Spithead concessions, he and pliant delegates drew up their own list. It was handed to Charles Buckner, port admiral at Sheerness, on 20 May when he visited the *Sandwich* to extend the Admiralty's promise of a royal pardon to the Nore dissidents. And the list seemed guaranteed to outrage. Composed as eight articles, it demanded not only the indulgences won at Spithead but more generous shore leave, a fairer distribution of prize money, amnesty for returning deserters, and changes in the Articles of War. In addition, in what was both an ominous reference to officers held hostage in mutinous ships and the ultimate in sheer impudence, "the committee in council on the *Sandwich* unanimously agree they will not give up their charges until the appearance of some of the Lords Commissioners of the Admiralty to ratify the same."

The Admiralty was already unhappy with the concessions to which Lord Howe had committed it and determined to approve no more. As for any of their lordships going cap in hand before the Nore rebels, that was unthinkable. But the location of the mutiny posed a strategic threat. The rebellious ships had arranged themselves in the Great Nore to form two crescents. Parker's men rowed into Sheerness and seized eight gunboats, from which they fired a parting shot as they left the harbor, and these vessels were placed in position at the formation's flanks. The Floating Republic had become a potentially intimidating force at the very gateway to the city of London. With this in mind, Lord Spencer rushed a letter to Duncan, whose own fleet at Great Yarmouth, according to the admiral, remained loyal and serene. Describing the ships at The Nore as "in the most complete state of mutiny," Spencer's letter hinted that Duncan might send some of his squadron to The Nore in the hope of bringing the mutineers to their senses.

Duncan ought then to have realized that but for his overly buoyant reports the Admiralty would scarcely have suggested such a thing. Duncan's ships were themselves close to "a most complete state of mutiny," according to Andrew Hardy, master's mate in the *Nassau*. Sailors ashore were breaking windows and frightening inhabitants. "Yarmouth is in an uproar," Hardy wrote on 20 May. "God knows where it will end." What helped feed Admiral Duncan's quite different impression was a statement from his people on the *Venerable* that they had "nothing to complain of" and would never, "as long as life will permit, see you or the flag insulted." In this spirit the *Venerable*'s crew would perhaps have fired on mutineers if so ordered. But not even Duncan, for all his professed optimism, could feel so sanguine about the rest of his fleet. In any event, he did not savor the Admiralty's idea and recommended an alternative. "You should get [the *Sandwich*] cast adrift in the night, let her go on the sands, that the scoundrels may drown." However, if there proved no other course than assigning some of his ships to The Nore, "I don't shrink from the business."

This was all very well, but it left the Admiralty still unclear as to the morale of Duncan's fleet. Their lordships decided that someone should go to Great Yarmouth and personally ascertain whether any of the ships there could be trusted to use force, if so ordered, against the sailors at The Nore. "Until we know what we can look to from your squadron," the Admiralty informed Duncan, "it will be very difficult for us to know how to act." The emissary chosen for this "very delicate business" was William Bligh, still without a ship.

Parker, meanwhile, continued to act with irrational boldness. He chastised the Admiralty peers for not coming to Sheerness in person and protested the reinforcement of the garrison as "an insult to the peaceable behavior of the seamen," words he would also have applied to the military detachments steadily deploying along the shoreline of northern Kent. On 26 May Admiral Buckner had reported that the mutineers were planning to blockade the Thames and the Medway. It was almost as if they were privy to a ruling just made by the Lord Chancellor, head of the British judiciary, that any pardon granted at Spithead did not automatically apply to The Nore. In these same hours, while the departure of Bridport's Channel Fleet had lessened apprehensions about a French move from Brest, the reported Dutch buildup at Texel strengthened the belief that the sooner Duncan's North Sea force resumed its blockade the better. "There is little doubt of a descent upon this country being in contemplation," wrote an anxious Pitt. To these dire developments his cabinet responded by increasing pressure upon the Admiralty to put an end to the general unrest.

Spencer had no option. As he had during the crisis at Spithead, the First Lord of the Admiralty had to show himself in person at the scene of a mutiny. But without waiting for Bligh's report from Great Yarmouth, the Admiralty also directed Duncan to prepare dependable ships for action against the Nore mutineers. It was a carrot-and-stick combination, one doomed to fail. Duncan's orders had not yet reached him when, on Saturday, 27 May, he signaled his fleet to weigh anchor, intending to return to the North Sea blockading station. Despite that friendly petition of a few days earlier, some of the *Venerable*'s crew balked at sailing, and Duncan had to summon his marines, who overpowered and ironed the ringleaders. The *Venerable* put to sea, and the loyal *Adamant* prepared to follow. The *Montagu* held back, her people complaining because she leaked so badly that they slept on sodden hammocks. The *Nassau* also refused to put out. "Our people now are desperate," wrote Master's Mate Hardy, and the captain's clerk logged "violent commotions." The *Nassau*'s commander transferred his flag to the *Adamant,* and "when he left the ship," noted Hardy, "tears were seen coming down his cheeks."

That same weekend Lord Spencer left London for Sheerness. On Sunday morning at the harbor commissioner's home Admiral Buckner informed the First Lord that Parker would permit his delegates to confer with him only if he had come in total submission. Discussions did take place, but Parker attended none. (Spencer is said to have refused to see him.) The First Lord may then have been tempted to return to London in disgust. But there had appeared among the ships signs of a faltering resolve as more and more men favored accepting the promise of a royal pardon and letting things go at that. Rumors of a wavering in the mutinous ranks very likely reached Lord Spencer, who stayed on in Sheerness through Monday morning.

He may not, even by then, have become apprised of events off Great Yarmouth, where Captain Bligh had arrived too late to see Duncan but after a visit to the *Nassau* concluded that the conduct of his sailors, if ordered to fire on their comrades at The Nore, would be "very doubtful and hazardous." Duncan's fleet was, in any case, disintegrating. The 64-gun ships *Repulse* and *Ardent* had followed him out on Saturday but then turned back. So had the frigates *Isis* and *Glatton*, also the *Agamemnon*, whose captain refused to call out the marines when the crew trained the guns on the quarterdeck because, as he told a mortified officer of the watch, "some of my men will be shot, and I could not bear to see them lying in convulsions on the deck." Conscious of "a disgrace which I believe never before happened to a British admiral," Duncan sailed into the North Sea with only two ships, the *Venerable* and the *Adamant*. Not that those that had deserted him tarried long at Great Yarmouth. Before nightfall on Sunday some were on the move again, southbound for The Nore and by no means with the purpose that the Admiralty had hopefully contemplated.

Bad weather prevented further meetings between the Admiralty's deputation at Sheerness and the mutinous delegates until Monday afternoon. Even then only two rain-soaked delegates arrived at the commissioner's house and said they were unable to make up their minds until informed what precisely had been done for the Portsmouth men. Admiral Buckner gave them a copy of the act of Parliament relating to pay and food rations. Still undecided, they returned to their ships, where the split in ranks had widened. More bad news was in store for them. When Lord Spencer returned to London, he left Buckner with sealed instructions for isolating the mutinous ships. No supply boats would be allowed to leave Sheerness, and seamen coming ashore to seek provisions were to be seized and imprisoned.

Even as Parker went ahead with his lunatic plan to blockade London, the great mutiny had begun to crumble. Parker assembled the crew of the *Sandwich* and appealed for continued support. The loudest cries in response were for giving up. On Tuesday two 36-gun frigates, never wholeheartedly mutinous and kept in place only by the superior firepower of HMS *Inflexible*, managed to escape. The *Clyde* slipped cables first and got into Sheerness on the flood tide. The *San Fiorenzo* erred in direction, and a fresh westerly wind carried her downriver through the middle of the rebellious fleet. She ran a gauntlet of musket fire and grapeshot. Emerging doggedly with shrouds torn and four topmen wounded, she rounded the coast with the aid of a pilot and made safely into Portsmouth.

The mutiny might have ended there and then. But even as the frigates escaped, the first reinforcements from Great Yarmouth hove into view, six sail of the line—the *Montagu, Repulse, Nassau, Belliqueux, Lion*, and *Standard*—all with red flags flying. According to a Lieutenant Watson, on board a tender that the mutineers had seized, Parker rejoiced, "seemed intoxicated with a sense of his own consequence." The Admiralty's refusal to negotiate had left him with only two courses of action: settle for the promised royal pardon and return to duty, or leave English waters for France or even America. The first alternative did not sit well with him, and his followers would probably have opposed the other. But the addition of Duncan's errant ships gave Parker a formidable force with which he dreamed still more obsessively of bringing the Admiralty to its knees.

Though London might not starve, Parker's blockade threatened ruin to merchants, brokers, importers, and exporters. More North Sea Fleet vessels had arrived at The Nore, Bligh's *Director* included. Parker thanked them "from the bottom of our hearts," probably not fully aware of how insecure their commitment to mutiny had become by then. The *Director*'s decks, for instance, were the scene of almost daily fights between mutineers and loyalists. Even so, Parker's force, augmented by the Great Yarmouth contingent, numbered almost two dozen warships that were, reported an alarmed Admiral Buckner from Sheerness, "stopping all traders bound for the port of London." Master's Mate Hardy on the *Nassau* wrote of the mutineers' determination to "stop the commerce of the country until their demands are met. This is a desperate undertaking." But the size of the mercantile flotilla halted at the Thames became too big for Parker to handle. For this reason and because his blockade had cost the seamen's movement popular sympathy as well as parliamentary support, Parker ordered that all merchant vessels be allowed free passage, only victualing ships to be detained.

At the same time the Admiralty's countermeasures were hurting his supporters. Not only were the seamen denied supplies from shore, but the post office was about to cease deliveries to disaffected ships. As the Admiralty calculated, "Nothing is more likely to bring them to reason than finding themselves cut off from the country." Precautions were in place and steps taken to foil escape attempts. A boom would be lowered across the Thames so that the mutineers could not get upriver, and the estuary's marker buoys would be removed and lighthouse lamps doused.

Along with the growing condemnation of the mutiny and the blockade was a continuing reluctance to blame the lowly seamen. They were "misguided . . . deluded," temporarily "seduced" by shadowy instigators. This was the theme of a royal proclamation alerting the country to political agitators and to new legislation, the Incitement to Mutiny Act, which carried the death penalty. Not everybody subscribed to the notion that Britain's sailors were fundamentally patriotic and the real villains sinister subversives. Many would have agreed with Rufus King, the American minister in London, who wrote that while "the seamen may have been tampered with," they were genuinely questioning traditional precepts and allegiances because "they have heard so much of the Equality and Rights of Man." Probably so, but they had not totally abandoned loyal traditions, and on a rain-swept 4 June, the king's birthday, every mutinous ship fired a royal salute and ran up the royal standard alongside its red flag.

Two days later, in the great cabin of the *Sandwich*, the central committee, with Parker at the head of the table, drafted a petition to the king. This contained a list of grievances, some soft soap for His Majesty—"We have the highest opinion of Our Most Gracious Sovereign"—and some startingly novel sentiments: "Liberty—the pride and boast of a Briton, has always been denied us. The Age of Reason has at last evolved." Also a warning: "We will sell our lives dearly. Starving us will not work, we have six months' provisions." The petition concluded with an ultimatum. The mutineers would "astonish their dear countrymen" with an unspecified action and withdraw "as outlaws" to another country if no response came to their petition within fifty-four hours.

Those defiant words hid bluff and desperation. Low on supplies and fresh water, more of Parker's people were for breaking away, and now he knew it. He may have learned of the efforts at his rear to seal off escape, the removal or destruction of buoys and the blackout of lighthouses and lightships. A confidently toughened Admiralty sent Captain Knight of the *Montagu*, who had delivered the delegates' ultimatum, back to Sheerness with a curt rejection. Parker and his committee toured a disillusioned fleet. Most of the ships greeted him respectfully, bands playing on some. But then he spoke of continuing the mutiny, told them that they had no option, that the government had ruled them traitors, that they could forget a royal pardon and expect instead the noose or a firing squad. More jeers than cheers greeted these remarks as the people wrangled among themselves.

For some, escape still appeared an attractive possibility. The ninth of June brought a determination to sail. HMS *Sandwich* made the signal, one gun fired and foretopsail loosened. The whole fleet answered, but without clear comprehension. "Where they intend to go, God only knows," wrote Andrew Hardy on the *Nassau*. "Some say to the Dutch, others say France, and others Botany Bay." Wherever they decided, "we [officers] will still be prisoners." Officers on HMS *Leopard* had other ideas. The first lieutenant had managed to slip from confinement and conspire with loyalists to retake the ship. They did so that same Friday afternoon, overpowering the rebel faction at gunpoint. After a struggle in which a loyal midshipman fell mortally wounded, eighteen mutinous ringleaders were locked in irons, and with the royal standard aloft in place of the red flag the *Leopard* bore upriver for Gravesend. The *Repulse* tried to follow but grounded, a sitting target for the *Monmouth* and the *Director*, the ships closest to her. Accounts vary as to what happened next. Parker may have boarded the *Director* and ordered her cannon brought to bear, howling with rage when the crew refused to obey. (Bligh would have been proud.) Parker is next seen on the *Monmouth*, whose guns certainly opened up at the *Repulse*, and he is said to have worked one himself. The firing lasted longer than an hour, and a lieutenant on the *Repulse* lost a leg. But by nightfall the ship had freed herself and got safely up the River Medway. The *Ardent* broke away next, and the following morning the *Nassau* was not the only vessel upon which, as Master's Mate Hardy recorded, the people "are all in an uproar afraid they will be left in the lurch."

Each vessel waited for the others to move first. So it seemed, at any rate, and some impatient members of the *Nassau*'s crew set forth among the remaining ships of the North Sea Fleet to spur a general abandonment of "Admiral" Parker's mutiny. Red flags still flew on seventeen sail of the line. By midday Saturday that figure was down to five. The mutiny was close to over, even on the *Sandwich*, where delegates fretted anxiously and a speechless Parker found himself in effect a prisoner. On Monday the twelfth a few holdouts like the *Montagu* and *Inflexible* still threatened to fire on ships poised to make off, but one after another of them slipped cables, the people releasing their officers, who promptly reasserted authority. As the *Standard* sailed upriver with royal colors flying, one of her delegates shot himself. The stubborn *Montagu* quit on the fifteenth, her log showing the following entry: "Took into custody 11 men called Delegates and Committee men and put them in irons." On the *Sandwich*, where so much had begun, Parker made a final appeal to the crew. He was shouted down. Faced by the newly released officers, he turned over the keys to the magazine and small arms and store room and was himself then taken below and the next morning put ashore in irons at Gravesend.

Richard Parker was the first of more than four hundred court-martialed for the mutiny at The Nore. The panel of thirteen judges of captain's rank or higher gathered in the great cabin of HMS *Neptune*

After portraying himself as a rueful martyr, Parker was hanged from the yardarm of the *Sandwich*. *(National Maritime Museum, London)*

late in June heard him protest that he had acted from the best of motives. But nothing could have excused his participation, widely observed, in the bombardment of one of His Majesty's ships. That monarch, when Parker was convicted and sentenced to die, wanted his body hung in chains at the scene of his infamy. But there could be found no legal grounds for this display. Not that it would have made any difference to Parker, who presented himself as a rueful martyr, amazed that he had ever become involved in helping the underdog. "The miseries [of] the lower classes are imputable in a great measure to their ignorance, cowardice and duplicity. Nothing short of a miracle would ever afford them any relief." He should have known better than to accept the leadership of the mutiny, and if anyone wondered how an educated man could have been so indiscreet, "tell them that Richard Parker, in his last moments, was pierced to the bottom of his soul with asking himself the same question."

After leading the successful mutiny at Spithead, Valentine Joyce had feasted with lords. Aboard HMS *Sandwich* on the morning of 30 June the leader of the failed Nore mutiny ate a good breakfast, received a glass of wine and a handshake from his captain and psalms from the chaplain, and then was hanged from the yardarm. Stories would circulate long afterward of how his wife arranged the theft of his body and its furtive transport to London for a Christian burial. Recaptured by authorities, it was finally interred, decently enough, in a Whitechapel churchyard.

The trials continued after Parker's death (their record fills thirty-two volumes in the British Admiralty's archives). Sixty mutineers were condemned to death, imprisonment, or flogging. Probably no more than two dozen were hanged, most of them from the *Sandwich*. The *Director*'s quota for conviction was reduced, thanks to her captain, who went to considerable lengths to secure pardons. This should have won him the gratitude and affection of his people and probably did, perhaps encouraging him to again assume that he was forever done with mutiny. And even yet this was for William Bligh to be by no means the case.

Six

Six

THE NIGHTMARE SHIP

That the Dutch crews blockaded at intervals by Admiral Duncan's North Sea Fleet were themselves far from models of discipline may be one of the reasons why they did not emerge during the Nore mutiny. They finally came to grips with the British at the Battle of Camperdown and were decisively beaten by ships that four months earlier had been hotbeds of mutiny. One was the *Director*, and though there were questions afterward about her performance under Bligh, his men and the former mutineers on other ships fought well, as if all the more determined to affirm their patriotism and loyalty.

As that perilous summer of 1797 waned, Admiral Earl Howe advised against any complacency or display of triumph at the Admiralty with respect to the mutineers at Spithead and The Nore. "If exultation is shewn . . . at the success on the part of the Government . . . it may increase the mischief." The Admiralty could certainly have derived a twofold lesson from those events, namely, that legitimate grievances of the lower deck were best promptly redressed and that impossible demands were best resisted without compromise. Yet their lordships still suffered from a blind spot. British sailors had beome aware of "rights" that they might secure through unified action. The Admiralty failed to admit or understand this phenomenon, and instances of collective insubordination continued, especially within squadrons on foreign stations newly augmented by ships from the troubled home waters.

Some of that revolutionary awareness lurked even behind incidents where lofty principles seemed not at stake. Early in July of that same year, 1797, men on the 90-gun *St. George*, one of the ships blockading

Cadiz, mutinied to protest the death sentence passed upon two of their number convicted of buggery. The two were hanged anyway, and four others were court-martialed for mutiny and similarly condemned. Their execution was set for a Sunday. Officers disturbed by the precedent of Sabbath hangings expressed their concern to the commander of the Mediterranean Fleet, Sir John Jervis, who had the most vocal of them sent home. Jervis, newly titled the Earl St. Vincent for his victory off the Spanish cape of that name, was a formidable if fair-minded officer determined to allow no lower-deck mischief to impede naval operations. He ruled that the executions proceed as ordered, and to Rear Adm. Horatio Nelson, employed on the same station, he wrote that had the criminals been granted the five days' stay they asked for, "they could have hatched five hundred treasons."

Nelson had not long shifted his flag to the *Theseus*, one of the ships involved in the mutinies at home, whose crew, however, had sworn devotion to him in writing. A contemporary was to say of Britain's naval hero that seamen invariably became attached to him and "in ten days time he could have restored the most mutinous ship in the Navy to order." Perhaps so, but Nelson was no less opposed than any fellow commander to submission to mutinous demands. Just before sailing off to make an amphibious assault on the island of Teneriffe, he congratulated Earl St. Vincent on his tough stance and hoped it would "end all disorders in our fleet." He added that events back home might never have so deteriorated had those in charge displayed "the same determined spirit." As for hanging offenders on holy days, "had it been Christmas Day instead of Sunday I would have executed them. We know not what might have been hatched by a Sunday's grog."

Toward the end of the year Earl St. Vincent felt he could report "every appearance of contentment and proper subordination." The respite was short-lived. In the spring of 1798 ten of his best ships were detailed for service under Nelson, who had returned to the Mediterranean after recuperating in England from the loss of his right arm and who was eager to challenge Bonaparte's fleet, which was fitting out at Toulon. The replacement ships sent to St. Vincent included HMS *Marlborough*, which was in a state of almost open mutiny. Forewarned, St. Vincent arranged his ships into two columns and ordered the *Marlborough* anchored between them upon her arrival. Mutinous ringleaders were quickly identified, court-martialed, and sentenced to death, St. Vincent adding a refinement. Each man must be hauled to the yardarm by members of the *Marlborough*'s crew, "no part of the boats' crews from other ships, as had been on similar occasions, to assist in the punishment." When the *Marlborough*'s captain voiced doubt that his men would obey, St. Vincent asked him if that meant he was unable to command his ship, for if it did, "I will immediately send on board an officer who can." He encircled the *Marlborough* with armed launches and the executions began, each carried out by the doomed man's own messmates. St. Vincent never deviated from this course and was to remain unmoved even by appeals for mercy based on a transgressor's good character. In the admiral's view, "No character, however good, shall save a man who is guilty of mutiny."

Britain's sailors had won for themselves improved pay and sustenance, somewhat better living conditions, and increased respect from their superiors. They could expect no more from the Admiralty. Further reforms or concessions were out of the question. When mutiny flared, the only sane response was of the sort exemplified by Adm. the Earl St. Vincent's suppressive measures in his Mediterranean Fleet. In 1798 at least fifty British sailors were hanged and as many flogged with from one hundred to four hundred lashes for mutiny, incitement to mutiny, and mutinous assembly, expressions, or behavior. The history of that short span of years embracing the end of the eighteenth century and the dawn of a new scintillates with British naval triumphs—at Camperdown, the Nile, Copenhagen, Trafalgar—each a testament to the tactical skill of commanding officers and the valor and loyalty of their seamen. And it is impossible to be sure that glory would have crowned any of those engagements without the stern, even ruthless, policy found necessary to keep mutinous spirits in check.

Among the British sailors hanged for mutiny in 1798 were four found masquerading under false names on a French privateer captured by HMS *Valiant* in the West Indies. They were betrayed by a fifth member of the privateer's crew, who served as prosecuting witness at their courts-martial. Following the executions their bodies were taken to specially built gibbets at Port Royal, Jamaica, for more prominent display. Their trials and confessions, with the fifth man's testimony, gave the world the first coherent details of a bloody revolt against a captain more truly guilty of the sort of quarterdeck sadism for which posterity would indict William Bligh.

Hugh Pigot came from a family whose wealth and political influence (his father had been on the board of the British Admiralty) were possible factors in his attainment of naval command at the age of twenty-two. It would be said in Pigot's defense that he was a skillful if ill-tempered officer who demanded proficiency from inferiors and too readily believed he could flog it out of them. In other words, a Bligh with a busier lash. Another assessment portrays him as a victim of self-doubts that could drive him to fits of passion and extreme cruelty. There is insufficient evidence for safe speculation, and it may be enough to presume that Pigot's was a character warped by a sense of insecurity and instincts of downright meanness.

The grisly drama of HMS *Hermione* was played out mostly in a tropical setting. Britain's precarious economy during her war with France depended substantially on the rich West Indian trade, the eastbound convoys that sailed regularly with sugar, molasses, coffee, syrup, cotton, and tobacco. Naval protection was of the utmost importance because the French had bases in those Caribbean waters, as did their Spanish allies. For Britain's navy men, service in the West Indies was a lonely, hostile, and pestilential exile, and the officers were scarcely any better off. And while the hardships and perils found on such pitilessly remote stations could have a pernicious effect upon those burdened with the responsibilities of command, characters already pathologically flawed were the most vulnerable. Hugh Pigot may have fallen into this category, and his average of two floggings a week on HMS *Success*, a punishment rate not really excessive, was to worsen rapidly after he transferred his command to the 32-gun frigate *Hermione* early in 1797.

On an autumn evening of that year as the *Hermione* and the brig *Diligence* patrolled the Mona Passage west of Puerto Rico, Pigot lost his temper with a young Irish midshipman, David O'Brien Casey, who had the temerity to answer back and was thereupon ordered under threat of the cat to apologize on bended knee. Casey refused and was stripped to the waist, tied to the bar of the capstan, and given twelve lashes by Boatswain William Martin. The *Hermione*'s crew had by this time endured months of brutal treatment. If an actual plot had developed, one of the early instigators would have been Lawrence Cronin, another Irishman, thirty-five, educated, and not long promoted by Pigot from able seaman to surgeon's mate. Pigot seemed not to have suspected Cronin, or anyone else. His harsh reaction to Casey's impertinence may have reflected some apprehensive knowledge of events back home, confided to him by Adm. Sir Hyde Parker, commanding the West Indies station. Parker, an aging widower who thought highly of Pigot, saw Irish plotting behind every sailors' protest and was certainly informed of the mutiny at Spithead. The virus had already reached his command. The crew of a Royal Navy schooner, the *Marie Antoinette*, had thrown its lieutenant and another officer overboard and sailed away into enemy waters.

Five days after Midshipman Casey's flogging the *Hermione* battled rainsqualls, and topmen out on the yards were gathering up canvas in the teeth of the gusty wind. From fifty-feet below Pigot bellowed curses at them through his speaking trumpet, apparently infuriated by their slowness. He threatened to flog the last man down. In the scrambling descent three mizzentopmen missed their footing and plunged to their deaths. Pigot ordered the bodies thrown overboard and blamed a dozen men for clumsiness aloft and had them all flogged. According to Casey's subsequent account, it was this tragedy that "hastened if not entirely decided the mutiny." While the flogging proceeded in front of all hands, a privateer the *Hermione* had been pursuing slipped out of sight. The better to find it again Pigot signaled the *Diligence* to bear away on a new tack. By nightfall the *Hermione* and her complement of some 170 uneasy souls sailed on alone.

All but the duty watch presumably slumbered, including Boatswain William Martin and his wife, whom Pigot had for unknown reasons allowed to join her husband on the patrol. The horror began just before midnight, but perhaps not according to a definite plan. If there was a genuine conspiracy below decks it amounted to no more than eighteen men, Surgeon's Mate Cronin among them. But more than twice as many were suddenly fervid for action. Emotions chiefly of hate took control, with the help of buckets of officers' rum stolen from the gun room. Some two dozen men of the starboard watch tramped aft to the captain's cabin, felled the marine guard, and smashed open the door. Pigot sprang from his cot. He was beaten back by knives, cutlasses, and tomahawks. In the dim glow of a lantern, the intruders practically fought each other to get at him. John Phillips, sailmaker, boasted afterward of how he had "stabbed the captain in the guts." Outside, the wounded sentinel dragged himself up the companionway and called out to Lt. Henry Foreshaw, the officer of the watch. A maintopman cowering between two carronades on the after part of the quarterdeck had heard cries of "Murder" from Pigot's cabin, and if they were not audible to Foreshaw, he was certainly aware of what had broken out when he ordered Master's Mate William Turner to go below and investigate.

Turner jeered at him. The master's mate was one of the mutineers. Realizing that contact had better be restored with the *Diligence*, the lieutenant turned to the helmsman with the appropriate commands. They were flung back in his face. Foreshaw at once knocked the man down but was quickly seized by a dozen or so who hauled him aft and slashed and hacked at him until he toppled over the side. In Pigot's cabin, meanwhile, the intruders continued their unspeakable handiwork.

His long nightshirt a bloody shroud, Pigot sprawled against the barrel of a 12-pound cannon, feebly brandishing a dirk. He is said to have recognized a former favorite among his attackers and pleaded with him, to no avail. Someone shattered the stern window. Though stabbed repeatedly, Pigot must still have breathed when thrust out into the sea, for his cries were heard aboard the ship, growing fainter as he drifted away into the blackness.

The bloodshed on the *Hermione* that night of 21 and 22 September 1797 is all but beyond belief. Old scores were brutally settled. Seaman John Fletcher took revenge on the midshipman he blamed for a recent flogging. Aided by other mutineers, Fletcher caught the screaming lad—he was no more than fourteen—near a hatchway ladder and all but hacked him to pieces. But much of the violence lacked any rationale. Mutineers shouting, "Kill the buggar" cornered Edward Southcott, the ship's master, in the gun room. His face split open by a tomahawk, he managed to duck and run, banging an alarm on the officers' doors. Lt. Archibald Douglas had already sped unclothed from his room to seek refuge in the cabin next door, that of bedridden Lieutenant McIntosh, marine commander, who was dying of yellow fever. When the mutineers rushed in, Douglas dodged them and raced back into his own cabin but had time only to don a dressing gown before the mob was upon him, chopping and hacking with a devil's assortment of bladed weapons. Still Douglas wrenched himself free. Trailing blood, he stumbled forward and got as far as the midshipmen's quarters before his howling pursuers overtook him. Huddled in a hammock, David Casey saw Douglas go down under flailing arms and the flash of steel.

The dead lieutenant was thrown overboard, as was the slain young midshipman. The mutineers thought they had done with Lieutenant Foreshaw as well, having forced his bloodied body over the side. But he had fallen into the mizzen chains, the projecting timbers to which a mast's lower shrouds are secured, and still conscious had crawled down to a gun barrel, then dragged himself through a port. Foreshaw's survival might have counted for a miracle, had any been acknowledged that dreadful night. Some of those who through loyalty or fear had taken no part in the uprising greeted Foreshaw's reappearance with genuine relief. But Boatswain's Mate Thomas Nash and Able Seaman John Farrel, an American, a foremost pair among those who had dispatched their captain, were quickly on the scene, leading a group with knives, tomahawks, and boarding pikes, and this time they made sure the lieutenant was finished before casting him into the sea.

Lasting no longer than thirty minutes and resulting in four deaths, that first round of savagery was a collective madness, emotions exploding and scattering all reason and moral sensibility. Not so what followed. Many of those drunk on rum staggered back to their berths and slept. Other more sober minds gathered in relative calm for serious planning. The boatswain's mates Nash and Thomas Jay, Master's Mate Turner—elected captain of the ship—and other ringleaders summoned a meeting in the gun room, where the remaining ten officers and warrant officers were grouped under armed guard, and the first order of business was to decide whether or not to kill them.

Lawrence Cronin, who had stayed in the background during the initial violence, climbed on a table and by lantern light read a prepared speech. It identified him as a Belfast Republican, charged the officers with tyranny, and pronounced them all deserving of death. Cronin was cheered. Few of the other ringleaders dissented. No one suggested that they deal with their captives as Fletcher Christian had with Bligh, casting them adrift in a boat. Midshipman Casey, according to his own account, had befriended the mutineer Nash and on this ground interceded on behalf of the ship's purser and surgeon. The effort failed. Thanks to a continuing popularity among the crew, Casey and Southcott, the ship's wounded master, were after some argument permitted to live. But the others were taken up one by one, stabbed and beaten, and alive or dead pitched into the sea. The surgeon had just carefully attended to the facial wounds of Samuel Reed, the *Hermione*'s first lieutenant. Both men went over the side, as did the dying marine commander, still wrapped in his blanket. Mutineers punched and kicked the purser as they hauled him up the ladder. For some reason, even the captain's clerk was a victim of the systematic massacre.

Quartermaster's Mate Richard Redman was overheard to cry, "By the Holy Ghost, the bo'sun shall go with the rest." Martin and his wife had locked themselves in their cabin. At Redman's call the mutineers broke in and emerged with the boatswain, whom they manhandled to the main deck and shoved through a gun port. But revolutionary ardor, blood lust, and thirst for vengeance were not, it seems, the only emotions running at a fever pitch in those hellish early morning hours. Instead of rejoining his fellow ringleaders, Redman returned to the boatswain's quarters and closed the door on himself and the freshly widowed Mrs. Martin. No one in the vicinity would report hearing a woman's screams. The ship's steward had watched Redman enter apparently unresisted, and "he remained in the cabin with the bo'sun's wife and I saw him no more that night."

The next day men swabbed the decks of blood while Nash, Cronin,

Redman, and "Captain" Turner conferred on the quarterdeck or over charts in Pigot's cleansed cabin. The *Hermione*, it was decided, would make south for the Spanish Main. The use of Captain Pigot's secret signal book might safely put off any British ship they passed. The nonmutinous portion of the *Hermione*'s crew had to be made sure of, and with this purpose Cronin administered an oath, swearing all hands to mutual loyalty. Their destination was La Guaira, on the coast of Venezuela, where they would anchor in the roadstead under the fortress guns with explanations ready for the Spanish governor—cruel maltreatment had forced them to mutiny, but they had set their officers adrift in a boat with provisions. Asylum would be requested, and perhaps, in return for the surrender of their valuable ship, a reward might be expected. And as these plans were being drawn up, the *Hermione*'s people fully realized that there was no longer a gold-braided despot on board to make their lives a misery. That realization outweighed any remorse at having committed a fearful crime, and the very night after the mutiny there was dancing on the quarterdeck to the joyful strains of a flute.

One month later the *Diligence* boarded a Spanish schooner several days out of Caracas. Thus was learned the fate of the missing British frigate. Some of the mutineers were housed in Venezuelan army barracks, but others on the loose ashore had blabbed to Spanish sailors. The governor at La Guaira had renamed the *Hermione* the *Santa Cecilia* and ordered her refitted and manned by twenty-five of her seamen under Spanish guard. Shocked by what he heard, Capt. Robert Mends of the *Diligence* felt some apprehension about his own crew, who, however, assured him that had they remained in company with the *Hermione* when the mutiny occurred, "they would have retaken the *Hermione* or perished with her."

Mends carried the grim news to Sir Hyde Parker. The commander-in-chief of the Jamaica station still fumed over the loss of the little *Marie Antoinette*. Also, the storeship *Grampus* had just arrived from The Nore with "seeds of the late wicked mutiny" there. To guard against "infection," Parker hanged an agitator found among the *Grampus*'s people. The admiral's reaction upon hearing what had happened to the *Hermione* and her officers was to address a stern letter to the Spanish governor at La Guaira, demanding the frigate's return. His report on events to the Lords Commissioners of the Admiralty had much farther to travel, and it was as a melancholy Christmas present that English newspapers made known "the most daring and sanguinary mutiny that the annals of the British Navy can recall." But there was an immediate resolve to exact retribution, which Sir Hyde Parker, understandably most earnest in this regard, feared they might escape "unless sound policy induces the United States to exert their power in apprehending these criminals."

Many of the *Hermione*'s crew were released from Spanish custody and dispersed in various directions. Some were forced into menial or backbreaking labor, others signed on in Spanish, French, or neutral ships. An unknown number indeed found their way into the United States. Mrs. Martin, the boatswain's widow, is believed to have taken this route, though not with her husband's murderer, Quartermaster's Mate Redman, who had locked himself in the cabin with her. Redman and the ship's butcher crossed the Atlantic in a Spanish ship, only to fall into British hands when she was intercepted off Portugal by one of His Majesty's frigates. Some of the *Hermione*'s people, at their own request, were sent as prisoners of war to the island of Grenada and exchanged there for an equal number of Spaniards. They included Master Southcott and Midshipman Casey, useful witnesses for the prosecution at the subsequent trials. By the spring of 1799 twenty-four mutineers had been recaptured and court-martialed. Fifteen were hanged, only two of them, Richard Redman and Seaman Thomas Leech, in any sense ringleaders. Another became the central figure in a cause célèbre with repercussions in American politics.

Along with Leech and Redman, Boatswain's Mate Thomas Nash was one of the gang that had murdered Captain Pigot. Following the surrender of the *Hermione* at La Guaira, he had signed on in an American schooner, *Tanner's Delight*, under a false name. But liquor loosened Nash's tongue, leading to his arrest when the ship returned to Charleston, South Carolina, and one of the crew told the British consul of Nash's drunken boasts. Through its minister in Washington, the British government requested that Nash be handed over, and President John Adams, having no objection, advised his secretary of state accordingly. But Nash insisted that he was actually an American citizen, impressed by a British warship, and that his role in the *Hermione*'s mutiny was just a bold if violent bid for freedom. Feelings ran high in Charleston, where Nash's case came to court on 25 July 1799, with a near riot when the judge decided against him. He was brought in irons aboard a British cutter, which promptly sailed for Jamaica, where he was hanged from the foreyardarm of HMS *Acasta* for "mutiny, piracy, desertion and murder."

In what had become general practice where mutineers were concerned, Nash's body was gibbeted on Gallow Point at Port Royal. It still hung there, one of the fifteen skeletons of the mutineers, at the close of the year when political campaigners in the United States cited Nash's extradition as an example of the Federalist Party's habitual kowtowing to the British. The charge was made repeatedly and doubtless contributed to Adams's defeat and the election of Thomas Jefferson when polling day came around.

America's national navy was still in its infancy, about to test its mettle in a "quasi war" with Britain's traditional foe, France. The *Constellation* was one of the country's first three frigates, and on her shakedown cruise Capt. Thomas Truxtun was apprised by the secretary of the navy of a seaman's letter that showed "there is a spirit of Mutiny in some part of your crew." The secretary directed Truxtun to seek out any grievances, including complaints of ill treatment by officers, and "to reform silently any Abuse of Authority. By causing full justice to be done to the sailors, you will be more justified in treating as they Merit . . . those turbulent and ungovernable Men . . . who can only be restrained by severity." Truxtun mustered his crew on the spar deck and lectured them on the evils of mutiny. In due course he discovered a tried and true mutineer on his ship, John Watson, formerly a quarter gunner on HMS *Hermione*, serving American colors under a false name. From what he had heard, Truxtun may have sympathized with anyone unlucky enough to be commanded by Captain Pigot, but as a stern disciplinarian who could never have condoned mutiny, against whatever flag, he handed Watson over to the British consul at Norfolk. Watson was hanged in July 1800.

The *Hermione* was by then back in British hands, thanks to the resourcefulness and courage of a boarding party from HMS *Surprise*. Capt. Edward Hamilton led six boatloads of men under cover of night into Venezuelan waters where the *Santa Cecilia*, née *Hermione*, lay at anchor. The hand-to-hand fight that raged throughout the ship left more than a hundred Spanish sailors dead. Hamilton and many of his people themselves bled from wounds as they brought the prize safely back to Jamaica. But of several of the mutineer's ringleaders, the conspirator Lawrence Cronin among them, no trace would ever be found. About sixty men had actually mutinied on HMS *Hermione*. Over a period of almost ten years, half of them, despite the new identities most had adopted, were caught or surrendered. Twenty-four were hanged, the last in October 1806, not very long after the *Hermione*, her own name changed by the Royal Navy first to *Retaliation*, then *Retribution*, was towed into the Thames dockyard at Deptford and broken up.

The British Admiralty's new attitude, blending severity in discipline with equity and reform (the Earl St. Vincent had become First Lord), did much to purge its navy of mutinous contamination. Mutinies became rare and isolated incidents and had lost whatever political coloration the

Cutting out the Spanish frigate that was formerly the *Hermione*. *(National Maritime Museum, London)*

Spithead and Nore outbreaks may have had. The crew of the *Temeraire* off Bantry Bay, Ireland, in December 1801 had conceived highly elaborate plans to seize the powder magazine, to alert other vessels in the squadron with rockets, and to use threats that they would blow up the ship unless their grievance was redressed. It consisted solely of a disinclination to sail for the West Indies, hostilities with France having just ended and many of the men being homesick after eight or nine years of sea service. The mutiny failed, and six convicted ringleaders were executed.

Rarer still were the signs of serious or widespread discontent following the short-lived peace secured by the Treaty of Amiens. The renewed struggle against France and her allies brought the fleet back into favor. If Britain needed reminding of how vital her navy was, Nelson's great triumph off Cape Trafalgar in 1805 was more than enough for the purpose. There appeared to be a linkage between such victories and the sailors' morale. The lash remained the chief instrument of shipboard discipline but was to be administered justly and in moderation. "Starting"—the deeply resented custom of beating with a rope's end to hurry seamen about their tasks—was about to be abolished, though only after a brief uprising against an ill-tempered captain who had introduced variations involving broomsticks and the application of salt pickle to lacerated shoulders. (The captain died during a fight with two frigates, and it was rumored that his own men had shot him.)

Not that mutiny was yet a thing of the past. In the month that saw the last hanging of the "Bloody Hermiones," that affair almost had an encore, and in the same West Indian waters. The incident occurred on the brig *Ferret*, whose commander, the Honourable George Cadogan, was in some respects a carbon copy of the late Hugh Pigot, but his people lacked the nerve to carry out their plans for killing him and shaping course, as had the *Hermione*, for La Guaira. They got as far as confronting Cadogan with cutlasses and boarding pikes, but he managed to cow them with a pistol, ignored their complaints of "ill-usage by flogging and starving," and had his marines arrest the ringleaders. In keeping with the more forceful policy of no quarter for mutineers, twelve of the *Ferret's* crew were hanged at Port Royal. Even so, the Admiralty lost little time before transferring Cadogan to another ship.

For most of that year, 1806, the one prominent captain who had survived the loss of his ship to mutineers was on the high seas, bound for Australia. The placid domestic life William Bligh had wished for ever since his experience on the *Bounty* had so far been denied him. His quietest spell was probably the three years after Camperdown, spent conducting hydrographic surveys for the Admiralty. In 1801, as commander of the 56-gun *Glatton*, he was with Nelson at the Battle of Copenhagen and afterward complimented on his contribution to the victory. Evidently apprehensive of some argument on that point, he had asked Nelson for a written testimonial, a request said to have caused the admiral some embarrassment. In command of the *Warrior* three years later, Bligh was accused by a junior lieutenant of "tyrannical, oppressive and unofficerlike conduct" and brought before a court-martial. He admitted to his hot temper and harsh language but ascribed these to zeal for the service, and he was merely reprimanded. Bligh nevertheless felt mortified, his accuser having been in his opinion nothing but an insubordinate malingerer. He probably welcomed with relief the assignment to the governorship of New South Wales, secured for him by Sir Joseph Banks.

The post had promised Bligh, by then in his fifties, better pay and a good pension. If he thought an untroubled tenure also among the prospects, he was sadly mistaken. While traveling out as a passenger on a transport convoy, he persistently wrangled with its commander, further evidencing his incurable vanity. Of the colony in his charge he wrote, "When I have done I think it will be a charming place." But his attempted reforms plunged him into conflict with a corrupt officer clique that monopolized the region's economy while trafficking in rum. And in the Rum Rebellion

After "a long and turbulent life," Vice Adm. William Bligh. *(Library of Congress)*

Bligh was again targeted for mutiny, deposed from command, and held captive for seventeen months. His principal foe, an army colonel, was brought back to England and cashiered, an outcome that went far to vindicate Bligh's conduct as governor. All the same, he returned home to find his character still in question, even among royalty. The Prince Regent had spoken of him unfavorably in a letter that leaked to the press. Bligh wrote to the Prince himself, protesting the letter and citing his services to crown and country. He did not, fortunately, lack for champions and was soon gazetted as a vice admiral of the Blue. With this honorary title Bligh could then have looked forward to a measure of quiet home life. But his wife, who had not accompanied him to Australia, died only two years after his return. He retired into the country with his four unmarried daughters, and in December 1817 came the end of what an artist who had sailed with him on the *Providence* called "a long and turbulent life. Let our old captain's frailties be forgotten. . . . View him as a man of science and an excellent practical seaman."

As a result of the distractions of Bligh's last years, he may not have spared much thought to the strange news from Pitcairn Island, although he surely became aware of it. He would have been in the middle of the Rum Rebellion when his countrymen at home first learned of where Fletcher Christian, his fellow mutineers, and Tahitians male and female anchored the *Bounty* after an eight thousand–mile Pacific search for an island sanctuary. The ship had not lasted long. There were plans to break her up and use the timbers ashore, but Matthew Quintal for reasons unknown set fire to her. Fits of gloom, perhaps madness, seem to have foreshadowed Christian's own extinction, and varied stories would account for his demise: He fell or threw himself off the rocks into the sea. He was shot while trying to flee in the ship's only remaining boat. The natives revolted against their masters, and he was among those slain, clubbed to death, perhaps on a day a third child was born to his Mauatua (Isabella). Certainly the Pitcairn commune had become a murderous encampment of fear, hatred, and jealousy. Two shipmates axed Quintal to death because he was greedy for women who belonged to others. Others were killed by the Tahitian males, who were themselves massacred by vengeful "widows." And on 6 February 1808 when the Nantucket whaler *Topaz* called at Pitcairn, the only man left alive to give her captain, Mayhew Folger, any coherent if never fully verifiable account of events there in the preceding nineteen years was Alexander Smith, calling himself John Adams. (Research shows Adams to have been his original name, Smith a false one.)

The one-time mutineer had become educator and Christian leader, a father to the community in more than one sense, indeed a source of life on the island inasmuch as he directed its agriculture. If, as some suspected, Adams shot Fletcher Christian, none who visited Pitcairn thereafter pressed the point. And he was evidently now loyal, swung his hat in the air and cried, "Old England for ever" upon hearing the news of Trafalgar. So the British navy decided to leave him where he was, and in 1829 he died there. Were Christian's bones also on Pitcairn?* Published letters allegedly Christian's and supposedly proving his survival were dismissed as forgeries. Still, gossip had it that he had somehow found his way back to England and was concealed by his family in the Lake District. Peter Heywood, who had narrowly escaped the rope and went on to become a captain, told of seeing Christian on a Plymouth street, but the man had fled before he was able to accost him. So the stories would persist and the fate of Fletcher Christian remain almost as much a mystery as the true genesis of his fabled mutiny.

* His genes and name certainly were. He had fathered three children with Mauatua, and their descendants live today on Pitcairn Island and elsewhere across the Pacific.

Seven

⁊

THE *SOMERS*

*M*ore than a hundred of the *Hermione*'s people, mutinous or otherwise, were never accounted for. Of those who drifted into the United States under new names, an unknown number entered the American navy. The mutineer Nash had been discovered and handed over to the British, with political consequences in the United States. Another identified on the *Constellation* was also forcibly repatriated. And further echoes of Captain Pigot's bloody overthrow would sound in the fledgling American fleet.

"Discipline is to be effected by a particular deportment much easier than by great severity." So wrote Commo. Thomas Truxtun in 1800, conveying his disapproval of James Sever as a naval commander. He had perforce to act on Captain Sever's report of a mutiny brewing on the frigate *Congress*, and as senior naval officer at Norfolk he reduced the resulting death sentences to flogging and dismissal from the service. Sever's real bane, it transpired after the *Congress* returned to sea, was Samuel L. Marshall, the ship's doctor, who allegedly expressed "warm approbation of the mutinous, murderous conduct of the crew of His Majesty's frigate *Hermione*." During a court-martial that acquitted him of Sever's charges, Marshall explained that he had merely voiced his opinion that men forced into naval service against their will could hardly be condemned for attempting to throw off the bonds of authority. In America it was different: men enlisted voluntarily and were generously paid. As Marshall put it, "The circumstances which attended the Mutiny on board the *Hermione* were different from anything that can possibly happen in our navy."

An opposite view to the doctor's comfortable assumption about American immunity emerged three years later on the frigate *President* anchored in Hampton Roads. Her crew sent the captain an unsigned letter, complaining of "horrid usage . . . enough to turn a man's stomach" and of conditions "at such a pitch as to exceed the *Hermione*." An alarmed Capt. Samuel Barron quickly produced an offender, Robert Quinn, who was sentenced by court-martial to have his head shaved and "MUTINY" branded on his forehead and to be flogged through the fleet for a total of 320 lashes. The boat carrying him from ship to ship had drawn alongside the *John Adams* when Quinn lost consciousness. He was returned to the *President*, the balance of his ordeal deferred until he revived. "I have no idea that [Quinn] could survive," wrote the purser on the *John Adams*. "It is to be sure most cruel punishment but the very existence of the Navy requires it."

Those words reflect a belief generally held that mutiny could ravage a naval force as effectively as storms or enemy action. This was the lesson to be drawn from the British experience at Spithead and Nore, more so than from the single if bloodier *Hermione* affair. It was doubtless borne in mind when in April 1800, two years after the establishment of a Department of the Navy, the American Congress passed an Act for the Better Government of the Navy, Article Thirteen of which stated that any member of the service who made or attempted to make "a mutinous assembly shall on conviction thereof by a court-martial suffer death." Did mutinous assembly constitute a mutiny? The very word mutiny occurred only once in Article Thirteen, that portion of it relating to anyone who "bearing witness to a mutiny" did not do his utmost to prevent or suppress it. This failure to define mutiny was either a legislative lapse or a dodging of the bothersome question of how many persons it takes to make a mutiny. One man could make "a mutinous assembly," but might not this fall short of mutiny?

By its appearance in Article Thirteen, the reference to a person who "shall treat with contempt" a superior while on duty carries a connotation of mutiny, and mutiny was the charge brought against William Johnson of the ketch *Dispatch*, who in 1812 at the Norfolk Navy Yard picked a fight with another seaman and cursed the midshipman who intervened. A lieutenant on the scene also came in for Johnson's abuse, liquor-induced by all accounts, and Johnson had to be gagged and double-ironed before marines could get him to the guardhouse. The court having judged Johnson's offense as punishable under Article Thirteen, he became the first United States Navy seaman condemned to die for mutiny. The conclusion of this case acknowledged mutiny as commitable by a single individual. As far as the record shows, the only question raised by the Navy Department was whether it fell within the province of the commander of the navy yard to have convened William Johnson's court-martial.

The view of many naval officers and bureaucrats was that assult upon a superior, verbal disrespect, or even simple disobedience on the part of one man alone could be interpreted as mutiny. Mid-nineteenth-century legal literature would authoritatively embody this broad interpretation. Mutiny was "not necessarily an aggregate offense, committed by many individuals, for it may originate and conclude with a single person and be as complete with one actor in it, as one thousand." Mutiny could begin and end with one alone.

No dispute befogged any instance where members of a crew wrested control from their commander and sailed away with his ship. This unarguable mode of mutiny, rare enough in the British navy, was virtually nonexistent in the American service, but a notable example occurred in the Pacific during the War of 1812. After hunting British whalers for twelve months, Capt. David Porter had decided to put in at the Marquesas to refit his frigate *Essex*, which with five prizes he anchored off Nuka Hiva, the largest of the island group. What ensued has a familiar ring—the prolonged stay in an island paradise undermined morale, and a rising against authority followed the renewal of the voyage.

The commanding officer hardly set a prudent example. The moment he stepped ashore amid a horde of tattooed islanders, "a handsome young woman of about eighteen, her complexion fairer than common, her bearing majestic," riveted Porter's attention. And he reported the predictable results of his liberal shore-leave policy with scarcely concealed glee, the crew's fraternization with native women "all helter-skelter and promiscuous intercourse." Porter's men got themselves mixed up in one or two tribal wars, but life at Nuka Hiva was mostly labor well seasoned with dalliance. When the *Essex* was ready for sea, Porter heard that the men would mutiny rather than sail. But if too lax during protracted idyll, Porter had few equals at mastering events turned suddenly touch and go. With all hands called to the quarterdeck, he announced that at the first sign of disobedience he would put a match to the magazine and blow them all to hell, himself included. He plucked a suspect at random from his silenced crew and dumped him over the side into a native boat. The *Essex* sailed without further trouble.

But not so one of the captive whalers Porter had left behind in the Marquesas with John Gamble, a marine lieutenant under orders to make his way homeward if no word of the *Essex* arrived within five months.

Gamble's was an astonishing experience. He sailed in the prize *Serangapatam* on 7 May 1814 with two midshipmen, a crew of thirteen, and six British prisoners. They had no sooner cleared the Marquesas than Gamble and the midshipmen were overpowered and with two loyal seamen set adrift in an open boat. The *Serangapatam* bore away, flying English colors, manned by an alliance of British tars and eleven American mutineers. Gamble's party managed to reach an island, only to be attacked by natives, who killed the two midshipmen. Gamble and his remaining companions escaped to Nuka Hiva, and with others of the *Essex* still stationed there they outfitted another prize vessel, which, under Gamble's commendable leadership, held together long enough to voyage 2,500 miles of Pacific Ocean and make a final landfall in the Sandwich Islands, where the British took his scarred and scorbutic people into custody. No trace was ever found of the *Serangapatam* and her mutineers.

That was a mutiny not attributable to sadistic officers. There were probably no Pigots in the American fleet. Even so, by its fifth decade, struggling belatedly through the transition from canvas to steam, the United States Navy stood in serious need of capable seamen, and the shortage coincided with stories of shipboard brutality and injustice. Early in 1837 an article in *The Naval Magazine*, lamenting a scarcity of thoroughbred Americans aboard American warships, conceded that "a harsh system" was one reason why the navy "is not now popular," but deemed this harshness necessary because of "the unlimited introduction of foreigners." The writer was Lt. Alexander Slidell, collaborating with his sister's husband, Capt. Matthew Calbraith Perry, and there is considerable irony here. Both men were naval officers in the vanguard of those advocating manpower reform and technical advancement. Perry supervised the construction of America's second steam warship at Brooklyn, and his simultaneous campaign for new forms of naval apprenticeship was conducted in alliance with his brother-in-law. Perry's greatest fame lay ahead, when he would take a squadron to Japan and open up that country to American trade. Slidell also sought the chance to gain renown in distant and unexploited waters. He would instead be pamphleteered as precisely the kind of officer that made the navy "not now popular," and as the principal figure in the century's darkest and most baffling naval controversy he would have to fight off comparisons with Bligh and Pigot.

The son of a New York merchant and insurance broker, Slidell had begun his naval career in 1816 as a thirteen-year-old midshipman, but since then his active service had been at best intermittent. There was reasonable excuse for this at first—Slidell was one of countless American naval men stricken with yellow fever while serving in the West Indies. In 1825, the year of his promotion to lieutenant, he took extended leave in Europe to improve his health. His intellect certainly thrived. After studying in France, he toured Spain and founded a lasting friendship with Washington Irving, then on the staff of the American legation at Madrid, by helping to research what became Irving's popular biography of Christopher Columbus. Irving probably inspired Slidell's own literary aspirations.

A fertile imagination assisted these aspirations, animating some of Slidell's travel writing. In Spain two robbers held up his coach and killed the driver and the mule boy. Closed windows in front and on the sides prevented Slidell from attempting a rescue, but "I could distinctly hear each stroke of the murderous knife as it entered its victim." The villains were caught and hanged separately. Spectator at the first execution, Slidell resolved not to attend the second, then did so after reflecting that an observant traveler could not afford to miss anything. On a return visit to Spain he viewed yet another execution, this time a garroting, which he described in meticulous detail. He had known that it would be "a spectacle full of horror and painful excitement, still I determined to witness it. I felt sad and melancholy, and yet, by a strange perversion, I was willing to feel moreso."

Slidell's first travel book, *A Year in Spain*, appeared in 1829. Besides two more, in circulation by 1836 (each in two volumes), he found time to write articles on naval affairs. He worked mostly at home, thanks to the "repeated indulgences" with which the Navy Department had responded to his many applications for furlough. Service on the USS *Brandywine* preceded more leave for European traveling. His travel was of some benefit to the navy, for Slidell collected information on the British construction of steam warships and passed it on to Washington, D.C. That done, he completed *The American in England* and married Catherine Robinson, the twenty-year-old daughter of a banker and lawyer. He also renewed his earlier efforts to secure a place in the government's plans for an elaborate naval expedition to the South Seas. He wished for a berth on one of the brigs, providing him "the leisure, the freedom from interruption and complete isolation in my solitary cabin" needed to produce a faithful record of events.

What Slidell was obviously after, the chance to write a best-selling account of an unprecedented voyage, posed a threat to Thomas Ap Catesby Jones, the appointed commander, an egocentric who wanted no rivals to the official history he would be expected to prepare. Also,

Jones was very likely one of the naval officers enraged by a recent published article in which Slidell had criticized the "system of deathlike stagnation" through which elderly officers maintained positions of command, to the detriment of ambitious juniors. Jones insisted that Slidell be dropped from consideration. Slidell turned to President Andrew Jackson for help. "The only disqualification I am aware of," he wrote, "is found in the fact of my having written several works." Washington Irving also addressed the White House, saying that Slidell's "literary exercise" had never interfered with his naval duties. All to no avail. "If belles lettre attainments are paramount to all other qualifications in commanders," Jones told the secretary of the navy, "why not draw from the nation's best resources in that line?" Thanks to what he called Jones's "malignity . . . low and unworthy intrigue against me," Slidell saw his dream of adding literary luster to the South Seas Surveying and Exploring Expedition fade. (Neither did Jones go on the great cruise, for his irascibility led to his withdrawal from its command, which went to Lt. Charles Wilkes.)

Slidell returned to active duty, serving as first lieutenant on the *Independence* and next commanding the fast new brig *Dolphin*. His health remained unstable. After almost two years of pursuing pirates in Brazilian waters he took another long furlough, during which, to qualify for the legacy of his maternal uncle, a bachelor named Mackenzie, he legally adopted Mackenzie as his last name. He bought an estate near Tarrytown, on which he settled his wife and two children, and wrote busily, beginning biographies of American naval heroes and volunteering ideas to improve the navy's apprentice system. Training periods sorely needed to be lengthened, and Alexander Slidell Mackenzie believed this best done at sea.

In 1841 Mackenzie, aged thirty-eight, was promoted to commander and assigned to the steam frigate *Missouri*, from which vessel he sent Abel P. Upshur, the new secretary of the navy, his most detailed program yet on the subject of apprentices. It entailed the deployment of a vessel manned almost entirely by boys, who would thus receive their training at sea, the vessel functioning both as schoolship and cruiser. He thought a suitable ship would be one of the navy's two new brigs, just completed at the New York and Boston navy yards. In his reply, dated 7 May 1842, Upshur replied that the department had been thinking along the same lines and had only awaited the availability of a suitable ship. That time had arrived: "The necessary orders will be immediately given to prepare the *Somers* for this purpose and you will be ordered to the command of her."

The *Somers* was a racily built brig-of-war, weighing little more than 250 tons and mounting ten 32-pound carronades on the spar deck. Like her sister, the *Bainbridge*, she was much oversparred—both vessels were fated to capsize and sink, with a heavy loss of life. The *Somers* measured 105 feet from prow to taffrail and 25 feet in the beam, her berth deck 17 feet wide with only 58 inches of head room. To some of the 166 men and boys, more than half of them aged seventeen or under, who boarded the vessel at Brooklyn that midsummer, her living quarters must have appeared dismayingly cramped. Some may also have soon felt that the captain was a figure to be feared. Mackenzie was apprehensive that the boys included "too many children of foreigners . . . brought up precariously, dull-witted and far from robust." And the severity of his rule was manifest at the outset.

During the six weeks of final work before the *Somers* left on her maiden voyage Mackenzie inflicted about fifty separate punishments. Some were for desertion or theft, for which he ordered a dozen lashes, the maximum allowed, with the cat-o'-nine-tails. The busiest punitive instrument was the colt, a three-stranded rope frayed at the ends, and he ordered shirt-clad adolescents whipped 422 times for blaspheming, being unclean, fighting, losing a hammock, spitting, throwing tea or tobacco on the deck, and most frequently "skulking"—which usually meant attempting to shirk duty.

Writers who have dealt with the *Somers* tragedy concentrate mostly on Mackenzie's judgment and interpretation of events, some perceiving him as a victim of his own hyperimagination. They leave unanswered the question of how he rated as a disciplinarian, and few seem aware that even before he took command of the schoolship, Mackenzie had been described in public print as having a reputation for cruelty. Mackenzie himself may not have known in 1841 of the pamphlet *An Exposition of Official Tyranny in the United States Navy* by Solomon H. Sanborn, a former seaman. As an example of "cruel, unnecessary and unjust punishment," Sanborn cited the case of a marine on the *Independence*, anchored off Brazil in July 1837, who threw orange peels into spit boxes on the spar deck. He received a dozen lashes ordered by the first lieutenant, "Alexander S. Mackenzie, better known as Lieutenant A. Slidell, the accomplished author." While on the same South American station Mackenzie had served as captain of the schooner *Dolphin*, giving refuge to American citizens and others fleeing the dangers of a Brazilian civil war. As the *Dolphin's* log shows, the cat remained busy under Mackenzie's command, one unfortunate receiving thirty-nine lashes for "desertion and mutinous conduct." During this same South American cruise, in temporary command of the sloop-of-war *Fairfield*, Mackenzie "was noted for his cruelty to the men for small offenses and trifling accidents."

The *Somers* sailed on 11 July 1842, and the punishments continued. At the close of the brief shakedown cruise to Puerto Rico and back the commander reported his novices as quick to learn, but too many were deficient in character, and some were so small as to be "utterly useless." Future recruits should be sought not so much in large cities as at less frequented coastal towns and inland rivers among citizens with offspring less flawed by "those vicious propensities conspicuous in many of our present crews." Mackenzie had also to report something else. One of the older apprentices, while on lookout duty at the starboard cathead, "falling asleep he by some means dropped overboard." A search party lowered in the second cutter failed to find him. "I did hope to have gone through the first stages of training the crew and performed the cruise without a single accident but this has been denied me."

The *Somers* was soon at sea again for the continued schooling of apprentices, now numbering seventy-four. Mackenzie had got rid of nearly half the original complement as undesirable. The newcomers included an eighteen-year-old midshipman, Philip Spencer, whose presence was at first something of a novelty to the six other "young gentlemen" with whom he shared steerage space because he happened to be a son of the secretary of war. By his own account Mackenzie had greeted Spencer cordially, but upon learning of recent drunken escapades had tried to have him detached. That effort was confined to the New York Navy Yard, there being no time to communicate with Washington, and it failed. Earlier the midshipman's uncle, the captain of the *Columbus*, had asked Secretary Upshur to have the boy ordered to his ship, where he could keep a filial eye on him. It may have been a pity for all concerned that Upshur did not comply.

The ship sailed in September, bound for West Africa. Something of a minor mutiny soon took place when eight apprentices refused to obey orders. Mackenzie punished them with the colt. One of the offenders, a fourteen-year-old incorrigible named Dennis Manning, was thrashed again the next day and twice more before the month ended. (During his thirteen weeks at sea young Manning received 101 lashes—"fourteen with the cat and eighty-seven with the colt"—a punishment record among Mackenzie's schoolboys.) During the three weeks it took the *Somers* to cross the Atlantic Mackenzie ordered forty-three separate floggings, a figure that would shock at least one veteran captain when he heard of it and that points to a tantalizing riddle. How could such a modernistic, reform-minded officer have so instinctively hewn to a punitive policy becoming more and more anachronistic, as were the reactionary commanders still prone to it? The question lingers notwithstanding testimony from the purser's steward, James Wales, that the real bully on the schoolship *Somers* was Boatswain's Mate Samuel Cromwell, a burly Virginian who while carrying out the punishments "would strike with all his might as though it was pleasing to him."

This was alleged long after the fact, when reputations were at risk and key witnesses, Cromwell for one, forever beyond interrogation. Among those of the brig with nothing but good to say of Mackenzie were Lt. Guert Gansevoort, his second-in-command, also Midshipman and Acting Master Matthew C. Perry, Jr., Acting Midshipman Oliver H. Perry II, Midshipman Henry Rodgers, and Midshipman Adrian Deslonde. The captain was related to all four.

Though schooling was the *Somers*'s main business, she had a specific assignment. A lone American warship, the *Vandalia*, patrolled the West African coast, where tribesmen had murdered American nationals. Mackenzie carried dispatches directing the *Vandalia*'s captain to show the flag and demand an apology, compensation, and punishment of the guilty. Mackenzie reached the island of Madeira on 4 October, apprehensive lest bad weather delay his mission. Before resuming the voyage, he had ten boys larruped for dirtiness and abusive language. The *Somers* sailed south for the Canary Islands, only to find that the *Vandalia* had just called there and departed. On Mackenzie's ship the punishments continued, nine one day, three the next, seven two days later. On 21 October the brig anchored in the Cape Verde Islands. That day nine of the crew felt the cat-o'-nine-tails, and more boys were whipped with the colt—for sleeping on watch, wasting fresh water, not having a white hat, being dirty—offenses grave and trivial alike. There were in all sixty punishments that month. On 10 November the *Somers* reached Monrovia (Liberia), where Mackenzie was informed that the *Vandalia* had left for home. With his dispatches undelivered, Mackenzie decided to do likewise, by way of the (then Danish) Virgin Islands.

The *Somers* sailed westward before fresh trades. Generally, the weather stayed calm. However harsh their regimen, for schoolboys learning the ropes from seamen twice their age, the experience might well have turned into a rare autumnal adventure, something of a lark. Instead there had grown a palpable discontent, a slackening of discipline. Hardly among the good times was the day the *Somers* had halted at Liberia, her log showing ninety-two pounds of condemned bread thrown to the fishes, Seaman William Fry confined in double irons, and

Precocious, strabismic, and fatally addicted to pirate yarns: Passed Midshipman Philip Spencer. *(Sea Dangers, Schocken Books)*

three boys lashed for insolence, dirtiness, and "not cleaning a battleaxe." Officers began to notice signs that, it was afterward submitted, while not conceived as such at the time gave evidence of a mutinous conspiracy set in motion by Midshipman Philip Spencer. He mixed too little with his messmates and too freely with the crew and apprentices, some of whom he treated to liquor and tobacco and whose palms he read. He was given to enigmatic smiles and "a strange flashing of the eyes"; he cursed the captain behind his back, babbled of piracy, and searched maps for the Isle of Pines, a buccaneers' hangout west of Cuba. Michael H. Garty, six months a marine and a sergeant by virtue of his post on the *Somers* as master-at-arms, would remember Spencer's rambling on about seizing the ship and throwing her officers over the side. The midshipman had also displayed considerable interest in how many of the muskets in Garty's charge were kept loaded. Why had Garty not thought any of Spencer's talk worth reporting to the captain? "Because I had no suspicion of him."

Midshipman Rodgers would tell of Spencer's "mutinous expressions" while unable to recall his actual words. Purser's Mate Wales remembered the words—Spencer said he would love to throw the captain overboard and, by God, would do it yet—but "did not know at the time that these were mutinous expressions." To another midshipman Spencer said it would be easy to murder the captain and seize the vessel, and he sketched a pirate ship complete with skull and crossbones. He got Boatswain's Mate Cromwell to state the best means of disguising the brig—"by shipping the bowsprit aft"—and in a reference that begs further amplification, Captain Mackenzie would recall someone's telling him that Spencer had amused the crew by making music with his jaw: he had the knack of "throwing his jaw out of joint, and by the contact of the bones playing with accuracy and elegance a variety of airs." Sinister or merely bizarre, these characteristics were allegedly observed over a span of some eight weeks. Yet the captain was unaware of trouble and "could not forbear treating with ridicule" the extraordinary report, made in his cabin by Lieutenant Gansevoort on Saturday morning, 26 November, that "a conspiracy existed on board the brig, to capture her, murder the commander, the officers and most of the crew, and convert her into a pirate, and that Acting Midshipman Philip Spencer was at the head of it."

Eight

⌐

A MIDSHIPMAN'S MANIA

Classmates with whom he attended Canandaigua Academy in western New York remembered Philip Spencer's "queer stories and sharp tricks." At another school he was musically minded, a loner who mastered Greek and Latin with ease. An unsuccessful operation for strabismus had left him with a permanent squint and "a fixed staring look." Books on piracy fascinated him, and he was given to oratorical outbursts and had a lively imagination. At yet a third college Spencer banded with other adolescent romantics to form a new secret fraternity.

Through the political influence of his father, John Canfield Spencer, who appears to have despaired of him as an estimable student, Philip entered the navy in 1841 with a midshipman's rank. (He had two brothers, one a sea captain's clerk, the other a budding lawyer.) Attached to the receiving ship *North Carolina,* he was soon in trouble, fighting with a senior midshipman named Craney, who not long afterward resigned, ostensibly because the secretary of the navy neglected to act on his charge that the son of the new secretary of war had been unruly. Actually, Midshipman Craney had himself been in the Navy Department's bad books for drunkenness and other failings, and as recalled by the *North Carolina*'s captain, Matthew C. Perry, the ruckus between the two had originated in a Manhattan brothel where Craney, about to treat his younger companions, Philip and John Spencer, found himself short eighty dollars. Back on the ship the next day he had accused the Spencer brothers of theft. Other than issuing a stern reproof, Secretary of the Navy Upshur took no measures against Philip Spencer for assaulting the senior midshipman, expecting that "your future conduct will atone for your late misbehavior." Spencer's next post was in the Brazilian Squadron, from which he was soon sent home, following a drunken altercation in Rio de Janeiro with a British officer. "This is my first offense and I know my last," a seemingly contrite Spencer wrote to Secretary Upshur, and he cited the pain that a court-martial would cause his father. "Because of your penitence," the secretary relieved him from arrest. And Spencer's next appointment was to the *Somers*.

Since Philip Spencer was never closely questioned about the conversation he had with James Wales, the purser's steward, while they were seated on the booms between six and eight in the evening of Friday, 25 November 1842, Wales would remain the prime source for the successive tides of testimony. Little is known of him other than that he was a former typesetter and accountant for New England newspapers and was never at sea on a man-of-war before joining the *Somers*. After that two hours' huddle on the booms with Spencer, the purser's steward had reported to neither the captain nor the first lieutenant, afraid he might be seen by Spencer or his confederates, for he had taken an "oath of silence," under threat of death if he violated it.

A published writer whose works reflect habits of keen observation and the correlative practice of note taking, Alexander Slidell Mackenzie might be thought to have kept a private journal, furnishing an immediate if not impartial record of events. Nothing of the sort came to light. Nor did Wales write down what he claimed Spencer had told him until much later, then for official inquiry and in considerable detail. Unable to get to the captain's cabin without being watched, he had waited until morning, when he went to the wardroom before breakfast and told Horace Heiskell, the ship's purser, that Spencer had told him he was planning a mutiny. Wales had not elaborated. "I merely gave [Heiskell] to understand that there was a mutiny on foot. I condensed Spencer's statement, and went up to the First Lieutenant on my own account, for fear the Purser would neglect it."

To Guert Gansevoort, who came from an old upstate New York family and was a first cousin of Herman Melville (whose own naval career was about to begin), Wales did not repeat even the "condensed" version of Spencer's mutinous disclosures—Boatswain's Mate Cromwell, Seaman Elisha Small, and others of Spencer's "conspiracy" were on deck and "gathered around as though they were watching me." He simply told the first lieutenant that Mr. Heiskell wished to see him in the wardroom. Gansevoort had thereupon gone below, was asked by the purser if he knew a plot existed, and was given "the information that Mr. Wales had given him." As the lieutenant would recall, it was to the effect that Spencer had twenty men in the plot and that they would stage a row on the forecastle and in the confusion murder the captain and his officers. This then was Wales's "condensed" version, and even at that Gansevoort "did not stay to hear all [the purser] had to say," instead hurried to the captain's cabin and "mentioned the circumstances." When Mackenzie received the news "with great coolness" and expressed doubts as to its truth, Gansevoort "asked him if I should see Mr. Wales myself and get the information from him. He said no—he did not wish to do so, or to say anything about it." Mackenzie offered no reason for this but directed Gansevoort to keep a discreet eye on everybody, especially Midshipman Spencer.

Assuming the truth of this not altogether convincing testimony, it does seem strange that Mackenzie had not acted on the lieutenant's sensible suggestion. By the time of the testimony Wales had spoken well of the captain and been recommended by him for promotion. But how the captain felt about the purser's steward on the occasion is something of a mystery. There had been an "altercation" between the two during the brig's shakedown cruise, which, when questions were put, each admitted to but avoided detailing. Mackenzie was to imply that Spencer had buttonholed Wales at the booms because he knew of that earlier "difficulty." But Spencer was not on the cruise to Puerto Rico, so if there is anything to this assertion it means that the captain's "altercation" with Wales had left a vestige of gossip among the crew or a still-lingering, and conspicuous, mutual antipathy.

This feeling might explain why Mackenzie never did summon Wales for personal questioning. According to Mackenzie, the doubts with which he had greeted Gansevoort's startling announcement quickly vanished when he reflected upon the lieutenant's "earnest and solemn manner . . . and the strong impression of the reality and imminence of the danger made upon the mind of Mr. Wales himself." Mackenzie wrote this months later, when somewhat desperately explaining his actions on the *Somers,* apparently forgetful or heedless of Gansevoort's testimony that in those critical hours on the brig he did not see the purser's steward much less speak to him.

Neither did Mackenzie interrogate the allegedly mutinous young mastermind himself. He left that to Gansevoort while ransacking his own memory for clues to Spencer's wicked intentions. The first lieutenant, as directed, kept a "strict lookout" that Saturday but missed Spencer from the deck at about 2 P.M. and discovered that he was in the foretop, "apparently deep in thought." Another seaman soon joined him there and "appeared to be engaged in pricking India ink in Spencer's arm." Spencer remained in the top for some while, and when he finally descended, Gansevoort found him sitting at the foot of the Jacob's ladder. "I immediately caught his eye, which he kept staring upon me for more than a minute, *with the most infernal expression I have ever seen upon a human face. It satisfied me at once of the man's guilt.*"

It hardly seems necessary to wonder if it was the eye with the permanent cast that so emphatically convinced the first lieutenant. At any rate, he reported these "circumstances" to the commander, whose own sworn testimony would claim that they amounted to somewhat more than Spencer's baleful glare and sojourn in the tops to get tattooed. Gansevoort had found out about the midshipman's nocturnal conferences with Cromwell and Elisha Small, as well as his gifts of tobacco and money to certain apprentices. From unnamed sources Mackenzie himself, presumably in those same midday hours, had learned that Spencer had cursed and threatened him, sketched a pirate brig, predicted Midshipman Rodgers's death, made music with his jaw, and "corrupted the wardroom steward by causing him to steal brandy from the wardroom mess." And there were incidents of his drunkenness while in the Brazilian Squadron. "These various recollections, added to what had been revealed to me, determined me to make sure at once of his person."

At evening quarters Mackenzie ordered all officers to the quarterdeck, where he beckoned Spencer forth and said that he had heard the midshipman aspired to the command of the ship. How he would gain it Mackenzie had no idea unless "by walking over my dead body and those of my officers." Spencer denied any such aspiration: "It is all a joke." To which Mackenzie replied that it was "joking on a forbidden subject" and might cost Spencer his life. Spencer's cravat was searched for the written mutiny plans that according to Wales he had crumpled and hidden there. Nothing was found in it. Mackenzie turned to Lieutenant Gansevoort and ordered Spencer's arrest. Gansevoort relieved the midshipman of his sword. An armorer brought up double irons, and when Spencer was fettered hand and foot, he was made to sit on the starboard arms chest. Placing Gansevoort in charge of the prisoner's security, Mackenzie told him to order his instant death if he tried to communicate with any of the crew. As entered in the ship's log by the captain's nephew, Acting Master Matthew Perry, the midshipman was arrested because he had been found "tampering with some of the crew of this vessel for the purpose of creating a mutiny on board."

It was a jumpy mood on the *Somers* that night. Armed with cutlasses and pistols, the officers of the watch made frequent rounds of spar and berth decks to ensure that all hands stayed in their hammocks. In the steerage Lieutenant Gansevoort and Midshipman Henry Rodgers searched Spencer's locker. Inside his razor case they found two sheets of paper containing Greek characters, which Rodgers was able to translate. Thirty-one names were listed under three separate headings. The four names under "Certain" included those of Spencer and Wales. Ten were headed "Doubtful," four of these marked as likely to join the "project," and the remainder "will probably join when the thing is done, if not, they must be forced." Wales was to dispute any intimation of himself as a conspirator by stating that his name must have been added to the "Certain" list after he met Spencer on the booms, when he had pretended to go along with the midshipman's scheming to learn more of it.

The next morning Mackenzie inspected the crew at quarters, particularly observing Cromwell and Small. According to the ship's medical officer, Small had reported sick, so he was unlikely to have been on deck. But in any event, Mackenzie's writer's imagination was clearly at work in his official report of the occasion, with Cromwell's "muscles braced, his battle-axe grasped resolutely, his cheek pale. He had a dangerous and determined air," while Small shifted nervously, "his battle-axe passed from one hand to the other, his eye wandered irresolutely but never towards mine. I attributed his conduct to fear."

The wind moderated in the afternoon, and Mackenzie ordered skysails and royal studding sails set. One of the apprentices who scrambled aloft was on the main-royal yard when through some mishandling the main topgallant mast went, taking canvas with it, and would have taken the boy on the main-royal yard had he not wriggled back safely to the topgallant yard, which remained in place. The accident may have been caused by a misunderstood or inappropriate order from Acting Midshipman Oliver H. Perry II, who directed operations. ("This is all your fault," someone heard the captain tell Perry.) It was confusion of this sort, Mackenzie professed to feel, that conspirators were likely to take advantage of, and after the deck was cleared of wreckage he received more food for suspicion. Cromwell, Small, and others on Spencer's list were seen clustered at the masthead, whence they had gone, Midshipman Rodgers would opine, "for plotting," and in the less succinct recollection of Captain Mackenzie they were aloft either from an unusual zeal for work "or for the purpose of conspiracy. The eye of Mr. Spencer traveled perpetually to the masthead and cast thither many of those strange and stealthy glances which I had heretofore noticed."

After supper the new mast was sent up and secured. And with dusk approaching Mackenzie had decided "that it was scarcely safe to leave

Cromwell at large. . . . the night was the season of danger." The same suspect group, Cromwell included, was gathered at the masthead. Mackenzie stationed armed officers about the darkened deck and had Cromwell arrested the moment he climbed down. The boatswain's mate denied charges that he had tried to communicate with the prisoner Spencer and said Elisha Small had. Mackenzie ordered both Cromwell and Small placed in irons on the quarterdeck with Spencer.

None of Mackenzie's official flashbacks suggest any other reason than fear for confining Samuel Cromwell. In manner and sheer physical bulk the boatswain's mate was probably the most intimidating member of the crew, a bully with a shady past, but there was really nothing to indict him as a mutineer. He was not named among Spencer's chosen. (One "E. Andrews" was listed, and since no one of that name was on the brig's muster roll, it was generally supposed to be Cromwell's alias.) But due process did not exist on that strange homeward voyage. Even in 1842 an accused was entitled to face his accusers and be fully told of the charges and specifications, and it was on this point that Midshipman Charles Hays would be asked if "any investigation into Spencer's guilt of any crime against the laws of the United States Navy was made by Captain Mackenzie or any other officer in Spencer's presence." The answer: "None that I know of, in his presence." Mackenzie had directed Lieutenant Gansevoort to "find out all I could" about the mutinous plot. According to Gansevoort, Midshipman Spencer admitted savoring the idea of mutiny on previous ships: "it was a mania with him." But the first lieutenant at no time searchingly questioned Spencer, either because the prisoner was "not disposed to talk" or for possible "other reasons" that Gansevoort said he could not remember.

To the extent that fear gripped Mackenzie and others on the *Somers,* it was now not so much of mutiny as of a mass attempt (itself mutiny?) to free the suspected mutineers. With "sullen" looks, some of the men gathered about the vessel, discussing their arrested shipmates and saying (recalled an apprentice) "that it was not right to put them in irons." Gunner's Mate Henry King expected an uprising at any moment and "was afraid to turn into my hammock." Sergeant Garty seldom left his, having been taken ill, and in his place Purser's Steward Wales acted as master-at-arms. Wales's recollections of those hours bristle with threat. He would kill any of the prisoners seen trying to communicate with one another, and he told a sailmaker's mate who acted suspiciously that unless he desisted "I should blow his brains out. . . . I had to bring three or four up for punishment."

These included one of the novices, charged with stealing sennit from another lad's hat, and the wardroom steward, Henry Waltham, accused of smuggling brandy to Midshipman Spencer—"vile offenses" in the captain's view, for each of which he ordered the maximum twelve lashes. Someone informed him that Waltham, while locked in irons to await his flogging, had told a seaman where three bottles of wine were secreted in the wardroom. This got Waltham a second dose of the cat.

All hands having been mustered to witness punishment, Mackenzie took the opportunity to lecture them on "the mysterious agency . . . at work since our departure from New York to corrupt the crew." Some were horrified to hear of Spencer's perfidy, others relieved to hear that his plot had been nipped in the bud, and a few, no doubt guilty but remorseful, shed tears. "I now considered the crew tranquilized and the vessel safe." Not for long. During the next night seditious mutterings were heard, "an insolent and menacing air was assumed by many," and there were absentees when the watches were called and mustered. "Where was this to end?" With the weather fine, there was already a "disposition" to rescue the prisoners. In bad weather, with loyal people occupied in shortening sail, might not the others make their move? Yet how many more could he safely arrest? Consulting with the first lieutenant, "I came to the conclusion that if the officers had to take care of any more prisoners, the safety of the vessel required that the first three should be put to death."

The next day the weather indeed worsened. The ship rolled heavily. A boom tackle was carried away. Midshipman Matthew Perry, who had charge of the deck, "took in the slack of the weather sheet myself, and without thinking of the prisoners I gave the order 'some of you lay aft.' " Fifteen or more did—at a rush, which became in Gansevoort's and Mackenzie's respective testimonies a mutinous assault to free the prisoners, checked only by the first lieutenant's brandishing of his Colt pistol and swearing to kill whoever stepped first upon the quarterdeck. Given the prevailing jitteriness, a boisterous response to Perry's unthinking order could well have been mistaken for a rebellious rush. That would-be mutineers roamed the ship, or so Mackenzie believed, was the essence of what he would seek to convey as his dilemma. Their continuing at large endangered the ship. But so would their arrest, producing an excess of prisoners, a problem only to be solved by the elimination of some. That dilemma he formally shared with his officers. In the forenoon of 30 November he addressed them in a letter, seeking their advice. Yet his mind was made up, he had "determined if necessary to do without counsel what I knew to be necessary to my duty to the flag and vessel."

He clinched the business that same morning by arresting four more suspects. Not much detail would illuminate this event. One of the men had intended but "failed to get up an outbreak in the night," and a knife found in his sailbag was "fit only to kill." The four had missed their musters, and all were named on Spencer's list, one certain and three doubtful. Now, in Mackenzie's words, "we had made more prisoners than we had the force to take care of."

Meanwhile, the seven officers whose advice he awaited were assembled around a small table in the wardroom and had apparently decided to act less as an advisory board than as a grand jury. Lieutenant Gansevoort was to say that Mackenzie's letter ordered them to investigate the guilt of Spencer, Cromwell, and Small. According to the ship's log, Mackenzie's injunction was not only to probe their guilt but, if guilt was established, suggest "the best mode of disposing of them under the existing circumstances." If this latter request is true, much of significance was conveyed verbally, for the letter itself contains no such specifics.

Thirteen witnesses were heard one by one. Not that "witnesses" is the correct word, except perhaps as applied to Purser's Steward Wales. In response to leading questions, their statements—taken under oath; noted in pencil by Purser Heiskell and Oliver Perry, the captain's clerk; finally read over to each; and signed or marked—consisted mostly of scattered thoughts and vague recollections, scarcely the substance even of gossip. Spencer and Cromwell had often been seen in furtive talk. The ship was not safe while they and Small remained alive. Some of the black galley cooks were in league with them. Some of the apprentices too. Cromwell was a desperate character; the damned son of a bitch should hang. "Mr. Spencer told me if he knew where the keys lay, he would first take the arms and then secure the captain and officers. . . ." This was from the ailing Sergeant Garty, evidently asked by no one why he had not alerted the captain. The fullest "statement" was that of James Wales, its purport the conversation on the booms. Spencer had begun by asking Wales if he feared death and could kill a man. Wales gave him a meandering reply. Spencer then described his planned mutiny. After killing the captain, "Mr. Spencer was to go down in the wardroom and there, with his own hands, murder the wardroom officers, while they were asleep." The brig would be taken to the Isle of Pines or another pirate haunt. (Wales's testimony said nothing of selecting females from captive ships and disposing of them after use. That was a much later embellishment.) Elisha Small had briefly attended the conversation on the boom. Replete with plotting, mutiny, murder, and hate, Wales's statement ended somewhat anticlimactically with, "On one occasion I found Mr. Spencer asleep on his watch."

The council in the wardroom carried over into the following morning, 1 December. Not every officer stayed throughout, some came and went. At no time were any of the prisoners brought before it. They did not even know that they were being tried. There is a story, impossible to confirm, that Lieutenant Gansevoort twice emerged to tell his captain that they had insufficient evidence of the prisoners' guilt and that each time Mackenzie sent him back to secure a conviction. With or without such pressure from the captain, the result was a unanimous conclusion, delivered to Mackenzie as a letter consisting almost entirely of a 212-word sentence. Spencer, Cromwell, and Small were guilty of an intent to commit mutiny. Since the extent of their conspiracy was unknown and contingencies were impossible to foresee, it was unsafe to carry them home, and for the sake of the ship and the lives of the rest "they should be put to death, in a manner best calculated as an example to make a beneficial impression upon the disaffected."

The letter also spoke of giving the condemned "sufficient time to prepare." But there was little of that. In Mackenzie's unapologetic words the conspiracy still existed, involving "at least" twenty of the crew. He had to consider the apprentices, schoolboys easily tempted "by the pleasures held out to them as accompanying the life of a pirate." His officers were too fatigued to have resisted any attempt made to rescue Spencer and company. And Spencer, Cromwell, and Small were the prisoners most capable of navigating a ship. Really, there was no dearth of motives for getting rid of those three. Thus would be Mackenzie's impassioned self-defense. His duty was to "carry [the council's] recommendation into immediate effect."

This Mackenzie certainly did. Noon approached when he received the officer's letter and the council's proceedings were read aloud to him. He issued orders to prepare for three executions and donned full-dress uniform. According to the ship's log, it was only 1:45 P.M. when all hands were called to witness punishment. The day was bright, the sea gently rolling, the ship holding to a westward course, some three days sailing from the Virgin Islands. Mackenzie's officers, fully armed, were stationed about the deck, as decided by a watch bill he had composed the night before. Men stood at three whips tackled to the main yardarms, ready to haul when the condemned were noosed and the command given. As Mackenzie subsequently reported, the officers were under his orders to "stab to the heart . . . cut down whoever should take even one hand off the ropes or fail to haul on them."

According to Mackenzie's first official letter making known the executions, prepared less than a week after they had occured, he personally

A Currier and Ives impression of Mackenzie's schoolship on the afternoon of the executions, with bodies hanging from the yardarm. *(U.S. Naval Academy Museum Library)*

told the condemned three of "my determination as to their fate and gave them ten minutes to make any arrangement of their affairs or send any messages they might wish." Daniel McKinley, one of Mackenzie's shackled seamen not marked for hanging (though as yet unaware of his luck), crouched about eight feet from where Spencer sat on the starboard arms chest. McKinley later testified, "The commander came out of his cabin in full dress uniform and told Mr. Spencer he had ten minutes to live." Mackenzie sent for a bible, three prayer books, and a camp stool. He also had pen and paper, and seating himself close to Spencer, he began a subdued exchange that evidently no one else, not even McKinley, was close enough to overhear. When the ten minutes had passed, Mackenzie was seen to be still talking quietly with Spencer and scribbling something. Oliver Perry, the captain's clerk, while "not near enough to hear their conversation," assumed that he was writing at the youth's dictation. Other than to assert that Spencer and Small (but not Cromwell) acknowledged their guilt and begged his forgiveness, Mackenzie would say nothing of any farewell messages in his first notification to the secretary of the navy, but eighteen days later confessional and penitent utterances that he attributed to Spencer were to form a lengthy and, to many, incredible portion of an official report to the secretary, that being "the least painful mode" of getting them to Spencer's father, the secretary of war. To still questions at that future date, Mackenzie would produce what he swore were his original notes.

In those final moments Cromwell was heard to protest his innocence and to express concern for his wife, Small to lament for "my poor old mother." Lieutenant Gansevoort thought that he heard Spencer ask the captain to consider whether he might be acting too hastily. Gansevoort's testimony, with that of Mackenzie and Purser's Steward Wales, would tell of final handshakes, some flow of tears, and pleas from contrite transgressors for forgiveness. The three were escorted forward and helped upon hammock netting stacked port and starboard near each gangway. A black neckerchief found in Spencer's locker was placed over his face, and a frock or jumper hooded each of the others. In the log's terse words, "bent the starboard outer whip onto Acting Midshipman Spencer, the inner one onto Seaman Elisha Small, and the larboard one onto Boatswain's Mate Samuel Cromwell." When the ropes were thus fastened about their throats, Mackenzie mounted the trunk house, from which dais he ordered the executions carried out. The log suffices: "At 2.15 fired a weather gun and ran the prisoners up to the yardarm."

Nine

■

A CRIME UNDEFINED

ackenzie's official (and belated) report of events aboard his schoolship would run to some thirteen thousand words, fully one-third of them devoted to the hangings and last rites. Readers acquainted with his travel books might have recalled, wonderingly, the writer's fascination with executions in Spain, the "painful excitement" he deemed "a strange perversion." One sure reaction to the report when it appeared was surprise and outrage over his stated belief that had he brought Spencer home alive, wealth and influence would have rescued the young offender from retribution. He had (Mackenzie said) told him as much in those final moments. "It is not in nature that his father should not have interfered. For those who have friends or money in America there was no punishment for the worst of crimes."

That exaggerated indictment sheds light on Mackenzie's prejudices. Like many a writer similarly handicapped he resented the fact that humble beginnings had robbed him of a liberal education. Four years of boarding school were little to boast about, especially since in class he was, according to his wife, "no student . . . not at all precocious," and when he entered the navy, scarcely twelve years old, "his education was necessarily incomplete." The opposite was true of Philip Spencer. Precocity indeed may have proved that young man's fatal attribute. The words Mackenzie said he addressed to his people, assembled beneath three gently swaying corpses, suggests something of the envy of the self-taught for those blessed with a handsome tutelage: Spencer, born into high society with appropriate advantage but "betrayed by ill-regulated ambition." Cromwell, "who must have received an excellent

education but lusted for gold." And Small, who "had enjoyed the benefits of education but could not resist the brandy."

The bodies were lowered after dinner and delivered to messmates
who prepared them for burial. The dead seamen were sewn up in their
hammocks, the midshipman accorded the dignity of a coffin, made from
two mess chests, and full dress attire except for the sword, "which he
had forfeited the right to wear." With dusk falling and battle lanterns
aglow, Mackenzie read the funeral services. When the bodies had been
committed to the deep, "I felt that I once more was completely commander of the vessel intrusted to me."

Yet for the next day or so he was seldom seen on deck, reported as
indisposed. The brig reached St. Thomas on 4 December, and it was
then that Mackenzie wrote for the secretary of the navy, "in great haste
and with a wretched pen," his first account of the occurrences. He must
have left a copy with the United States consul, if not the master of some
American merchant vessel (The USS *Vandalia* had not yet reached St.
Thomas), because should bad weather, "collision in the night, or other
accident cause us never to be heard of, I am desirous that the Navy
Department should not be unaquainted with recent developments on
the *Somers*." He added that if his ship never reached port, "be assured
that it was not because of her capture from the officers." Mackenzie later
asserted that discipline was fully restored after the executions, that when
piped down from witnessing punishment, and called upon to give three
cheers, the crew had responded heartily. However, if this had signaled
a release of tension it was but momentary. On that final passage home
Gunner's Mate King "never unbuckled [his] arms." Punishments continued. Seven apprentices were whipped on 7 December, three men flogged
the next day, and on the ninth the charge of "not going aloft to furl the
maintopsails," which earned eleven boys a dozen colts each, almost
suggests a mutiny in miniature.

The *Somers* dropped anchor in the East River on Wednesday night,
14 December. Mackenzie at once arrested six apprentices and two seamen as suspected mutineers, to bring the number of men in irons to
twelve. Civilian visitors were barred from the ship. There was, wrote a
metropolitan diarist, "a strange mystery about this vessel." Using a
friendly newspaper, Mackenzie got his side of the story out quickly. It
was a much less informative account, confined to mutiny charges and
the simple fact of the hangings, that he had sent to the secretary of the
navy. Upshur, not up to the task of confronting his cabinet colleague,
John Canfield Spencer, with the harrowing news, delegated it to
Spencer's son-in-law and private secretary. The secretary of war was in

the midst of attending to treaties with the Chippewa Indians. Stunned by what he heard, he and his heartbroken wife withdrew from public activity. But anger infused Spencer's grief, to be vented with a pen almost as busy as became that of the captain who had ordered his eighteen-year-old son hanged.

Spencer was probably the author of an article signed "S" that was published in *The Madisonian* one week before Christmas and that bluntly proclaimed Mackenzie's guilt. "The laws of Congress proscribing the navy regulations forbid the taking of human life, even by sentence of a court-martial, without the sanction of the president of the United States or of the commander of the fleet or squadron." And while the newspapers' first reaction had largely favored Mackenzie, second thoughts produced adverse headlines. The *New York Herald,* which had labeled the executed three as "desperadoes," conceded less than forty-eight hours later that "the [mutinous] plot was merely in embryo. The officers would seem to have acted under a panic." Even among those related to Mackenzie through marriage, someone ventured to say that he "only did his duty, perhaps a little hastily."

Mackenzie hoped the navy's formal inquiry would protect his reputation. Three veteran officers made up the court, with a civilian judge advocate appointed by Secretary Upshur to give the right impression of impartiality in "a case without precedent in our history." The hearings were held on the receiving ship *North Carolina* in the Brooklyn Navy Yard and from Mackenzie's standpoint got off to a bad start. That prolix report of his, late in reaching the Navy Department, was read into the record and was thus soon in the public domain. It was at once widely deplored for its sanctimony or scoffed at for its florid manner—"bad taste . . . a singular mixture of folly, silliness and blasphemy," the *New York Herald* called it, while James Fenimore Cooper wrote to his wife that Mackemzie "has actually got in one of the prayers he read to his crew." But Mackenzie was less bothered by aspersions upon his literary style than "statements going the rounds that I was cruel on the *Independence* and as acting commander of the *Fairfield*." Such charges obviously strengthened the belief that he could drive men to mutiny. "As all the mutinies on record," he told the court, "have been provoked by injustice toward the crew or by gross tyranny or incapacity on the part of the commanding officer, it concerns me to show that no such causes existed on the *Somers.*" Legitimate grievances had led to Britain's naval revolts in home waters, a captain's barbarity had provoked bloodshed on the *Hermione,* and the *Bounty* affair was of a similar cast. (That Mackenzie would equate those latter two mutinies indicates how already well rooted

"Assailed by malignity," Alexander S. Mackenzie appeared before the court of inquiry. From a sketch published in the *New York Weekly Tribune,* 21 January 1843. *(U.S. Naval Institute)*

was the image of William Bligh as tyrant.) But, Mackenzie insisted, there was nothing like that on his schoolship.

Secretary Spencer expected that the *Somers* "mutiny" would appear to have been nothing but "a phantom of Wales's perjury and Mackenzie's fears." Unfolding testimony promised as much. That of the purser's steward was more than a shade too lurid for ready credence, his version of the conversation on the booms now expanded to include Spencer's telling him that apprentices who refused to assist the revolt would be made to "walk the plank," that captive women would be ravished then disposed of, and that captured vessels would be plundered then sunk with their crews because "dead men tell no tales." Philip Spencer, evidently, had not been the only member of the schoolship's company familiar with pirate yarns.

Portions of the *Somers*'s logbook appeared in the press, horrifying readers with their disclosures of 2,265 lashes inflicted across the backs of mostly boys within a period of six months. In the *North Carolina*'s cabin an agitated Mackenzie demanded action against whomever was responsible for the leak. He suspected officers of the receiving ship. When the court demurred, he cried, "I shall take care then to call the attention of the Secretary of the Navy to the matter—that I shall!"

But Upshur's sympathy for the beleaguered commander may have begun to wane. He probably resented a letter that Mackenzie had written to chide him for having (as had been reported) "passed the greater part of the day subsequent to the receipt of the dispatches from the *Somers* in conference with the Secretary of War." Neither could Upshur have felt comfortable with the officer s attempts to make public some charges of theft and other harsh reproofs leveled by Secretary Spencer at his reprobate son in letters that Mackenzie had found among the boy's personal effects and read. (He sent copies to Francis Lieber, a noted authority on economic and public ethics, who read them presumably without compunction and pronounced the Spencers "a shocking breed," the late young Philip "a villain . . . scamp.") Mackenzie, indeed, had at first declined to return the letters to the dead boy's father, claiming "they are necessary to me . . . for my protection against the malignity by which I am already assailed." He finally surrendered them, "yielding to considerations which may not be appreciated . . . but . . . have duly authorized copies of all . . . excepting only those which decency forbade my asking anyone to copy."

When the court of inquiry exonerated Mackenzie, holding his "immediate execution of the ringleaders demanded by duty and justified by necessity," cynics apprehended a whitewash. Simon Cameron, a future successor to John Spencer in the War Department, called the hanging of his son "cowardly butchery" and anticipated Mackenzie's upcoming court-martial as another "mockery of justice." Mackenzie requested that procedure himself to head off his arrest and trial for murder in a civil court, something the family of Boatswain's Mate Samuel Cromwell, covertly goaded by Secretary Spencer or his friends, had taken steps to bring about.

"Careworn and anxious," Mackenzie stood again in the great cabin of the *North Carolina,* charged with murder, illegal punishment, oppression, cruelty, and conduct unbecoming an officer, to all of which he pleaded not guilty. Heard by a panel of fourteen officers, most of the testimony echoed that of the court of inquiry. Sergeant Garty of the marines reiterated his belief that mutiny was planned and that an attempted rescue of Mackenzie's prisoners was likely to have succeeded. Discussion turned on whether they could have been carried into St. Thomas and transferred to another American vessel of war. Mackenzie's pen was again at work, on a hurried document for the court. St. Thomas was distant by some ten days' sailing when he had to contend with "the daily and hourly increasing insubordination of the crew." Besides, he could not be sure that the *Vandalia* or some other American man-of-war would be in harbor. It went without saying that from no other source would he have sought help. "A naval commander can never be justified in invoking foreign aid in reducing an insubordinate crew to obedience."

The trial had lasted about two months when Mackenzie's counsel read his defense. Even the evidence of "seemingly trifle incidents . . . looks and motions . . . significant enough to those who see them" bore out the existence of a mutinous conspiracy: "Such is the character of mutiny." And in this instance, mutiny beyond the reach of statute law and with ever-growing prospects of success. "Never was a crew where malcontents could have had a fairer chance of making proselytes." Alone on the ocean, unable to invoke a regular court-martial, what was the commander to do? Given all circumstances, he had only one choice. "Necessity stood stern umpire." The judge advocate agreed, his closing remarks offering yet another definition of mutiny: "The intent or act to supersede lawful authority, or resist it, or bring it into contempt." Mackenzie was acquitted of all charges.

Three days after the verdict was announced, Surgeon Leacock of the *Somers,* who despite his failing health had joined his fellow officers in public support of their accused captain, was found dead of a self-inflicted wound in the brig's gun room. Mackenzie was not remotely the type to have sought release from woe in suicide, but his spirits were sorely tested in the months and years that followed. Hardly had the trial ended when Secretary Upshur removed him from command of the *Somers,* an action that Mackenzie, considering the legal vindication he had won, found "mortifying." And when an obviously impatient Upshur inquired of him about the twelve prisoners for whose expected trial the court remained in session, a weary Mackenzie replied that he no longer wished to prefer charges against them. They were released and the court adjourned.

The *Somers* affair launched passionate and prolonged debate and was even dramatized onstage at New York's Bowery Theatre. Mackenzie paid little heed. At his home overlooking the Hudson River he worked quietly on a biography of Stephen Decatur and awaited sea orders, with steadily declining hopes of ever getting any. Notables in the literary, legal, and political spheres who waged wordy skirmishes about his conduct and culpability included James Fenimore Cooper, considered by Mackenzie an "unscrupulous and unmanly enemy" ever since the two had battled in print over Oliver H. Perry's performance on Lake Erie in the War of 1812. Cooper used influential contacts in Washington to get his review of the *Somers* case, in Mackenzie's words "a malignant commentary," bound right in with the published transcript of the commander's court-martial. Cooper conceded that Spencer had plotted mutiny but only half seriously, Mackenzie and Lieutenant Gansevoort thereupon so overreacting that "a mutiny was required in order that the officers might escape ridicule." Richard H. Dana, writer, jurist, and former seaman, expressed a kindlier view, deciding after a visit to the *Somers* that on such a small vessel Mackenzie's concern was understandable: "You feel as though half a dozen resolute conspirators could have swept the decks and thrown overboard all that opposed them before aid could come from below."

Mackenzie might never have gone to sea again had it not been for the failure of his brother's mission, on behalf of the United States government, to purchase Mexican territory. (John Slidell had pursued a lucrative legal career in Louisiana and would later win prominence as an agent of the Confederate government in the Civil War.) In the conflict that followed, Mackenzie served as commander of the steamer *Mississippi,* returning home in April 1848 with his never-robust health again weakened. He died five months later after one of his solitary horseback rides. Guert Gansevoort, his uneasy ally on the *Somers,* continued a career not altogether free from further controversy. In January 1856, commanding the 16-gun sloop *Decatur* in Seattle Bay, Washington Territory, he assisted in the rescue of settlers menaced by hostile Indians, but aspects of his conduct on this occasion drew charges of "unpardonable delinquency" from a fellow commander. Gansevoort was subsequently suspended from command of the *Decatur* for being intoxicated. During the Civil War his cousin Herman Melville wrote that he was "Brave as a lion and I hope he will yet turn out the hero of a brilliant victory." Nothing of the sort happened. But Gansevoort attained the rank of commodore before his death in 1868, and it is anybody's guess whether, as was said of him, his role in the *Somers* affair had left him "prey to unavailing remorse."

Melville had returned from his own fourteen months' service in the United States Navy to produce the semiautobiographical *White-jacket: or, The World in a Man-of-War.* It champions the lot of the common sailor, but its two references to the *Somers* reflect an uncertainty upon her captain's conduct. Perhaps Melville had not wished to offend Gansevoort, whom he obviously admired. It is in his novella, *Billy Budd, Foretopman,* written near the close of his life and first published in

1924, that Melville scholars search for similarities with the tragedy on Mackenzie's schoolship, a daunting task leading inevitably to a straining for parallels. Melville's Billy Budd is the personification of goodness and innocence, no devilishly mischievous or mutinous Philip Spencer. Yet the *Somers* certainly figured in Melville's meditations. It is "under the lee of the booms" that we find Billy first accosted by "a mysterious emissary." When later, in the forechains, he stammeringly rejects efforts to bribe him into mutiny, the would-be intriguer decamps, "disappearing in the direction of the mainmast in the shadow of the booms." And officers who must, in the end, decide Billy's fate are "not unlikely brought to something more or less akin to that harassed frame of mind which . . . actuated the commander of the brig-of-war *Somers.*"

Not in the symbolistic Billy Budd has Philip Spencer achieved immortality but rather through the myths attached to the Chi Psi fraternity of which he was a cofounder. As for the ill-fated ship on which he served, she took forty officers and men to the bottom in 1846 and still lies on her starboard side in 110 feet of water off Veracruz. Her voyage as a schoolship under Alexander Slidell Mackenzie's command was a foredoomed experiment in cadet training within the American navy. The melancholy outcome had the effect of quickening steps toward a more efficient scholastic system. That a major result of the *Somers* affair was the founding of the United States Naval Academy adds perhaps a crowning irony, for such an institution had long been contemplated, with Mackenzie one of its earliest and most earnest advocates.

What happened aboard the brig *Somers* was the most discussed mid–nineteenth century naval episode of any that bore an imprint of mutiny. Little enough could be said of an occurrence connected with the 18-gun sloop-of-war *Warren* in 1846 because of the disappearance of all hands directly concerned. The *Warren*'s launch had sailed out of San Francisco Bay with a small crew under the command of a midshipman and a purser's clerk, brothers named Montgomery. It headed for the mouth of the Sacramento River. The launch carried gold coin for payment of the army garrison at New Helvetia, the colony lately developed by John Sutter, and although the Montgomery brothers were reputedly unpopular, greed was doubtless the reason why the vessel never reached its destination. No trace of launch or occupants was ever found except for a midshipman's jacket sighted a few years later as part of a prostitute's wardrobe in the goldfields east of Sutter's Fort.

News of a mutiny from that same far western region in 1849 contained echoes of Alexander Mackenzie's troubles inasmuch as it afforded another example of the dilemmas besetting a commander with no resources but his own to cope with a perceived erosion of discipline. The officer was Thomas Ap Catesby Jones, the same contentious captain who had thwarted Mackenzie's hopes for a literary role in the South Seas Exploring Expedition.

Flying his flag on the 74-gun ship-of-war *Ohio,* he commanded the Pacific Squadron after the Mexican War and was in Californian waters at the height of the gold fever, which, by infecting his low-paid sailors, sustained the threat of mass desertions. Jones saw to it that his marines kept their muskets loaded and midshipmen in charge of shore-going boats their revolvers conveniently holstered. But on the night of 13 September, although Midshipman William Gibson of the schooner *Ewing* landed a San Francisco dinner party safely ashore at the Clay Street Wharf with "pistol in each hand," he unwisely set the weapons aside on the return trip. "In a few moments the after oarsman John Black threw his oar out of the rowlock and himself on me." Black's fellow oarsmen, four in number, including one Peter Black who may have been a brother, joined in, and they flung Gibson over the side. An English merchantman picked him up later. His attackers rowed ashore at San Pablo Bay and plunged inland in the general direction of the gold mines. Search parties overtook them, and the following month, before a court-martial assembled on board the *Warren,* all five were convicted of mutiny and desertion and sentenced to death.

Commodore Jones was well aware that the Articles of War stipulated that to proceed with such executions inside the territorial jurisdiction of the United States required presidential review and approval. But communication with Millard Fillmore in Washington would have taken months. The commodore's situation was not unlike that pleaded in defense by Commander Mackenzie, namely, that time was running out, discipline was crumbling, and the people were in need of an immediate object lesson. The two cases differed principally in their locations, one on the high seas, the other in American territorial waters. Jones took a bold chance, deciding for himself that California was remote enough from the seat of government to qualify as a foreign station, one on which he as commander had the necessary authority to review and approve sentences. Three of these he reduced to flogging, loss of pay, and confinement. John Black was hanged from the foreyardarm of the *Ewing* and Peter Black from that of the *Warren.* Little more than a year later a panel of his peers absolved Jones of charges that he had exceeded his authority in carrying out the executions. But it was subsequently learned that while on the Pacific station Jones had misused public funds, and five years' suspension closed a long and turbulent naval career.

Among naval officers, viewpoints upon the nature of mutiny continued to vary. What hardly brought consensus any closer was, in too many
examples where the offense was alleged, the problem superiors had of
deciding whether affirmations or denials of mutiny were soberly made
or sprang from processes no more judicious than self-interest or personal
spite. An 1848 episode illustrates the point. The 44-gun frigate *United
States* was moored off Port Mahon, in the Mediterranean Sea, where
Spain allowed American naval vessels to winter and take on supplies.
One January midday Lt. Roger Perry aroused Capt. Joseph Smoot at
his lodgings ashore, reporting that half of the flagship's crew had gathered on the gun deck, triced up the fore and main hatches, and refused
to work. When Perry mentioned mutiny, the captain interrupted, saying
that "Jack only wants to frolic." All the same, he returned to the *United
States* in haste and called forth the marine detachment, and having
managed to assemble his dissident people on the quarterdeck, he opened
negotiations.

Besides forty-eight hours' furlough, the men each wanted ten dollars
of spending money. Smoot suggested eight, still three more than his
squadron commander, Commo. George Read, had authorized. The men
accepted his offer, along with permission to raise more funds by selling
their pea jackets. Seventy-four satisfied sailors thereupon marched
ashore, but this settlement left Smoot's first lieutenant, George A.
Prentiss, a self-professed "lover of strict discipline," thoroughly out-
raged. The commodore himself was on board but had refused to intervene, remaining "serene and tranquil in his cabin," according to Prentiss,
and allowing Captain Smoot "to submit to all or nearly all the demands
of the mutineers." Between Prentiss, Smoot, and Commodore Read,
bad blood had long existed, not to mention more recent ill feeling (or
envy) over well-founded rumors that Smoot kept a woman in Port
Mahon. Whatever his real motives, Prentiss in due course sent to the
secretary of the navy a lengthy diatribe directed at Smoot and Read that
charged them in particular with failing to suppress a mutiny.

Smoot countered by having Prentiss put on trial for falsehood and
disrespect. Prentiss, who had escaped conviction seven years earlier
when court-martialed for alleged bullying and neglect of duty, emerged
this time too with only a light reprimand. His judges had to grapple
with gnawing questions. How was mutiny to be proved? Who most
possessed the power of infallible determination? Captain Smoot argued
that naval regulations contained no precise definition of the term, that
mutiny's presence or otherwise was left solely to the conclusion of the
commander, a prerogative Smoot clearly believed must not be shared
with a first lieutenant.

Prentiss conceded the absence of anything like an incontrovertible definition. The Thirteenth Article of War, which dealt with mutiny, only prescribed punishment. Prentiss, in his defense, attempted to remedy this omission, drawing from past judicial interpretations: "The crime of mutiny or revolt consists not in simple disobedience but in organized and concerted resistance to lawful authority, aiming at the subversion of the power of those legally entitled to command." An *act* of disobedience was not required to constitute the offense. Conspiracy to disobey was sufficient. Disobedience was mutiny only when "done by a common combination, or to effect a common purpose. The parties must act together." The absence of specific ringleaders in the present case was significant. As even Captain Smoot had testified, "it was a general thing." So (Prentiss continued) disobedience had proceeded from "concert and combination. The offense of mutiny was thus consummated . . . was perfect and complete, and no less real because [the mutineers] were checked in their course by threats or promises or bribes."

As Lieutenant Prentiss's acquittal on the falsehood charge suggests, a majority of the court tended to agree. But no subsequent action was taken against Smoot—nor, for that matter, against the mutineers, whose only sin, in the captain's stated view, had been a perfectly understandable desire to "frolic" amid the fleshpots of Port Mahon.

What appears to have most disconcerted those in the business of defining mutiny was a compulsion to develop a special coloration, to isolate "mutiny" from such clearly defined offenses as conspiracy or simple disobedience, while retaining these as obligatory ingredients. In his two-volume *Military Law,* 1886, the West Point professor of law, Lt. Col. William W. Winthrop, sought to resolve the problem in terms of emphasis or *intent*. The reason for the inadequacy of existing definitions, for mutiny's confusion with other crimes, was "the characterizing intent not being sufficiently recognized." Disrespect shown or violence done to a superior officer, defiance of his orders, threats directly against him or voiced at protest meetings, these were offenses in and of themselves, but none constituted mutiny unless "characterized by deliberate purpose to usurp, subvert or override military authority."

Not even Winthrop could altogether avoid ambiguity, and on the question of how many persons it took to make a mutiny he was no more than tentative, perhaps preferring to leave that poser to a contemporary, Andrew Allen Harwood, whose *The Law and Practices of United States Naval Courts Martial,* published in 1867, had focused on conspiracy as a usual element in mutinies. No one could disagree that conspiracy requires more than a single individual, "and so, in mutiny and sedition, two or more persons are frequently parties thereto." Fre-

"Here was mutiny." Daniel Ammen quelled it with revolver and bullets.
(U.S. Naval Institute)

quently—not always. What might be inferred from Harwood's writing is that while evidence of conspiracy eases the task of definers, the absence of such evidence cannot rule out the possibility that mutiny has taken place. However convenient the detection of conspiracy is to the evidential process, "it does not follow that it requires more than one to commit [mutiny]. The offense may begin and end with one individual." So this reasoning, after all, removes conspiracy as a prerequisite, and it seems to have had considerable appeal within the United States naval community, where the concept that one person alone can be guilty of mutiny would prevail well into the twentieth century, albeit shakily, for it was always vulnerable to challenge.

There was nothing ambiguous about the uprising on the *Ocean Queen* in 1864. Few afterward doubted that a conspiracy to seize and plunder the 3,000-ton Atlantic and Pacific Mail Steamship Company's vessel existed, or that only Comdr. Daniel Ammen's clear judgment and forthright action averted disaster to its civilian passengers. On Friday, 13 May, the *Ocean Queen* had taken on a draft of 220 naval replacements, in Ammen's charge, bound via the Panama Isthmus for assignment to ships-of-war on Pacific coastal patrol. Army transfers made up part of

The steamship *Ocean Queen,* Panama-bound with eight hundred civilians and a mutinous naval draft. *(Courtesy of The Mariners Museum, Newport News, Virginia)*

the draft, many of them a bad lot looking for excuses to mutiny as soon as the ship cleared harbor. Around midnight two leaders of the malcontents, John Kelly and Alfred Bussell, sent for and told Commander Ammen that crowded as they were to the starboard side of the ship, forward of the wheelhouse and beneath the hurricane deck, sleep was impossible. The commander promised to speak with Edward Tinklepaugh, the vessel's master, about the matter, sternly dissenting, however, when Kelly suggested that an issue of whiskey would help.

The next evening, after the unruly element had found fault with their food, roughed up the ship's stewards, and thrown pots and furniture over the side, Tinklepaugh reminded the commander that the safety of his eight hundred first-class and steerage passengers must be considered, and he proposed that Ammen dump his troublemakers ashore at Fortress Monroe in Hampton Roads. But that was too far off course, and Ammen, in any event, was not the type to be deterred from his duty. When on Sunday morning Kelly and others told him that they intended to break open the spirits room, he replied with equal bluntness that if they tried, he and his assistant, Boatswain Thomas Bell, would not hesitate to shoot them.

No effort was made at this stage to arrest the ringleaders, something Ammen and Tinklepaugh felt would touch off a mass revolt. Without a ship's arsenal or marines, the officers and crew would be quickly overpowered, the *Ocean Queen* and her innocent souls, women and children among them, placed at the mercy of mutineers. Also, when the replacements assembled for dinner—hard bread, roast beef, roast potatoes, and tea—Boatswain Bell heard no complaints and told the commander that he thought further trouble unlikely. Ammen and Tinklepaugh were not so easily taken in. After dinner half a dozen men led by Kelly and Bussell crept off, and while twenty or thirty others clustered abaft the foremast, apparently waiting to see how things went, this group soon appeared at the light wooden grating erected in the port gangway to protect the passengers' quarters aft from unlawful intrusion. A guard at the barrier was easily dealt with, but Tinklepaugh, the ship's engineer, and three or four armed passengers stood braced on the other side, awaiting the first man to break through.

Shouts brought Commander Ammen rushing to the scene with his revolver drawn. He found a hand-to-hand struggle in progress at the barrier. He immediately ordered fire and discharged his own revolver. There were other shots, at close range, and the mutineers fled, leaving Kelly and Bussell both dead, one on each side of the grating. A third man was shot and wounded as he raced to join the uncertain crowd abaft the foremast. Ammen afterward placed five men in irons and lectured the rest of his troublesome draft on the hurricane deck. A minister was found among the passengers to recite the appropriate words, and the dead ringleaders were buried at sea. There might still have been disorder. Fortunately, the *Ocean Queen* fell in with the screw steamer *Neptune,* a newly commissioned Union vessel that was patrolling Cuban waters where the feared rebel cruiser *Florida* was reported on the prowl. The *Neptune* took Ammen's prisoners off his hands and convoyed the *Ocean Queen* all the way to Panama. Not that disembarkation there ended the commander's worries. While the ship was crossing the Isthmus 10 of his replacements jumped off the moving train and fled, leaving a total of 202 when Daniel Ammen, no doubt with the utmost relief, finally delivered them to a receiving ship on the Pacific station.

Having quelled a mutiny on the high seas in wartime, especially with hundreds imperiled and an enemy raider lurking over the horizon, Ammen had no fear of the kind of criticism leveled at Alexander Mackenzie. But as Mackenzie had done, he moved to forestall civil proceedings by requesting a court-martial. "A court of inquiry," he wrote to the secretary of the navy, "would not free me from possible civil prosecution afterwards." His request was granted. At the court-martial, before which he was charged with murder, Ammen's defense contended that "here was mutiny. I did not hesitate to give the order to fire upon the mutineers. I fired twice. Had I failed in my duty the narrative of the *Ocean Queen* might have been added to the book of horrors." The court agreed and judged the killings "justifiable homicide."

* * *

In Great Britain at this time the Naval Discipline Act was about to replace the old 1749 naval code, but as with the United States Navy's successive generations of naval law, the traditional term "Articles of War" remained in vogue. Mutiny in the British navy was still punishable by death, though only for ringleaders when the offense was not accompanied by acts of violence. Under this distinction a nonviolent mutineer might get off with imprisonment. Nor did "making a mutinous assembly" carry the death penalty. Incitement to mutiny did, whether committed by service personnel or civilians if the latter were "on board any ship of Her Majesty." As in the United States, an incontestable definition for mutiny continued to elude the ablest legal minds. The British jurist Theodore Thring, whose *Criminal Law of the Navy* was published in 1861 and deemed important enough to warrant a second printing sixteen years later, stated that resistance by one or more persons to superior authority *implied* mutiny. But "this crime had not been defined by any statute, and it has been doubted whether a single person, unaided by any accessory, can be guilty of the offence."

Thring pointed out that Sections 10 and 11 of the Naval Discipline Act, by their repeated use of the word *join*, "necessarily imply that there must be more than one person engaged to constitute a state of mutiny." At the same time, Section 14 ruled that a single person could be punished for making "any mutinous assembly." Wherein did the two offenses differ? To some poor wretch hauled before a court-martial the issue was by no means one of hairsplitting semantics but could be a matter of life or death. No arbitrary definitions were provided. One had to compare the tenth and eleventh sections with the seventeenth, which dealt with insubordination, to draw some reasonable inference of what was meant by mutiny. Thring settled for defining it as "a combination of two or more persons to rise against the authority of their superior officer, and effect their purpose . . . by resistance, either active or passive." Concerted disobedience Thring deemed conceivable as mutiny.

Not everyone agreed. Some years earlier another British legal sage, William Hickman, in his *Law and Practice of Naval Courts Martial,* had directed attention to a court's determination in the trial of a sailor charged with striking an officer. The act could be construed as mutiny. Mutiny took many forms, from mass insurrection to "debating together on any subject of discontent." It might also be "a murmuring, or muttering even, against the exercise of authority." It did not have to be "an aggregate offence [but] might originate and conclude with a single person." This consideration of mutiny as commitable by one person would take hold more securely in the United States. In Britain, however, it became generally accepted, indeed codified into law, that the essence of mutiny was collective insubordination.

What added urgency to the need for a clear definition of the term was a jittery perception of the British Board of Admiralty, especially among its old-guard members, that the new methods adopted by the lower deck to air grievances were themselves forms of mutiny thinly disguised. Ever since the Spithead mutiny, which might never have broken out had sailors' complaints received prompt and serious attention, direct petitioning to the Admiralty or Parliament was an accepted manner of pressing for reform. But as the nineteenth century drew to a close the Admiralty moved to outlaw the practice and tended to regard any collective manifestation of protest as tantamount to mutiny. Britain's sailors reacted by forming lower-deck societies, whose resemblance to labor unions further alarmed the Admiralty.

More properly entitled benefit societies, they had their origin in the need to aid the families of ratings who died or were invalided, such dependents in most cases receiving no pensions. The societies were formed of separate naval trades or groups of trades, the Naval Artisans Death Benefit Association, for instance, being made up of blacksmiths, coopers, painters, and plumbers. They subsisted on quite small membership fees, but with increasing fleet expansion and modernization their strength grew and interests diversified. Besides having a charitable function, they began to serve as recreational or social clubs, promoters of solidarity among the different naval trades, and to the uneasy gaze of some in the British naval hierarchy were potentially dangerous advocates for the claims and gripes of their members.

The lower-deck societies drew inspiration from a former naval petty officer named James Woods, who after narrowly escaping a court-martial for shipboard agitation bought his discharge and in 1898, under the new name Lionel Yexley, founded the *Bluejacket and Coastguard Gazette.* Seeking a more effective medium through which to lobby the government for redress of sailors' grievances, Yexley in 1904 cofounded *The Fleet,* a monthly magazine devoting more space to alleged abuses and injustices aboard His Majesty's warships.

Mindful that senior naval officers thought him a troublemaker, Yexley took pains to give *The Fleet* a character innocent of subversion. While campaigning for general improvement and reform, he made a point of emphasizing lower-deck loyalty, an approach that secured him the consistent support of Adm. Sir John Fisher, a First Sea Lord well attuned to the importance of sailors' morale in an increasingly complex and stressful nautical environment. Yexley's alliance with Fisher explains in part why lower-deck organizations and Yexley's *The Fleet* survived with minimal interference from Whitehall's bureaucrats. But another and perhaps principal reason was the recognition that they served as useful safety valves. Only a few years earlier crews on HMS *Majestic* and other warships had demonstrated their discontent by throwing gun sights over the side and committing other mutinous acts. Letters to *The Fleet* and petitions from benefit societies were more agreeable forms of protest. And the avowals of patriotism that so often accompanied these letters afforded a modicum of relief to the British naval establishment at a time when revolutionary pressures were building in the combat fleets of other monarchies. One had only to look at events in Imperial Russia.

So Yexley and the reform movement he represented were tolerated—but with private misgivings. Certain admirals still felt that while purporting to moderate and properly channel the views of the lower deck, Yexley and his ilk actually inflamed them. In fact, Britain was experiencing severe industrial unrest, with a concomitant rise in political radicalism bound to have affected the lower ranks of her defense forces. And the naval discontents of which Yexley so often warned Whitehall were all too real, as indicated by a high rate of desertions, almost two thousand annually between 1903 and 1905—a period when ratings mutinied at the Portsmouth Naval Barracks. The commander blamed Yexley—"a very dangerous man . . . raising mutiny and discontent"—and he described his barracks as a volcano ready to erupt. But it was in 1905 that Russia provided the world with a classic example of how, given a seething populace at home and confused or embittered sailors afloat, little more than the issuance of spoiled meat from the galley can touch off such eruptions.

Ten

❧

THE *POTEMKIN*

R ussia had tried ever since the Crimean War to make a sea power of itself. Notwithstanding years of advancement in naval organization and warship design and construction, when tsarist expansionism and Japan's vigorous response led to the twentieth century's first great naval contest, the Imperial Russian Navy was sadly ill-prepared. The immediate toll was high enough: twenty warships sunk or disabled and ten thousand sailors lost. The price paid on Russia's home front ran higher yet as the news from the Straits of Tsushima strengthened opposition to the Tsar's war and fueled the fires of revolution.

Russian naval conscripts were drawn from the peasantry, but not overwhelmingly so, and it was a stereotypical exaggeration to have characterized the Russian sailor as "simple, childlike," a dull-witted subordinate going about his duties "in his own melancholy way," as did an English observer in 1899. By 1905 one-third of Russia's navy consisted of men with industrial working-class backgrounds, among them personnel skilled in marine engineering and other branches of a fitfully modernizing fleet. Lower-deck illiteracy was widespread, but probably less significant a factor in the dangers threatening the Tsar's navy than its officer material, an aristocratic, closed-in breed with its own layers of discontent, chiefly among the junior ranks, related to wardroom jealousies and an unjust system of promotion. The men they led were docile but only up to a point. By the first years of the century revolutionary cells were forming below decks on ships not busily employed, especially those at such politically radicalized outposts as the Imperial Naval Base at Sevastopol.

The most powerful warship of the Black Sea Fleet: The *Kniaz Potemkin Tavritchesky*. *(U.S. Naval Historical Center)*

Even before the unpopular and mismanaged Pacific war Russia's Social Democratic Party had adherents aboard ships of the Black Sea Squadron. This force had played no part in the hostilities but had pursued instead a humdrum role of coastal patrol and repeated maneuvers. Such routine only bred monotony, ever pernicious to morale and particularly so among members of a fleet that lacked any strong naval tradition.

Near the close of June 1905, some three weeks after the disaster at Tsushima, the 12,600-ton battleship *Kniaz Potemkin Tavritchesky* steamed out of Sevastopol and shaped course northwest for Tendra Bay to undergo gunnery exercises. The rest of the squadron would join her later. Only a year in commission, carrying four 12-inch and twelve 6-inch guns, the three-funneled *Potemkin* was the squadron's most powerful vessel. Manned in large part by semiliterate sailors customarily obedient to superiors, the ship was a prime target for radical infiltration. The loyalty of subordinates when instinctive and unquestioning is ever more fragile than when hard-won and nurtured and is safely secured only through authority's reciprocal concern for their welfare. This truism was lost on the *Potemkin*'s captain, executive officer, and ship's doctor, or they would not have so loftily insisted that the borscht served for the crew's midday meal was fit to eat when practically all of the *Potemkin*'s six hundred men swore that it was made from maggot-infested meat.

Officers' fare being of higher quality, Capt. Evgenii N. Golikov had

The *Potemkin's* officers and petty officers before the mutiny. Captain Golikov is front center, with executive officer Giliarovskii on his right. *(Bettman/Hulton)*

just enjoyed his own lunch when informed of trouble below deck. Golikov seems not to have been a harsh commander, but like so many Russians he took his people's loyalty for granted, and it would have shocked him to learn that sailors of the Black Sea Squadron had already plotted mutiny and awaited only a prearranged signal to strike. Also, perhaps Golikov's thoughts just then mostly concerned his wife, who was following the battleship on board the naval transport *Vekhia* and was expected to join him ashore at Odessa.

Golikov reacted to the reports of lower-deck turmoil with an attempt to convince the crew that the meat was edible, as vouched for by Smirnov, the ship's doctor. The people, whom Golikov addressed from a capstan in the center of the quarterdeck, were then dismissed, and the captain had himself started back to his cabin when the executive officer, Comdr. Ippolit Giliarovskii, a younger man, aristocratic and of more ruthless cut, shouted for the men to return and ordered the boatswain to summon the marine guard and bring a tarpaulin. The captain had now disappeared, and Giliarovskii, presumably angered by his kid-glove treatment of insubordinate sailors, had taken over with the intention of teaching them a lesson.

So goes the prevalent version. The business of the tarpaulin either signaled that the executive officer was actually about to order certain men shot or was meant to scare the crew into believing this was his intention. There was a long-discarded practice in the Russian fleet of covering offenders with a tarpaulin or sailcloth before they were shot. According to Sergei Eisenstein's naval consultant during the making of his film *The Battleship Potemkin,* the purpose of the tarpaulin used in the old Russian navy during a shipboard execution by firing squad was to protect the deck from bloodstains. Contemporary official accounts make no mention of a tarpaulin, and in any event the *Potemkin*'s senior officers were well aware that sailors in the Tsar's navy could not be put to death without a court-martial. A tarpaulin may have been called for as a means of instilling terror into the protesters. So with a twelve-man rifle squad in nervous attendance, the situation on the quarterdeck of the *Potemkin,* lying off the bleak and uninhabited island of Tendra that Tuesday afternoon, was conceivably one of bluff, fear, and confusion—ideal from the standpoint of Engineer Quartermaster Afanasii Matiushenko, twenty-six, a revolutionary organizer secretly enjoined to begin a mutiny when the rest of the squadron caught up but unable to resist an opportunity such as now presented itself.

As Giliarovskii talked with quiet urgency to a midshipman beside him, perhaps about to order the marines into action, Matiushenko

"The moment we had waited for." Afanasii Matiushenko, ship's engineer and mutiny's ringleader. *(Bettmann/Hulton)*

beseeched them not to fire upon their comrades. Several of Matiu-shenko's followers lunged for the marines' rifles. Others dashed off to the ship's armory, including perhaps Gunner Grigori Vakulenchuk, like Matiushenko a seaman politically radicalized during technical training in the navy. Vakulenchuk is said to have fired the first shot, but almost simultaneously Commander Giliarovskii fired twice, and Vakulenchuk collapsed, bleeding. The executive officer next aimed at Matiushenko, who was, however, also armed. Giliarovskii died in a quick exchange of shots. A midshipman fell, mortally wounded; so did the gunnery officer who had hurried up from the wardroom. Lt. Wilhelm Tonn, also just on deck, surveyed the carnage and at once proposed a ceasefire. Matiushenko followed him aft down the gangladder and into a 12-inch-gun turret. But shots instead of discussion sounded from within, and when Tonn abruptly emerged, the waiting men killed him at once.

Then Matiushenko came out unscathed. He ordered the lieutenant's body tossed overboard and the other dead officers similarly disposed of. More officers climbed up on deck, some to dodge the mutineers and throw themselves into the sea. They were promptly used for target practice. Mutineers discovered Lieutenant Alexeyev, the assistant navigation officer, in the main magazine, about to fuse the ship's mines as ordered (he said) by the captain. Swearing his true support for the uprising, Alexeyev begged permission to join it. Matiushenko appointed him captain under the revolutionaries' direction. Captain Golikov meanwhile had darted from one cabin to another. He was cornered and hauled on deck. One account has him stammering for forgiveness and pleading that the shooting stop. He was himself put to death. After his body had gone overboard, the seventh and last officer to die was Surgeon Smirnov, dragged from his quarters after a failed suicide attempt, brutally manhandled and taunted about rotten meat. Only the necessity of attending to Vakulenchuk and other wounded seamen saved the doctor's assistant, Golenko, from following him over the side.

Some of the officers in the water were rescued by Torpedo Boat *N267,* which had accompanied the battleship from Sevastopol. Informed of the mutiny, *N267*'s commander, Baron Klodt von Jurgensburg, ordered top speed back to the naval base. But rebels manning the *Potemkin*'s guns sent a 3-inch shell through the torpedo boat's funnel. This changed Klodt's mind, and with his officers and those he had plucked from the water he was brought on board the battleship and locked below under guard.

The slaughter on the *Potemkin* bears comparison with that on HMS *Hermione* more than a century earlier. And after the bloodletting, while decks were scrubbed, the mutineers experienced the same sense of exhilaration as had Captain Pigot's slayers. They did not comprise the whole crew. Probably a hundred were actively engaged. Many were bullied or otherwise persuaded into collaborating. About one-third—more than two hundred men—shrank from the violence but were helpless to prevent it. For the most part they held their peace as Matiushenko, orating from the quarterdeck where Captain Golikov had not long stood, pictured all Russia as waiting to throw off the chains of slavery. The rest of the squadron would shortly join the *Potemkin* in rebellion, and "we will link up with our brothers ashore."

He meant in Odessa, where strikers and revolutionary groups clashed daily with police and the Tsar's troops. The *Potemkin* anchored four miles outside that terraced port while Matiushenko and a ship's committee of a dozen or so ideological soul mates savored officers' cigars and wine in the admiral's stateroom and drew up plans. The ship must be properly run, normal routine adhered to as far as possible. This required the retention of petty officers and a few of commissioned rank like "Captain" Alexeyev and Lieutenant Kovalenko, the engineering officer, a Marxist since his university days. In Odessa the *Potemkin* rebels would establish contact with Social Democratic organizations and make efforts to subvert the police and the military. And they had secured a martyr—despite the ministrations of the assistant surgeon, Comrade Vakulenchuk had died in the night.

He would be made to serve the cause in death as he never could have in life. His body was ferried to the pier at daybreak and placed on display under a tent at the foot of the twelve flights of white sandstone steps that rose to the statue of the Duc de Richelieu overlooking the harbor. This crude bier was an immediate rallying point for radical demonstrators and orators, curiosity seekers, and soldiers, but these last were, however, driven off by sailors' threats to signal the *Potemkin* and bring her guns into action. The same warning capped an ultimatum addressed to the military by the ship's revolutionaries, announcing their determination to "free the people of Odessa and of all Russia."

For the radicals ashore who were convinced that strikes and demonstrations would prove no match for the Tsar's legions, the arrival of the *Potemkin* in a state of mutiny spurred hopes. A student leader named Constantine Feldmann was soon on board the battleship with half a dozen comrades and proposed that Vakulenchuk's funeral be turned into a mass effort by the *Potemkin*'s crew to win over the army and police. In his euphoria Feldmann had yet to perceive that the *Potemkin*'s sailors, notwithstanding Matiushenko's incessant proselytizing, were concerned more with events aboard their ship than with the grandiose goal of overturning Russia's ruling class. Told that splitting up the crew would place the ship in jeopardy, Feldmann acknowledged this rejection of his plan as indicative of sound tactical thinking. His colleagues, on the other hand, seemed to have sensed not only a lack of true revolutionary fervor on board but even a resentment of their intrusion, for they soon took the boat back to shore.

It was still forenoon when General Kokhanov, military commander at Odessa, received a telegraphed ukase from the royal palace at St. Petersburg proclaiming the "disorder at Odessa and in the neighbouring localities . . . a state of war." (The real war with Japan was not yet over.) Thus emboldened, when Kokhanov heard that mobs around the seaman Vakulenchuk's bier had coalesced and were starting up the Richelieu steps, he ordered his cossacks into action. They galloped from their bivouac in Cathedral Square to the Nikolaevsky Boulevard, dismounted in the crescent at the head of the steps, and in orderly ranks began a downward march, rifles poised and bayonets fixed. Some demonstrators had already reached the topmost flight when the first bullets struck among them. Those not killed instantly fell back into the horde surging up from below. The cossacks continued their steady descent, pausing only to crouch and fire, or bayonet more frequently as congestion increased on the lower steps. When it was all over, the governor of Odessa informed foreign consuls that the cossacks had been obliged to fire when the insurgents threatened to take over the town. He estimated the death toll as five hundred.

The massacre on the Richelieu steps prompted fresh demands for the *Potemkin* to intervene in the strife ashore by sending landing parties and firing her big guns. Matiushenko continued to argue that such action would endanger the ship. The revolution would truly get under way when the other ships of the Black Sea Squadron came up and joined the *Potemkin* in mutiny. But the only fresh arrival that tense evening was the fleet auxiliary *Vekhia* carrying Captain Golikov's wife—or widow, as she was about to learn—and newborn baby. Her husband's slayers put her ashore with the officers they had held captive. Dusk fell, pierced by searchlight beams, the *Potemkin*'s and shore-based. In Odessa the last vestiges of civil order had snapped, the bloodshed on the Richelieu steps but prelude to a night of looting, arson, and wanton killing. On the *Potemkin,* sleep was impossible, if only because of the constant arguing and insurrectionary rhetoric, Feldmann in particular badgering the crew in an attempt to sustain, or generate, the required revolutionary ardor. Under growing emotional strain, all hands awaited the arrival of the rest of the Sevastopol squadron.

At Sevastopol earlier in the day Vice Admiral Krieger, deputizing for an absent commander-in-chief, had responded to a cable from Odessa that reported mutiny on the *Potemkin* by first checking the loyalty of his remaining crews. That on the battleship *Catherine II* was shaky at best, and she was confined to harbor. The battleships *Tri Sviatitelia (Holy Trinity)*, *Dvenadsat Apostoloff (The Twelve Apostles)*, and *Georgi Pobjedonosets (George the Conqueror)*, with the light cruiser *Kazarsky* and four torpedo escorts—these were the vessels Krieger assigned to suppress the mutiny and get the *Potemkin* safe and sound into Tendra Bay forty-eight hours hence, by which time he would also have arrived in his flagship *Rostislav*. Under the command of Admiral Vishnevetsky, this force left Sevastopol shortly before midnight. It was still at sea the next morning while Cossacks sniped at citizens seeking their dead among Odessa's ashes and the *Potemkin*'s ship's committee secured permission to bury their own. Twelve unarmed sailors accompanied Grigori Vaku-lenchuk's body to the cemetery. They were ambushed on the return, and only nine got back to the *Potemkin*. An enraged ship's committee, acting on information that Odessa's military commanders were to meet that evening in the Municipal Theater, ordered that it be shelled. The brief bombardment at 7:30 P.M. wrought no damage, the gun controller later claiming that he had purposely misdirected the fire. And that same evening the American consul, after training his binoculars upon the open bay, telegraphed Washington: "Something very like the Black Sea Fleet seems to be slowly moving this way. Whether with crews only or officers as well, God only knows."

There was uncertainty too on the *Potemkin*. Were the crews on those approaching ships obedient to their officers, they might still draw the line at firing upon the mutineers. But no one could be sure. Clustered on the bridge in the wan light of dawn, Matiushenko, his committee, and the civilian Constantine Feldmann reached accord for once. The *Potemkin* would not yield. Matiushenko told his appointed captain, Alexeyev, to get the battleship under way, and she steamed for her sister ships, flying defiant signal flags and clearing her decks for action.

Admiral Vishnevetsky was himself by no means confident that his men would fire if ordered to. That necessity he hoped would not arise. The fact that his crews were sufficiently loyal to have brought their vessels to Odessa in a show of strength was enough to make the rebels see reason. Such very likely were Vishnevetsky's expectations—dashed in a hurry by the sight of the battleship coming out prepared to fight. Vishnevetsky could have forced the issue. Even against so formidable an ironclad as the *Potemkin* his combined firepower would surely have carried the day. He decided not to try, influenced by the unreliability of his people no less than by the obvious determination of the mutineers. He swung his flotilla southward for Tendra Bay. His official explanation upon reaching that rendezvous empty-handed—that he sought rein-forcements—would fail to save him from an official reprimand. But neither had Vishnevetsky's apparent retreat signaled victory for the *Potemkin*'s revolutionaries, who were obliged to cut short a musical celebration on the quarterdeck when early in the afternoon the ships were sighted coming back to Odessa.

Five first-class warships this time, Vishnevetsky's augmented by the

Sinop and Admiral Krieger's flagship *Rostislav*. They approached in two columns, with auxiliary vessels trailing astern and the light cruiser *Kazarsky* centered in the forefront. Again the *Potemkin* thrust her bows seaward to meet a superior force, tension rising on every vessel as the distance between them narrowed. A radio message was rushed to Matiushenko on the *Potemkin*'s bridge. Krieger demanded immediate surrender. Matiushenko's response was to keep the battleship on course. Still no guns fired. Krieger's columns were spaced five hundred yards apart, a channel into which the *Potemkin* now boldly plunged, the *Kazarsky* swerving to avoid getting rammed. And as the *Potemkin* steamed past ships on both beams, a stunned silence among their crews gave way to cheers from hundreds on the *Georgi Pobjedonosets, Dvenadsat Apostoloff,* and *Sinop* who came pouring from below decks and out of turret hatches.

Brief bewilderment on the *Potemkin*'s bridge gave way to joyful realization. There would be no shooting. The men on those ships were demonstrating solidarity with the mutineers. Thus it seemed to Matiushenko, who would recall his emotions: "This was the moment we had waited for. This was the beginning of the Revolution." On the flagship *Rostislav,* whose people remained nervously at their stations, Krieger and his officers could only watch in helpless disbelief as the *Potemkin,* having cleared the rearmost vessels, came about and once more passed between the two lines of ships, her mutineers evidently alert to the danger of being cut off from Odessa. She reached the bay with the *Georgi Pobjedonosets* steaming in her wake and flashing by signal lamp a request to join the mutiny. And that was enough for Admiral Krieger. Fearful of losing any more ships to the mutineers, he took his depleted squadron back out to sea and made full speed for Sevastopol.

Matiushenko's jubilation would prove premature. When he directed the men on the *Georgi Pobjedonosets* to place their officers under arrest, the message winked back that they, the people, were not yet in complete control. The revolutionary leader boarded the *Georgi Pobjedonosets* to see for himself. He found a confused crew, with petty officers below plotting counterrevolutionary moves—and the battleship's captain, Goosevitch, still on the bridge. But all it took was an intimidating burst of Matiushenko's oratory, and Goosevitch threw up his hands in despair. Other officers did likewise, not including one lieutenant who, rather than tear off his epaulets at gunpoint, drew a revolver and shot himself. Goosevitch was sent ashore. Still the battleship was far from revolutionized. Constantine Feldmann went on board to convert the hesitant, and his fever-pitch delivery ended only at dawn, when fatigue had reduced his voice to a croak.

Emotions on the *Potemkin*'s bridge had swung from optimism to uncertainty. Some refused to lose hope. "Our minds were at ease," one mutineer wrote. "Now we had our revolutionary squadron—two [battleships] with six 12-inch guns, a torpedo boat and the *Vekhia*." They would establish a free government in Odessa, organize a people's army, march to Kiev, Kharkov, then on to Moscow and St. Petersburg. But that vision quickly evaporated. Despite Feldmann's marathon oratory, at daylight on 1 July the *Georgi Pobjedonosets* remained a divided ship. By noon counterrevolutionaries were gaining the upper hand. On the *Potemkin* the surgeon Golenko volunteered to try and secure the other battleship's support. Golenko had hitherto avoided political discussions, confining himself to his medical duties. But perhaps all along he had awaited an opportunity to thwart the mutineers. At any rate, once on the *Georgi Pobjedonosets* he threw in his lot with the petty officers and left Matiushenko and Feldmann, who had returned to the *Potemkin,* unaware of what was afoot until the *Georgi Pobjedonosets* hoisted a signal for sailing and invited the *Potemkin* to follow.

Coaling from a barge lashed to her side, the *Potemkin* was in no position to mount and dispatch a boarding party. Matiushenko ordered the guns manned. A threat of attack signaled to the departing *Georgi Pobjedonosets* brought her obediently about, and the crisis seemed over, but only for an instant. Instead of stopping at her previous anchorage, the errant battleship steamed right past the *Potemkin* into the harbor, and near the outer mole she struck a mudbank. In the hours since the mutiny broke out the mood below decks on the *Potemkin* had varied from fear or confusion to vague joy. The sudden loss of the *Georgi Pobjedonosets* after her surprising acquisition as an ally now stirred a more pronounced disillusionment. It was felt in some degree on the bridge as well. Taking Odessa was now out of the question. The garrison commander, as Matiushenko may have been informed, had brought up fresh mortar batteries. Heavy artillery occupied the hills. And now landing parties would also have to face a battleship's guns turned seaward. Once again argument divided the *Potemkin*'s mutinous command, visionaries like Feldmann wishing to continue the revolution in another locality. At least there was general agreement that to remain off Odessa would be folly.

Moreover, while the majority of the ship's six hundred men lost whatever radical zeal their ideological ringleaders had managed to stoke among them, few if any favored surrender. Future direction might be unclear, but there was no turning back, not to the near certainty of a firing squad. Matiushenko correctly believed that the people would take their ship to Romania for water and supplies if he asked them. Even so, the revolution would have to be postponed. Constantine Feldmann feared its outright abandonment, and with laryngeal hoarseness he begged for the crew's unwavering support. Seamen never fully won over by his impassioned sloganeering scoffed at him. Unscholarly and nonpolitical though many of them were, some may have detected an absurd naïveté in this student's presumption that what was essentially a sailors' revolt against bad food and insensitive officers would serve as an impulse for a nationwide uprising. Though Feldmann could not have known it, most Russians were in fact ignorant of the events in the Black Sea, and even on the fourth day of the mutiny only a handful in the capital, St. Petersburg, had heard anything about it. For Feldmann it was enough that the outlook for his precious revolution had turned sour. As the *Potemkin* and her small entourage steamed southwestward for Romania's sole Black Sea port, Constanza, he fled to the wardroom, "pursued by phantoms" and tormented by a sense of failure when "all Russia was hanging on our decision."

Pessimism was also felt at Sevastopol, where news of the latest developments off Odessa had yet to arrive. "I am afraid the sea is controlled by rebels," lamented Admiral Chukhnin, commander-in-chief. But forty less-defeatist junior officers had vowed to retake the *Potemkin* or perish in the attempt. With Chukhnin's sober blessing, this self-styled "suicide squad" led by a Lieutenant Yanovitch set forth at dusk on 1 July aboard the fast new destroyer *Stremitelny*. She hugged the Crimean coast, steaming without lights, and reached Odessa twelve hours after the *Potemkin*'s departure. More determined than ever, convinced of a holy mission to avenge the blood of their brother officers and expunge disgrace from the Cross of St. Andrew, they quickly got to sea again.

Mutineers on the *Potemkin* meanwhile wondered how Romania might greet them. Perhaps they would be seized and sent back to Russia. Some believed, correctly, that the Tsar's government must now be pressuring its Balkan neighbors into treating the *Potemkin* as a pirate ship. But at Constanza two Romanian naval officers met them politely, coming out in a launch and agreeing to place their list of requirements before the Romanian prime minister. An anxious overnight wait followed, during which Matiushenko's party learned from other vessels in the harbor that ships of the Black Sea Squadron were out looking for them. Matiushenko would have suspected as much. And when the next morning a telegraphed appeal from King Carol I to surrender accompanied the Bucharest government's refusal to approve supplies,

The *Potemkin*'s rebels enjoy Romanian hospitality in exile. *(Bettmann/Hulton)*

the *Potemkin* hurried back to sea, her revolutionary committee once more split, some for returning to Odessa, others for seeking fuel and sustenance elsewhere. Only hours after the battleship had left, the *Stremitelny* put in. A little later so did the battleships *Sinop* and *Tri Sviatitelia*. All were on the same mission of vengeful pursuit, these near misses heightening the anticipation of an imminent capture, though none could to more than guess the fugitive ship's next port of call.

In search of sanctuary: the travels of the *Potemkin* mutineers. *(Bill Clipson)*

Her sleepless and increasingly despondent leaders had decided upon Feodosiia, on the eastern side of the Crimean peninsula. That meant steaming perilously close to Sevastopol, but risks had to be courted. The need for food, fresh water, and coal had become vital. The *Potemkin* could not remain indefinitely at large, adrift in a sea 750 miles long and 380 miles wide, with ships on the prowl for her and the exit to the Mediterranean barred by Turkish batteries at the Dardanelles. Feldmann and other ideologues envisioned Feodosiia as a stopping place on the way farther east to Caucasia, a fertile ground for revolution. Other ringleaders had no idea what to do after Feodosiia. As for the crew, lacking political motives from the outset, they had, in a sense, less to feel sorry about, and they passed the time like good sailors, maintaining regular ship's routine, obedient to their petty officers' insistence that decks be kept scrubbed and brass polished.

At Feodosiia the *Potemkin* was amicably welcomed, the ringleaders feted at the town hall—a reception that again proved deceptive. Warnings from St. Petersburg against assisting the mutineers had reached the little coaling port, and all its mayor would offer was fresh water. On the *Potemkin*'s bridge by this time exhaustion and bitter despair had ruled out further niceties, and Matiushenko sent the mayor an ultimatum: coal and supplies within twenty-four hours or Feodosiia would be blown off the map. Townsfolk fled to the hills. As the hour of the ultimatum's expiration approached, Matiushenko and Feldmann took a party of sailors with towing gear to a coaling barge. They were freeing its anchor when surprised by soldiers on the quay who opened fire. Three sailors died on the barge. Others made off in the *Potemkin*'s launch. The firing continued. A wounded seaman fell out of the launch, and Feldmann dove in after him. The launch kept going, and it was the Tsar's soldiers who dragged Feldmann and the half-drowned sailor ashore.

This affray as much as anything marked the end of the mutiny on the *Potemkin*. Its leaders were drained of spirit. Some among them realized no doubt that the chances of their shipboard revolt's proving inspiration for a great national rebellion had vanished when the *Georgi Pobjedonosets* changed her mind about defecting. Now it was all over, "only the Black Sea witnessing our broken hearts and tears," Matiushenko would remember. None had worked harder than he, or plotted more ruthlessly, for a successful revolt. It should have led to the overthrow of the Romanov autocracy, Matiushenko's dream. That cataclysmic event was not very far off, although he would not live to see it.

The destroyer *Stremitelny* hove to off Feodosiia only three hours after the *Potemkin*, her ultimatum abandoned, raised anchor and returned to sea. The "suicide squad" was denied its goal of destroying the mutineers—it had been prepared to shoot on sight—but soon had the satisfaction of learning that the mutiny had collapsed. Something like collapse also overtook the *Stremitelny* when her engines broke down under the stress of that twenty-six–knot zigzag hunt across the northwestern reaches of the Black Sea.

The *Potemkin* was back at Constanza on 8 July with Torpedo Boat *N267*, which had accompanied her throughout. Matiushenko ordered the battleship's seacocks opened, then he marched ashore at the head of his committee to seek the hospitality of the local Social Democratic party. Three days later Black Sea Squadron vessels raised the scuttled *Potemkin* and towed her to Sevastopol. Inactive during the First World War, she would be sunk finally in 1919 by naval officers to keep her out of Bolshevik hands. By then about five hundred of her former crew were living quietly in Romania, many of them, however, the focus of suspicion during periodic civil strife in that country. Of those who had surrendered to their own authorities, seven convicted mutineers received death sentences. Others were banished to Siberian penal colonies. Lieutenant Alexeyev, the *Potemkin*'s erstwhile "captain," was among a number of officers who successfully pleaded that their participation in the mutiny had been forced at gunpoint.

Contantine Feldmann, captured at Feodosiia, escaped from jail and found temporary sanctuary in Austria. When revolution at last succeeded in Russia, the Nikolaevsky Boulevard in Odessa, above the Richelieu steps, would be renamed for him. Afanasii Matiushenko wandered through different countries, including France and the United States, where he worked briefly for the Singer Sewing Machine Company, living meanwhile among Russian radicals on New York City's lower east side. "There are many Socialists here," he wrote to a friend, "but very few real people. I think a lot about the happiness of the people and I shall never cease to do so." In 1907 he returned to Russia with a false name and passport and joined the outlawed anarcho-syndicalist movement. Just one week after the second anniversary of his mutiny Matiushenko was arrested, and later he was hanged at Sevastopol. He would soon be forgotten, but not the ship he had served on. Vladimir Ilyich Lenin would declare, "Of all the arts for us, the camera is the most important." Thus Lenin's observation on film as propaganda. A schoolboy in Latvia at the time of the *Potemkin* mutiny, the filmmaker Sergei Eisenstein was destined to give Lenin's words dramatic affirmation, his epic motion picture ensuring that the world had by no means heard the last of that ill-starred naval uprising.

Eleven

Eleven

∎

IMPERIAL FLEETS

ensible comparisons between the Russian navy and its western counterparts in the pre–First World War years are not easily drawn. Even so, it is safe to assume that had ships of the Black Sea Squadron been permitted lower-deck societies on the order of those in Britain's Royal Navy, the fracas on the *Potemkin,* insofar as it related to the sailors' distaste for spoiled meat, might not have escalated into bloodshed. Lower-deck societies were not a feature of the United States Navy either. But then, the Navy Relief Society had just been organized in Washington, D.C., its prime object the succor of deserving dependents, its funds derived from the proceeds of the annual army-navy football game and the dollar-a-year membership fee charged enlisted personnel. Moreover, there was some truth in *Our Navy's* boast that "Uncle Sam provides for his bluejackets with a bountiful hand."

Founded in 1898 by Yeoman Ray C. Shepherd on the naval training station at Yerba Buena Island, San Francisco, this periodical began as a hand-mimeographed sheet called *Naval Flashes.* It appeared as *Our Navy* in 1906, and by adopting a journalistic tone that blended professional pride, sentimentality, and simple patriotism with frequent bold protest, it would bear a certain resemblance to its British contemporary, Lionel Yexley's *The Fleet.* One difference was that whereas Yexley welcomed political support in obtaining better conditions for British tars, Shepherd editorially scorned outside help as unnecessary interference: "Any man who has a REAL grievance can always secure a favorable hearing. There are too many imaginary grievances for the good of the entire service." Moreover, in Shepherd's view, attempts to portray the American bluejacket as underpaid and overworked were too often traceable to alien agitators. As a New York–based slick magazine widely circulated throughout the fleet and attractive to advertisers, *Our Navy* would in time display more audacity—"The service needed a fearless publication"—and find itself, like *The Fleet,* charged with provoking discontent below decks. But in 1910 its perception that an anarchist campaign was subverting the American navy through the furtive distribution of eight-page pamphlets was more in line with the views of Britain's First Lord of the Admiralty Reginald McKenna. Mass insubordination had broken out on the British cruiser *Leviathan,* and four sailors were convicted of "making mutinous assembly." McKenna blamed "the mischievous socialist literature that our men had been flooded with."

McKenna's successor, Winston Churchill, took a more enlightened view, enlisting the counsel of Sir John Fisher and, albeit without that one-time First Lord's zest for making enemies, vigorously pursuing his determination to "enlarge, improve and modernize the Navy." Churchill and Fisher together profited from Yexley's experience and advice—he was still tub-thumping in *The Fleet's* pages—and their joint efforts won fairer disciplinary procedures, higher promotion rates for the lower deck, and the first pay raise in sixty years.

More responsive than his predecessor with regard to sailors' grievances, Churchill nevertheless shared the general suspicion that His Majesty's ships were vulnerable to left-wing contamination. Some discerned such a threat in the sailors' proposals to amalgamate their benefit societies and link up with the newly founded Labour Party. To clinch that pay raise (a smaller one than he had pressed for), in 1912 Churchill had to warn the cabinet of "a deep and widespread sense of injustice and discontent throughout all ranks and ratings in the Navy. It is rendered more dangerous by every successful strike for higher wages on shore." As if to underline Churchill's warning, trouble broke out the following year on HMS *London.* Articles in *The Fleet,* citing complaints from members of the crew, blamed the battleship's new commander for the ship's being "in a state of incipient mutiny." The captain was "blinded with a sense of his own importance . . . he seems to have run amok . . . the laughing-stock of the service." Certainly a moralistic disciplinarian, the *London's* new captain was also a tough veteran officer, and he promptly sued for libel. Yexley lost the case and had to pay heavy damages, to the satisfaction of those who thought he should have been silenced long ago and who moreover believed the Admiralty too timid by half when dealing with lower-deck unrest.

The Board of Admiralty had in fact paid little consistent attention to the mood and welfare of its seamen. Even during Churchill's tenure what mostly preoccupied the Sea Lords were questions of warship design and construction, gunnery science and battle tactics, and the comparative merits of coal and oil as fuel for ships' engines. Discussions on these matters became more and more infused with urgency as the British perceived themselves to be in a naval arms race with an increasingly arrogant Germany. In the process, lower-deck morale seldom appeared on the Board's agenda, and should some mutinous display remind their lordships that lower-deck loyalty and obedience were essential to fighting efficiency and ought not to be taken for granted, it was that same concern over German naval expansion that brought about a hasty accommodation with the seamen, easily mistaken for appeasement. In March 1914 stokers on the battleship *Zealandia* refused to perform extra duty given them as punishment for slackness during coaling operations. A court-martial on the spot resulted in eight convictions with prison sentences. This touched off an uproar among the crew, whose dissatisfaction apparently focused upon the vessel's newly appointed executive officer. The Admiralty wasted no time before relieving him of his post—in mortifying fashion because the order to that effect was read aloud before the ship's officers assembled on deck. The stokers' prison sentences were set aside.

Disquiet among British sailors continued well into the war years. In 1916, the year of the Battle of Jutland, incidents were reported from at least four vessels, those on the *Teutonic* and *Fantome* described as nonviolent mutiny. The next year "excessive punishment" was protested through a show of mass disobedience on the *Amphitrite*, while rumors and anonymous petitions worried officers on other ships. The signs of discontent proliferated mostly during periods of inaction. As was traditionally the case, grievances and grudges were apt to be forgotten at moments of actual combat, banished by sheer desperation or an instinctive response to duty. Nothing remotely resembling mutiny, at least nothing reported, occurred on British decks off Coronel and the Falklands in 1914, Dogger Bank in 1915, nor during the Jutland engagement with its cost to the Royal Navy of fourteen ships and more than six thousand men. Just as exemplary was the other side's showing.

But months of relative idleness followed Jutland's severe losses to both Germany and Great Britain, allowing complaints to fester within each fighting force. Soon Lionel Yexley felt it necessary to send the king, the cabinet, and the Board of Admiralty a confidential statement of sailors' discontents, portraying the lower deck as "one combustible mass" ready to "burst into flame." Sir Eric Geddes, Churchill's successor on the board, admitted to "a certain amount of dissatisfaction on the Lower Deck" but denied that it was of serious magnitude. All the same, the mutiny that, according to retired Sir John Fisher, Britain's naval hierarchy would have to contend with "sure as fate" might indeed have broken out had not a convulsion within the Kaiser's High Seas Fleet mercifully hastened the war to an end.

Like its sanguinary predecessors in what had become known as the Great War, the year 1917 was characterized by massive and generally futile land offensives on the Western Front, in Russia, in the Balkans, and in Asiatic Turkey. Naval warfare was confined almost solely to Germany's submarine operations, which by the spring had reached their maximum effectiveness and also brought the United States into the conflict. Yet it was naval activity of a sort, a revolt against discipline and authority, that more than any other development of the bloody year signaled the beginning of the end of the great world struggle. Mutiny was but a specter haunting Britain's naval establishment. In the German and Russian navies it materialized decisively. While instigating factors differed, all three cases evinced a marked strain of lower-deck boredom or war weariness. Somewhat less of a common element though present in varying degree was a leftward political consciousness traceable in the German and Russian examples to the growth of Social Democratic parties throughout continental Europe.

Germany had no vital need for a seagoing navy. It was created as Kaiser Wilhelm II's personal toy, with no purpose other than to challenge Great Britain's naval supremacy. A majority of its conscripted personnel doubtless understood, and resented this goal. They were on disagreeably familiar terms with imperial arrogance, cultivated as it was by an officer corps squarely modeled upon the Prussian caste system. To a lower-deck class peopled more and more by technicians and skilled artisans with burgeoning political awareness, the indifference or outright callousness of their superiors was an additional burden in an already oppressive environment. That may have been the German navy's undoing, the willful perpetuation of an outmoded aristocracy within a complex modern combat arm. Lower-deck living conditions that had not kept pace with a hundred years of technical revolution compounded the danger. Little had changed beyond the reversal of crews' and officers' quarters, which in recent dreadnought design placed the men aft and the officers forward, two different worlds separated by a midships section, two-thirds of the overall length, devoted to engines, boiler rooms, gun turrets, trunks, and magazine spaces. The officers' quarters were appropriately commodious and comfortably equipped, while seven or eight hundred men far aft ate and slept in cramped fashion much the same as that of their historical forbears under canvas.

As early as 1915 groups had formed on some of Germany's newest capital ships to press for better living conditions. When their protests went unheeded, they developed toward their elitist superiors a more unified hostility, which, after Jutland, thrived on the monotony of prolonged confinement to port. Wiser and more competent officers who might have checked this trend were drawn into destroyer and submarine service, leaving too many class-conscious amateurs in command of the battleships. The seamen's emotions were further inflamed because they and their loved ones at home bore the brunt of the poor harvests and the British blockade while the officers continued to enjoy the sensual benefits of shoreside canteens and exclusive clubs. All things considered, a mutiny in Germany's High Seas Fleet was perhaps bound to have occurred sooner or later.

That it broke out when it did in 1917 owed much to the more-publicized upheaval in the east. Russia's Baltic Fleet had recovered sufficiently from its 1905 war losses to meet the initial challenges of the 1914–18 conflict. But the revolutionary surge aborted by the *Potemkin's* misfired mutiny then regathered strength. What had failed to mature in the Black Sea would get a second chance, this time in northern waters, emerging out of a protest against an unpopular war blamed for domestic hardships and, it seemed, waged solely to prop up a corrupt tsarist regime. To these identifiable causes might be added a more fundamental ingredient, a violent and uncompromising revolutionary ardor with which the men of the Kronstadt naval base, on Kotlin Island in the eastern corner of the Gulf of Finland, appear to have been generously imbued.

In the second week of March (late February by the old Russian calendar), almost simultaneously with the strikes and rioting occurring thirty miles away in the capital, Petrograd (formerly St. Petersburg), sailors of the Torpedo and Mining Training Detachment in Kronstadt rose up against their officers, left several for dead, then marched out of the barracks to rally the First Baltic Fleet Depot Troop. By dusk the whole port garrison was in revolt. At least two score officers and a dozen petty officers were slain, including an admiral who was dragged to Anchor Square, bayoneted, and mutilated. Overnight Kronstadt's naval hierarchy died. Within forty-eight hours the town had quieted and was in the hands of a revolutionary committee. But the mutinous fever had reached the nucleus of Russia's Baltic Fleet, seven capital ships and a number of smaller vessels frozen in at Helsingfors (Helsinki) 160 miles across the gulf (Finland was still part of the tsarist empire). Admiral A. J. Nepenin commanded the fleet, and the new provisional government in Petrograd, a product of the political upheaval, at once challenged his deep-rooted loyalty to the Romanov rulers when it summoned his support for its plan to buy civic stability with the Tsar's abdication. Nepenin sensed approaching disaster for his fleet. To maintain discipline he ordered it placed on battle alert, and at the same time he struggled with his personal dilemma.

Reluctantly, he opted to join those pressuring Nicholas II to abdicate. Late on Thursday, 15 March, from the converted two-funneled armed yacht *Kretchet,* which served as his flagship, Nepenin telegraphed his decision to Petrograd, adding, "With enormous difficulty I control the fleet and retain the trust of the sailors." But he had failed to keep those sailors at Helsingfors informed of events in their capital. They knew little enough even of the carnage at Kronstadt. It was a news blackout bound to have spawned ugly rumors that, with revolutionary ardor, shipboard grudges, possibly enemy agents—Russia was still at war with Germany—and a thoroughly demoralized element in two or three of Nepenin's battleships, must be taken into account to explain the savagery about to erupt.

Nepenin was informed early Friday of the Tsar's abdication. A dynasty had collapsed. Not until late afternoon did the admiral release this awesome news to his fleet, and the great hush said to have fallen upon it was but a stillness short-lived. Across the frozen harbor at the Sveaborg fortress where the Second Battleship Squadron was docked, sailors on the *Andrei Pervozvanny* and *Imperator Pavel* simply ran amok, shooting at officers with the weapons they had obtained by breaking the locks on the ships' rifle racks. Some officers sought help from the squadron commander, Vice Adm. Arkadii Nebolsin, but by nightfall he was himself shot to death at the dockside. Mutineers on the *Imperator Pavel* accused their navigating officer of being an agent of the secret police and bayoneted him, then killed the ship's executive officer. The bodies were thrown overboard onto the ice.

The *Andrei Pervozvanny*'s captain and others found themselves besieged below decks. A hail of bullets met each attempt to ascend the ladder. "We heard firing and the last screams of new victims," the captain would recall. He was finally released and got to the upper deck: "On all ships sinister red lights were burning and on our neighbour *Pavel* flashes of fire were continually seen coming from rifle shots." A revolutionary committee hastily formed on the *Petropavlovsk,* the flagship of the First

The *Imperator Pavel* was the setting for a massacre of officers within hours of the Tsar's abdication, as was the *Andrei Pervozvanny*, whose captain, besieged below decks, heard "the last screams of new victims." *(U.S. Naval Historical Center)*

Battleship Squadron, signaled to other ships that officers were to be disarmed only, but this plea came too late for some forty who had died, mostly on the *Andrei Pervozvanny* and the *Imperator Pavel*. The slaughter was tragically meaningless. A number who fell were not altogether in opposition to the antiwar, antimonarchy clamor then sweeping the motherland. A distraught Admiral Nepenin summoned a meeting of sailors' delegates to the *Kretchet,* and over a hundred attended, but his orders that the imprisoned officers be released and the murderers arrested were lost in the sailors' demands for freedom to choose their own commanders and immunity from disciplinary action. And by dawn on Saturday revolutionary councils on the battleships were calling for Nepenin's own ouster.

Not only were his hours in command numbered. On the other side of town, where minesweepers were docked, sailors had elected as fleet commander A. S. Maksimov, an admiral who had a good war record and was popular among the ratings but was known as "a bombastic opportunist" among his brother officers. When Maksimov arrived alongside the *Kretchet* in a red-ribboned automobile, Nepenin at first refused to relinquish command. But he was persuaded to follow Maksimov in a procession to the Helsingfors railway station to attend a grand reception for government officials coming from Petrograd. Nepenin was approaching the harbor gates on foot when bullets struck him from behind. He died instantly, his killer never to be found, and at 3 P.M. that same day a cablegram from the new war minister confirmed Maksimov's appointment as commander-in-chief of the Baltic Fleet.

Maksimov's status was tentative and largely titular. Control of the Russian Baltic Fleet had passed from the wardroom's gold braid to committees formed of rough-hewn stokers and dockers. It was a young docker, Pavel Efimovich Dybenko, who chaired the first meeting of the ruling body, the Tsentrobalt, one April night aboard a verminous little transport, the *Viola,* tied up at Helsingfors. The eldest of six children of a Ukranian peasant family, Dybenko had joined the Bolshevik faction of Russia's Social Democratic Party and, carrying his radical message into the navy, had already served six months' imprisonment for stirring his shipmates into revolt. Tall, bearded, and organ-voiced, Pavel Dybenko was destined for a hectic career well into Russia's revolutionary era.

The first news of the Russian Revolution coincided with the politicizing of a discontent by this time thoroughly rooted within Germany's High Seas Fleet. Germany contained the oldest and most effective of Western Europe's Social Democratic organizations, founded in 1875 as

A member of the Petrograd government addresses Helsingfors sailors, March 1917. The bearded officer third from the right facing the camera is Vice Admiral Maksimov. *(National Board of Antiquities, Finland)*

From lower-deck radical to first Commissar of the Red Navy: Pavel Efimovich Dybenko. *(Harper & Row, Barnes & Noble Import Division)*

the Socialist Workers Party. By the outbreak of the war its membership
exceeded five million, many of whom sided with the Russian radicals in
their demand for an armistice and in the spring of 1917 had just broken
away to form the Independent Social Democratic Party (USPD). It was
to this movement that lower-deck activists in the High Seas Fleet looked
for inspiration and support. But while the more erudite among them
were as influenced by the writings of the militant socialists Karl
Liebnicht and Rosa Luxembourg as were the pundit mutineers of Spithead in 1797 by the ideas of Thomas Paine, plans could have evolved
only from instinctive resistance to some perceived violation of justice.

On 6 June aboard the battleship *Prinzregent Luitpold* the meals
served to the stokers were so wretched that they refused to eat or work.
Only upon a promise of improved rations were they persuaded to call
off their hunger strike. As a result the Berlin government authorized
Menagekommission—food supervisory committees made up of ratings
and petty officers. But High Seas Fleet commanders were in a distinctly
counterrevolutionary mood. A number had joined the rightist Father-
land Party. The Baltic Naval Command at Kiel had ordered a ban on
the distribution of left-wing literature within the fleet. And the authority

to permit *Menagekommission* was largely ignored. That elitist spirit was at work, characterized by disdain for or fear of the inferior community, many hundreds strong, sullenly going about its duties when not crowded unseen at the far end of each battleship.

Many sailors first heard of the government's concession on the question of food committees over beers in the taverns of Kiel and Wilhelmshaven. The discovery led to feelings of betrayal and sharpened the lower deck's resentment of the officers. As the sailors' attitude assumed the character of a movement, leaders emerged and included two of the most politically radicalized men in the fleet, both serving on the *Friedrich der Grosse*. Willy Sachse, a twenty-two-year-old stoker petty officer, had belonged to a socialist youth organization before the war. Seaman Max Reichpietsch was of the same age but had five years in the navy, his record of punishment for petty theft and urinating on deck somewhat redeemed by dutiful conduct at the Battle of Jutland. The two decided that they would establish a food committee on their ship. First, however, Reichpietsch would use his next furlough in Berlin not only to see his working-class parents but to consult the deputies of the Independent Social Democratic Party. Servicemen routinely called on their Reichstag representatives, often with complaints, but Reichpietsch's purpose was more ambitious, to forge a direct link with the party's central leadership.

Foes of the Socialist movement afterward charged that its leaders had planted in Reichpietsch's mind the idea of organizing a naval mutiny. More likely he was humored at party headquarters, with Deputy Wilhelm Dittmann even embarrassed by the naïve young sailor's visit. Dittman just then was anxious to project himself publicly as a moderate before attending the peace-seeking socialist congress about to be held in Stockholm. Perhaps Reichpietsch misinterpreted Dittmann's words and those of the other socialist deputies. Then again, in his revolutionary zeal, falsehood or exaggeration would have come easily to him. At any rate, back on the *Friedrich der Grosse* he told shipmates importantly that the USPD regarded him as its representative in the fleet, with the authority to sign them all up as party members.

Reichpietsch and Willy Sachse were next in contact with a more realistic pair of lower-deck demagogues. Albin Köbis and Johann Beckers, stokers on the *Prinzregent Luitpold,* were in fact not socialists but anarchists, wary of political affiliation, and at their instigation shipmates had determined upon not merely a food committee but a sailors' council to plan strikes and protests. Albin Köbis was to justify these moves as "a counter-action against the [officers'] Pan-Germanic propaganda."

Köbis accompanied Willy Sachse on a visit to Berlin. They did not get to see Deputy Wilhelm Dittmann, who was ready now with excuses to avoid any further encounters with dissatisfied sailors. The pair returned to their ship embittered or, in Köbis's case certainly, confirmed in the belief that party politicians should never be relied upon. This difference in outlook contributed to a rivalry for leadership that developed between Köbis and Beckers on the one hand and Sachse and Reichpietsch on the other. At a sailors' meeting in the Meilenstein Tavern in Kiel on 14 July Beckers presented a written constitution aimed at correcting shipboard abuses and affirming support for the Stockholm peacemakers. This drew general applause, but when Reichpietsch urged that action be taken in concert with the USPD, both Beckers and Köbis vehemently objected.

Two weeks after that tavern gathering the German Admiralty ordered an investigation into reports of naval unrest. The Admiralty bureaucrat appointed to head it must have gone about the task perfunctorily at best or he would scarcely have reported on 7 August that shipboard grouses were not to be taken seriously. Five days earlier at Wilhelmshaven, forty-seven stokers of the *Prinzregent Luitpold* had walked off their ship to protest having been denied a promised film show. When they had returned, Capt. Karl von Hornhardt had ordered eleven of them arrested at random. That same evening in an empty freight car on the dock Albin Köbis had addressed delegates from the *Friedrich der Grosse, Kaiser, Kaiserin,* and *Pillau* and secured their support for a wildcat strike. The next morning Köbis had led six hundred men ashore. They had tramped beyond town to a favorite tavern, and on that occasion it had taken naval shore patrols and a police posse to persuade them back to their ships. More "ringleaders" had been borne off under arrest. Displaying the same stubborn refusal to deal with genuine grievances, Captain von Hornhardt blamed these and similar disorders on "widespread agitation and recruitment by the Independent Social Democratic Party which has undermined the patriotic spirit and military bearing of the crew." But each walkout had ended on a generally peaceful note, suggesting that there was less truth in the captain's assertion than in the plea of one of his sailors that "we did not want a revolution, only our human rights."

The refusal or inability to perceive that war weariness, ill-treatment, and poor food were responsible for the lower-deck discontent extended even to the High Seas Fleet commander, Rear Adm. Reinhard Scheer, who had quite competently led his ships and men at the Battle of Jutland. But reports from a naval lawyer named Dobring, attached to the Fourth Squadron, who had conducted interrogations among different crews no doubt influenced Scheer's perspective. Beckers, Köbis, Reichpietsch, and Sachse were among the sailors questioned and apparently threatened with death unless they cooperated. Out of cunning or plain funk Sachse did so freely, claiming to have been led astray by left-wing politicians. On 9 August Scheer stated that "without a doubt there is a connection between the [lower deck] movement and the Independent Social Democratic Party." Four days later under Dobring's relentless grilling Max Reichpietsch blurted, probably with embellishments, the details of his meeting in Berlin with socialist deputies. Solidarity foundered altogether with further "confessions" from Albin Köbis and Johann Beckers.

The destruction of key documents made it difficult for postwar naval historians to piece together exactly what occurred during this wartime burst of unrest in the German High Seas Fleet. Official historians numbered only four battleships affected and called the incidents merely "irregularities that arose when food was limited and routine dull." A private account told of "insubordination, mass desertion, hunger strikes and acts of sabotage in which some five thousand men were involved." The record shows two hundred arrests and a series of courts-martial with seventy-seven convictions and nine death sentences, of which Admiral Scheer commuted all but two. (Willy Sachse was among those who at that time escaped death, but he was executed in 1944 for his alleged complicity in the plot to kill Adolf Hitler.) Convicted of "treasonable incitement to rebellion," Max Reichpietsch and Albin Köbis were taken to the Wahr Firing Range near Cologne and early on 5 September shot to death by a twenty-man firing squad.

Thus had collapsed the enlisted men's movement, such as it was. But sullenness and resentment only worsened. Circumstances gathered for a real mutiny, among them the transfer of presumed troublemakers from ships to shore installations at Kiel and Wilhelmshaven, already breeding grounds for radical discontent. "This danger is averted for the moment," wrote Scheer in a secret memorandum to his officers. "Our most important duty now is to prevent its reappearance." And it was for little more reason than to preoccupy ships' crews and keep them out of mischief that the German Admiralty mounted an amphibious strike against Moon and Dagö, two of Russia's island bases in the Baltic. That it was successful—"my troops melted away," explained a mortified defending admiral—illustrated the decline of the Imperial Russian Navy as a loyal fighting force, the same fate that was in store for Kaiser Wilhelm's.

The German foray in the Baltic occurred in mid-October. It coincided with a decision reached by Vladimir Ilyich Lenin and his henchmen to attempt another coup. Outlawed since July by the provisional

The ship whose one blank shot heralded the birth of the Soviet republic: the cruiser *Avrora*. *(U.S. Naval Historical Center)*

government in Petrograd, the Bolshevik leader had taken refuge in Finland, living in Helsingfors near the harbor—conveniently placed to pursue an interest in the warships and garrison. Lenin and Leon Trotsky knew the value of a discontented fleet, and when they finally moved against Alexander Kerensky's government in the first week of November, what most historically dramatized the event was the participation of Russian naval vessels and personnel.

Kronstadt's irrepressible element took an active role. Never reconciled to the new regime, the Kronstadt Soviet on Kotlin Island had eagerly awaited Lenin's call. He had slipped into Petrograd and set up headquarters in the baroque Smolny Institute scarcely a dozen blocks from the Winter Palace, where Kerensky's cabinet had installed itself. When Lenin signaled action late on Tuesday, 7 November, sailors barracked in Petrograd seized control of the golden-spired Old Admiralty building, the main post office, and the Nikolai Bridge, lowering this drawbridge to allow Red Guard units over from Vasilevsky Island into the city. Naval support was more firmly secured by the arrival of the destroyers *Samson, Zabiiaka,* and *Metroy,* with five smaller craft, ordered up the Neva by Pavel Dybenko's revolutionary Tsentrobalt at Kronstadt in spite of protests from Rear Admiral Rozvozov, commander of the Baltic Fleet. Rozvozov had no better luck with the *Avrora,* notwithstanding that this vessel, a veteran of Tsushima, was scheduled for important engineering trials. Her 578-man crew had voted instead to join the uprising, and at 3 A.M. on Wednesday the 6,700-ton cruiser entered Petrograd under the control of a Bolshevik ship's committee and anchored downstream from the Nikolai Bridge.

The assault upon the Winter Palace was in fact delayed pending the arrival of the ships and men from Kronstadt. Early Wednesday evening Trotsky's military revolutionary committee sent Kerensky an ultimatum. The Winter Palace was surrounded by more than three thousand sailors with hundreds of army comrades, and trained upon it were the guns of the Peter and Paul Fortress across the Neva, besides those of the *Avrora.* The government made no response. At 9 P.M. the *Avrora*'s 6-inch bow gun fired a blank, at which signal began the storming of the great 1,100-room edifice built for Catherine the Great. But the fighting was brief, the palace defenders consisting mostly of military cadets and a women's battalion. As an overture to a long and eventful epoch the day was comparatively bloodless. Kerensky fled. Lenin proclaimed the dictatorship of the proletariat. Pavel Dybenko, named Commissar of the Red Navy for the occasion, described his Kronstadt sailors as "spoiling for a fight on the barricades." It would not be long before they would be giving him a rough time. But now the only significant naval gunfire had been the *Avrora*'s blank. Even so, the mutinous crews could claim much of the credit for overthrowing what propaganda had convinced them was a reactionary administration. And the *Avrora* would remain moored in the Neva, a naval monument to the founding of the Soviet Republic.

Twelve

◢

CATTARO TO KRONSTADT

rmies had mutinied. In 1917 French troops by the thousands threw down their weapons and marched away from the Western Front. Two Russian infantry brigades transferred from the east to bolster those crumbling units had themselves rebelled and were subdued only by the guns of their allies. But the French had mutinied out of disgust for a blundering command responsible for dreadful casualty rates. Russian army revolts sprang from similar causes, although quickly politicized and absorbed along with the naval outbreaks into the general revulsion for the Romanov dynasty. What most nourished the growth of a mutinous spirit within the belligerent fleets were sheer boredom, meager or unpalatable food, resentment of oppressive superiors, and political soul-searching. No doubt these factors contributed to disquiet among the land forces, but the record shows that navies were most susceptible to them and that demoralization and indiscipline, especially within squadrons long idled in home waters, were more likely to result in the navy than in the army.

Even a shortage of soap and shoes could detonate long-smoldering vexations. This occurred among men of an Austro-Hungarian cruiser squadron located off the coast of Montenegro early in 1918. Rumors of an approaching mutiny had circulated throughout the bleak Balkan winter, but as with contemporary revolts in other navies there seems not to have been any serious advance planning. An ethnic mixture of Hungarians, Serbs, Croats, and Slovenes, these were dispirited sailors, war-weary and troubled by news of hardships at home, where famine and riots attended the dissolution of the Hapsburg monarchy. At midday

Disorder on the *Sankt Georg* symbolized the dissolution of the Hapsburg monarchy. *(Innere Front, R. Oldenbourg Verlag)*

on 1 February aboard the armored cruiser *Sankt Georg* the officers were lunching in the wardroom, the ship's orchestra playing for them in the lobby outside, when reports of a disturbance among the ratings sent the executive officer hurrying on deck. He was immediately shot and wounded. Seamen raided the ship's rifle racks, confined the officers to their cabins, and hoisted the red flag.

If the outbreak on the *Sankt Georg* had a ringleader, he was Franz Rasch, a reservist once active in Social Democratic politics. But when other ships joined the revolt—the armored cruiser *Kaiser Karl VI,* two light cruisers, and several of the flotilla's two dozen destroyers and torpedo boats—Anton Sesan assumed firmer leadership. Formerly a merchant seaman, Sesan was a somewhat theatrical twenty-five-year-old sublieutenant attached to the naval air station ashore at Kumbor. He boarded the depot ship *Gäa,* once a Hamburg-Amerika Line express steamer, and set up his command post in what had been the ladies' saloon. It was probably on Sesan's orders that the *Kronprinz Erzherzog Rudolf,* an obsolete battleship but heavily gunned, took position at the mouth of the Gulf of Cattaro to prevent loyal ships from escaping to sea.

Sesan's mutineers assured their captive superiors that what they were about was not revolution but a demonstration for peace. Along the coast at Castelnuevo, however, the garrison commander was taking warlike precautions, telegraphing for reinforcements, evacuating civilians, and preparing his forts to bombard the mutinous ships. This they began when the *Kronprinz Erzherzog Rudolf* was sighted making ready to use its own guns on the railroad station where the troop train was expected. Shells struck the old battleship and killed two of her people. Not yet forty-eight hours old, the mutiny crumbled. Officers on the light cruiser *Novara* were the first to regain control and, ignoring Sesan's signals to stay where they were, took their vessel farther up the inner fjord toward Cattaro. With three revolvers tucked in his belt, Sesan returned to the air station and tried to talk fliers into an air attack on the Castelnuevo forts. They refused to listen. By then twenty-four companies of infantry had arrived—seaborne reinforcements as well, a loyal squadron of three battleships with seventeen escorts steaming into the Gulf. *Kaiser Karl VI* lowered her red flag and ran up the white one of surrender.

Sesan fled to Rome. Intervention by the Austrian Social Democratic Party secured pardons for most of the seamen charged with insurrection but failed to save Franz Rasch and three other mutineers, who were taken to a mountainside village overlooking the Adriatic Sea, lined against a churchyard wall, and shot.

If any word of the mutiny off Cattaro (now Kotor) reached Austro-Hungary's principal ally, its lessons went unheeded. Perhaps it was too late anyway to prevent the disintegration of the German High Seas Fleet, a process hastened by the collapse of General Ludendorf's spring offensive. By late summer the Allies were advancing on the Western Front, and Germany's defeat loomed as inevitable. Yet despite warnings from the Berlin Admiralty against providing the men with causes for discontent, officers continued to foolishly flaunt their superior way of life. Their better food and living conditions were not the only factors bound to have sharpened the lower deck's sense of unjust deprivation. One can imagine the morale of the boat crews taking officers ashore for visits to Kiel's brothels and ordered to await their return. And one may wonder how in the world certain admirals could have expected their people to act like loyal sailors when they themselves began to plot a mutiny of their own.

Under Prince Max of Baden, the new German government set the plot in motion by announcing a policy to seek an end to the fighting. An armistice, most German admirals felt, might bring untold ignominy upon the inactive High Seas Fleet, including its breakup and parceling out among the victorious Allies. The admirals' conspiracy, for such it was, hinged upon the idea of a last-ditch battle that, if it did not dramatically turn the tables through victory, would in defeat preserve the honor of the German navy. In the words of one admiral, anything was better than having the fleet "bargained away or allowed to die in disgrace." Admiral Scheer had become the Imperial Navy's chief of staff. His top aide, Capt. Magnus von Levetzow, drafted a secret memorandum, recommending an immediate move against Britain's naval force. With Scheer's endorsement the proposal was relayed to Adm. Franz von Hipper, his successor as commander of the High Seas Fleet, who at once summoned his captains and drew up the plans. Destroyers would first raid enemy shipping in the English Channel. This would draw the British squadrons from their North Sea anchorages. They would find themselves in mine-infested waters, stalked by submarines, and then the High Seas Fleet would pounce. Within twenty-four hours it should all be over.

Total secrecy was impossible. Young lieutenants had talked freely at Wilhemshaven dinner parties. And when light cruisers were ordered into Cuxhaven to load mines, the seamen themselves sensed something big afoot, their imagination troubled by reports from stewards of solemn toasts in the wardroom. The officers had determined on a Wagnerian climax to the Great War, a death ride of the big ships, a sacrificial final engagement. So ran the rumors. Long afterward Scheer insisted that nothing so suicidal had been envisaged. The intention was to sever British communications, securing a trump card for Germany at the impending armistice negotiations. But Scheer could not have denied the insubordinate nature of the admirals' scheme. They kept Prince Max and his government in the dark, gave even the Kaiser only slight inkling, and would claim that he nodded approval. It was certainly a gamble and far from calculated. That nothing could ensue without lower-deck obedience seems not to have been seriously considered. Wisdom might have suggested that commanders address the men frankly, appeal to their patriotism, explain the project as designed to preserve the honor of the service of their troth. It might have worked. But nothing of the sort was essayed, the officers perhaps resigned to its futility, sharing Hipper's apprehension, formally expressed on 18 October even as he contemplated a last heroic battle, that their crews might revolt at any moment and storm out of the war.

Reinhard Scheer (1863–1928). For the honor of the High Seas Fleet his admirals planned their own mutiny. *(U.S. Naval Institute)*

On the twenty-eighth, as units of the High Seas Fleet prepared to get under way for the assembly areas in Schillig Roads, it would have been hard to tell who were more keyed up, the officers or the men. By the next morning, alert to what their superiors had in store for them, sailors on the *Markgraf,* flagship of the Third Battle Squadron, gathered angrily in the forecastle. The officer of the watch intervened, was promptly surrounded, and had to be rescued by the master-at-arms and ship's police. Cheers then echoing across the gray waters of the Wilhelmshaven Basin meant no eagerness for steaming out against the British but mutinous disorders on the *König* and *Kronprinz Wilhelm*. By sundown twenty-two capital ships and a dozen light cruisers with seventy destroyers were gathered in the waters off Wilhelmshaven, and few if any lacked men ready to show how they felt about being sent into battle on the eve of an armistice.

Yet even as sailors on the First Battle Squadron ships *Thüringen* and *Helgoland* smashed anchor windlasses, while stokers dumped coals from boilers onto deck plates and hosed them down, officers still dreamed of *Flottenvorstoss,* the fleet's climactic thrust. Gathered at 10:00 P.M. for a final briefing by Admiral Hipper on his flagship *Baden,* some of them discounted reports of lower-deck disturbances as merely isolated instances of surrender to pacifist propaganda. Sailing was in any event postponed because of fog. This delay provided a last chance for officers to shed their elitist crust and make a bold call upon the men to stand with them as fellow Germans, proud and unconquered. No one grasped the opportunity. The *Thüringen*'s captain may have thought of it the next morning when he agreed to receive a lower-deck deputation, but by midday he was signaling the flagship *Ostfriesland* that he had lost control of his own ship. This dire news reached Admiral Hipper on the *Baden* at about the same time as a message from Admiral Krafft of the Third Battle Squadron warning that any attempt to force his men into action would bring open rebellion.

At Jutland, Franz von Hipper had led his cruisers into the very heart of the British formations. But a commander who shows daring and gallantry in conventional combat may be utterly nonplussed when confronted with hostility from those he commands. The best Hipper could think of now was to separate his squadrons, hoping thereby to halt the spread of insurrection. He detached the Third Battle Squadron to Kiel. The big ships passed through the Kiel Canal and once anchored at their home port unloaded hundreds of malcontents, to the dismay of Vice Adm. Wilhelm Souchon, newly appointed governor of the Imperial Fortress, whose hands were already full with hungry civilians and demonstrating dockyard workers.

Meanwhile, on the *Kaiser Wilhelm II,* to which old battleship he had transferred his flag, Hipper still clung to the idea of *Flottenvorstoss,* if a somewhat modified version involving only the First Battle Squadron and a submarine flotilla. But the *Thüringen*'s and *Helgoland*'s crews

Revolutionstaumel in den Straßen Kiels
Abordnungen der Kriegsschiffbesatzungen mar-
schieren zum Stationsgebäude Ostsee mit Plakaten,
die den Bürger zur Ruhe mahnen

Der Vertrauensmann der Meuterer: Kuhnt

Die Flotte meutert — Der rote Wimpel am Mast

Defiant German sailors, red flags at their ships' mastheads: Hamburg, November 1918. *(Ullstein Bilderdienst, Berlin)* refused to cooperate. Mutineers on the *Thüringen* had barricaded them-selves in the forward battery. A well-placed shell in that area would have at once reestablished discipline. So thought the commander of submarine *U-135*, which, with five destroyers and two fleet tenders carrying a marine detachment, sailed out of Wilhelmshaven at Hipper's orders on that dismal Thursday afternoon to position themselves about the defiant battleships. A different emotion was that of a seaman on one of the destroyers who "felt a helpless rage when we trained our guns on our comrades." Those sailors were leaning out of forecastle scuttles, staring uncertainly at the surrounding craft. Some of the destroyers might well have opened fire but for the presence of officers exposed on the *Thüringen*'s bridge. Moreover, as Hipper must surely have borne in mind, what those men were rebelling against was an unauthorized operation, which a future board of inquiry might conclude was itself nothing short of mutiny. But the marines were sufficient. Two hundred of them clambered aboard the *Thüringen* with rifles and fixed bayonets. One by one the sailors emerged through a forecastle hatch and were hustled over the side into a waiting tender. The scene was repeated on the *Helgoland*. "What a terrible day," wrote Hipper in his diary. "Our people went on strike."

The outcome was less peaceful at Kiel, where naval mutiny bur-geoned into popular revolt. The Third Battle Squadron had anchored on 1 November. The following morning hundreds of its sailors gathered in a conference room at Trade Union House to hear Karl Artelt, an aggressive young socialist and naval conscript thought by some to be crazy. But he was an effective speaker, who rallied his audience into supporting demands for the release of the men arrested as mutineers, and the next day, after finding Trade Union House padlocked at Admiral Souchon's orders, he harangued a still larger crowd on the Waldwiese, an open space on the outskirts of town. Aroused by Artelt's oratory, the mixed horde of sailors and dockyard workers followed him in a march through Kiel toward the naval detention barracks. Along the way they met a squad of nervous shore-based marines, whose lieutenant ordered fire when Artelt's men refused to halt. The encounter left eight dead and forty wounded. An unhappy Admiral Souchon urged that the Third Battle Squadron be sent back to sea. The answer he got was that its crews would refuse to sail. Souchon then appealed to Berlin, where a bewildered new navy minister, Vice Adm. Ritter von Mann, tried to make sense of reports from Kiel and Wilhelmshaven telling, on the one hand, of massed lower-deck disobedience and, on the other, of officers having themselves planned an illegal coup de main.

"This bloody business must end." Gustav Noske addressing dissident U-boat crews at Kiel. *(Ullstein Bilderdienst, Berlin)*

To calm things in Kiel the Berlin cabinet voted to send a socialist member of the Reichstag, a former basket weaver and newspaper editor named Gustav Noske. He got there none too soon. Warships and barracks were in insurgent hands, prisoners were set at large, red flags flew everywhere, and crews deserted their vessels in droves to roam the rain-swept streets. Motoring about town in a commandeered staff car adorned with a crimson banner, Karl Artelt distributed instructions on how to elect soviets along the Russian pattern and formulate demands for general amnesty, the Kaiser's abdication, and an immediate end to the war. When Noske arrived on Monday morning, 4 November, Admiral Souchon was probably only too relieved to surrender authority to him. Not that Noske's task as peacemaker was simple. Most admirals would have no truck with the sailors' soviets, some pressing for Ritter von Mann in Berlin to order a land and sea blockade of Kiel and "suffocate the mutinies with blood and iron." The sailors too had their hotheads. While attempting to prevent the hoisting of the red flag on the *König,* in drydock, the ship's captain and two other officers were gunned down. But Noske rapidly secured the trust of extremists on both sides, Karl Artelt included. "This bloody business must end," Noske declared.

By the end of the week, so it had. The town of Kiel returned to

"The saddest voyage." With admirals and mutineers sharing command, the High Seas Fleet steams into Allied captivity. *(U.S. Naval Institute)*

normal. Artelt's Sailors' Council proclaimed victory. The admirals' pipe dream of *Flottenvorstoss* had long faded, and pardons were promised for not only those who had opposed it but men still imprisoned for the 1917 mutinies. But although Kiel was quiet, the sailors' uprising begun there had spread to other ports and garrison towns, to Bremerhaven, Hamburg, Cuxhaven, Cologne, and Berlin itself, and become part of a nationwide antiwar revolt. The navy's role in it had repeated that of sailors in Russia's revolution. The objectives matched, cease-fire and the dissolution of a ruling monarchy. The Kaiser abdicated, as had the Tsar, exile for one, execution for the other. But the drama then played out differently. Russian ships had remained more or less a national force, though weakened and submissive to the new Bolshevik government. Under the Armistice signed on 11 November the Germany navy, complete with admirals in nominal command and revolutionaries in effective control, would become subject to the decisions of a conference of wrangling victors. In the meantime its fate was internment. Seventy-four ships steamed across the North Sea into the Orkney Island basin known as Scapa Flow—what a mechanic's mate on the *Prinzregent Luitpold* called "the saddest voyage ever made by an undefeated fleet."

Hipper had appointed Hans Ludwig von Reuter in charge of it. Few admirals in history could have had a more melancholy or humiliating assignment. While complying with British whims and wishes, von Reuter had also to get along with the "workers' councils," those sailors' soviets on his eleven battleships. Any violent disorder would give the British an excuse to seize the fleet, destroying the last shreds of German naval pride. Von Reuter was an officer no less adamant than Alexander Slidell Mackenzie, three-quarters of a century before him, in the belief that a naval commander must never rely on foreign help to quell a mutiny. One wonders whether the admiral might have savored irony in the fact that while his fleet lay in a state of suspended mutiny the lower-deck morale of its custodians was not all that secure—if evidence ever reached his attention. The Royal Navy's sailors checking the German vessels for hidden arms were forbidden to fraternize with their crews—one German destroyer lieutenant thought British officers "terrified" of the risk of revolutionary contagion to their own men.

Perhaps only a few of his closest officers became aware that Admiral von Reuter had determined to expunge all dishonor to the fleet with one bold stroke. Winter had passed, and pale sunlight glinted off the hulls of the silent ships. Through long months von Reuter had shared uneasy command with the lower-deck councils, some of whose members thought nothing of routinely insulting their officers. Few if any had ever saluted. On one of the smaller vessels a plot to murder the captain had been discovered. And a repatriation program begun by the British had moved too slowly to satisfy the councils. But something else had spurred the admiral's decision, early May's news that Allied peace terms would effectively reduce the German navy to a contemptible token force. The following month two thousand ratings were sent home, leaving little more than caretaker crews to man the interned fleet. Von Reuter decided to wait no longer. On 17 June he drew up detailed instructions for scuttling every ship. Four days later he appeared on the *Emden*'s quarter-deck in full dress uniform, wearing all of his medals. The morning was warm and misty. At ten o'clock he gave the signal. It sped around the fleet by semaphore flags and Morse-flashing lamps, and the ships began to fill. Von Reuter's old flagship *Friedrich der Grosse* sank first, and by five o'clock in the afternoon the rest of the High Seas Fleet had followed her to the bottom.

The end of hostilities against Germany did not mean the end of all fighting for Allied land and sea forces. In March 1918 the new leaders of a demoralized and strife-torn Russia had signed a peace treaty with the Germans, posing a very real threat that Germany might gain access to Russian wheat and oil and thus escape the effect of the Allies' western blockade and prolong if not win the war. Moreover, the Germans might lay hands on the thousands of tons of food, clothing, and ammunition shipped from Britain and the United States to Archangel, Murmansk, and Vladivostok. Allied intervention appeared imperative. "Since Russia cannot help herself she must be helped by her friends," wrote Arthur J. Balfour, Britain's foreign secretary, and plans for intervention were completed even as the German army launched its spring offensive on the Western Front. They were not canceled when that offensive failed. The result was that when Bolshevik forces resisted this latest penetration of their homeland, British, French, and American soldiers and sailors found themselves fighting Russians long after the news of Germany's surrender, and the potent war weariness that had already generated storms of protest and insubordination was to further the mutinous chronology.

Among Americans, whose entry into the European conflict dated only from 1917, fatigue and disgust were not so rampant, although United States sailors on patrol off Archangel and Murmansk could have mustered no measurable zeal for this bleak, confused, and undeclared war. And War Department, Military Intelligence Division, memoranda of June 1919 on the subject "Mutiny Among the American Troops of the N.R.E.F." (North Russica Expeditionary Force) indicate that American land forces were by no means free of a near-mutinous resentment against being forced to meddle in Russia's internal affairs. These memoranda contain references to "one or more mutinous occurrences" among American infantrymen on the Archangel front. With a view to guarding United States personnel against further rebellious impulses, the troubles of the other Allies were to be discreetly studied, the Office of Naval Intelligence, for instance, asked to disclose "what they have concerning mutinies in the French navy."

They could have had quite a lot. In November 1918 the crews of French warships had refused to shell Odessa's revolutionaries, and by the following spring sympathy for workers' soviets had combined with such hatred of this new round of hostilities as to produce instances of actual cooperation between French enlisted men and Marxist forces on shore. On 12 April 1919, the eve of Easter Sunday, the crew of the 25,000-ton battleship *France,* on station off Sevastopol, was ordered to prepare for coaling the next day. This was a profoundly discontented ship's company. They had not touched a French port in eighteen months, for much of that time laying off Corfu, the ship's officers living in comparative luxury and the lower deck miserably victualed and homesick. Instead of orders for home and demobilization, the armistice had brought deployment into the Black Sea and conflict with former allies. That Saturday afternoon four hundred seamen gathered on the battleship's foredeck and declared against coaling the next day. And when an admiral from the battleship *Jean Bart* came on board to perch himself beside a gun turret and scold them for their conduct, they swayed toward him, murmuring death threats.

The next morning the *France* flew a red flag. Seamen ashore fraternized with Sevastopol's workers. Some joined demonstrations and ran into oddly mixed opposition. Six matelots died under machine-gun fire from Greek conscripts commanded by an ensign from the *Jean Bart*. Angered by the killings, the *France*'s lower-deck complement demanded that their ship be ordered home. The Ministry of Marine in Paris doubtless heeded the warning signs, for within a fortnight the *France* was detached from Black Sea service and ordered to Toulon. Twenty-three mutineers were tried and convicted, but popular sympathy was to force a reduction in their jail terms.

The firebrand who most unnerved French commanders in the Black Sea was André Marty, whose entrance into naval service as a known anarchist says much about the lack of a screening process in the recruitment or draft systems of that period. Marty's serious activism afloat began when his ship, the destroyer *Protet,* prepared to shell Crimean revolutionaries and he was caught attempting to flood the ammunition hoists. He had, it turned out, formed a subversive cell on the *Protet* and written "a complete manual for sabotage." Marty was arrested and thrown into a Romanian jail but sowed discontent among his guards and was sent back to the fleet. On 23 April while imprisoned aboard the *Waldeck Rousseau,* flagship of the French cruiser squadron off Odessa, Marty decided "we must win this vessel for the Red Flag." Again working upon his guards, he organized a one-hundred-man secret society on board and circulated a message: "The war on Russia is illegal—the only enemies are your own officers." Marty was soon hustled back to the *Protet,* but the damage was done on the flagship, which followed the *France* home, with disorder breaking out during calls at Constantinople and Bizerte.

A good deal of self-generated myth conceals the true details of André Marty's mutinous career, and it can only be guessed to what degree his mischief led to the French fleet's withdrawal from involvement in the Russian imbroglio. Discontent plagued French ships at other locations than the Black Sea—off Greece and Syria, even in remote Vladivostock. For his own contributions, Marty was court-martialed at Constantinople and sentenced to twenty years' imprisonment. He served only four, then launched a lively career in radical French politics. Active in the Spanish Civil War, he achieved notoriety for the alleged butchering of General

Firebrand of the French Black Sea Fleet: André Marty. *(La Révolte de la Mer Noire,* Editions Sociales-Messidor, 1949)*

Franco's followers—he makes an appearance in Hemingway's *For Whom the Bell Tolls.* Later he so rebelled against the rigid discipline of his own Communist Party that it had finally to expel him, which suggests that if lonely and embittered at the end, as noted by his obituaries, André Marty must also have died a congenital mutineer.

British service personnel felt, as their French counterparts did, that with the Central Powers defeated it made no sense to fight the Russians. Britain's sailors had additional and longer-standing grievances. They were upset over their pay. In the war years many had associated with American and Australian navy men, whose pay scales were substantially higher than theirs. Emulating coal miners, police, cotton workers, and other civilians at home who had struck, sometimes successfully, for better wages, men of the Royal Navy had thought seriously of staging a general strike even before the war with Germany had ended. Taking a cue from the civilian work stoppages, they contemplated the value of

The *Jean Bart, France,* and other mutinous French battleships in the Mediterranean, 1919. *(U.S. Naval Historical Center)*

unity. Early in 1919 a member of the Board of Admiralty warned privately of "an organized attempt by socialist and syndicalist circles to introduce into the Navy a Lower Deck Union on Trade Union lines." To head off trouble, the Board appointed a panel to study lower-deck grievances, its chairman Rear Adm. Sir Thomas Jerram, who had commanded a battleship at Jutland and knew that fairness was essential to lower-deck morale. Jerram's committee toured home ports, conducting interviews, and he made a point of talking with seamen's delegates. There was little time to lose, especially in view of the mounting opposition to Allied entanglement with Russia's civil war.

Early in the year the crews of several small vessels disobeyed orders to put to sea. At Milford Haven eight men of the patrol gunboat *Kilbride* were court-martialed for "non-violent mutiny." Refusals to weigh anchor for Russia were recorded at Invergordon, Rosyth, Devonport, and Portsmouth. Discipline among British crews already in Russian waters began to crumble at about the same time mutinies were shaking the French naval command. Rear Adm. Sir Walter Cowan, a veteran officer whose combat experience reached back to gunboat battles on the River Nile in Queen Victoria's day, headed the Royal Navy's contingent. Some found Cowan a tiger to serve with while cool under fire. Meek in appearance, quiet-voiced, and of short height, Cowan had habitually cultivated the companionship of the lowly fighting man. He was not the only officer to develop a shipboard affinity with inferior ranks only to find himself at some loss when it abruptly soured. Not that disciplinary and morale problems were altogether new to Admiral Cowan—in 1914 he had commanded HMS *Zealandia* when her people had demonstrated against their new executive officer.

The 645-ton gunboat *Cicala* had been ordered up the River Dvina, a dangerous passage exposed to fire from Bolshevik inland water craft and gun batteries along its wooded banks. The *Cicala*'s crew of fifty, having already wintered in the White Sea, said no. Cowan sent his chief of staff with word that force would be used if needed to make them obey. The *Cicala* sailed. But the incident left Cowan acutely disturbed. He was himself unsure of how best to command in what was, to his orderly mind, a highly anomalous situation. He wrote to the Chief of Naval Staff in London, who in turn inquired of the British cabinet: Were their forces in Russia to consider themselves at war with the Bolsheviks? Prime Minister David Lloyd George's affirmative reply was unlikely to have improved matters, if only because in this case the government did not provide the usual wartime pension for the survivors of any men who were killed.

The cruiser *Vindictive* left for northern Russia in June with a thousand men on board, three hundred more than her normal complement. She ran aground in the Baltic, then bad weather ruled out shore leave at Copenhagen. Officers talked an angry gathering out of a strike. But one day while gale force winds buffeted the ship an engineering officer came across some stokers interfering with the cruiser's fans. He brandished a wrench, and the men retreated. A court-martial later convicted two ratings of "mutiny accompanied by violence."

Disorders persisted throughout the summer. In September two entire companies of the Sixth Battalion, Royal Marines, after covering the Allied evacuation of Murmansk, refused further duty in the Lake Onega region, and ninety of their number were convicted of mutiny. There were thirteen death sentences—speedily commuted. By that autumn British ships had fought against Russian destroyers and cruisers and had been shelled from shore batteries, attacked by aircraft, and torpedoed by submarines. More than a hundred men had died. Trouble erupted on Admiral Cowan's own flagship, the newly commissioned cruiser *Delhi,* and the convicted ringleader of a dissident group of men who locked themselves in the recreation room would draw eighteen months hard labor and dismissal from the navy for "joining a mutinous assembly and uttering words of sedition." In a memorandum to all ships dated

29 October 1919 Cowan put the best face he could on why they were in the Baltic Sea. It was "to keep order and prevent oppression." The task was harsh and unpleasant, the more so because his ships' crews had admittedly earned a respite. "Yet our Navy has scarcely ever had a worthier aim . . . so I ask you to help me see it through."

If such appeals won Cowan some temporary relief from threats of mutiny, probably none could have mollified the war resisters back home. In the Firth of Forth that same month, when the destroyers *Velox*, *Versatile*, and *Wryneck* signaled to prepare for departure, their rumored destination the Baltic, nearly a hundred ratings deserted. Half of them boarded a London train at Edinburgh with the intention of petitioning the Admiralty in person against Russian service. They were forming up at Kings Cross Station to march upon Whitehall when police closed in and arrested them. Ten men court-martialed for "desertion and non-violent mutiny" were thrown out of the navy and jailed.

That was the last display of British naval revolt against the policy of intervention. Why had such involvement persisted beyond 1918? Only because of an obligation to help "allies whose cooperation with us . . . had lately been so welcome." Thus Lloyd George's explanation. "When it became clear that their bid for power was doomed to failure and that the choice of the Russian people was definitely swinging to support a Bolshevik regime, our withdrawal was inevitable." Moscow's version, soon in print, was that "the Soviet Republic successfully repulsed all foreign imperialist attacks thanks to the heroic efforts of the ruling Communist party." Distortion, of course, yet hardly more reprehensible than the Allies' failure, in their official accounts, to admit that the threat of a large-scale breakdown in morale and discipline, ashore and afloat, was a factor in their decision to abandon the Russian misadventure and bring their troops and seamen home before the year ended.

What closed a cycle of naval mutinies that may be said to have begun with the *Potemkin* revolt and its attempted politicization was an uprising in 1921 against the Bolshevik masters by the very sailors who had assisted them into power, the recalcitrants of Kronstadt. Revolution and civil war had left little remaining of the original Baltic Fleet. Four battle cruisers and a cluster of destroyers lay off Kotlin Island, manned by sovietized crews with an ineffectual handful of officers still haunted by the memory of 1917's massacre. One of the battle cruisers, the *Petropavlovsk,* sat uselessly on an even keel in the shallows, disabled by British torpedoes. But the sailors were politically restless, convinced like large segments of the populace elsewhere that the "dictatorship of the proletariat," now based in Moscow, had shaped into as despotic a regime as the tsarism that it had bloodily replaced. Workers and peasants had already staged protest demonstrations. But Kronstadt took the center stage, its immediate target the council of commissars that had taken over from the Tsentrobalt. Led by Stephen Maximovitch Petrichenko, a senior clerk on the *Petropavlovsk,* Kronstadt's latest mutineers displayed characteristically perverse motives, proclaiming themselves staunch supporters of the soviet system while yet opposed to political totalitarianism.

A handsome Ukrainian with a magnetic personality, Petrichenko assembled his comrades on the *Petropavlovsk's* quarterdeck, where they voted to demand a greater say in the national government. On 1 March their resolutions were read at a gathering of sixteen thousand sailors, Red Army men, and workers in Yakorny Square, an event attended by Communist Party officials from Moscow, on hand to cow the movement with threats and intimidation. They were unheeded or, attempting to speak, shouted down. At a later meeting in Kronstadt's school of marine engineering, ships' delegates elected fifteen men as a "provisional revolutionary committee," with Petrichenko its chairman.

With more zest than sober thought Petrichenko's presidium determined that Kronstadt's sailors would run the naval base themselves, in effect seceding from the central government, until Moscow agreed to their demands. It was swiftly obvious that this also meant placing themselves under siege to whatever forces Leon Trotsky, commissar of war, might bring to bear. The island naval base had three principal forts facing the Russian mainland across five miles of frozen channel. A chain of batteries and smaller forts added up to a total of 135 cannon, with scores of machine guns. There were also the icebound ships, the two dreadnoughts *Petropavlovsk* and *Sevastopol,* each with twelve 12-inch guns and twenty 5-inch guns. The rebels numbered about fifteen hundred sailors, soldiers, and dockyard workers, many no doubt aware of their limited supplies of food, fuel, and ammunition but stubbornly hopeful of holding out until the ice broke and allowed outside help to reach them.

The first round of fighting might have buoyed such hope. On 8 March when twenty-five thousand of Trotsky's whiteclad troops swarmed in crouching waves across the ice, they met a barrage of fire that hurled them back and left hundreds dead. Not until more than a week later was a second attack launched, double the strength of the first, and by that time the defenders were running out of ammunition. The fortress batteries and battle-cruiser guns fired their last shells. The fighting, which had begun at 3 A.M., lasted all day, resistance collapsing when it was discovered that the leaders, including Petrichenko, had fled north

Kronstadt revolt, 1921. The *Petropavlovsk, Sevastopol,* and other dread-noughts of the Baltic Fleet, frozen in off Kotlin Island. *(National Board of Antiquities, Finland)*

over the ice to Finland. Hundreds of Kronstadters took the same route to escape. Six hundred had died in the battle. Red troops marched hundreds more to eventual imprisonment in Petrograd jails and Siberian labor camps. Condemning the rebels as counterrevolutionaries in the pay of the Whites and of foreign governments, Pavel Dybenko took command at Kronstadt, and it was doubtless on the authority of the Tsentrobalt's original chairman that scores of his former comrades, mutineers for a second time, were sent to their deaths. Petrichenko published unrepentant articles in Finland, was repatriated to Russia in 1945, and died in a prison camp. Dybenko's ultimate fate was equally grim. The inceptive Kronstadt mutineer and first Red Navy commissar would hold a number of high Communist posts and assist Joseph Stalin's 1937 purges, only to be executed himself the following year on Stalin's order.

The warships principally involved in the Kronstadt rebellion, the *Petropavlovsk* and *Sevastopol,* were in due course extensively refitted and renamed the *Marat* and *Pariskiya-Kommuna.* In 1941 German bombs wrecked the *Marat* where she lay off Kotlin Island. Her sister ship survived, a floating reminder of a sailors' revolt that was the last serious internal challenge to Communist domination in Russia until the popular uprisings of the late 1980s.

Thirteen

RED PLOTS AND PAY CUTS

E ven after the withdrawal of its units from Russia, the British Admiralty could by no means guarantee shipboard serenity. The Admiralty's welfare program was recognized for what it was, an attempt to undermine lower-deck societies, which more and more appeared to resemble trade unions. These were feared in some quarters as downright subversive, and in due course the Director of Naval Intelligence placed them under surveillance. The publication in *The Worker's Dreadnought,* a left-wing sheet, of an article headed "Discontent on the Lower Deck" led to a raid on the publisher's office by a security squad. In 1921 Adm. Sir Walter Cowan, who had known his share of mutinies, warned that discipline in the Royal Navy "hangs by a very slender thread" because of "the mass of mischievous and revolutionary literature which floods the country." That year there were court-martial trials in the British fleet for "suspicion of mutiny in preparation," "concealing mutinous practice," and "incitement to mutiny."

But the findings of the Jerram Committee appointed to investigate lower-deck complaints would lead to better rates of pay and to monetary allowances indexed to the cost of living. At the same time, such were the postwar cuts in military spending and service strength, with a corresponding increase in civilian unemployment figures, that sailors were soon considering themselves fortunate to at least have a secure job with regular wages. With the continuance of this more satisfied atmosphere aboard His Majesty's warships, the Admiralty found it easier to impose restrictions on those too-leftist lower-deck societies, whose memberships thereupon steadily declined.

In the United States, meanwhile, efforts to better conditions for the navy's enlisted men brought forth, as in Britain, charges of socialist influence. *Our Navy* was at the center of one such controversy. Throughout the war this magazine had retained its safely patriotic and inspirational tone while yet making proposals bound to have raised hackles here and there. Prospering from the wartime increase in naval personnel strength, which enlarged its circulation, *Our Navy* had boldly proclaimed the American sailor's constitutional right to the same civil liberties that other citizens enjoyed: "He lost none of the privileges of American citizenship by holding up his right hand and donning the blue shirt, neither did he bargain to do so."

As far back as 1914 *Our Navy* had campaigned for direct representation of the enlisted men before Congress. It revived efforts in this direction with the advent of peace and under Ray C. Shepherd's continuing editorship urged as an initial step the formation of a committee on every ship "to harmonize demands and condense the wishes of the crew." Chief petty officers had organized such bodies for their own welfare and recreational purposes. They should cooperate in securing "a DEFINITE PLATFORM for the enlisted men." The novelty here is that *Our Navy* derived encouragement for its saucy radicalism from Secretary of the Navy Josephus Daniels, whose overt solicitude for the lower deck irritated tradition-bound admirals almost as much as did the lack of any nautical experience in his personal background.

Warning signals had not gone unheeded. On 9 April 1920 the chief of the Bureau of Navigation told a Senate committee that disaster would overwhelm the whole navy unless Congress approved an immediate pay raise. The desertion rate had reached seven hundred men per month, and good recruits were difficult to get. The following year wages were duly improved. Still *Our Navy* went on preaching heresy. In its April issue the magazine reiterated in full detail its plan for a system of ships' committees that would give the lower deck a voice in the running of its affairs. Moreover, the committees should combine to elect a representative who would have a permanent position within the Navy Department, where, with office space and clerical help furnished, he would be conveniently available to the secretary for advice on personnel problems. By this time, however, the Department had a new chief, one of decidedly more traditional stock than his predecessor. Prior to gaining some eminence as a Detroit automobile maker and politician, Edwin Denby had worked his way up from private to major in the Marine Corps. Having given lectures on citizenship, the flag, and the spirit of *semper fidelis,* he was unlikely to have applauded *Our Navy's* dictum that "the

American bluejacket is, as he has a perfect right to be, the master of his own destiny." The weekly *Army and Navy Register* denounced such notions as fostering "sovietism" in the fleet, and that Secretary Denby heartily agreed is inferable from the manner in which he handled the case of Captain Stearns.

Discipline as a subject is not much easier to define than mutiny. Clark Daniel Stearns had made a special study of it and was perhaps freer than the average United States Navy officer in giving voice to his views. A graduate of the Naval Academy in the class of 1891, Stearns had held an assortment of posts when in early 1918 he was appointed to the *Roanoke,* one of eight converted merchant vessels making up the navy's minelaying force in the North Sea. During this command, which earned Stearns the Distinguished Service Medal, he had authorized an election by the minelayer's four-hundred-man crew of two committees, one of petty officers, the other a "ship's committee" composed of one enlisted man for each division. The committees' function was to investigate doubtful cases at "captain's mast," the shipboard method of adjudicating minor disciplinary offenses, and to make or convey, on behalf of the people, complaints and suggestions concerning the "health, happiness and comfort of the ship's company." In Stearns's opinion, the fact that sailors on his minelayer performed their tasks with quiet competence and speed—"all movement on duty is habitually done in double time by everyone"—and were singled out for praise by a British port admiral proved the experiment's success.

Stearns believed that unrest on ships and shore stations was all too frequently traceable to "the lack of cooperation between the officers and enlisted personnel in matters relating to discipline and the general welfare." Josephus Daniels, while secretary of the navy, openly favored the formation of ships' "morale committees" consisting of petty officers and enlisted men. While not depriving the commander of "the power to discipline," such a body would, the argument ran, promote mutual understanding between the wardroom and the lower deck. Not long after leaving the *Roanoke,* Captain Stearns conducted a survey of naval prisons, criticized the navy's penal system as archaic, and recommended among other things the creation of an Office of Discipline. And upon his next assignment as captain of the prewar dreadnought *Michigan* he proceeded once more to implement what Josephus Daniels might have applauded as a fine idea but what others regarded as dangerously unorthodox.

Clark Stearns's command of the USS *Michigan* lasted precisely 107 days. What abruptly curtailed it was Order No. 17, which the captain issued on 3 May 1921 as the ship lay off Tangier Island in the Chesapeake Bay. The order began with an attempted definition of discipline. "Discipline does not mean punishment. [It] is systematic training with a view to right conduct . . . implies intelligent cooperation or willing submission to law and order through unity of purpose." Instructions followed for the formation of a "Ship's Morale Committee." They embodied those employed on the *Roanoke,* with an additional provision for an executive committee of seven chief petty officers, petty officers, and nonrated men to screen cases of alleged indiscipline and decide which should be brought to the captain's attention. Coming at the beginning of a period marked by general nervousness in western countries over Muscovite attempts to subvert their fighting forces, the introduction of such an innovation so suggestive of "workers' councils" set off alarm bells. There was no telling where it might lead. Thus, evidently, reasoned the admirals of the Atlantic Fleet and the battleship squadron of which the *Michigan* was part, for they jointly recommended to Secretary Denby that he take appropriate action. Denby did not hesitate. For issuing an order "prejudicial to discipline," Clark Stearns found himself detached from command of the *Michigan,* transferred from the East Coast to the West, and placed in command of the navy yard at Puget Sound, Washington.

Newspapers picked up the story. Stearns's superiors had concluded that the *Michigan*'s experiment in shared authority, with ex-Secretary Daniels's endorsement, was reflective of "a Soviet spirit [which] had crept into the Navy." Mention was made, without details, of a recent case in which a commander had actually left it to his men to decide at which port they would next dock, an unheard-of example of permissiveness for which the captain was privately reprimanded. Such events, or what he took them to signify, led Secretary Denby to warn, in a special memorandum to the navy, of a "sinister propaganda" at work to undermine sailors' morale. "In the hearts of discontented men false doctrines find ready acceptance." Everyone at sea was subject to homesickness, occasional dejection, imagined ill-treatment. But a sailor must not allow these natural burdens to lead him into "such folly as desertion or resistance to lawful authority." Instead, he must be ever on guard against "the preaching of sovietism, communism, and anarchy."

In support of Denby's warning, the *New York Times* assured its readers that sailors' pay was generous, that "promotion [was] within reach of any well-behaved enlisted men," and that their quarters and rations were far better than might be found on any foreign warship. The lower deck's favorite magazine, *Our Navy,* would have disputed

No strangers to mutiny: Brazil's mighty battleships *Minas Geraes* and *São Paulo*. *(U.S. Naval Historical Center)*

none of this but nevertheless perversely insisted that "the Navy's personnel problems continue to pile up. Contentment is not what it should be."

The only real naval mutiny of those immediate postwar years occurred on one of two battleships that were no strangers to mutiny, a pair of the world's most powerful dreadnoughts whose guns trained if not fired on each other but never at a foreign foe. They were the Brazilian navy's pride and joy for forty years, the *Minas Geraes* and *São Paulo,* British-built at Messrs Armstrong and Messrs Vickers shortly before the First World War.

The very appearance of these two 20,000-ton capital ships off Rio de Janeiro in 1910 would have been enough to convince Brazilians of their debut as a twentieth-century naval power, had the country not then been in the throes of social and political upheaval. And the ships had no sooner arrived than mutiny broke out on board. According to British engineers who crossed the Atlantic on the vessels, the immediate cause was a brutal flogging given a Brazilian sailor. The navy had outlawed capital punishment a dozen years earlier, but the *chibata,* a fierce leather whip, was back in use to control overworked crews—each ship, reported the American consul at Rio de Janeiro, carried only three hundred seamen, less than one-third the proper complement. Plotted briefly in secret, the mutiny started at 10 P.M. on 22 November when Captain Neves of the *Minas Geraes,* returning from dinner aboard a French navy training ship, was fired upon as he climbed the gangway ladder. He managed to draw his sword but died before he could raise it. The crew then turned on their remaining officers and put them ashore. Some resisted. On the *São Paulo* it was the same story. By the next morning five officers lay dead, and the squadron of two dreadnoughts, four cruisers, and five destroyers, guns aimed at Rio, was more or less under the command of a seaman named Jean Candido, who telegraphed to President Hermes da Fonseca an ultimatum demanding the abolition of the *chibata,* higher pay, shorter work hours, and amnesty for every mutineer.

There was no immediate response. Not until after the *Minas Geraes's* 12-inch guns had hurled a few shells into the Brazilian capital did Fonseca's government agree to the demands. An American envoy wrote disapprovingly of the rebel sailors' treatment ashore as heroes: "It may be asked what assurance the government can feel that these same seamen won't rise again." As in fact many did, less than a month later. Once more the ships were "in command of their crews." It was not quite a renewed outbreak by the same men. A large number were replacements for the original mutineers, many of whom, despite the government's promise of amnesty, were confined to a prison on Villegainon Island—where in January 1911 it was reported that forty-five, including Jean Candido, had suddenly died from gangrene, sunstroke, and suffocation.

The second mutiny to strike Brazil's sole two battleships occurred in 1924 and sprang from no lower-deck discontent, did not even directly involve the inferior ranks. The mutineers were six junior lieutenants, the leader Hercolano Cascardo, age twenty-four, who had caught an insurrectionary fever already rampant among army troops and who believed that "destiny decreed that I should assume command of the *São Paulo.*" The opportunity arose on 4 November after the captain had gone ashore with a party, leaving only three senior officers on board, none of whom resisted when Cascardo and his colleagues ordered them placed under lock and key. Cascardo then hoisted the red flag. What the five hundred or so ratings thought of it all (others were on shore leave) went unrecorded, although about half seem to have thrown in their lot with the young lieutenants. The first threat to Cascardo's plans, such as they were, came when government forces raided the Naval School of Aviation, presumed a hotbed of revolutionaries, and arrested officers and cadets from whom Cascardo had expected help. Neither was the support that Cascardo's revolt got from the *Minas Geraes* anything but short-lived. When rifle fire drove off a launch carrying the Brazilian minister of marine and others desirous of remonstrating with the *São Paulo*'s rebels, the launch headed for the *Minas Geraes,* where the minister's mission was successful enough for it to appear that she might begin firing upon her mutinous sister ship.

At the same time, for reasons that perhaps only the *São Paulo*'s lower ranks could have explained, the ship's electrical and hydraulic equipment malfunctioned and her Babcock boilers drained of steam. Immobilized, the dreadnought lay for two hours in Guanabara Bay, uncomfortably close to the *Minas Geraes* and also within range of presumably loyal forts. After nightfall, when the *São Paulo* managed to raise enough steam pressure to make for the outer harbor at limited speed, several shore batteries opened up. The *São Paulo*'s big guns replied. In a brief exchange of shells, no hits were registered on the dreadnought—"either the harbor defenses are in a lamentable condition," reported a United States consul, as apparently disgusted with Brazilian events as his 1910 predecessor, "or the forts deliberately intended to avoid hitting the vessel." By then the *São Paulo*'s engines were turning more rapidly. She cleared the harbor entrance at twenty knots.

The mutinous young junta had a battleship on its hands with no clear notion of what to do next. Cascardo's wild dream of leading an alliance of warships, aviators, and army divisions quickly faded. "The revolution should have become general," he would say, "but everything had failed." His immediate objective now was escape into foreign waters. All that night the *São Paulo* stole southward for Uruguay. The *Minas Geraes,* with the minister of marine on board and an escort of destroyers, set out in belated pursuit. The pursuing ships were only at the coast of

Santa Caterina when the fugitive dreadnought, some eight hundred miles ahead, neared the mouth of the River Plata, Cascardo and his mutineers straight-facedly appealing for refuge from Brazilian persecution. Uruguay's government said yes. Seven junior officers with 250 lower-deck followers were promptly landed at Montevideo under local army custody. Six officers and about two hundred of the crew remained on board, swearing loyalty to the Brazilian flag when the *Minas Geraes* finally arrived to take her runaway sister back to Rio de Janeiro.

"The naval prestige of Brazil has sustained a great blow." Thus concluded the American naval attaché, pained by what he thought an insufficient display of popular shame "at the spectacle of a modern dreadnought mutinying and proceeding to sea flying the red flag." Some with a broader sense of humor than local *Yanqui* diplomats deemed the affair a farcical and foredoomed escapade by youngsters whose allegiance to the national government and respect for naval tradition just happened to have succumbed to an audacious impulse. Certainly they were never punished for it and probably slipped back into Brazil to join diehard insurgents. The main thing was that Brazil still had the most powerful South American navy by virtue of those two formidable if erstwhile mutinous battleships. But their guns no more discharged in anger. The *Minas Geraes* finished her days as an administration ship for the navy's commander-in-chief. The *São Paulo* met her end less meekly. Sold for scrap in 1951, she was crossing the Atlantic, bound for the Clyde, when at the height of a storm she tore loose from the two tugs that had her in tow, and the old dreadnought was never seen again.

For more than a dozen years after the First World War few observers in either Britain or the United States noticed any signs that another and still greater conflict was approaching. National crises were, in the main, domestic and of a social and economic nature, with foreign threat defined not so much in terms of overt attack by land, sea, or air as through subversion or insidious propaganda, invariably Moscow-inspired. During the General Strike in Britain anxiety arose over how military and naval forces would conduct themselves if the emergency required their involvement. Most labor unionists and the radical press urged sailors and soldiers never to attack their striking brothers. This sort of rhetoric, had circumstances taken that grave a turn, might have qualified as incitement to mutiny. Happily, no such contingency developed, and notwithstanding dark mutterings about scabbing and strike breaking, Britain's naval personnel acquitted themselves loyally as they helped keep vital services running.

All the same, it was felt that there must be no lowering of the guard against the peril of Bolshevik infiltration. In 1926, the year of the great labor stoppage, Scotland Yard's Special Branch uncovered a "Red plot" to distribute motion pictures conveying the wrong kind of ideology. Customs officers were warned to look out for movies that the government deemed subversive. Not surprisingly, the proscribed list included Eisenstein's *The Battleship Potemkin,* rejected by the British Board of Censors because "it dealt with mutiny against properly constituted authority." Germany also banned the film because of scenes "corrupting to law and order." Somewhat mild controversy and mixed reviews greeted its opening in the United States, where, in contrast to Edwin Denby's day, the naval establishment, at least for the time being, showed no inclination to panic over reports of Red agitation. At a secret conference of the Communist International in Germany an American delegate calling himself "Jack Wilson" boasted that ten Communist cells flourished below decks in the United States Navy, an "improvement" over recent years that compared favorably with the results in navies of other capitalist countries—thirteen and fourteen cells were active, reported delegates, in the British and the French navies. Such figures buoyed the meeting's expectation of a rash of mutinies in the near future. They were totally discounted at the Navy Department in Washington, where a cursory check turned up no Communist "Jack Wilson" in the service, and Secretary Curtis D. Wilbur diagnosed, "The heart of the Navy is sound."

British Intelligence took such reports more soberly. In 1930 Britain's security service MI5 decided that "communist efforts to tamper with HM Forces are on the increase." They probably were. Unfortunately, the attention paid to the genuine grievances that might encourage political subversion among the military and naval ranks was more often than not inadequate. Even so, some members of Britain's naval establishment were habitually apprehensive lest the pendulum swing too far in the other direction, toward greater leniency, and this was especially true after the Socialists had come to power and appeared all too ready to cave in when confronted by indiscipline among soldiers and sailors.

Such criticism was heard following an incident on the submarine tender *Lucia* in early January 1931. The vessel was at Devonport, preparing to join the rest of the Atlantic Fleet on spring exercises in the Mediterranean. Bad weather had forced delays in work schedules. Most of the crew had missed Christmas leave but expected time off on the first weekend of the new year so that they could bid their families farewell. Instead, they were ordered to remain on duty and paint the ship. That Sunday morning, when told to turn to and clean the ship in readiness for painting, a number of angry sailors closed the main hatch and sealed themselves below. It took an armed guard from the Royal Naval Barracks to get them off the vessel under arrest. The naval command at Plymouth issued a characteristic warning. "It can be said at once that the word mutiny would be unjustifiable." The *Lucia*'s officers thought otherwise. But under Britain's Naval Discipline Act, mutiny, even if unaccompanied by violence, was punishable by death for the ringleaders and imprisonment for any who joined or failed to suppress it. Such stern punishment would not have sat well with the Labour government's working-class constituency, and it was no doubt the decision of A. V. Alexander, a Socialist First Lord, that mutiny charges were not applied. Four sailors convicted of willful disobedience were dismissed from the navy and jailed.

Things had not ended there. Under pressure from left-wing politicians who preferred to think that the *Lucia*'s officers, not the lower deck, were to blame, Alexander appointed a committee of inquiry, which concluded that "want of tact and consideration on the part of the captain and executive" had caused the incident. Also, petty officers aware of the lower-deck mood had failed to inform their superiors. As a result, an order "ordinarily met with cheerfulness was made the occasion of a concerted refusal of duty." The Board of Admiralty thereupon quashed the punishments, while humiliating the *Lucia*'s captain, executive officer, and boatswain by terminating their appointments and placing them on half pay. Politically, this outcome reinforced the ruling party's reputation for siding with the underdog. But admirals and others foresaw consequences extending beyond the damaged careers of the *Lucia*'s officers. They read in the present Board's lenient attitude toward lower-deck dissidence a prescription for further trouble. And they had ample claim for justification of those fears when only a few months later the news from Invergordon staggered the nation.

Some fresh strain of subversion may have infected sailors of the Royal Navy's Atlantic Fleet when its Second Cruiser Squadron undertook a Baltic cruise that summer. This, at any rate, was the surmise of observers who called attention to the visits that the British ships had made to German ports where radicals instrumental in the 1917–18 naval revolts were still active. Fraternization was allowed. British tars in Hamburg were entertained at the International Seamen's Club, said to be a Communist rendezvous. But what all this probably signified was nothing more alarming than an Englishman's instinct to seek the company of class equals. It certainly implied a class consciousness, which explains why the average British sailor, at least during those years between the wars, identified more comfortably with civilian laborers ashore than with his own ship's officers.

This did not necessarily betoken class hostility nor reflect upon that simple patriotism with which the British navy's lower deck was traditionally and bountifully blessed. Some accounts state than when warships going home from their Baltic cruise passed through the Kiel Canal, radicals at Cuxhaven raised a huge red banner on which was written in white letters "Sailors and Marines—Turn Your Guns on Your Officers." British sailors seeing this appeal are likely to have guffawed. If Britain's warships harbored any political agitators eager to exploit the slightest grievance, they did not constitute a decisive entity. Those who should have known better brought about the trouble that autumn at Invergordon. Neither foreign instigation, antiauthoritarian impulses, nor anything else could have proved more effective in touching off the sailors' fury than the plan of their own national leaders to reduce pay scales and the maladroit manner in which this news got to the Atlantic Fleet.

Like the rest of the industrial world, Britain struggled to cope with the Great Depression. Three weeks after the return of the Second Cruiser Squadron from the Baltic a new coalition government, under the same Socialist Party leader Ramsey MacDonald, faced the task of implementing a royal commission's proposals to save money by drastic economies. The salaries of the fighting forces would not escape the axe. The commission's view was that "no officer or man serving His Majesty has any legal right to a particular rate of pay." A. V. Alexander had warned the cabinet that if pay cuts were ordered, the navy might mutiny. MacDonald was to say that "as far as I can charge my memory," the advice he got from the Board of Admiralty was that the men would loyally accept the cuts provided similar reductions were made in the salaries of other public servants. Whatever the case, Sir Joseph Austen Chamberlain, a sixty-seven-year-old politician of no great distinction, replaced Alexander in the new administration. Chamberlain was embittered because he had wanted not the Admiralty but the post of Foreign Secretary, and he was unaware of his predecessor's apprehensions until too late to have done any good.

Chamberlain subscribed to the general notion that sacrifice must be shared. In 1925 a drop in the cost of living had meant that the 1919 naval pay rates fixed by the Jerram Committee were too high, and they had accordingly been reduced for enlistees thereafter. What the present government intended was that the lower rates be universally applied. For sailors in service in 1919 and those entering before 1925, all of whom presumed that their pay scales were guaranteed to be permanent, the new proposals would mean cuts of up to 25 percent. This could be taken as a breach of contract, but whether Chamberlain realized it is doubtful. Utterly new to the job, he was also probably not as well briefed by his Sea Lords as he should have been.

The question confronting the new head of the Admiralty was how most painlessly to convey his government's decision to the sailors. He favored an immediate fleet order giving out the details but was told that it could not precede the emergency budget statement scheduled for 10 September, when Parliament reassembled after its summer recess. It was decided, however, that naval commanders-in-chief should be alerted to the coming announcement. On 3 September each was sent a telegram "for confidential guidance." That addressed to Sir Michael Hodges, commander of the Atlantic Fleet, did not reach him personally, for he was on furlough and in failing health. The telegram lay in his cabin on the flagship *Nelson* at Portsmouth, awaiting his return. This happened to be a busy week for the Atlantic Fleet because its ships were getting ready to sail for Scotland and begin exercises in the North Sea.

The economy proposals themselves were not unknown. They had been published earlier that summer and were the subject of a pseudonymous letter that appeared in *The Fleet* on 1 September. (Lionel Yexley, still preoccupied with lower-deck morale despite his own poor health, identified the writer as a sailor on the destroyer *Acasta* with the Mediterranean Fleet.) In tone, the letter recalled the memorial sent to Adm. Earl Howe by the Spithead sailors in 1797: "We all sincerely hope that many solemn promises Parliament made to us . . . will not be broken . . . this matter is exercising the minds and discussions of the Lower Deck to the almost exclusion of anything else. . . . In the meantime we are all asking what is going to happen—IF?" Seamen of the Atlantic Fleet were asking themselves the same ominous question as their ships prepared to leave home ports for the north. And many who had read that letter in *The Fleet* were especially absorbed that same week with the popular dailies, which while mostly headlining Britain's financial crisis shared column space with reports of a rebellion in the Chilean navy— over pay cuts.

For what they called "the worst mutiny in the history of South America," some United States diplomats on that continent came close to blaming the British. British officers had trained the Chilean navy. "Did they not teach discipline?" asked the U.S. naval attaché in Santiago. There were other connections. The battleship principally involved, the 30,000-ton *Almirante Latorre,* was British built and had only recently

The central ship in Chile's naval revolt: the 30,000-ton *Almirante Latorre*.
(Ted Stone)

returned to Chile from an extensive refit lasting eighteen months at the Devonport shipyard. During this period the *Lucia,* a mutiny of her own just ahead, had provided the battleship with logistical support. In the opinion of the American military attaché at Santiago, the Chilean crews became infected with communism during their British sojourn. Even the London *Times* presumed that Red agents "under instruction from Moscow and Berlin established contact with the underpaid Chilean crews."

When the mutiny began, the *Almirante Latorre* lay with other vessels off Coquimbo, three hundred miles north of the capital. On the last day of August, while most officers and men were ashore attending a prizefighting tournament, what a Chilean commander afterward described as "a small circle of extremists," including petty officers, huddled among the hydraulic equipment and agreed upon seizing the whole flotilla to dramatize their demand for restoration of the pay cuts. The conspirators included crew members from other ships, notably the forty-year-old, three-funneled armored cruiser *General O'Higgins,* also British-built. Both ships were in mutinous hands by midnight. Minor resistance on the *General O'Higgins* left two wounded. Some destroyers were reluctant to join the revolt until boarding parties from the big ships closed the wardroom hatches and made captives of their officers. Abel Campo, the flag admiral on the *Almirante Latorre,* was locked in his

Air power halts a mutiny: Coquimbo Bay, Chile, September 1931. *(Library of Congress)*

cabin. His clerk, Ernesto Gonzales, one of the ringleaders, replaced him as commander of the flotilla.

Within forty-eight hours the mutiny had spread to Chile's southern naval base at Talcahuano. Unaccountably, the commander there had ordered all officers ashore, in effect surrendering their ships to the rebels. Mutineers also gained control of Talcahuano's naval citadel. There followed a midweek interval of indecision among both the rebel leadership and Santiago's ruling politicians. Adm. Don Arturo Wilson, a veteran naval hero of a nineteenth-century war against Peru, boarded the *Almirante Latorre* and begged the mutineers to see reason: "Your old admiral makes this appeal from the depths of his heart." It did little good. But by then Santiago no longer dithered. A government shake-up had produced a new minister for war, Gen. Carlos Vergarra, an unequivocal hard-liner who sent army troops to retake the naval citadel at Talcahuano and assembled an aerial strike force to end the mutiny off Coquimbo.

It was a motley squadron, formed of Curtiss Falcons, a Junkers, a Vickers Vixen, and other aircraft of old and foreign vintage, commanded by a Chilean air force colonel trained at Langley Field, Virginia, who probably welcomed an opportunity to demonstrate the superiority of bombing planes over battleships. His orders, however, were to avoid direct hits because officers were still on board. Vergarra's planes caught the mutinous flotilla on Sunday morning as it attempted to clear the harbor. The *Almirante Latorre* met them with antiaircraft gunfire, forcing one plane to retire with a damaged radiator. But the Vickers Vixen dropped a three-hundred-pound bomb close enough to the battleship to shower her people with spray and shrapnel. That was enough for the destroyer crews, half of whom had remained loyal anyway. They overcame the mutinous faction and freed their officers, and by the next morning the mutiny had also collapsed on the big ships. But none of the death sentences awaiting Gonzales and his henchmen would be carried out. A reformist government took power and granted the ringleaders general amnesty while a number of their officers, charged with laxity or secret sympathy for the mutineers, were reprimanded, dismissed, or forced into retirement.

The Chilean mutiny that first week in September 1931 was at first reported in the British press as a typical South American "comic opera" episode. Then coverage grew more serious. Men of the Atlantic Fleet, on the point of leaving their home ports of Portsmouth, Devonport, and Chatham for the north, read in the *Daily Herald:* "Planes Bomb Mutinous Fleet." And before another week had passed, action taken by those same sailors would produce headlines telling startled Britons of rebellion within their own cherished navy.

Fourteen

INVERGORDON

hen Adm. Sir Michael Hodges returned from leave to his flagship *Nelson* on 7 September 1931, he at once came down with pleurisy and was rushed ashore to the naval hospital at Portsmouth. Control of the Atlantic Fleet passed to his senior aide, Rear Adm. Wilfred Tomkinson, who commanded the battle cruiser *Hood,* at 42,000 tons the world's largest warship. Tomkinson and his ships were off England's east coast, heading north, when on the tenth of the month Britain's chancellor of the exchequer announced his emergency budget, which included deep reductions in unemployment benefits, decreases in police and teachers' salaries and pensions, and cuts in pay scales for the armed services—a fiscal retrenchment made still more depressing by the higher duties to be imposed on alcohol and tobacco.

Tomkinson doubtless knew about it from the BBC that same evening—ships' wardrooms had radio sets, but not the crews' quarters. And the admiral is likely to have heard rumors of pay cuts in the offing. But he had no plan ready for gently breaking the news to his people, perhaps because of the additional work and thought required of him by his unexpected assumption of responsibility for the whole fleet and its impending exercises. The Admiralty's signal of "confidential guidance" in this matter might properly have jogged his attention. But it was still in the office of Admiral Hodges's chief of staff on HMS *Nelson,* which had yet to leave Portsmouth harbor. An Admiralty letter dated 10 September, intended for distribution to all ships, might have been even more useful toward bracing Tomkinson's crews for the blow. It sought to explain the purpose of the pay cuts and appealed for the men's understanding and cooperation. (Army and air force heads sent similar letters to their commands.) But the Admiralty's letter did not get to Tomkinson right away. As it was directed to the commander-in-chief, Atlantic Fleet, it followed the earlier telegram by going to the battleship *Nelson*. Far to the north, on the afternoon of Friday the eleventh, Tomkinson's ships entered Cromarty Firth on the eastern coast of the Scottish Highlands—the *Hood, Rodney, Warspite, Malaya, Repulse, Valiant, Adventure, York, Dorsetshire, Norfolk,* and *Exeter,* names already distinguished in a past war, several to gain luster or be mourned in another less than a decade away. Once the ships were attached to their buoys off Invergordon, parties went ashore for mail and newspapers. Many returned frowning with puzzlement or anxiety.

But there were some twelve thousand lower-deck personnel in the Atlantic Fleet. Coming from civilian sources ashore without confirmation from their own trusted superiors, the news took time to sink in. The next day passed with no trouble to speak of. According to Len Wincott, an able seaman on the cruiser *Norfolk,* when the men turned in that night, "there was nothing further from our minds than mutiny." While Wincott's veracity on certain points would be seriously questioned, those weekend hours do seem to have provided a good opportunity for Admiral Tomkinson to have tactfully alerted his men. By all accounts, he sympathized with them, his feelings fostering later speculation that he might have decided to let events take their course instead of intervening. Of somewhat short stature, Tomkinson was a quiet-mannered officer who had specialized in torpedoes and earned a gold medal for rescuing a sailor from drowning. He had commanded the *Hood* for only two months and was not well known outside that vessel. When taking over as commander-in-chief from the hospitalized Hodges and briefing himself hurriedly on preparations for the North Sea war games, Admiral Tomkinson appears to have been left pretty much on his own.

Details of the pay cuts were promulgated in an Admiralty Fleet Order. It reached Admiral Tomkinson that same Saturday night and was posted on ships' notice boards the next morning. Able Seaman Wincott, like others aboard the *Norfolk,* saw it on his way to breakfast. He later recalled it as a complicated sixteen-page document and its impact "one of complete shock." Wincott heard that the men would meet at the seamen's canteen in Invergordon. "I felt I must go and try my hand at speechmaking." What influence Wincott and Fred Copeman, a politically minded shipmate on the *Norfolk,* exerted throughout the unrest would become a matter of debate. There was no professional

Newspapers tell the British of their sailors' discontent. *(Library of Congress)*

agitation, no rebellious conspiracy. If uttered at all, the word mutiny probably arose in reference to the recent events in Chile. This is not to say that some of the Devonport contingent who had formed friendships with Chilean sailors during the *Almirante Latorre*'s prolonged visit did not indulge in wild talk of following their example. But what was most evident in the crowded canteen that Sunday afternoon, as sailors smoked and drank—luxuries expected to soon cost more—or sprang upon chairs with heated calls for a work stoppage, was a spontaneous and forseeable response to the news, tactlessly imparted, that their pay would be docked and their families thus exposed to further hardship.

The *Nelson* arrived about then, putting Tomkinson in possession, belatedly, of the Admiralty's earlier and confidential messages. He had also some inkling of what was under way ashore in the canteen but took no positive steps to intervene. Some activity on the *Warspite*, presumably aimed at assembling a shore patrol to break up the meeting, is unlikely to have been at Tomkinson's direction. In any event, the canteen emptied at a decent hour, some of the men singing as they strolled back to their ships. The next morning Tomkinson informed the Admiralty of "a slight disturbance in the Royal Naval Canteen," to which he attached "no importance from a general disciplinary point of view." That same fore-noon he told all ships' captains to read to their people portions of the Admiralty's letter. In 1925, when pay scales were pegged to a drop in the cost of living, "men already in service were nevertheless allowed to retain the advantages of the existing higher rates." In the present eco-nomic crisis "it is impossible to permit this concession to continue." According to a lieutenant commander on the *Hood*, the letter of "explana-tion" exacerbated rather than tempered the men's anger. At that point nothing could have persuaded them that the Board of Admiralty had not betrayed them.

On board the *Hood* that Monday evening Tomkinson dined with his ships' commanders. Some firm rapport with the lower deck might have been more to the admiral's advantage, but the opportunity for securing this had flown. It was not too late, however, for him to call off the North Sea maneuvers, on which the first of his ships were scheduled to sail at daybreak. Confronting the three admirals and ten captains at his table, Tomkinson probably invited and would certainly have welcomed their counsel. But apparently Adm. E. A. Astley-Rushton, who flew his flag on the cruiser *Dorsetshire*, recommended that he cancel operations. And Astley-Rushton was perhaps not the best source of advice—only one day junior to Tomkinson in rank and with more command experi-ence, he is said to have resented the other's authority.

Meanwhile, in the mist-wreathed little town of Invergordon, the sailors were holding another meeting. About three hundred men crowded the naval canteen and heard more agreement then dissent to stop work as a protest against the pay cuts. The lieutenant of a shore patrol who forced his way into the canteen and tried to stop the speech making was nonviolently but firmly thrust back outside. Still more

The flagship of a troubled rear admiral: the mighty battle cruiser *Hood*.
(Imperial War Museum, London)

seamen thronged a soccer field adjacent to the canteen, and Able Seaman Copeman of the *Norfolk* was among the speakers who addressed them from the roof of the pavilion. Unity was a pervasive theme, to halt the taunts exchanged between the men who were arguing over whose ship most contained the fortitude needed to down tools. Back on board, the sailors continued their discourse. Lower-deck meetings on the *Nelson, Repulse,* and *Valiant* lasted until well after midnight. Younger ratings whose pay was little affected played no part and for safety's sake held their peace.

Admiral Tomkinson was not aware of everything taking place. And such information as he possessed might well have left him at considerable loss as to how best to proceed. It was the belief of at least Adm. Sir Reginald Tyrwhitt, a veteran of Jutland, that "Tomkinson made a bloody balls of it all through sheer inactivity." There is, though, another line of thought. With no particular devotion to the new head of the Admiralty and his triumvirate of elderly admirals, a bureaucratic body he held accountable for the fleet's agitation, Tomkinson may have simply decided to take the path of least resistance. Dutifully he signaled White-hall at 1:45 A.M.: "I am of the opinion that it may be difficult to get the ships to sea for practice this morning."

At 6:30 the battle cruiser *Repulse* ventured out on schedule, to the accompaniment of boos from the other ships. Half an hour later the crew of HMS *Nelson* listened respectfully to their captain until he made some hapless remark about their wives' having to take in washing. Perhaps it was an attempt at jocularity or even a caustic slap at the Board of Admiralty. Whatever their intent, his words were ill-chosen and touched off an angry muttering, and he hurried back to his cabin, thereafter to be seldom seen outside of it. From the cruiser *Norfolk,* as Able Seaman Wincott remembered, not all the other ships were visible in the murk of a Scottish morning, but loud cheers echoed across the firth from one vessel to another. Wincott's messmate Copeman described how things "worked out simply. Go on the forecastle. No one else can get there. The hatches from the seamen's mess deck lead directly to the forecastle. If the marines are with you no one can do anything about it." Such a clear-cut strategy may not have been in everyone's mind, but in one warship after another that Tuesday morning orders to work were disobeyed.

On the *Valiant,* which should have sailed at eight, only petty officers and a few leading seamen turned out when piped for duty. Lt. Comdr. Charles Drage was among a group of officers who tried to raise the anchor by themselves. Three years earlier Drage had delivered a lecture at the Military Staff College entitled "Some Modern Mutinies." At Invergordon the spectacle of determined sailors from his own lower deck who "flooded on to the forecastle and sat on the cable, just like that," effectively immobilizing the 35,000-ton battleship, enriched his knowledge of the subject.

The *Repulse* and two other ships at sea were recalled. At 9:30 Tomkinson officially canceled the exercises and so informed the Admiralty. At about noon their lordships signaled their approval but directed that the men should be given to understand that sacrifices were required from everybody: "Unless these are cheerfully accepted the financial recovery of the country will be impossible." The day advanced without any signs of overt hostility. "The attitude of all ratings towards their officers is correct," Tomkinson assured the Admiralty. When ships' bands played the national anthem, striking sailors jumped to attention. Men on the *Rodney* hauled a piano from the recreation room to the forecastle, not so much for entertainment as to let other crews know by continued playing that the work stoppage went ahead. The strikers persuaded the cooks to carry on working so that meals could be served as usual.

As at The Nore and Spithead so long ago, all the sailors refusing duty at Invergordon would have declared themselves fundamentally

HMS *Norfolk*. The captain's clerk typed out a statement of grievances dictated by "We, the loyal subjects of His Majesty. . . ." *(Imperial War Museum, London)*

patriotic—probably even Len Wincott, whose subsequently self-proclaimed animus against the officer class was more of a post-mutiny development. He had a hand in composing a statement of grievances, which the captain's clerk on the *Norfolk* typed out, and it began, "We, the loyal subjects of His Majesty, The King, do hereby present to our Lords Commissioners of the Admiralty, our earnest representations. . . ." Still, it emphasized solidarity: "We are resolved to remain as one unit, refusing to sail under the new rates of pay." Such action had been made necessary to prevent "tragedy, poverty and immorality amongst the families of the Lower Deck." This document accompanied others of similar nature collected for the fleet's chief of staff, Rear Adm. R. M. Colvin, to take to London. He set out at 1 P.M., waving cheerfully from his launch.

Half an hour later Tomkinson signaled the Admiralty that until the men were promised a revision of those pay cuts, "discipline in the Atlantic Fleet will not be restored and in my opinion may further deteriorate." This appeared not to impress the Board, which waited six hours before replying that while representation of hardship would be considered, ships' companies in the meantime must be left in no doubt of their lordships' expectation that they "will uphold the tradition of the service by loyally carrying out their duty." If, as seems likely, Tomkinson's messages to the Board were not merely to keep it informed but to seek its positive direction so that he alone would not have to bear responsibility for the consequences, the Admiralty failed to accommodate him. Instead, it urged that the fleet exercises be quickly resumed and in lengthly detail attempted to minimize the impact of the cuts on the sailors and demonstrate that they were not being singled out: "Reductions on a precisely similar basis are to be put into effect in the Army and Air Force." The difference, as the Board should have known, was that the cuts fell upon almost 75 percent of naval personnel, whereas only about one-third of the army's were affected and still fewer in the Royal Air Force.

In its first statement to the news media on the events in Cromarty Firth, the Board of Admiralty appeared to distance itself from Tomkinson's decision to cancel the fleet exercises. Then, as if in afterthought or at somebody's prodding, it assumed its share of responsibility with a second announcement that same evening, stating that it approved of the exercises' being "temporarily suspended." The next morning's headlines to this effect were disquieting enough, but in keeping with officialdom's implied wish, newspapers generally avoided the word that had sprung to most minds. They employed the Admiralty's less upsetting choice, "unrest." A notable exception was the conservative *Morning Post,* which while editorially opposing the sailors' course gave euphemism short shrift: "To use plain language, which is not fashionable nowadays, [the lower ratings] committed a mutiny."

Crowds had gathered on previous nights in Whitehall to enjoy the unprecedented spectacle of government buildings floodlit for the centennial of Faraday's electromagnetic discoveries. But there was more gloom than celebration in the halls of the Admiralty that Wednesday morning as the Sea Lords met to deal with the crisis at Invergordon. It had dawned on Austen Chamberlain that "my caretaker's job was going suddenly to become a centre of danger and interest." Perhaps the caliber of the admirals about him did not encourage the First Lord, for they had brought to their short-term bureaucratic posts little humor or imagination and scarcely any of the foresight and understanding now so urgently required of them. Perhaps recalling how speedily bombing planes had ended the Chilean mutiny, one of them suggested that artillery be hauled up the hills around Cromarty Firth to threaten the mutineers into submission. Something of the sort was evidently considered. Admiral Colvin had arrived in London by air from Scotland and gave his opinion that the fleet would not budge without some concession on the pay cuts. But when Chamberlain took him before an eleven o'clock cabinet meeting, they found considerable willingness among certain officials to use force rather than yield to mutinous demands. According to leaked information in the American press, these hardliners included J. H. Thomas, Dominions Secretary and Minister for Unemployment, who wanted to "make an example" of the dissident sailors instead of allowing them to "sovietize the British Navy."

A "most immediate" telegram from Admiral Tomkinson warned that without favorable word from the Admiralty, "the situation will get entirely out of control." (Some of his own crew on the *Hood* had joined in the mutiny.) A still more disturbing message followed. Aboard some ships men were massing on their forecastles. Crews exchanged cheers as if egging one another on. The next step might be unrestricted traffic between rebellious vessels and acts of sabotage. The tone of these signals was exaggerated, perhaps intentionally so. Still blaming his superiors for the whole mess, Tomkinson may have succumbed to a notion that overheated rhetoric would compel them to prompt and ameliorative action. On the ships themselves the sailors' wrath had taken no perilous turn. Even when Admiral Astley-Rushton toured his cruisers—in a picket boat manned by petty officers—and lectured the crews with stern profanities, no one booed him. They simply wandered off out of earshot. (He seems not, however, to have boarded the *Adventure,* being turned back by jeers from the men lining the rail.) The *Norfolk*'s captain, "a broken man," had already pleaded with his people to return to duty, and although none of them did, some went out of their way to console him with expressions of sympathy and regret.

The Admiralty concluded, and impressed upon the cabinet, that one order the Invergordon men were sure to obey was to return to their home ports. Chamberlain announced in Parliament that measures would be taken to help the men with families most likely to suffer from the pay cuts. And to conduct personal investigations of such hardship cases was the reason given out for the Admiralty's order recalling the Atlantic Fleet from the north that same afternoon. Moreover, that the sailors' behavior thus far would go unpunished was indicated in the stipulation that "any further refusals to carry out orders will be dealt with under the Naval Discipline Act."

Yet it was following the government's decision to bring the ships home that the risk of violence sharply increased. Many sailors feared arrest the moment they docked. Others were unwilling to quit their strike merely on the pledge of an investigation into hardship cases. Not everybody felt this way, and the mess decks rang with arguments that here and there erupted into fistfights. Such signs of dissension among the men emboldened the officers into taking a tougher line. A dozen hours earlier in his daily report, the *Nelson*'s captain had described how his people "collected in a tight, compact, silent and respectful body around and on the port bower cable and cableholder making it impossible to weigh anchor without using force. To have enforced this order would have been a most unspeakable folly. We are not at war. . . ." That was yesterday. Now he and the commander of the *Hood* let it be known that to get their ships to sea they were prepared to part the anchor cables, regardless of the physical danger to crew members rooted stubbornly to the foredeck. On the *Valiant,* when a similarly defiant crowd refused to disperse, the captain ordered his marines to remove them by gunfire if necessary. Only then did hundreds of men drift aft, where they congregated to hear him guarantee that when they reached home port they would not be treated as mutineers.

Admiral Tomkinson had signaled London that although sailing was due to start at 9:30 P.M., "I am not at all sure that all ships will leave." Faced with continued rebellion, the government might well have resorted to military force, for which plans had been secretly drafted. But fleet command now regained some initiative. Many of the men still suspected that the business of returning south was a trick, but as even Len Wincott acknowledged, it was a risk that had to be taken. Led by the *Hood,* the Atlantic Fleet finally put to sea. On Friday night all ships were home, the *Repulse, Valiant,* and *York* at Chatham; the *Rodney, Malaya, Dorsetshire, Norfolk,* and *Exeter* at Devonport; and the *Nelson, Hood,* and *Warspite* at Portsmouth, their crews reading with mixed feelings that what they had done off Invergordon had so shaken overseas faith in Britain's stability as to stimulate an international flight from the pound.

Chamberlain meanwhile had made it official. "The past is past," he told the House of Commons. The "disturbance" at Invergordon should be forgotten. There would be no penalties. Nor would there be a formal inquiry. But behind the scenes, alarm grew rather than abated because of reports or rumors of fresh and more determined mutinous conspiracy. Seamen coming ashore at Devonport and nearby Plymouth had been quickly buttonholed by agents of MI5 and Naval Intelligence, not to mention local detectives—altogether a more formidable spy force than the single London magistrate who, for the same purpose of tracing foreign agitation, had sought to ingratiate himself with Spithead's sailors in 1797. And as on that earlier occasion, tipsy or mischievous ratings fed the agents a good deal of lurid nonsense.

Even so, discontent still festered within the Atlantic Fleet. The ships' return to home ports offered Tomkinson further opportunity to do something, perhaps to establish a more personal contact with his aggrieved people. But he was never, in his own words, "a popularity Jack with the Lower Deck. Those who are, or aspire to be, with very few exceptions have done a great deal of harm to discipline generally." At the same time, Tomkinson claimed to have made more friends among the inferior ranks than had most officers. If true, this claim applied to a far earlier day. Given the short time he had been with the Atlantic Fleet, not even a "popularity Jack" could have won himself much of an affinity below decks. At any rate, in keeping with his character, Tomkinson seems not to have made any great effort.

But of these deficiencies of command, such as they were, nothing was publicly known. Other causes were to blame for the continued dissatisfaction within the Atlantic Fleet, whose sailors found themselves close to stigmatized because of the difference between their reactions to the pay cuts and those of the other combat branches. For instance, seamen on the China station and in the Mediterranean were reported to have received the news of the cuts "philosophically." (On the North American station, unrest aboard the light cruiser *Delhi,* which had previously been briefly mutinous in 1919, forced the cancellation of a scheduled visit to New York.) There was some grumbling among the soldiers, but as one Aldershot colonel disdainfully remarked, "The Army does not follow the example of the Atlantic Fleet." Little wonder that intelligence agents, if not the general public, convinced themselves that this fleet, particularly those of its ships and crews based at reputedly radical Devonport, was prone to a specific form of subversion.

Forming the basis for secret reports to the cabinet from MI5 and the Director of Naval Intelligence, the new talk of an uprising at the home ports helped scare the government into granting the objectives of the original mutiny. Those reports described the lower deck of the Atlantic Fleet as thoroughly organized under Communist influence and determined to resist the pay cuts. Even the officers, wrote the cabinet secretary in his diary, "considered it essential to limit the cuts." And by then so did Austen Chamberlain, who was "prepared to tell the cabinet that I could not remain First Lord unless they granted our requests." The government hastily "accepted my view," and on 21 September, less than a week from the beginning of the sailors' strike, it authorized his Board of Admiralty to restrict the cuts to a maximum of 10 percent.

Officially, no one was punished for the mutiny at Invergordon. But the Admiralty, courting further charges of pledge breaking, set about purging the fleet of alleged undesirables, some four hundred of whose names were duly supplied to MI5 by Naval Intelligence. Wincott and Copeman were among thirty-six seamen taken from their ships and confined to the Naval Barracks at Devonport on a "disciplinary course" they likened to penal servitude. Perhaps significantly, they were not released and discharged from the service, to thereupon give their version of events, until after the national elections held in October. It was to be expected that Wincott would assert that the government, not the sailors, was responsible for the mutiny. But there were officers who privately agreed with him, including Admiral Tomkinson, who uttered, "The men had no other course than the one they took," realizing with chagrin that he was being made a scapegoat for the whole affair.

Blame had not attached itself to him right away. Tomkinson had no reason to fear that he had fallen from the Admiralty's grace. It had initially approved his cancellation of fleet exercises, and after the mutiny he was sent on a cruise to the West Indies in command of battle cruisers. Moreover, Chamberlain resigned as First Lord within two months of the mutiny and accepted partial blame for it—"We did not use all the sources of information at our disposal and did not show . . . foresight." Also, a discreet investigation by Tomkinson's successor in command of the Atlantic Fleet deemed the Admiralty culpable and the men's actions excusable. But this view did not sit well with a new Board of Admiralty. It was all Tomkinson's fault. Events might have taken a better turn had he acted on the Admiralty's telegram of 3 September (this criticism indicating real or pretended ignorance of the fact that it had reached him four days late). He should have been alerted by the shore meetings, ordered the canteen closed, and addressed the men in person.

At least two members of the Board under Austen Chamberlain were unable to escape serious damage to their careers, while seven captains of the Atlantic Fleet lost their commands. But the principal victim was Admiral Tomkinson. Five months after the mutiny, when about to dine one evening at Goverment House in Trinidad, he was mortified to hear over the radio that his new appointment had been cut short. A "personal and confidential" letter arrived belatedly, conveying the Admiralty's official explanation: "Their Lordships are unable to relieve you of responsibility for a serious error of judgement in omitting to take any decided action . . . when dissatisfaction [at Invergordon] had begun to show." The "failure of discipline"—their euphemism for mutiny—would in all probability not have occurred "if the situation had been well handled . . . instead of being allowed to drift."

Tomkinson vented his bitterness in letters to his friends. He had been "definitely censured" while refused any chance of defending himself, "treated in a very unfair and underhanded manner." He would "take steps" to let the Admiralty know how he felt. But there was little he could do. And perhaps he soon suspected that the Admiralty's reprimand, though directed at himself, resulted from its irritation with some of his stalwart allies, who pursued a vendetta of their own with the Board by harassing it for an inquiry into his case in full knowledge that their Lordships wished to let the matter drop. Subsequently, only a veiled threat put forth in a letter from the new First Lord silenced them. Public confidence in the navy had been restored and sympathy improved between the Admiralty and naval personnel: "A great responsibility will rest on anyone who now takes steps to disturb these relations by controversy." A more candid letter to Tomkinson's presumably well-meaning friends warned that such steps would do the admiral more harm than good.

As things were, Tomkinson's naval career was irreparably damaged. After three years on half-pay he was placed on the retired list. His Second World War service was mostly confined to managing ships in the Bristol Channel. His death in 1971 at the age of ninety-three briefly revived the debate over the Invergordon mutiny, to which Len Wincott made his proletarian contribution in a letter to the *Times* that bore a Moscow postbox address. After the mutiny Wincott had joined the Communist Party (so had his messmate Fred Copeman) and finally settled in the Soviet Union, to become an effective propagandist. Wincott's old ship *Norfolk,* like others of Invergordon memory, acquitted herself well in the Second World War, taking part in the pursuit of the *Bismarck* along with the battleship *Repulse,* later sunk by Japanese torpedo-bombers in the China Sea, and the *Rodney* and *Dorsetshire,* the latter having the honor of finishing off the *Bismarck* with two torpedoes. And that German battleship's most notable victim was Admiral Tomkinson's short-lived command, the mighty *Hood,* her magazines exploding under shellfire and sending her to the bottom of the Greenland Sea with all but three of her entire complement.

Fifteen

◢

PORT CHICAGO

*T*he mutiny in Cromarty Firth occurred near the close of that short period separating the cease-fire of one European war and the gathering clouds of another. Disarmament treaties recently signed put a brake on naval expansion. Totalitarian governments were not yet recognized as overt international threats. Domestic affairs preoccupied Mussolini's Italy. The militant bloc headed by Adolf Hitler in the German Reichstag was still a minority. In Western Europe and the New World, social confusion characterized this span of hardly more than a dozen years as postwar fiscal boom rapidly ended in a slump. Except perhaps for a growing American perception of Japan as a future foe, nations tended not to fear one another as much as they did internal strife and economic collapse. If the major industrial powers apprehended any danger at all from beyond their respective frontiers it was a common one of ideological subversion, the source Soviet Russia. The British Empire's first line of defense was its naval squadrons scattered around the globe. They feared no direct onslaught. A surprise attack upon the navy of a nation at peace was scarcely imaginable and would remain so until Pearl Harbor, a decade or more ahead. Naval vulnerability could, however, be defined in other terms. Especially after Invergordon, many in Britain felt that their Royal Navy had become a target for covert assaults directed from Moscow.

Since the tactics employed were understood to be contingent upon the sailors' morale, Britain's naval hierarchy frowned upon lower-deck expressions of discontent as tending to play into insidious hands. They had, therefore, to be discouraged. In this connection, some thought sterner command the only answer. "For the last four or five years," wrote Adm. Sir Walter Cowan within a fortnight of the Invergordon crisis, "[The Admiralty] have failed to check a growing looseness of discipline." Cowan, whose earlier brushes with lower-deck disaffection may not have improved his reasoning for dealing with the problem, was by this time chief naval aide to King George V. "As regards the men, there has been far too much talk of increased privileges, comfort, food, etc., and too little of achievement and efficiency." Some who thought likewise wondered why their Lordships at Whitehall had not resigned in toto when the government ruled out reprisals against Invergordon's mutineers. "The habit of grousing," wrote Admiral Tyrwhitt to the Board, "has become the fashion and any grievance is better than none."

A drive was duly mounted against individuals or organizations suspected of exploiting those grievances to generate open revolt. Scotland Yard arrested the head of a small left-wing publishing house for trying to "seduce persons serving in H. M. Forces from their duty and allegiance to His Majesty and to incite and stir up such persons to commit acts of mutiny." Three civilians seized in Portsmouth were reminded that the Incitement to Mutiny Act of 1797, under which they were held, had once imposed the death sentence, later changed to transportation for life in colonial penal settlements, and that it could still put them permanently behind bars. This trio had tried to work up a mutiny on HMS *Warspite* and had accosted a telegraphist, promising, in return for his cooperation, a continued career at that trade in Russia—hardly an irresistible inducement, and the sailor had instead notified his commanding officer, who advised him to string the men along. These small-time efforts to subvert were ineffectual, but authorities were not amused by the testimony, which told of secret meetings in railway station lavatories, contacts identifiable from prominently displayed yellow breast-pocket handkerchiefs, and coded telegrams—"Come at once, Mother ill" meant money would be found and "Bottle of fizz" that the deal was off. A later discovery by MI5 and Naval Intelligence that pamphlets smuggled into the Mediterranean Fleet contained "a gross incitement to mutiny" heightened the belief that a genuine Bolshevik campaign to undermine British naval strength was in progress.

The Netherlands government had cause for similar concern about its naval security, especially after the mutiny on the *De Zeven Provincien* in 1933. The timing of this event supplies naval history with three major mutinies—befalling the Chilean, British, and Dutch navies—one after another, each with the same immediate cause, resistance to pay cuts, and all arising from the common scourge of world economic depression.

A second mutiny quelled by air power. The battleship *De Zeven Provincien,* February 1933. *(The Illustrated London News)*

The 6,500-ton twin-funneled battleship was based in the Netherlands East Indies, a once-productive region then suffering from a decline in exports. Sailors' pay had been reduced by 10 percent. Protest meetings followed, ashore at Surabaja and on the ships. The mood below decks grew uglier when rumors spread of even larger cuts ahead, in keeping with those just ruled for the civil service. Trouble first broke out on board the cruiser *Java.* Not until Dutch colonial troops took off the most dissident members of her crew was the ship able to sail as scheduled. But word of the incident reached the *De Zeven Provincien,* at a solitary station off the northwestern tip of Sumatra, and on the night of Saturday, 4 February, while their captain relaxed ashore in the port of Uleelheue, the most determined of the ship's mixed European and Javanese people decided to act.

It was afterward said that the film *The Battleship Potemkin* had influenced some of them. It is still more likely that they remembered the outcome of the Invergordon mutiny as a victory for British mutineers. Also, perhaps they had little to fear from the ship's commander, Captain Eikeboom—he had reacted to previous warnings of dissatisfaction below decks with apparent indifference. Even when notified by messenger of a genuinely serious uprising on his ship, the captain, enjoying himself at a party in the Afjeh Club, merely sent back a note to his first lieutenant, telling him to keep a particularly close eye on the native Javanese, who comprised more than half the lower-deck strength of 228 men. Such seeming unconcern may have disgusted the first lieutenant, for within minutes after crew members had hauled in the boarding ladder and broken out the ship's guns, he took to a raft with the announced intention of informing the captain to his face that the *De Zeven Provincien* was in a state of mutiny.

The ship's remaining fourteen officers gathered on the captain's bridge. The younger among them favored firing on the mutineers. Seniors overruled them, but a junior lieutenant headed for the wireless shack, intending to signal the fleet commander at Surabaja. A corporal, Dutch like himself, drove him back, waving a pistol. Though begun chiefly among the native Javanese, the revolt was quickly augmented by Dutch messmates. The mutineers made their plan public by means of the ship's wireless. It was to make for Surabaja and demand restoration of the pay cuts and freedom for the *Java*'s jailed dissidents. With any loyalists safely locked up, the mutineers took over the engine room and got up steam in the Yarrow boilers, and the ship proceeded slowly down the western coast of Sumatra.

The first lieutenant, meanwhile, had blurted his news to Captain Eikeboom ashore. Eikeboom promptly boarded the East Indies Government steamer *Aldebaran* with a party of armed infantrymen and set out after his runaway vessel. There was little that the *Aldebaran*, an 830-ton craft with a complement of forty-five men, could do other than follow in the battleship's wake and keep naval headquarters at Surabaja hourly informed of her position. But this proved essential for the deployment of a task force consisting of the *Java*, two destroyers, two submarines, and three Dornier flying-boats, assembled at Batavia (Djakarta) and held in readiness to halt the *De Zeven Provincien* as she approached the Sunda Strait.

To settle this sailors' revolt of their own, authorities in The Hague could avail themselves of two recent object lessons. Chile's naval mutiny had been crushed by force, Britain's had ended in appeasement. The Dutch followed Chile's example, a decision probably influenced by growing alarm over the spread of radical propaganda. Amsterdam socialists were about to subsidize performances of a banned play, *Mutiny at Cattaro*, based on the Austro-Hungarian episode in 1918. Pamphlets reported to be circulating at home ports urged sailors to form councils on the Soviet model. Orders from the Netherlands government to its distant colony were, therefore, uncompromising, and the result a brief but brutal encounter off the Sunda Strait. With the *Aldebaran* following at a safe distance, the *De Zeven Provincien* had voyaged along the coast for four days before one of the flying boats sighted her. The *Java* was on the scene and radioed for the mutineers to surrender unconditionally. In response, they professed peaceful intentions, a wish for fairness. There was no further exchange. The Dorniers were overhead.

A 100-pound bomb struck the *De Zeven Provincien*'s port top deck, blowing it and a funnel to fragments and killing eighteen men, mostly Javanese. All that remained for the *Java* and her consorts to do was haul wounded seamen out of the water. And at home the government set about applying stern justice with an even hand. After courts-martial that dragged on for more than a year not only did forty convicted mutineers go to jail, but several of the *De Zeven Provincien*'s officers were judged guilty of dereliction, and they included Captain Eikeboom, sentenced to four months' imprisonment and dismissal from the navy.

That same year in Great Britain the rumors and intermittent evidence of Red plots to weaken the national defense had produced the Incitement to Disaffection Bill. This was an extension or reinforcement of the Incitement to Mutiny Act of 1797, adopted out of a similar uneasiness over foreign subversion, and it carried a maximum penalty of life imprisonment. Such legislation may have helped stave off Communist infiltration but did little to restore British lower-deck morale, still a fragile quantity eight months after Invergordon when the Admiralty's "Notes On Dealing With Insubordination" directed that at any sign of discontent likely to escalate into mutiny "the action of all officers must be such as to indicate unmistakeably that they intend to retain or regain control and to uphold discipline." The use of force could not be ruled out, with "shooting to kill," of course, to be regarded only as a last resort. Fortunately, the Invergordon crisis had caused many captains to take a greater interest in the problems of the lower deck. Certain members of the Board of Admiralty themselves paid visits to ships and shore establishments. But there persisted too inadequate an appreciation of the realities of lower-deck life, and the continued hesitation to redress grievances appears to have reflected a fear of encouraging unionist sailors to flout traditional authority. If such was the case, this fear too was a legacy of Invergordon, no carefully calculated mutiny, yet one creating a spontaneous unity that had confounded admirals, defied the cabinet, and challenged the Crown.

The same sort of alarm was to be found in the United States, where in 1934 the House Un-American Activities Committee listened soberly to stories of agents' boarding United States warships as sightseers and smuggling inflammatory propaganda into the sailors' quarters, and of pretty girls' dating enlisted men to seduce them from their proper allegiance. The effort to subvert the United States Navy was, by these accounts, better organized than heretofore. One navy commander testified, "No matter where the fleet may go we find, usually, that the agitators had arrived ahead of it." Another officer described how San Francisco Communists sought to "cultivate men from ships of the fleet" by entertaining them at parties. A group of sailors from the dreadnought *Pennsylvania* and other ships then at San Francisco were picked up on Market Street and taken by taxi to an address on Haight Street where, after being presumably tranquilized by drink, card games, and an improbable "eleven-year-old tap dancer," were plied with pacifist talk. According to the assistant secretary of the navy, Col. Henry L. Roosevelt, "a great deal of undercover propaganda is carried on in nearly every port of call of Navy ships, in navy yard towns, and in some cases on the ships themselves."

Congress considered a bill "To Punish for Exerting Mutinous Influence upon the Army and the Navy." Its proponents emphasized that propaganda activity among civilians would not be affected. The purpose was to "insulate against disloyalty" sailors and soldiers who "by their own voluntary enlistment [form] a class distinct from any other in the nation." If their minds were turned into "instant debating societies," if they were perniciously conditioned to question orders, then the country's defense expenditures would go to waste; indeed, "we might be building up and training a Frankenstein to destroy our Government." But not even grave reminders that "the revolutions in Russia and Germany began in their respective navies" were enough to quiet opponents of the bill, who called it un-American itself, a threat to constitutional freedoms and an insult to the nation's servicemen. Existing laws against conspiracy and sedition were sufficient protection against any attempted subversion of the fighting forces, efforts that in any event were quite evidently proving futile. In the joint view of minority members on the House Military Affairs Committee, "This bill, then, proposes to use a twelve-inch gun to kill a gnat." It failed to pass, but identical legislation was proposed four years later when, according to FBI exchanges with Naval Intelligence, the Communist party was stepping up efforts to radicalize American service personnel, with "special concentration within the National Guard and the Naval forces."

By that time, while western democracies in general clung to the suspicion that domestic agents controlled by Moscow tampered with their men in uniform, they were also obliged to consider the danger posed by other totalitarian regimes, principally Germany's. Hitler had become chancellor one week before the naval mutiny in the Netherlands East Indies and soon made known his intentions: reintroducing compulsory military service, creating a new German air force, and resuscitating the German navy—all in defiance of the Versailles peace treaty. Because of the resultant spurt of war preparations and attendant anxieties, lower-deck complaints tended to dwindle. But those in positions of authority had not forgotten concerns about morale. Britain had been at war with Germany scarcely three months when Churchill, First Lord of the Admiralty, coupled a decision that the navy would forgo pause to celebrate the Christmas holiday with an admonition that "every effort should be made to ease the strain upon the destroyer crews." Smooth arrangements at Devonport provided the men of the flotillas coming in from patrols with immediate relief—"two or three days rest in port brings them round in wonderful manner," Churchill wrote. Everything should be done "with the intention of comforting those crews to the utmost extent operations permit."

Especially for vessels escorting merchant shipping, the tense or hectic nature of those operations kept dutiful sailors so on their toes they had little disposition or opportunity to brood or gripe. Weeks of inaction at sea during wartime can be vastly different from periods of idleness and confinement in port. Under both conditions sailors become bored. Under the latter, as we have seen, their mood may turn restless and ugly. But at sea the extreme vigilance required of wartime crews on convoy duty and their ever-present sense of imminent peril can rob boredom of its baneful potential or banish it completely. For crews on ships of every class, in every navy of the Second World War's principal belligerents, actual clashes with the foe were apt to occur more frequently than in previous conflicts. As many British destroyers were sunk during the first two years of Hitler's war as were lost throughout the entire fifty months of the 1914–18 hostilities.

After Pearl Harbor, the United States Navy was just as grimly busy. Not since the Barbary Wars and the War of 1812 did it voyage so extensively and fight so many battles. And the fact that feelings of dissatisfaction with lower-deck life invariably dissolve in the heat of combat was demonstrated time and again. Sullen thoughts vanish as self-preservation, past indoctrination, and instinctive performance of duty combine to dictate action. There is nothing like hostile fire to convince a serviceman of his importance and that of the job assigned him. On the deck of the destroyer *Borie,* locked bow to bow in a death struggle with the submarine she had just rammed, the commander found little need to give orders and none at all to repeat them. Wrote war reporter John Hersey of the *Borie*'s last battle: "All through the ship men acted on their own . . . responded to months of careful training [and] their own initiatives. Everyone found something to do." Even on larger vessels where hundreds of men cooped below are denied the excitement of participating in events topside, it was possible to instill the necessary sense of involvement. Many an officer, using his ship's loudspeaker system, would broadcast a blow-by-blow narrative of the action. (Perhaps significantly, one such combat commentator, the damage-control officer on a cruiser fighting off Guadalcanal, was in peacetime a psychology professor.)

All things considered, it is hardly surprising that records show no instance of mutiny on the high seas in the United States Navy during the Second World War. For a celebrated "mutiny" aboard an American warship in that conflict we must refer to fiction, and even on the USS *Caine* it was not so much a matter of lower-deck protest against harsh conditions or tyrannical command as it was the officers' collaboration to depose a pathetically manic captain. The novel invites parallels with the *Bounty*—for instance, the *Caine*'s commander's obsession with allegedly stolen strawberries recalls the coconut incident in the British vessel. But Queeg was no Bligh, and it would be in a future (undeclared) war when an actual occurrence on an American destroyer, complete with suggestions of wardroom conspiracy and command neuroses, brought both the fictional commander and the real-life captain of the breadfruit brig sharply to mind. Yet there was indeed a legally confirmed mutiny in the United States Navy during the war against the Axis Powers, a mass one at that, qualifying, if measured by the number of court-martial convictions, as one of the three or four largest in naval history.

After the First World War it was the navy's unwritten policy to discourage the recruitment of black Americans. Those accepted served for the most part as stewards. At the time of Pearl Harbor there were no black officers and very few black seamen above the steward level. (The *Caine*'s chief steward and steward's mates are black and stereotypic.) Wartime conscription produced a wider acceptance of blacks, who were, however, still subjected to segregated training and assignment. By the middle of 1943 there were more than one hundred thousand black enlisted men in the navy and still no black officers, an abnormality impossible to ignore. The navy's Bureau of Personnel issued a letter deeming it "important from the standpoint of morale that Negroes be assured the same opportunities for promotion as other enlisted personnel." Plans were implemented for appropriate officer indoctrination. Even so, a disproportionate number of blacks, educated and illiterate alike, were shunted into dead-end or unpopular shore-based fields. And this is the reason why, only three months after thirteen black men became the first of their race to receive officer's commissions in the United States Navy, all fifty of the same service charged with conspiracy and mutiny were also black.

Since its construction in 1942 as a subcommand of the Naval Ammunition Depot at Mare Island, twenty miles north of San Francisco, the Port Chicago loading base had been manned almost entirely by black seamen supervised by white officers. Some of the facility's personnel may have understood that their work was of decisive importance to the outcome of distant land, sea, and air battles, but theirs was a thankless, depressing, and dangerous line of work that none of them, black or white, were likely to have relished. For the officers, periodic relief was possible in jaunts to Oakland or San Francisco. Commercial transport into Port Chicago served the black workers, but they found that war-bred settlement to be no haven of hospitality.

Subsequent court testimony would describe "the colored enlisted personnel [as] neither temperamentally nor intellectually capable of handling high explosives." They were "poor material for training"—this toward explaining why they had been given no preliminary stevedore instruction. To make up for this deficiency, some of the officers had instituted weekly training sessions, but by and large they themselves, like their men, had to learn on the job, their only textbook a Coast Guard manual entitled *Regulations Governing Transportation Of Military Explosives On Board Vessels During The Present Emergency*. Known as the Red Book, it was quickly outdated and had little useful to say about the TPX-loaded Mark 47 depth bombs being hoisted from four of sixteen railroad boxcars and lowered through the hatches of the 7,212-ton Liberty Ship *E. A. Bryan* on the night of 17 July 1944.

The loading proceeded under floodlights. Half the men engaged were on the dock, the rest in the *E. A. Bryan*'s five holds, receiving the cargo. On the other side of the five-hundred-foot-long pier another ship, the *Quinalt Victory*, awaited, and about seventy crew members of both vessels were present, also sentries. By 10 P.M. nearly five thousand tons of explosives had been loaded—antiaircraft shells, incendiary clusters, and fragmentation bombs, besides the Mark 47 depth bombs. These latter were of a relatively new type and not to be confused with the conventional TNT-primed depth charges, which the Red Book said

The shock waves were felt fifty miles away. This photograph shows Port Chicago after the explosion. *(San Francisco Public Library)*

could be loaded aboard ship in ordinary cargo nets without protective trays to cushion the shock of landing. TPX always had to be handled more gingerly than TNT. A dent in the outer covering might be enough to detonate the material, as the navy's Bureau of Ordnance conceded, citing " 'container dent' sensitivity . . . new to the literature of explosives" as one of the two fatal elements in what occurred at Port Chicago, the other being "a careless act of someone who perished." A hoist might have been allowed to swing against the ship's side or been dropped from too great a height into the hold. Perhaps the absence of those protective trays under the depth bombs was to blame. Only conjecture suggests why the Liberty Ship suddenly exploded.

Generating shock waves felt fifty miles away, the first blast was enough to have killed all who could have provided eyewitness testimony. Other explosions followed, destroying the *Quinalt Victory,* railroad cars, the pier, and a fire barge. Boiling gases mushroomed 12,000 feet into the summer night sky, and of the 320 dead, two-thirds of them black Americans, only 51 bodies would be found sufficiently intact for identification.

"As was to be expected, Negro personnel performed bravely . . . carried on in accordance with our service's highest traditions." Thus declared Adm. Carleton H. Wright, in command of the Twelfth Naval District, praising survivors within a week of the disaster. As for those who had died, "their sacrifice could not have been greater had it occurred on a battleship or a beach-head." Scarcely a month later his tone had changed, the admiral warning scores of black sailors manifestly averse to further hazarding such sacrifice that mutinous conduct in wartime bore a fearful risk of its own, that of a firing squad.

The Port Chicago explosion had injured more than four hundred men. Psychological scars were to be expected as well. Secretary of the Navy James Forrestal believed that putting fit survivors immediately back to work at handling ammunition was "the preferred method of preventing them from building up mental and emotional barriers which, if allowed to accumulate, become increasingly difficult to overcome." They had not gone back to work at once, if only because of the devastation to the Port Chicago facility. But neither were any given furloughs, despite the survivors' jumpiness, dazed manner, and other symptoms of trauma. The loading divisions were instead quartered at local installations, such as the Camp Shoemaker naval training center and the naval barracks at Vallejo.

On 8 August, twenty-two days after the explosion, the ammunition carrier *San Gay* arrived at Mare Island Ammunition Depot and berthed at Pier 34 East. Railroad boxcars filled with shells and detonators drew up alongside. The ship was rigged for loading, hatches were opened, and the dispersed divisions were alerted that evening for a resumption of their ammunition-loading duties. Thereupon, the officers in charge discovered that in the three weeks of unrelieved confinement since the explosion at Port Chicago the men had developed a distinctly uncooperative mood.

At about noon the following day Lt. Ernest Delucchi of the fourth loading division reported personally to Comdr. Joseph R. Tobin, who was in charge of the Vallejo naval barracks, that instead of boarding the ferry to Mare Island as ordered, practically all 105 of his men had drifted off in the opposite direction and halted at the mess hall. When the lieutenant returned from the commander's office, he found them listening impassively to a chaplain, who offered to stand alongside them on the loading dock if only they would go back to work. Obedient to a point, the men allowed themselves to be lined up on the parade ground, where appeals were made to their racial pride. They were next ushered into the recreation building and marched upstairs to the chaplain's office, which doubled as a movie-projection room, where Commander Tobin began to tell each man individually that unless he returned to work disciplinary action would surely follow. The commander had not progressed very far when he was informed by telephone of disorders in other divisions. The message was more or less the same. The men would obey any order except that which put them back on loading ammunition. By nightfall those who still refused numbered 258. They were separated from the rest, berthed on a lighter tied up at the pier, and assembled the next morning on the baseball diamond, to be addressed by the commanding officer of the Twelfth Naval District.

Admiral Wright had held that assignment for eight months. He had come to it straight from a Pacific war zone, where almost half of his cruiser flotilla had been blasted out from under him by Japanese destroyers. With such experience fresh in mind he was unlikely to have felt much sympathy for the men who stood before him. Even so, out of fairness he probably recognized that they may not have fully apprehended the gravity of their conduct. Here was a situation calling for plain language. He reminded the men that GIs on Saipan were in desperate need of the ammunition they refused to load. He warned them that continued refusal amounted to mutiny and concluded with the fearsome thrust that though loading ammunition was risky, they were now courting a greater hazard, that of death by a firing party.

The admiral's blunt delivery had an effect. Mutiny? Said one black loader, "We thought mutiny was like when you kill people or take over something . . . that it could only happen on a ship on the high seas." When the admiral finished talking, division officers once more ordered a return to work. The men divided themselves into two groups, those willing to obey and those who felt otherwise. Some wept as they made their choice. The obedient group now proved the far larger, numbering 208. They were not yet in the clear. Having originally refused orders, they were taken to Camp Shoemaker for interrogation and summary courts-martial. The holdouts, fifty still defiant, were also borne off, to confinement in the guardhouse. And what ensued during the balance of the month would extend the controversy over the original conduct of the black ammunition loaders to include doubts concerning the propriety of some of the navy's investigative and judicial methods.

The compliant 208 were interviewed separately and in the presence of armed guards. Replies were extracted under the threat of a general court-martial. Men were coerced into testifying against one another. The questioners drafted statements, which several of the men refused to sign, protesting that their words were twisted.

A legal officer interrogated the recalcitrant fifty in the Camp Shoe-maker brig, asking if they knew the definition of mutiny. Apparently none did, so "I read the definition from Courts and Boards. I read, I think, part of section 46." (Section 46 of the current Naval Courts and Boards defined mutiny as "unlawful opposition or resistance to or defiance of superior military authority, with a deliberate purpose to usurp, subvert, or override such authority.") One of the men expressed his fear of loading ammunition. "I told him 'you failed to obey orders, that's mutiny and is about the same as looking down a gun barrel.' "

And thus Capt. Nelson Goss, commanding officer of the Port Chicago installation, formally reported it to Admiral Wright. "A refusal to obey orders, sufficiently concerted and sufficiently persisted in to appear mutinous . . . occurred on the part of three divisions of (negro) personnel . . . followed [by] the two remaining divisions." Agitators were "undoubtedly" involved, the men having been subject to "outside propaganda . . . subversive influence." All along the men had "exhibited the normal characteristics of negroes" but lately had begun showing a "persistent disposition to question orders, to argue, and in effect attempt to bargain." Their joint action and continued disobedience "indicated a mutinous attitude."

When official reports of the case reached his desk, the president of the United States suggested that only nominal sentences be imposed on the penitent 208, for they had acted out of "mass fear and . . . this is understandable." Perhaps equally understandable, considering the enormous wartime pressures he was under and his unpublicized declining health, is Franklin D. Roosevelt's omission, in his brief comment, of any reference to the fifty prisoners whose initial disobedience had been motivated by the same fear. Evidently no one drew his attention to the anomaly either. Charges were drafted: "Having conspired each with the other to mutiny against the lawful authority of their superior naval officers . . . by refusing to work in the operation of loading ammunition [they] did . . . make a mutiny . . . in that they did . . . wilfully, concertedly and persistently disobey, disregard, and defy a lawful order with a deliberate purpose and intent to override superior military authority, the United States then being in a state of war."

Sixteen

NO BULWARKS OF PRIDE

News of the impending trial of fifty young black sailors for mutiny touched off protests from organizations and private citizens alike. The National Association for the Advancement of Colored People sent Eleanor Roosevelt a brochure fiercely critical of the navy's action. It "seems a sad story," wrote the president's wife to Secretary of the Navy James Forrestal, and she hoped "special care will be taken." The navy was certainly reacting to charges that the work of loading munitions was deliberately assigned to black personnel. Admiral Wright felt that there was no more "racial discrimination" at Port Chicago than at another loading facility in his Twelfth Naval District that exclusively employed whites. All the same, forwarding his initial report to Washington, the admiral had stated that while it was perfectly "logical" to use blacks at ammunition sites, some means of biracial rotation should be considered to check an unjustified impression that they were singled out for such work. Forrestal endorsed the idea in a memo to the White House. The assignment of more whites to ammunition-handling duties would "avoid any semblance of discrimination against Negroes." By the end of the year white and black Americans were taking turns on the rebuilt Port Chicago loading pier—without, of course, any integration of units. All this was a separate development, unconnected with the court-martial proceedings, throughout whose thirty-three autumn days the subject of racial discrimination arose fleetingly if at all, the principal arguments turning upon the nature of mutiny and whether the accused could be shown to have committed it.

They had understandable cause for fear. Their minds may have

Yerba Buena, California, 14 September 1944. Largest mutiny trial begins.
(Library of Congress)

rebelled against the notion that their own government would order them all shot to death. Neither, perhaps, did the legal officers involved in the case soberly believe that things would get that far. But they might. Those sailors who had thought that mutiny meant only trying to take over a ship now knew better. Some had believed at the time that when their superiors at Port Chicago had talked of a firing squad, they were using exaggeration to scare them into obedience. Now they realized that because of their conduct on that occasion they might indeed die. It was possible.

The trial was conducted within a converted marine barracks on Yerba Buena Island and was open to the public as if to indicate that, notwithstanding the wartime need for secrecy, in this matter the navy had nothing to hide. The defendants were provided with a skillful five-man legal team, one lawyer for each group of ten. But the court was no less capable and of a more hard-shelled character, seven officers of senior rank presided over by a rear admiral brought out of retirement. A future district attorney, tough on antiwar protesters in the 1960s, led the prosecution as judge advocate. Once again viewpoints clashed over definitions, interpretations, and shades of meaning. Both sides drew earnestly upon William Winthrop, "recognized," declared defense counsel, "as the leading authority on military law." That luminary had identified mutiny as essentially requiring "a deliberate purpose to usurp, subvert or override superior military authority." As the accused had entertained no such aim, the case against them should be dismissed. The judge advocate, Lt. Comdr. James F. Coakley, brushed this motion aside. It was not the prosecution's duty to prove the required motive, which was sufficiently implicit in the men's disobedience. Joint, collective, and persistent refusal to work might commonly be termed a strike when indulged in by civilian stevedores, but in the military it was mutiny. And there were those statements, more than fifty of them, amounting to full confessions.

Those statements, already suspect, escaped close examination. Even the question of disobedience lost its clarity when Commander Tobin admitted under defense's persuasion that he could not assert from personal knowledge that any sailors except the six or seven he had interviewed were positively ordered to work. Neither were the prosecution's arguments claiming conspiracy all that compelling. While the wording of the charge presupposed conspiracy, the actual charge was of "making a mutiny." In this light, and ignoring the judge advocate's protests against hairsplitting, the defense considered itself bound only to disprove mutiny, defined by the specification as willful, concerted, and persistent disobedience with a view toward overriding authority. The defense went about this task by getting the seamen to testify one after another that although frankly too scared to load any more ammunition, they had not jointly plotted refusal to do so and had indeed received no direct orders. Where, then, was the specific intent to override, Winthrop's "essential element," ratified as such by *Naval Courts and Boards*? That intent may be openly declared in word or implied in deed, neither of which was manifest in the conduct of the defendants. All that could be established was that following the "destruction and carnage" of the July explosion each man "of his own initiative" decided against handling ammunition.

Perhaps nothing could have better mirrored the ambiguity surrounding legal definitions of mutiny than the confidence, matching that of the defense counsel, with which the judge advocate also invoked Winthropean precepts. Coakley focused on that same "essential element" to which the other side attached so much importance. "A combination . . . to refuse or perform military service . . . if persisted in after due warning, may certainly be treated as mutiny." Specific intent? Such refusal was clear proof of it. The disobedience of one man alone could not amount to mutiny. "But," Coakley continued, "when you have a large number, as in this case, in a mass or group refusal to obey an order, you have an extraordinary case of conspiracy . . . an extraordinary case

The future U.S. Supreme Court Justice who appealed a mass mutiny conviction: Thurgood Marshall. *(Library of Congress)*

of mutiny." His line of reasoning prevailed. When the trial concluded on 24 October, the court deliberated only eighty minutes before returning a verdict of guilty for every one of the Port Chicago fifty.

No death sentences were handed down, but the penalties imposed were harsh enough—fifteen years' imprisonment and dishonorable discharge. (The 208 given summary courts-martial had drawn bad-conduct discharges and three months' forfeiture of pay.) Admiral Wright reduced some sentences but only minimally, to eight-to-ten years' jail terms, with the dishonorable discharges left standing. By this time, however, the National Association for the Advancement of Colored People was actively involved. An NAACP lawyer flew west, met the prosecution and defense teams, and interviewed the convicted men. The lawyer was Thurgood Marshall, at thirty-six already prominent in the NAACP, having recently argued his first case before that highest judicial body of which he was destined to become a member. Marshall lost no time in denouncing the trial as racist and unfair. In a forceful appeal brief to the Judge Advocate General of the United States Navy he insisted that "there is no set rule as to what is mutiny." He was, moreover, disturbed by the short time it had taken the court to reach a verdict that blanketed fifty Americans with ignominy. They were, under the law, entitled to individual consideration. Their court-martial was "the largest . . . that has ever been held. It is the first in this war for mutiny." Racial pride hung in the balance. The convictions would "forever stand as a disgrace to the entire Negro personnel of the United States Navy. I do not know of any crime that civilians hate more than mutiny. . . ."

The questions that naval lawyers involved in the Port Chicago appeal process privately asked one another reflected Thurgood Marshall's reminder that there existed "no set rule" governing mutiny. Had the development of separate rules specifying disobedience, neglect of duty, etc., so narrowed the crime of mutiny that it could now mean only acts to subvert or override superior authority? Was the actors' aim to secure dominance in their sphere of activity, "for example, confining the ship's captain and taking over the operation of the ship?" Could disobedience of one order, and obedience to all others, constitute mutiny?

It was a case that would not die easily. When Forrestal ordered the court reconvened on the grounds, brought to his attention by Marshall, that it had relied excessively upon hearsay evidence—"twenty-three pieces of testimony . . . were inadmissable"—it nevertheless stuck to its findings. But as the end of the war approached, the dissatisfaction registered by black Americans in army and navy service loomed as an urgent problem. Racial disorders had broken out on the island of Guam. More than seventy black soldiers were court-martialed in Honolulu for refusing to work. At Camp Rousseau in California a thousand black members of a naval construction battalion (Seabees) staged a two-day hunger strike against "racial discrimination," and while no charges were brought against the strikers, the base commander was transferred. The navy issued a fifteen-page booklet, "Guide to the Command of Negro Naval Enlisted Personnel," directing officers to avoid stereotyped views and the use of derogatory terms. At the same time, it hoped to put the Port Chicago affair to rest with a conspicuous display of lenity. Prison sentences were reduced to one year. The war had been over for five months when the Navy Department restored all but a hospitalized three of the fifty convicted to active duty and promised them honorable discharges if they behaved themselves.

Improvements emerged. Dated 27 February 1946, an edict, while by no means ending de facto discrimination in the navy, stipulated that "Negro personnel . . . henceforth shall be eligible for all types of assignments, in all ratings, in all facilities and in all ships." The repaired installation at Port Chicago would survive for another twenty years, until the navy razed it completely to construct an expanded loading base—employing civilian stevedores—for the supply of U.S. forces fighting in the Vietnam War. What remained unaltered on the navy's books were the mutiny convictions of the Port Chicago fifty.*

The veteran sea commander and naval historian Edward L. Beach has committed to print what every true sailor knows but few might acknowledge without embarrassment, that there is "always something mysterious and beautiful about a ship on the bosom of the sea, something which makes men fall in love with her." That love can encompass a pride born of one's long service on a particular vessel and a conviction both of the rectitude of her business and the value of one's role in its pursuit. When pride is lacking, toil and privation that might otherwise have been stoically endured are more likely to enrage and produce real trouble. As a British student of naval affairs observed, "The cultivation of pride therefore is a bulwark in the prevention of mutiny." Whatever else was subsequently left to doubt, it seems all too clear that no such bulwark existed on board the ex-cargo ship HMS *Lothian* during some twenty bedeviled weeks in 1944.

What set the course for this melancholy affair was a telegram from Adm. Ernest J. King, the American chief of naval operations, to the British Admiralty in London in the summer of that year. The telegram seemed to betoken a change of heart. It was no secret within the echelons of the Allied High Command that Admiral King jealously regarded the sea war against Japan as an all-American enterprise, to which the British were not invited. He was now, three or four weeks after the D-Day invasion of Europe, asking if six British landing ships could be spared for immediate transfer to the Pacific war zone to help train American troops. The likeliest explanation for King's surprise request is that he was under pressure from President Roosevelt to appease Winston Churchill's desire for British naval representation in the Far East struggle. Half a dozen landing ships were a modest enough beginning. Furthermore, King might have felt confident that because of the early date by which he purported to need the vessels, the request was unlikely to be fulfilled.

---

* In the summer of 1990 a number of American congressmen asked the secretary of the navy to review the case and set aside the convictions if they seemed unwarranted. Controversy broke out anew, some surviving veterans recalling the trial proceedings as unjust. Other black Americans who had obeyed orders to load ammunition after the explosion claimed that if any at Port Chicago were deserving of praise and sympathy it was themselves, not the mutineers. The congressmen's request, at the time of this writing, has not been met.

But the British hastened to comply, not even pausing to consider any possible incompatibility of British methods and equipment with those of the Americans. And perhaps it was Admiral King's turn to be surprised when informed by London only two weeks after his telegram that the landing craft he had asked for, designated Force X, were assembling in the River Clyde and that "if you have no objection these ships will be placed under command of a flag officer, in which case HMS *Lothian* will be added to the Force as his flagship."

The known service record of Rear Adm. Arthur George Talbot, R.N., suggests that he hardly deserved such a lusterless and anticlimactic assignment. A fifty-two-year-old Yorkshireman, in the navy since age twelve—his family before him had produced five admirals—Talbot had conducted submarine operations at the start of the war, gone on to command three aircraft carriers in turn, and had most recently directed amphibious forces off Sword Beach during the D-Day landings. An Admiralty memorandum seems to show why he was chosen. Rushed preparations for Force X would impose "a great deal of inconvenience" upon its personnel, and to sustain their morale and efficiency required "a strong personality." Perhaps Talbot's, unbeknownst to the Admiralty, had after so many years of loyal and arduous service lost some of that strength. But in any event, each of the landing craft in his force already had a capable and experienced captain. Since the ships would steam more than halfway around the world to be placed at the disposal of Vice Adm. Thomas C. Kinkaid, commander of the U.S. Seventh (South Pacific) Fleet, the decision to give them a headquarters ship with its own British admiral on board may indeed have been a chauvinistic indiscretion.

British court-martial records and proceedings are concealed from the public for seventy-five years. The British Admiralty files accessible to researchers tell next to nothing about the history of the ill-starred Force X. One of the *Lothian*'s crew published a lower-deck version of events. Scattered references to the landing craft and their deployment in the South Pacific are found among U.S. Navy records. Such are the slender sources from which to weave a coherent account.

Among the sure ingredients for trouble was the familiar one of resentment against orders to a remote war zone considered principally someone else's province. British and French sailors and soldiers had objected to involvement in Russia's monumental fratricide after the 1918 cease-fire with Germany. Something of the same mood could be sensed in Britain as the end of yet another long bout with the Germans approached. Despite bold high-level pronouncements of continuing

From peacetime freighter to mutinous flagship: HMS *Lothian,* née *City of Edinburgh.* (Allied Landing Craft of World War Two, *Arms and Armour Press, 1985*)

Allied unity, there flickered here and there within the war-weary British lower ranks a reluctance to shoulder the further burdens of fighting Japan. This mood was mostly confined to the home front and expressed by servicemen of substandard military caliber. But such apparently predominated among the crew of the Force X flagship *Lothian,* a converted 12,790-ton (fully loaded) freighter armed with twin 4-inch guns at the bow and aft, whose designed carrying capacity of 450 men was greatly exceeded by the addition of an army signals detachment and about 100 air force personnel.

These units joined the *Lothian* on the assumption, it is said, of their required use in combat, but this rationale is curious in the light of Admiral King's original telegram, which had mentioned only training purposes. At any rate, one result was that the *Lothian* carried an unusual number of officers, including Admiral Talbot's own staff, for a vessel of her size and class.

Numbering seven craft including the headquarters ship, Force X steamed into the Atlantic on 3 August 1944 as part of a large convoy. The reaction of Talbot's people when he told them of their destination was not total dismay, thanks to the prospects of a scheduled first stop at New York. For the British crews, after five years of blackout and food shortages, New York's lights (only partially dimmed), unrationed eatables, and other long-denied pleasures would be close to heavenly. This was the eager anticipation—until Force X was safely docked at Manhattan's piers and too many of the *Lothian*'s people could only watch with chagrin from the ship's rail, their liberty restricted, while assorted officers and the Royal Air Force men strolled freely ashore.

Joined at New York by the American destroyer escorts *Machias, Sandusky,* and *Charlottesville,* the British Force X officially became a task group, under orders to report for duty with the U.S. Seventh Fleet after clearing the Panama Canal. A hurricane threat that drove all the ships into Charleston, South Carolina, for shelter delayed Force X's arrival in the Canal Zone. By this time the hurried preparations for sailing had begun to exact their price. The *Lothian*'s fresh-water system kept breaking down. Ventilation was inadequate for her complement of more than seven hundred disgruntled men. The food issued to the British crews was bad enough, the more so when contrasted with that supplied to the units of American servicemen who had boarded two of the landing ships, the *Arquebus* and *Empire Battleaxe*, at New York. A signal from Admiral Talbot to the Admiralty in London warned that "invidious comparisons" drawn between British and American messing standards were having "an unfortunate effect on morale and discipline."

But Talbot himself was now the chief object of lower-deck discontent. The overcrowded conditions, foul air, tainted water, and poor food were all felt to be the admiral's fault. The ship had a captain, Christopher Petrie, and an executive officer, Lt. Comdr. Kenneth Buckel. But at age fifty-one, following a long and grueling career in amphibious warfare, Captain Petrie had become detached in manner, even reclusive. Buckel could do little to redress grievances, though sympathetic as befitted one who had worked himself up from the lower deck. The conspicuous target for bitterness and derision was the gold-braided man at the top, apparently oblivious to lower-deck distress, holding court in the shedlike cabin especially built for him forward of the *Lothian*'s bridge or emerging all too often to pace purposefully fore and aft as if determined to make of vessel and crew an attack weapon to be reckoned with.

The admiral's own story of his ill-conceived expedition would never be made public. Talbot may have come to regret his appointment to Force X even before the ships completed their transatlantic crossing. He is said to have suffered from insomnia. Of a brief call he paid upon Admiral King in Washington, D.C., while Force X berthed at New York, nothing can be gleaned. It is fair to assume that Talbot dutifully resolved to make the best of a bad job. He may be pictured as a tradition-bound admiral with a flagship crew picked by and large from the bottom of the barrel—"jail-sweepings" and sullen ex-soldiers reported to be among them—and conceivably with a captain and executive officer whose fading zeal for their mission had drained with it the support they might otherwise have given him. With the hour steadily approaching when he would formally submit his men and ships to foreign command in a combat zone, the compulsion Talbot felt himself under to have them by that time in honorable shape may very well have become intense. But that would have been before Force X entered the Pacific Ocean. At least where the flagship was concerned one can only wonder if Arthur George Talbot's hopes for putting up a good show before the Americans could have fully survived the occurrence among his people at Balboa, Panama, on a sweltering Friday afternoon, 1 September 1944.

A dutiful but frustrated rear admiral: Arthur George Talbot. *(Imperial War Museum, London)*

That was the date set for the departure of Force X. The next scheduled landfall was Bora Bora in the French Society Islands, 4,500 miles distant. Force X had been in the Canal Zone for one week. The first signs of disobedience appeared when most of a hundred men sweating and grumbling in the heat of the ill-ventilated mess deck sat tight when ordered by senior ship's policemen to go topside. There were catcalls and rebellious singing. Lieutenant Commander Buckel came down the ladder with an admonition about where their conduct might lead, but it had little impact. Admiral Talbot was on deck, playing host to visiting American officers. Buckel managed to draw him aside and report the lower-deck situation. Talbot, it seems, thought of ordering the detachment of Royal Marines on board to fire their weapons through the hatchway. Buckel returned below with one last appeal to reason. He uttered the dread word mutiny. Apparently without his sanction the captain of marines descended as well, inflaming emotions. There ensued a confrontation with weapons. But some of the men were momentarily cowed. Buckel returned on deck, and the hatch was battened down with marine guards posted.

In response to the incessant hammering from below, the hatch was soon reopened. The men swarmed on deck. As if confident that the marines would not be ordered to fire on them in full view of the locals and American sailors gathered along the quayside, they crowded the foredeck and blocked access to the anchor hawsers and winches. Captain Petrie appeared. He told them that they were committing mutiny and threatened force unless they dispersed. When they responded with jeers and curses, he stated his determination to continue the voyage, without them if need be, adding that for all he cared they could leave the ship at once.

This a number proceeded to do. Ignoring the marines lined up on the main and boat decks with bayonets fixed, they strode aft and down the gangplank to the quay. A squad of army signalers with a sergeant in charge was ordered to follow and induce them to return. For the soldiers it was an uncomfortable task that ended in scuffles. The signalers were withdrawn, and an officer replaced them on the quayside, standing in the burning sunshine and reading aloud from the Articles of War. He had not finished when the more level-headed among the sailors decided that they had made their point, and some also possessed enough nationalistic or service pride to feel a degree of shame at the spectacle they were presenting in front of a mixed foreign audience. They returned on board. Seventeen remained ashore, still defiant, until a party of marines marched down the gangplank. There was some resistance, including some foolhardy attempts to grab the marines' rifles. But it was soon over, to be briefly noted in a military war diary, one of the few accessible official references to the incident. "A case of mass insubordination occurred. A number of seamen refused duty on sailing and moved to the jetty. . . . the three ringleaders and fourteen other ratings were placed under armed sentry by the Royal Marines."

Still in company with its three American escorts, Force X steamed across the South Pacific. Nothing untoward had occurred among the people of the other British vessels, named *Glenearn, Clan Lamont, Empire Battleaxe, Arquebus, Empire Mace,* and *Spearhead.* Shipboard conditions could not have been all that much more tolerable than on the *Lothian,* but perhaps their crews were of a superior quality and contained fewer malcontents. Throughout this stage of the protracted voyage there was a sense of uncertainty and estrangement on the *Lothian*'s lower deck. The seventeen arrested men were confined within a makeshift prison formerly the stewards' quarters. The others who had rebelled were kept apart, as much as possible, from the rest of the crew and the army and air force detachments, and they could only nervously speculate upon what might be in store for them. The *Lothian*'s officers congregated amidships, passageways to which were blocked by marine sentries, and a court of inquiry pressed fitfully ahead, with Admiral Talbot's chief of staff presiding. Witnesses summoned to testify were sworn to silence. Lieutenant Commander Buckel had been relieved of his duties as executive officer and was now seldom seen, and rumors floated about that he would be held responsible for the breakdown of discipline.

In far-off Quebec just then the Allied war leaders were meeting in conference. With a reduced need for naval operations in European waters, Winston Churchill wanted the British navy fully involved in the war against Japan. Roosevelt gave unhesitating assent, thus "overruled Admiral King's opinion," according to Adm. Sir Andrew Cunningham, who was present at the conference. But although "resigned to the use of our fleet in the Pacific," the U.S. chief of naval operations "made it quite clear that it must expect no assistance from the Americans. From this unhelpful attitude he never budged." While King's anglophobic views may not have percolated through all levels of the American naval command, the flotilla of British landing craft steadily ploughing toward the Pacific war zone would hardly have merited priority on anybody's list. In any event, Admiral Kinkaid was busy preparing his Seventh Fleet for its important role in support of Gen. Douglas MacArthur's troops, who were about to invade the Philippines. Kinkaid had been informed that Force X was coming out but had been given no specific instructions for its use. On 31 August—the eve of the mutiny on HMS *Lothian*—he was notified that "a general reserve group has been set up under your direct command with R/Admiral Talbot, R.N., in charge." Force X would be Kinkaid's to employ as he wished.

The ships arrived at Bora Bora on 14 September as scheduled. The next day the *Lothian* fired a gun to signal that a court-martial was under way. Again proceedings were conducted in the tightest secrecy. (Given the depressing circumstances, it may have escaped the notice of anyone involved that their present island anchorage was the approximate setting for the mutiny on the *Bounty,* also that the date happened to be the thirteenth anniversary of the mutiny at Invergordon.) The trial was that of the seventeen men in custody. Afterward they were hustled off the ship and locked up on other vessels. Talbot's flotilla next set course for Dutch New Guinea, where landing craft and transports with legions of troops were assembling for the planned strike on Leyte just five weeks off. It would take two of those weeks for Force X to reach its destination.

There was on HMS *Lothian* a small American navy signals team with its own private quarters; presumably, it was in regular touch with its own command. A 22 September message to the Seventh Fleet from General MacArthur's headquarters is evidence that the disposition of Force X had come under some sort of American review in those preinvasion days. Plans were to "employ Force X almost continuous in forward operational areas participating in training and assault operations. Improbable [that] force will return to mainland between operations." Admiral Talbot's knowledge of these plans might explain why he put his crews through intensified drills, with frequent calls to battle stations, during that final lengthy passage across the Pacific. None of this improved his standing with the lower deck, especially that sizable number whose status as defaulters technically under arrest ensured them no exemption from duty. As one of her company recalled, the *Lothian* was by this time a most despondent flagship, and the cheerlessness was not confined to the crew's quarters either. The officers crowded on board were rumored to be at odds with one another, and their captain unhappy and disgusted. And there was now a general belief that Talbot's inquiry had concluded that the *Lothian*'s executive officer had mishandled the disturbance at Balboa and that he was headed for a court-martial.

The admiral's emotions can only be conjectured. Less than four months earlier, off the Normandy beaches, he had taken HMS *Largs,* the combined command center for Sword Sector, through volleys of bombs and torpedoes. It would have been in character for him to have bent every effort to make the *Lothian* combat ready. Had the admiral been able to discharge his duty under Japanese fire as commendably as he had performed in the English Channel, it may well have restored honor and pride to his present command. He would be denied the opportunity. His ships finally reached Hollandia, the main assembly area for the Leyte invasion fleet, at the close of September. Nearly five hundred assorted vessels thronged the harbor, a spectacle that may well have quickened Talbot's pulse as he reported his arrival to Rear Adm. Daniel Barbey commanding the Seventh Amphibious Force. Barbey, however, privately sized up the newcomers as "a pretty sorry lot. They are not prepared for tropical duty. Communications equipment is awaiting installation, their cargo handling facilities are inadequate and their material condition poor." Another confidential American assessment described their "cleanliness and sanitation . . . not up to the standards maintained by ships of the U.S. Navy." What Admiral Talbot was formally told was wounding enough. His ships were of the wrong design to carry American assault boats, and the alterations required would not be practicable. They might be helpful for training purposes but were quite unsuitable for combat operations.

When news of Force X's exclusion from the imminent grand assault filtered below decks, some among the *Lothian*'s crew inevitably attributed it to the stain of mutiny. The unhappy affair had yet to run its course. The *Lothian*'s "defaulters" were mustered on deck for a summary hearing conducted by a weary captain, who sentenced them to 180 days of punishment drill. At about this time the men learned that the seventeen court-martialed earlier had received from ninety days' to one year's imprisonment, relatively light sentences handed down, it was suspected, in the hopes of keeping matters as quiet as possible. The *Lothian* next sailed some distance out of the busy harbor for still another court-martial, that of her executive officer.

The British minelaying cruiser *Ariadne* was at Hollandia as part of the invasion armada. On the eve of its departure for Leyte her captain, surely with distaste, found himself summoned to preside over the court-martial of a junior officer charged with not having exerted "his utmost endeavors" to suppress a mutiny. Admiral Talbot's chief of staff served as prosecutor. The charge was hardly sustainable because those earlier court-martial convictions were for insubordination, not mutiny. According to the 1942 edition of Stephen T. Banning's *Manual of Military Law*, considered a bible on the subject, mutiny *was* "collective insubordination" and the essence of the offense the combination to resist authority. But no one was of a mind to drive this point home at the trial of those seventeen, the prevailing circumstances being hardly propitious for going by the book. This would have been the case with Lieutenant

Commander Buckel's court-martial as well. It was all over within forty-eight hours, the officer convicted only on lesser counts, of tardiness in singling out the ringleaders and of attempting to appease them. Captain Petrie delivered a belated tribute to Buckel's proficiency as executive officer, but his words had little effect, and the lieutenant commander was dismissed from the *Lothian*.

At sundown on Friday, 13 October, Admiral Talbot and his crews watched the great invasion fleet get under way for the Philippines without them. Two weeks later, following the success of the Leyte operation, Admiral Barbey returned to Hollandia and learned that even in a training capacity the British force left much to be desired: "I doubt if the training value of these ships balance their absorption of our limited maintenance facilities." They could be used for ferrying troops around in the rear areas, "but I don't suppose they would take kindly to that idea." Admiral Talbot certainly did not. He still wanted his force to show its mettle under fire. Late in November Barbey wrote, "I am very sympathetic with Admiral Talbot's desire to have his ships take part in combat operations [but] the work required to make them ready may be so extensive as to make it advisable to employ them 'as is' in the rear area." Four were kept in use for training despite "bothersome . . . differences in landing force technique." Others were reduced to carrying troops, cargo, and mail between Australia and the Pacific islands. For a brief period the *Lothian* filled a useful berth as flagship for the fleet train supporting the British Pacific Fleet, which had come into robust being and would win even Admiral King's approbation. The ship was at Sydney in February 1945, by which time Talbot, the captain, and his former executive officer had all left the vessel. She returned to England under a new commander, who had been shocked by conditions on board.

After the war Talbot retired from the British navy with honors and took up farming. He died in 1960, and the following year the *Lothian*, reconverted to a freighter, was sold for scrap. Extensively voyaged, haplessly manned, never in combat, she had been the setting for an obscure episode of the Second World War that may be considered, in all justice, as but a sad if interesting footnote to the wartime record of a navy distinguished, in the main, by superb gallantry and noble sacrifice.

Seventeen

⌐

THE CALCULATED RISK

If pride and high morale are a fighting unit's best shields against the threat of mutiny, they are also the most susceptible to corrosion from war weariness and just plain homesickness. Spells of actual combat place too many demands upon thought, instinct, and reflexes for discontent to set in right away, but the mental stresses accumulated during life-and-death crises can work their harm later as a kind of insidious aftermath, a postaction proneness to even the smallest grievance. And the absence of some restorative, ideally in the form of home furlough if not complete release from active service, becomes a grievance of itself, with the appropriate potential for mutiny.

It is a psychological sequence more prevalent in wartime than official records show, and the anxious report from a medical officer aboard the USS *Kilty*, a fleet auxiliary on Pacific service in 1945, could doubtless have been duplicated in other commands and all theaters of combat. The *Kilty*'s crew had been in the thick of the Philippines campaign and had long been deprived of shore liberty. "The prolonged combat experience has reflected itself medically [and in] an increasing number of disciplinary problems. The men feel no one is vitally interested in what happens to them." They were "punch-drunk." Five had deserted. There had to be "prolonged rehabilitation outside the forward area, preferably in the United States," to avoid risk of "serious damage to the ship." The *Kilty*'s captain affirmed his medical officer's words. "Psychological" problems on board had reached "alarming proportions," and he was "personally apprehensive of the success of the vessel's future missions, the safety of the ship . . . and of its crew."

It may well be a matter of uncertainty whether those antimutiny bulwarks of pride and high morale could have survived had hostilities dragged on beyond 1945. Among the danger signs in those final months was the reaction of enlisted men in the U.S. Seventh Fleet when told that henceforth furloughs on home soil would be severely limited. The resultant "discontent and a general lowering of morale" so concerned Admiral Barbey that he urged "leave parties to Australia at every opportunity." And when all the shooting stopped, the morale of the lower ranks, more manifestly ashore than afloat, declined instead of improved because of the slowness of military demobilization. The streets of Manila in January 1946 filled with American soldiers protesting the needless delays in their return to civilian life. Four thousand GIs in Frankfurt-am-Main, Germany, marched upon their headquarters and were halted only at bayonet point. United States marines in Honolulu signed a petition to President Harry S. Truman, demanding their prompt passage home, and six convicted troublemakers went to jail. Gen. Dwight D. Eisenhower, newly appointed army chief of staff, investigated the Manila disorders, found the cause "acute homesickness aggravated by the termination of hostilities," and described the dissident men as "not inherently challenging discipline or authority."

That few such expressions of postwar homesickness appear to have seriously troubled American warships may be due in part to the United States Navy's having assumed throughout preceding generations the character of a permanent force, equally on guard in peace as in war, whereas the nation had never maintained a large standing army—although the Cold War was about to create one. Among America's allies, tardy demobilization touched off similar displays of impatience, again primarily among army men conscripted for war service. One naval exception may be noted, a reported mutiny in December 1945 on the British destroyer *Javelin*, some of whose crew refused to parade for inspection when ordered. But this was evidently an isolated incident, a show of sailors' displeasure with officers who were over eager to get their people back into a peacetime "spit and polish" mode.

Logistics and bureaucratic sloth were mainly responsible for the slow release of men in uniform, but growing tensions with the Soviet Union were also to blame. These, moreover, revived old fears, bordering at times on paranoia, of subversive infiltration controlled from Moscow. The uncovering of a Soviet spy ring in Canada prompted Glenn Howell, the United States naval attaché in Ottawa, to file a secret report with the intelligence division of the chief of naval operations. The attaché recalled how, as a naval intelligence officer in 1929, he had reacted to the appearance of leftist posters on notice boards in American warships by launching an investigation that resulted in a raid on Communist party headquarters in New York City. Now, in 1946, he again had reason to believe that "there is a decided infiltration of communists into the United States Navy." One sure means of thwarting their designs to spy and sow disaffection was by identifying the types of U.S. naval personnel "susceptible to subversive influence." The vigilant attaché listed these easy marks as "(a) Men of recent European origin. (British Isles alone excluded.) (b) Certain Jews, particularly those who come under category (a). (c) All Negroes. (d) Ex-college professors or ex-schoolteachers now commissioned as officers. (e) New Dealers of the Henry Wallace type, now commissioned as officers. (f) Officers who have inherited money and who have never, through their own ingenuity or effort, earned any other than what the Navy has offered them. (g) Officers of every rank who are in debt." These vulnerable unfortunates, most of them, were "probably all right, but they are also more open to the devious methods employed by the Soviets."

How seriously the higher reaches of the Navy Department regarded such "intelligence" is beyond estimation. But as the Cold War intensified, concern over communist subversion of the armed forces gathered strength, and not only in the United States. Late in February 1949 sailors on the Canadian destroyer *Athabascan,* on a spring training cruise to the Caribbean, staged a nonviolent demonstration, and the following week, in Far Eastern waters, so did about one-third of the 150-man crew of HMCS *Crescent.* The *Athabascan* was one of the escorts of the aircraft carrier *Magnificent,* thirty-two of whose ratings, on 22 March, refused to muster for mess-deck cleaning duty. In all three cases the men had banded together in protest against long work hours, inadequate shore leaves, shortened meal periods, and bad food. One retired Canadian naval commander blamed "poor bloody management by the officers." But "subversive elements" were also suspected, and while the findings of a secret inquiry into the affair were never published, and no disciplinary action was taken against the "mutineers," a broader and equally secret investigation sought to discover whether "red agents" were busy within the Canadian fleet.

In the United States at mid-century the creation of a Department of Defense, effectively unifying the management of the fighting services, obliged a corresponding uniformity in the definition and application of military law. The Uniform Code of Military Justice replaced the army's Articles of War and the navy's Articles for the Government of the Navy, also its *Naval Courts and Boards,* as separate entities. Among other improvements, the UCMJ established an identical and rather more democratic system of courts-martial for all branches of the national defense. But although its penal codes describing offenses and punishments are set forth in greater detail and with more attention to legalistic nuances than antiquated checklists of rules and regulations, this body of laws falls short of liberating the question of mutiny from its traditional murk. One might almost suspect that the word itself, still reminiscent of lower-deck uprisings against tyrannical captains in the era of sail, had with the advent of nuclear-powered aircraft carriers and fully automated missile-launching systems acquired too anachronistic a flavor to warrant further semantic effort in the search for a satisfying definition.

There has been no quarrel with Colonel Winthrop's assertion that mutiny is "the gravest and most criminal of the offenses known to the military code." In the United States armed forces, death is still the maximum punishment for mutiny, also for failure to prevent or report its occurrence. But as to what mutiny is, or is not, viewpoints and interpretations continue to differ. In Britain, army and navy law codes still reflect the influence of Winthrop's British equivalent, S. T. Banning, who wrote that because the combination to resist was the "essence" of mutiny, a single individual, however insubordinate, could not commit it. Banning's "collective insubordination" is the basis for Section 8 of Britain's current Naval Discipline Act, which describes mutiny as a combination between two or more persons to overthrow or resist lawful authority in Her Majesty's forces, or to disobey such authority in a manner subversive of discipline and duty. With few exceptions the British view has historically been that it takes two or more persons to make a mutiny.

Not so in the United States, where the Uniform Code of Military Justice, Article 94, admits the possibility that a single person can be so convicted. It says: "Any person subject to this chapter who, with intent to usurp or override lawful military authority, refuses, in concert with any other person, to obey orders or otherwise do his duty or creates any violence or disturbance is guilty of mutiny." A careful reading shows that thanks to the inclusion of the third "or" and the following qualifying words, this article defines two distinct types of mutiny. One is mutiny by disobedience or refusal of duty and involves concert of action. The other is mutiny by creating violence or disturbance and may be committed by one person acting alone. Both forms of mutiny require the intent to usurp or override. This was a departure from the long familiar Section 46 of *Naval Courts and Boards,* which held that while mutiny did not require concert of action, "it will be rare that this is lacking," and from the United States Army's 66th Article of War, which had stated flatly that "mutiny . . . necessarily includes some combination of two or more persons."

The first significant occasion for a close study of the provisions of the UCMJ's Article 94 arose following disorders at an army camp in Georgia. During the course of court-martial proceedings involving mutiny charges, the defense counsel pointed out that Article 94 embraced two forms of mutiny, one commitable by a single person. "The other, with which we are here concerned, requires the same intent [to usurp, etc.] but also necessitates concert of action." Winthrop was then invoked, to show that the intent, like the action, must be shared. Mutiny's most distinguishing feature was mutuality of intent. Mutiny by disobedience or refusal to perform duty was "a specialized type of mutiny in which the co-actors must share a common purpose. There must be concert of action and concert of intent. To hold otherwise would mean that mere joint disobedience constitutes this gravest of military crimes."

This argument won out, and the mutiny convictions were overturned, the case thereupon furnishing a useful precedent for defense tactics in future hearings, including a well-publicized trial in 1969 of twenty-seven soldiers stationed at the Presidio army base, San Francisco. Defense counsel reproved the court's judge for failing to make clear to the court that a conviction of mutiny required proof of shared intent. In one case after another, mutiny indictments were challenged, usually with success, because there was insufficient evidence to show both collective action *and* collective purpose. Yet it seems to have repeatedly escaped notice that this Winthropean dogma is not at all reflected in Article 94's definition of mutiny. The wording nowhere couples "refusal in concert" with Winthrop's "specific concerted intent," a fact plainly acknowledged in discussions of the article presented by successive editions of the United States *Manual for Courts Martial*. That Article 94 presupposes two types of mutiny is affirmed. One allows for the commission of the offense by a single person through the creation of "violence or disturbance." The other form may be a persistent disobedience, but while it has to occur in concert, thus "imports collective insubordination . . . this concert of insubordination need not be preconceived." It can occur spontaneously, without Winthrop's "concerted intent." Perhaps that should have sufficed. Unfortunately, the *Manual,* a federal guidebook on military law, rather muddies things again by adding that this kind of mutiny "may consist simply of a persistent and concerted refusal . . . with an insubordinate intent [inferrable from] words . . . acts done or . . . surrounding circumstances."

We have legislated against mutiny without establishing an unassailable definition for it. The standard work, *Black's Law Dictionary*, offers the following: "To rise against lawful or constituted authority in the naval or military service." Obviously this cannot suffice, if only because mutiny may take passive form with no one having to "rise against" anything. One wonders how members of the United States Supreme Court would reason if called upon to decide in a mutiny case. They might appear as stumped as when obliged to define obscenity. This latter challenge has been deferred to whim or taste, resulting in a consensus that amounts to "I cannot define obscenity, but I know it when I see it." Likewise, perhaps, mutiny—which, however, would lead back to the question of who is best qualified to "know it" on sight. It has become by no means a matter of course to accord this prerogative to the superior officer on the scene. The period of the Vietnam War produced two significant examples within the United States Navy of the higher level's refusal to accredit a commander's dogged insistence that mutiny had occurred on his ship. And in one of them, regard for an objective appraisal of facts and implications was all but lost in the attention focused upon the captain himself as a bizarre figure hitherto encountered only in the pages of popular fiction or in television farce.

In February 1966, during naval operations off the South Vietnamese coast, the captain of the destroyer *Leonard E. Mason* delivered a "Confidential—For Officers' Eyes Only" message to his task force commander, stating that the destroyer escort *Vance* had repeatedly fouled his ship's gun range and had spent useless firepower by hurling shells at sand dunes and barren rocks. Superior intervention at this point, perhaps a stern warning to the captain of the allegedly offending vessel, might well have prevented the development of a public tragicomedy that did nothing to enhance the prestige of the American navy.

Career recommendations are sometimes founded as much on a person's aggressive zeal and powers of imagination as upon his or her academic attainments. An abundance of the former qualities can often make up for deficiencies in the latter. But when a selection board weighs these intangibles, its decision may amount to what a confidant in United States naval service told Marcus Aurelius Arnheiter had applied in his case: "Your assignment to command," wrote Capt. Richard Alexander, "was, quite frankly, a calculated risk."

Arnheiter had originally contemplated a career in the army. When his first step in that direction proved unpromising, he turned to the navy, graduating with average distinction from the United States Naval Academy at Annapolis in 1953. While classroom luster continued to elude him, and unsatisfactory fitness reports delayed his promotion, he appears never to have lacked in audacity (afterward said to be his favorite word), stubbornness, and a breezy self-esteem perhaps envied while ridiculed. Arnheiter evidently excelled—and would later revel—in gunnery, for it was as gunnery officer on a destroyer in 1956 that he earned a special fitness report that secured him full lieutenancy. In the early 1960s Arnheiter put in time behind a Pentagon desk, specializing in the study of antisubmarine warfare and publishing his opinions with scant regard for the wrath they were bound to have aroused in certain quarters. His verbal flair for criticizing established priorities recalls the similar indulgence of another U.S. navy lieutenant long before him. And as Alexander Slidell Mackenzie had done in his day, so must Arnheiter have sown seeds of dislike.

Even so, in July 1962 he was promoted to lieutenant commander, and not long afterward, following study at George Washington University, he obtained a master's degree in personnel administration. In 1965, as executive officer of the USS *Ingersoll,* he earned a favorable fitness report from that vessel's captain. But evidently it was only through the active involvement of Captain Alexander, his old friend and principal advocate, that a clearance board for ship command, later that year, gave Marcus Arnheiter its seal of approval. To those who questioned whether Arnheiter possessed the psychological stamina to bear the responsibilities of command, Captain Alexander would argue that he was the type of officer whose potential brilliance requires precisely that kind of pressure to manifest itself. It would become a matter of dispute whether, as some stated, the board's approval was restricted to giving Arnheiter a command only in emergencies when no other qualified officer was available. The chief of naval operations sent Arnheiter his congratulations, "the board [having] decided in your favor, albeit with reservations." And on 22 December 1965, at Pearl Harbor, Lieutenant Commander Arnheiter had assumed command of the USS *Vance.*

Built for service in the Second World War, the ship saw action in the Mediterranean and Atlantic, and after ten postwar years in mothballs she was refitted for Cold War picket duty in the northern Pacific. The escalation of the Vietnam conflict saved her from the scrap heap, and when Marcus Arnheiter took charge she had not long returned from her first patrol in the Gulf of Tonkin. Arnheiter's reputation at this point was more or less intact, molded by his performance on the *Ingersoll.* On

Lt. Comdr. Marcus A. Arnheiter. Audacity was said to be his favorite word.
(Bettman)

the other hand, the good name of what would be Arnheiter's first and only sea command was not so secure, with suggestions of a decline in discipline. The stage, then, was perhaps already set for trouble, with a tired ship, lackadaisical personnel, and an overweening new commander in whose book glory hunting was no crime. Arnheiter certainly intended to make an impression, if only because at forty-one he was among the oldest Annapolis graduates of his rank.

Discontent on the *Vance* might have been understandable. She was not a large ship, 306 feet long, only 37 feet at the beam, and 1,850 tons fully loaded, her 105 ratings if not their 15 officers competing for space with the newest communications and surveillance equipment. Her latest cruise in South Vietnamese waters had been six months of almost unrelieved boredom for her people. But morale on the *Vance* before Arnheiter took charge never became an issue. All the attention would concentrate on his supposed aberrations and knaveries, catalogued in detail by his detractors, who gave an overall impression of dangerous eccentricity. Considered separately, some of the commander's foibles

Arnheiter's command for ninety-nine days: the USS *Vance*. *(U.S. Navy)*

might not have deserved such grave coloration—for example, his demand as soon as he arrived on board that a white toilet seat replace the regulation black one in his private bathroom. This is said to have embarrassed the executive officer, Lt. Ray S. Hardy, and when word of it spread to have in some strange fashion discomforted the ship's crew. But it was merely one item of a subsequently well publicized list. On his first visit to the engine room Arnheiter showed little interest in or knowledge of the *Vance*'s propulsion system. Not content with the ship's sole whaleboat, he ordered the purchase of a secondhand fiberglass speedboat, using ship's recreation funds. Other examples of alleged dubious behavior or "idiosyncracies" included an obsessive insistence upon neat dress and correct table etiquette and temper tantrums at the sight of coffee stains, spilled cigarette ash, and "girlie" magazines aboard his ship.

With her new commander's promise, dinned into the ears of his junior officers, to "take them where the action is," the *Vance* sailed on 28 December, and five days later he conducted the first of his controversial character-building sessions on the fantail. As Arnheiter described them, "They would last twenty minutes or so. Someone would open with an invocation—the Prayers at Sea from the United States Naval Institute book, for example—and then I would speak. The idea was to prepare the men to go into battle. I would ask them to reflect on the heritage of fighting men, like Stonewall Jackson, George Washington, Douglas MacArthur. If this happened on a Sunday we would close with the Navy hymn 'Eternal Father, Strong to Save.'" No one could have called the ostensible intent unconventional. Precombat pep talks have been standard practice among military leaders from Alexander the Great to Gen. George S. Patton, a warrior Arnheiter inevitably got around to quoting. The trouble lay in his use of religious adjuncts, soon causing the *Vance*'s operations officer, Lt. William T. Generous, to complain privately that the fantail sessions were nothing but thinly disguised Protestant services.

During a nine-day voyage to Guam, the *Vance*'s first stop en route to the war zone, more of her captain's "peculiarities" emerged. He had the crew awakened each morning by an overamplified recording of a fife-and-drum reveille instead of the traditional boatswain's whistle. And under absurdly secretive conditions he held periodic "war councils." In Operation Market Time, the U.S. Navy's program to shield the South Vietnamese coast from seaborne infiltration by the Vietcong, the *Vance*'s role was to patrol an alloted area, intercept and search suspect vessels, and destroy known landing facilities. It was a limited though important assignment, which Arnheiter apparently interpreted as an opportunity to win glittering battle honors for the *Vance,* and at those wardroom "war councils" he dazed his officers with portrayals of how, using the fiberglass speedboat as well as the whaleboat as decoys to lure junks and sampans within range of the *Vance*'s 3-inch guns, he would lay waste the enemy's shipping up and down the coast.

At Guam the *Vance* took on board empty oil drums and sandbags in preparation for Arnheiter's planned target practices. Some of his officers, Generous included, also came away from the island's naval station with two silver candelabra and a silver coffee server, stolen from the officers' club, allegedly at Arnheiter's urging, in the course of a party he had staged—and paid for with mess-fund money. The candelabra were returned with an apologetic story of a drunken prank. The coffee server stayed in the *Vance*'s wardroom.

The *Vance* sailed from Guam on 14 January. For target practice Arnheiter had organized a thirty-man "Special Fire Team." Huddled behind stacked sandbags and directed by the commander from the top deck via a microphone, the men blazed away at yellow-painted oil drums cast overboard, the ship, meanwhile, under Arnheiter's incessant orders, maneuvering so crazily at top speed that once an overheated diesel had to be shut down before it exploded. Factually recalled or exaggerated in retrospect, the commander's extraordinary behavior seemed to have no limit. He set up a "Boner Box" to receive fines levied upon his officers for such faults as sloppy dress, unshined shoes or belt buckles, and lax discipline in their respective divisions. Seated at the head of the table, he talked interminably of battle plans but was always ready to berate or fine for misplaced cutlery or wrongly sliced bread, so wardroom meals became an ordeal his officers sought ways to dodge. And about one week out of Guam, as the *Vance* approached the central South Vietnamese coast, the captain took up a position behind his flag-draped lectern as all hands save those on duty were mustered aft for more of his "moral guidance" or "character-building" ritual.

Actually, this was only the third fantail session. Lieutenant Generous had missed the first, being officer of the deck that morning. The next one appears not to have been another Arnheiter performance but was conducted by Hardy, who spoke harmlessly enough of God and the universe and who prudently eschewed hymns. "But today's gem was no more nor less than a Protestant service." Those were Generous's words in a letter he addressed that same Sunday, 23 January, to a Roman Catholic chaplain at Pearl Harbor. The fantail sessions were "euphemistically church calls" and so upsetting to him that he had already written the captain a letter asserting his "constitutional right" to absent himself from them. Lieutenant Hardy had declined to forward it to Arnheiter, advising Generous instead to seek counsel anonymously from outside the ship.

A graduate of Brown University who had obtained his commission through Reserve Officer Training Corps, Generous possessed a faultless service record. He had once suffered "a temporary emotional disorder" but upon recovering was certified "fully fit to handle the responsibilities of a naval officer." A friendly interviewer later thought him "highly strung . . . more than average neurotic but no psychotic plotter." On the *Vance* he could have tried another written complaint to Arnheiter, this time making sure he saw the letter by sidestepping the executive officer and thrusting it personally into the captain's hands. But he feared Arnheiter's cunning propensity for so twisting things as to place his own career in jeopardy. Perhaps an officer less traumatized by his superior's improprieties than Lieutenant Generous appears to have been would have taken them in his stride, nursing any sense of grievance until the opportunity arrived to air it before the proper higher authority. But Generous, clearly, could not wait to get things off his chest. In his private letter to the chaplain he declared that only concern for his wife and children prevented him from ignoring the order to lay aft. Not wishing to openly disobey, yet unable to accept "illegality and infringement of my constitutional rights," he labored under a burden from which he sought relief "anonymously . . . for the sake of my family." Of his right to challenge an order he deemed improper, the lieutenant felt in no doubt: "The Nuremberg Trials settled for all time the loyalty a military man must show his superior."

Upon arrival in South Vietnamese waters, Arnheiter sought immediate action. Sighting a horde of natives on the beach, he decided they were hostile and sent an armed party ashore in the whaleboat. The Vietnamese fled. It turned out, according to Arnheiter's officers, that they were refugees from a napalmed village, but the captain was officially commended for his "alert and aggressive action." Operation Masher had begun, an amphibious offensive against Vietcong and North Vietnamese units active mostly in a region north of the *Vance*'s patrol zone. The *Leonard E. Mason* and other gunfire destroyers had this stretch of coastline under attack. Despite orders to stay within his assigned zone, Arnheiter took the *Vance* into the *Mason*'s firing area, telling his operations officer, meanwhile, to send the navy's coastal surveillance center at Qui Nhon false position reports. Generous felt his best course was to obey but noted the ship's true position in his combat information center log. The *Mason*'s gunners just then had enough to contend with from adverse weather, low-lying fog that made marksmanship difficult, but the *Vance* repeatedly charged close to and even between the *Mason* and the shore targets, not only fouling her gun range but arousing her captain's concern lest the *Vance*'s unauthorized fire strike friendly forces operating less than a mile inland.

It was at this point that the *Mason*'s captain filed his official complaint. Arnheiter, on the other hand, claimed in a press release that his ship, "whose watchwords are Seek Out, Engage, and Destroy," carried out a "highly accurate bombardment" of enemy trenches and bunkers. Citing "major discrepancies," the captain of the *Mason* later characterized Arnheiter's words as "greatly at variance with what took place."

Even though there was nothing more than the report of the incensed captain of the *Mason* to go by, it seems a pity that no prompt action was taken to check the *Vance*'s activity under Marcus Arnheiter. A still more deplorable picture emerged from the testimony of Lieutenant Generous and his fellow officers: their captain on the top deck, in helmet and flak jacket, with a bone-handled revolver strapped to one hip, shouting excitedly and at one point so mistaking the ricochets of the *Vance*'s fire for hostile response that he ducked behind a gun-control shield for cover, as his crew watched in stupefied disbelief, the junior lieutenants exchanging remarks that dripped with contempt for their commanding officer. Arnheiter was to charge bitterly that even before these events off Vietnam his officers had begun their "conspiracy to mutiny." If what they recalled did in fact occur, at that stage a real mutiny erupting as traditionally from the lower deck might have come as a blessing to halt such a wretched scene.

More would be alleged. Arnheiter liked to stand on the top deck and via the ship's loudspeaker system provide his crew with a battle commentary—hardly censurable in itself, but one day off the Tom Quan peninsula he became so fascinated by jet planes and helicopters' strafing of coastal villages that he forgot to correct the *Vance*'s course and would have put her on the rocks had not the executive officer, after screaming unavailingly at his bemused captain, dashed into the pilothouse and ordered the helmsman to bring the ship about. And after each madcap attempt to lure enemy craft into gunnery range Arnheiter no longer hauled in the whaleboat but kept it under tow, the men still in it and soaked with spray from the destroyer's zigzagging wake. The sailors nicknamed him "Mad Marcus." Several who recalled *The Caine Mutiny* jokingly wondered when he would get out the ball bearings. The gunnery officer, Ens. Louis Belmonte (the "third major conspirator," according to Arnheiter), obeyed a suggestion from Lieutenant Generous and began listing the captain's aberrations, sort of a "Mad Marcus Log"—"not really a log . . . just a scribble here and there."

When these tales were publicly aired, comparisons with the fictitious *Caine* were inevitable. That they were also drawn on the occasion depends on the accuracy of reminiscence and sworn testimony. The Pulitzer prize–winning novel was published fifteen years earlier, but paperback reprints, a stage dramatization of the *Caine* court-martial, and a film with an all-star cast had kept Captain Queeg's image alive. Some of the published memoirs of Arnheiter's command might have strained credibility. But even if only partly true, they could well have justified the old cliché about life imitating art—except for one intriguing difference. Even in fiction, on the *Caine* under Queeg, it took at least ten months for "mutiny" to germinate, whereas the stress of serving scarcely sixty days under Arnheiter was enough, it seems, to have inflicted the executive officer with an ulcer and driven the operation officer to write of the captain that "the guy is paranoid."

Lieutenant Generous had grown distraught, and his state of mind impaired his efficiency, bringing him yet more and more under the verbal lash of his faultfinding commander. (The operations officer's written lament of being "in constant hot water for weeks" is an unconscious paraphrase of Fletcher Christian's memorable wail about weeks of living in hell.) The gunnery officer felt harassed. The executive officer sought impossible escape from his captain's endless talk and nagging. In consequence, the performance of the men in their respective divisons seriously deteriorated. Ensign Belmonte likened the ship to "a concentration camp." Arnheiter was everywhere, all the time, and none could elude him—except, according to other testimony, during inactive periods when he locked himself in his cabin, secretly drinking whiskey, not emerging before noon. His three principal victims—with the possible exception of Lieutenant Hardy, struggling to exercise a restraint appropriate to his position as second in command—found ways of mocking him behind his back, a ukulele-strumming operations officer composing songs of derision. Disrespectful cartoons were run off on a copying machine in the radio room and distributed among both officers and men.

The chief protagonists in the sad affair were commissioned officers. Arnheiter would name Lieutenant Generous as the instigator of a clandestine mutiny, and the captain in turn was lampooned or vilified as a freakish tyrant. From neither source could much be reliably gathered of the mood below decks. What the *Vance*'s people, more than one hundred sailors, thought of their unusual captain was left to speculation. Testimony showed two ratings (one of them while drunk) to have separately harbored murderous intentions toward him. But no palpably mutinous spirit appears to have flourished within the crew. No one complained of bad food or living conditions, infrequent shore leave, excessive work hours. From the accounts of the swimming and beer parties that Arnheiter staged for the lower ranks, it might be surmised that they good-naturedly tolerated his eccentricities, at worst took them as comic relief. In any navy, the lower deck seldom considers wardroom tensions much of its concern. Enlisted men on the *Vance* may have been merely confused by divided loyalties. And any of the people who made Arnheiter the butt of ribaldry were only following an example set by junior lieutenants presumably more cognizant than they of Article 89 of the Uniform Code of Military Justice, which declares that "any person . . . who behaves with disrespect towards his superior commissioned officer shall be punished as a court martial shall direct."

After a four-day rest at Bangkok the *Vance* resumed her patrol in the

Gulf of Siam. The official ship's history records "thirty boardings daily
. . . no contraband found" and some first-aid dispensation among
native crews. Hostility toward Arnheiter now took the form of petty
thievery: he lost his pipe and sunglasses. Meanwhile, the letter that
Generous had written earlier, complaining of the captain's fantail sessions, had gone through channels, and in the first week of March, off
An Thoi, South Vietnam, Lt. George Dando, a Presbyterian minister
with six months' active service, visited the ship. Disturbed by what he
saw and heard concerning their captain, he advised the ship's officers to
draw up court-martial charges against him and "fight it out." This
they were unwilling to do, "completely cowed," according to Dando,
"withdrawn to the point, psychologically speaking, where they were
dangerous." The chaplain attempted to work on Arnheiter himself but
was outtalked during a four-hour interview. Arnheiter admitted that he
may have gone too far in his efforts to tighten up a sloppy ship but
insisted that morale had improved under his command, and he summoned several chief petty officers to the cabin, each of whom agreed.
Dando felt that they were lying, perhaps to avoid endangering their
careers. Cautious about his own future, Dando waited a week before
deciding to report the frightening situation on the USS *Vance*.

In the meantime, there had occurred on that ship what some were
to assail as Arnheiter's crowning outrage. They were no doubt unaware
of a previous message from the commander of the Seventh Fleet's flotilla
of cruisers and destroyers to the effect that in the distribution of medals
the navy lagged behind the other services and that captains should do
their best to catch up. Arnheiter may have needed no such official
persuasion. But all he did, according to his subsequent testimony, was
to suggest citable phrases from examples in navy regulations when
Lieutenants Hardy and Generous came to him with their proposals for
ensuring that the *Vance*'s personnel received their quota of awards. His
alienated officers told an altogether different story. It was "solely as a
result of implicit direction" that they signed an eight-page citation
praising Arnheiter's courage and resourcefulness and recommending
that he be given a Silver Star, the navy's third-highest combat medal.
The whole idea, swore the officers, was Arnheiter's, and they went along
solely "to preserve peace in the ship."

By that time Lieutenant Dando's alarming words were before
Commo. Donald Milligan, commander of destroyer escorts at Subic
Bay in the Philippines: "When [Arnheiter] has the conn he is . . . a
menace. . . . misuse of recreation funds . . . submitting false reports. . . . two men tried to go after [him] while I was aboard. One

had a shotgun. . . . He does not appear to be as stable as an officer should be for command . . . he needs help." Milligan briefed his superiors on the situation as he understood it, and they sent a request to the Bureau of Naval Personnel in Washington for authority to relieve Marcus Arnheiter immediately, pending investigation. The *Vance* lay in Manila Bay, having just arrived, her three junior officers by their own admission in a highly emotional state, drinking nightly and plotting harebrained schemes against their captain. Early on 31 March, exactly ninety-nine days after taking over the *Vance,* Arnheiter received a coded teletype informing him that he was about to lose her. At eight that evening Commodore Milligan came on board and formally relieved him. With the commodore's permission, Arnheiter mustered all hands and gave a short farewell address. Such was the extraordinary spleen he must be presumed to have created in the wardroom of the *Vance* that even after his departure the ship's operations officer engaged with others to produce and circulate spurious documents holding him up to ridicule.

Eighteen

◢

NELSONIAN TRADITION
OR TYRANNICAL WHIMSY?

The manner in which Lieutenant Commander Arnheiter was hustled off the *Vance* left some members of the naval establishment feeling uneasy. It appeared to violate regulations requiring that charges and complaints against an officer be given one in writing before the drastic decision to relieve one of command. A more acceptable course would have been just to separate him from his ship while the charges were being investigated. The navy tried to still doubts by emphasizing wartime needs. Formalities had to be sacrificed to speed. The *Vance* must be back on Yankee Station upon the completion of her repair work at Manila. This controversy was in one respect a reminder of how far things had progressed since the early years of the American navy. Arnheiter was summarily dismissed from the *Vance* but remained in the service. Matters were not always handled this fairly. During the Quasi-War with France at the close of the eighteenth century a captain was expelled from the United States Navy without trial. Even his dismissal required an order from the president of the United States, and as James Fenimore Cooper, ever alert to real or fancied injustices in the navy, wrote four decades later, "It is at all times a dangerous and in scarcely any instance a necessary practice."

In any event, the furor over Arnheiter and the *Vance* had only begun. It would be said that by so swiftly removing him from a command he should never have been given in the first place, the navy corrected that original error just in time to prevent a real mutiny. But obliged now to continue the legal process, it invited criticism almost every step of the way. Commodore Milligan gathered statements for and against

Arnheiter and sent them to Capt. Ward W. Witter at Subic Bay, who conducted an informal one-man hearing. Assisted by a navy lawyer, Arnheiter was allowed to cross-examine all witnesses, but there were no fewer than forty allegations against him, clear evidence in his opinion that his officers had plotted "a new kind of mutiny . . . designed for the Modern Navy." The hearing lasted six days and concluded with the lone judge's recommendation that Arnheiter never again be given naval command, "either ashore or afloat."

In due course the results of the Subic Bay investigation came before Rear Adm. Walter H. Baumberger, commander of the cruiser-destroyer force in the Pacific, to whose San Diego office Arnheiter had been temporarily attached while the navy pondered his fate. Baumberger dismissed all but three of the findings, and those trivial, and proposed that Arnheiter be given another chance to prove himself. Doubtless not only an earlier personal association with Marcus Arnheiter but the weight of sentiment he had recruited to his cause influenced Baumberger, for several retired admirals perceived him as a victim of the sort of radical, pacifist, and generally unwholesome spirit daily manifest in college-campus riots and antiwar demonstrations.

Arnheiter now set about defending his character with a zeal the equal of any he had displayed on Yankee Station. With legal assistance and a thick file that included favorable affidavits from ten enlisted men of the *Vance,* he accused his former lieutenants of "mutiny and conspiracy to commit mutiny," charges that Admiral Baumberger, by then harboring second thoughts about his controversial friend, induced him to withdraw. At the same time the commander-in-chief of the Pacific Fleet endorsed the Subic Bay findings on Marcus Arnheiter, and the case next came before Adm. Benedict J. Semmes, head of the Bureau of Naval Personnel. Arnheiter meanwhile was transferred into bureacratic exile at the Treasure Island naval installation, San Francisco. Early in 1967 Semmes seemed to close the case by officially affirming the judgment of Arnheiter as unfit for command. Even Capt. Richard Alexander, the commander's erstwhile mentor, advised him to forget the navy and prepare for a new career.

But Arnheiter had no intention of giving up the fight. He sent a letter, dated 1 September 1967, subject heading "Additional evidence concerning subversion, mutinous activities and conditions aboard USS *Vance* before, during and after my command," to the secretary of the navy. It charged that subordinate officers had "covertly sabotaged" his efforts to rehabilitate a ship of whose poor disciplinary record he had been earlier apprised by the commandant of the 14th Naval District at

Pearl Harbor. This officer had "most strongly encouraged me to initiate a Command Guidance Program." He quoted another admiral, the deputy chief of the navy's logistics division, who had expressed uneasiness over "the method of [Arnheiter's] relief, and the possible ill-effects on Navy discipline and esprit de corps." He enclosed affidavits from petty officers on the *Vance;* a typical one read, "The trouble was people had been too used to being lazy and didn't want to change. As soon as [Arnheiter] left the ship everything slumped again." Also among Arnheiter's "evidence" were two or three of the papers his officers had faked—someone had sent Arnheiter a sample—designed and circulated to make him a laughing stock: "[They] show a shocking resistance to my efforts at getting a mess of a ship squared away." Arnheiter very likely saw to it that Captain Alexander knew about all this material. Certainly Alexander read some of the pro-Arnheiter affidavits from the *Vance's* lower deck. He thereupon retracted his earlier defeatist advice to Arnheiter, deplored it as "a pusillanimous step," and took a dramatically different tack, moving in Arnheiter's defense with such boldness that he all but shattered his own career.

After spending more than half his life in naval service, the forty-five-year-old Alexander had just been handed a plum appointment, command of the 54,000-ton *New Jersey,* the world's only operational battleship, under refit for South Vietnamese war service. Alexander interrupted his supervision of the work at Philadelphia to plead Arnheiter's cause in person before Secretary of the Navy Paul Ignatius. He left him a twenty-seven–page summary that pulled no punches. Arnheiter had been outrageously mistreated, the victim not only of professional assassination committed by "liars and disloyal officers," whose "slovenly and unseamanlike lives" he had disrupted by enforcing discipline, but also of the "improper, cowardly and peremptory" action of superiors who had used "flawed and extra-legal means" to remove him from command. His operations officer had written "hysterically to a junior chaplain . . . invoking the Nuremberg trial to support his acknowledged disloyalty." That chaplain's report was a pack of "hearsay complaints . . . distortions . . . falsehoods." Not even the *Vance's* previous captain escaped Alexander's broadside: the vessel was "a scroungy tin-can" that became "a first-class fighting ship" only under Arnheiter's command. Alexander concluded with a challenge: "Mr. Secretary, what all of your officers will demand to know is just how in hell could this happen in the U.S. Navy?"

That parting shot alone might have signaled a halt to Alexander's professional advancement. But in puzzling ignorance of or disregard for time-honored naval codes of discretion, Alexander had passed along copies of the letter to more than a dozen congressmen and reporters.

The reaction of the naval hierarchy was foreseeable. Within six weeks Captain Alexander had lost command of the *New Jersey* and was, like Arnheiter, permanently beached, his exile a staff job in the Boston Naval District.

Thanks as much to the navy's mishandling of his case as to his news media campaign, Marcus Arnheiter was widely perceived as a hero or a martyr. Impressed by his insistence that he had been cashiered for prosecuting the war too vigorously, one columnist titled an article, "He Could Have Been Another Halsey." A retired admiral in Arnheiter's corner predicted that wardrooms would echo with expressed fears that the navy was no longer "a safe harbor for officers with guts and forthrightness." An ambitious New York congressman held three days of hearings intended to force Secretary Ignatius into convening the court of inquiry that Arnheiter demanded. The congressman called on Ignatius to resign, but what so enraged the navy that it opened certain of its unflattering files on Arnheiter to inspection was his public charge that it had victimized him through lies and illegality.

The navy's newly aired material included the damaging Subic Bay testimony; told of the false position reports, the unauthorized shore bombardments, and the white for black toilet seat; and in yet another bizarre suggestion of the *Caine* mentioned a young ensign whose apparent inability to keep his shirttail tucked in drove the captain to distraction. Enough of a serious nature was revealed to imply justification for removing Arnheiter from command, but left unanswered was the question of why the navy had not court-martialed him or at least held a court of inquiry. Perhaps it did not want to expose its own lapses in judgment and procedure. But this was a period in which the naval service was acutely sensitive to public criticism. A series of ship mishaps had occurred in recent months. Nuclear submarines had collided in the Caribbean, and a destroyer had struck an aircraft carrier in the Mediterranean. Another carrier had rammed a submarine and shortly thereafter grounded on a sandbar. A wayward amphibious vessel had peeled some of the top off of the Chesapeake Bay Bridge-Tunnel. These and other accidents had received much press coverage, to the embarrassment of navy chiefs, who understandably might have wished the latest "scandal" over and done with. But with its angry (and successful) move to counter public support for Arnheiter with a more blemished image of him, it tended to perpetuate the affair.

A hitherto sympathetic or evenhanded newsman used the navy's disclosures to dig further. His published article detailed, among Arnheiter's other "aberrations," the alleged attempt to coerce officers into recommending him for a medal. The reporter later expanded his research into a book. Lawsuits followed, but none brought Marcus Arnheiter the vindication that he continued doggedly to seek long after both he and his "disloyal" officers had left the navy and the *Vance* was back in mothballs, to be finally disposed of in 1976.

The Nuremberg war-crimes trials effectively put to rest the concept that military orders must in all cases be obeyed without question. This fact had been recalled on the USS *Vance,* after less than a month under Marcus Arnheiter's command, to justify a contemplated disobedience of his orders. But the so-called Nuremberg ruling must be handled gingerly and never presumed a convenient method of escape from the dictates of an eccentric, even paranoid, commander.

There is still considerable relevance in the old United States Articles of War, which, although the Nuremberg principle may be thought a product of a more enlightened age, substantially anticipated it by almost a hundred years: "While obedience is the life of an army . . . an order contrary to the law need not be obeyed." But it is then implied that the illegality of an order issued does not necessarily embrace obedience to that order. In other words, if Arnheiter broke the law by ordering men to attend quasireligious fantail sessions, it did not automatically follow that the act of compliance was also illegal. Unless compliance was itself a clear "breach of law, human or divine," the subordinate's duty was to obey, "expressing his right, if he sees occasion, of protesting, at the proper time and in a proper spirit, and appealing to the common superior to right any wrong which he may think he suffers. No other course is officer-like or consistent with discipline."

Reviewing his experiences on the *Vance* after his return to civilian life, William T. Generous used the Nuremberg determination to support his argument that a captain could not legally enforce an order the subordinate recognized as unlawful. But it was not, he conceded, "a simple situation." No doubt it became clearer to the former operations officer during the study he made and subsequently published that traced the development of the Uniform Code of Military Justice. Today's UCMJ succinctly equates willful disobedience of a lawful command by a superior commissioned officer with common assault upon him, such offenses when committed in wartime punishable by death. The problem arises from the modifier *lawful*. During the brief war in the Persian Gulf in 1991 a young American officer claimed the right to disobey (assignment to the battlefront) because of a conscientious feeling that the order was "unlawful." A retired officer commenting on the case went further, claiming that in consequence of the Nuremberg Trials the

UCMJ *requires* a member of the United States armed forces to disobey an order he or she considers unlawful. In fact, this body of law admits of no such right or requirement, and the *United States Manual for Courts Martial* states that "an order requiring the performance of a military duty or act may be inferred to be lawful and it is disobeyed at the peril of the subordinate. This inference does not apply to a patently illegal order."

The key phrase here is "patently illegal." Obviously, this would describe an order to kill unarmed and nonthreatening civilians, the sort of crime that produced the Nuremberg principle in the first place. (Outright theft is also "patently illegal," and to return to the *Vance*, it may be wondered why the order or persuasion to steal candelabra from the officers' club at Guam was not resisted on "Nuremberg" grounds.) Except for very rare instances, then, a commander's order may be inferred as lawful. And this holds uniquely true at sea, where the captain of a ship, today as in the past, functions to all intents and purposes as guide, parental figure, and adjudicating deity.

That is all very well, but if the captain is for some reason incapable of properly shouldering those responsibilities, the same isolated environment may compel drastic action on the part of subordinate officers. Arnheiter's second-in-command had considered swearing out court-martial charges against him for falsifying his position reports but gave up the idea, convinced that the captain would somehow block this process. Since by their own admission they believed themselves in thrall to a psychologically unstable commander, one or two of the officers may also have thought of seizing control of the ship from him, as was done on the fictional *Caine*. For a brief moment something of the kind did occur when the *Vance* headed for the rocks and the executive officer, unable to get a coherent response from his allegedly mesmerized captain, took it upon himself to order the necessary change of course. The *Caine* had also faced disaster, and her executive officer had acted under the then-operative Articles of War, which permitted him to relieve his captain from duty by placing him under arrest or on the sick list—such action, however, to be justified only by the "most unusual and extraordinary circumstances" and never to be taken "without the approval of the Navy Department or other appropriate higher authority, except when reference to such higher authority is undoubtedly impracticable."

Sixty years before anyone had heard of Captain Queeg or the *Caine*, Herman Melville conjured an example of the dilemma posed by doubts about a captain's sanity. Melville's imagined vessel was HMS *Indomitable* (or *Bellepotent*, his later choice of name), whose commanding officer,

Captain Vere, was apparently shocked out of his senses when his stammering angel of a foretopman, Billy Budd, struck the master-at-arms dead. Recovering his voice, Captain Vere ordered a drumhead court-martial, in the surgeon's opinion an irrational decision. The right thing to do was to place Billy in irons and postpone further action until the ship rejoined its squadron, when the admiral could deal with the business. The *Indomitable*'s lieutenants agreed. But the captain must not be disobeyed, unless his peculiar behavior was in fact a symptom of madness. The surgeon deliberated: "Was Captain Vere suddenly affected in his mind, or was it but a transient excitement? Was he unhinged?" Assuming he was, how could it be proved? Nothing could more baffle a subordinate officer than to suspect his captain to be "not mad indeed, but yet not quite unaffected in his intellect. To argue his order would be insolence. To resist him would be mutiny."

Marcus Arnheiter's accusation that his officers conspired to mutiny is unlikely to have survived close judicial examination, though charges of gross disrespect might have made some headway. The proper course for any of the *Vance*'s people who felt wronged was to have first applied to their captain for redress and, if refused, to convey their grievance "to any superior commissioned officer who shall forward that complaint to the officer exercising court-martial jurisdiction over the officer against whom it is made." The complaint would be studied and appropriate action taken. It is that simple but quite evidently did not appear so to Arnheiter's officers, who, unable to contain their emotions for as long as due process would have required, had sought relief in deriding or vilifying him behind his back and writing to a junior chaplain.

Defending his manner of command, Arnheiter had recalled Adm. Lord Nelson's boast that he could make a naval officer out of any lout: "It occurred to me that I should attempt to follow through in the Nelsonian tradition as best I could." His reward was to be publicly portrayed as "a real-life Queeg . . . who ran his ship with tyrannical whimsy," unable to tell right from wrong, unknowingly driving his junior officers half out of their own wits. A naval court of inquiry complete with psychiatric appraisal might have shed more light on the affair and stilled any disquieting questions of why it took such a singularly short time for two or three officers to develop hostile if not mutinous feelings against a commander it was their bounden duty to respect and support. As it was, everyone connected with the *Vance* affair seemed to have their say (not including the lower deck to any great extent), and the navy was only too willing to declare the case closed. If mystery still lingered, the truth was perhaps only explicable in terms of human psychology, and while clues and parallels were sought through copious references to a novelist's USS *Caine,* they might just as well have been looked for aboard HMS *Bounty.*

The *Vance* affair coincided with, and some thought may partly have reflected, the social turbulence of the late 1960s. Not for generations had Americans felt so conscious of a revolutionary spirit, feared no less than welcomed as traditional values were overturned and age-old loyalties questioned. It was a period of national agitation, and in no way could the defense forces of the United States have remained unaffected, especially since the two most combustible elements at work on the American scene were the demands of racial minorities for fair recognition and a mounting controversy over the Vietnam War.

Antiwar and generally countercultural movements employing a busy "underground" press advocated sabotage and outright mutiny. News sheets titled *Counterpoint, Fatigue Press, Ultimate Weapon, Open Sights,* and *Last Harass* circulated on army camps and found their way aboard naval craft. A sailor named Roger Priest prepared his subversive newsletter at the Department of Defense desk where he worked, and knowledgeable of a seaman's rights, he had his personnel file altered to designate a pacifist organization as beneficiary for service-oriented life insurance and death gratuities. Through his press releases Priest urged other sailors and soldiers to follow suit, exulting in the presumption that were he to be shipped off to Southeast Asia and killed, the War Resisters League could expect a check from the Pentagon. *Open Sights* declared at its editorial masthead, "This paper is your personal property. It cannot legally be taken from you. If anybody tries, demand a signed receipt from your commanding officer." The conventional news media, meanwhile, ran disturbing stories from the distant war zone of "fragging" incidents, murderous assaults by army subordinates on their own officers. Considering the enormous size of America's overseas forces, the extent of such mutinous phenomena was minuscule. Even so, Gen. William Westmoreland resorted to soldierly understatement when he warned early in 1969 of "deliberate efforts . . . to introduce the divisiveness found in our society into the Army."

He might also have mentioned the navy. When in autumn 1971 the 60,000-ton aircraft carrier *Constellation* prepared to return to the Southeast Asian war zone, pacifist groups worked very hard to keep her at home. According to the commander-in-chief of the Pacific Fleet,

The aircraft carrier *Constellation* was a special target for antiwar campaigners in 1972. *(U.S. Navy)*

"never was there such a concerted effort to entice American servicemen from their posts." It had no measurable success. Of the carrier's 2,700-man operational crew (air squadrons brought the total ship's complement to 4,500), only nine seamen deserted, and although the Non-Violent Action Committee claimed that a thousand men had petitioned their officers to allow Jane Fonda and other entertainers on board to perform an antiwar show, the captain said that he had counted only thirty-two signatures.

Still, it was an impressive campaign. Sailors were plied with leaflets and invitations to picnics and private parties (usually accepted) and preached at from the San Diego dockyard gates by political activists. Twenty-five hundred letters of peace propaganda arrived on board the *Constellation*, addressed to individuals not by name but as members of various divisions. This prompted the vessel's commanding officer to order them all destroyed as "undeliverable"—which got him into hot water with the United States Postal Service because each envelope bore a return address. Bumper stickers ashore and posters on boats in the harbor called upon the *Constellation*'s people to disobey sailing orders, and even as she headed for sea on 1 October a light plane flew overhead trailing a 125-foot banner with the words "Constellation Stay Home For Peace."

The carrier sailed under a new captain, John D. Ward, over whose signature there shortly appeared an order on the subject "Handling of Dissident and Protest Activities," which prohibited officers from bargaining with any so-called serviceman's union. The order derived from United States Navy Regulations, Article 1247—"Combinations of persons . . . for the purpose of influencing legislation, remonstrating against orders . . . complaining of particular duty . . . are forbidden." No guidance was offered about how officers might cope with such "combinations" should any develop. That such directives had to be posted at all was an indication of the navy's hasty arousal to situations unlikely to have been foreseen even two decades earlier. Changes had occured to compel fresh thinking on the meaning and application of discipline.

Traditional precepts were fast becoming obsolete. For instance, in a 1955 officers training manual Rear Adm. Arleigh Burke, warning of a "depersonalization of the Fleet," had stated that "a paramount duty" of a warship's division officers was not so much to function as specialists as to "fulfil their responsibilities to their subordinates." Each officer must display "continuous concern" about his men "as individuals." Few advocates of an efficient fleet would have argued otherwise. But in an age of increasingly complicated naval structure and weaponry, the admiral's conclusion that "a successful navy requires a unique and close relationship between officer and man" suggested an ideal ever more difficult to attain.

In March 1972 the *Kitty Hawk,* a carrier of the same vintage but on her sixth war deployment, joined the *Constellation.* Other United States war vessels massed in the Yankee Station area. The reason for the naval buildup was that while America's ground involvement in the Indo-Chinese conflict had begun winding down, intelligence reports told of massive preparations under way by North Vietnamese troops to cross the demilitarized zone into South Vietnam. When they finally attacked in April, the ships already on Yankee Station were able to respond at once with round-the-clock aircraft strikes against Vietcong military and supply facilities. This meant a punishing work schedule for carrier crews that were partly composed of black Americans disillusioned with navy life and sensitive to anything construable as a racist affront. And as the Communists' Easter offensive turned into a protracted summer campaign, its effect of keeping the American ships on station beyond their scheduled periods of deployment aggravated a lower-deck racial polarization noticeable even before their arrival in the Gulf of Tonkin. The minority-affairs officer on the *Constellation* was to testify that her captain "never, in my opinion, fully realized the potential powder keg he was sitting on."

For the United States Navy it was an unprecedented situation. While conducting operations against an acknowledged foreign foe, Seventh Fleet aircraft carriers in the Pacific had also to contend with a less publicized internal strife that had its roots in antiwar sentiment and racial frustration. Years later a secretary of the navy, John F. Lehman, would recall that during his active service on the *Saratoga* off Vietnam in 1972 "no white officer would walk unescorted on the second deck where the enlisted men's mess was." In July fires were started on the *Forrestal* and *Ranger,* the eighteenth instance of sabotage aboard the latter vessel, a prime target back home for peace activists' "Stop Our Ships" agitation. All told, by the close of that year the United States Navy would log seventy-four instances of sabotage, more than half on aircraft carriers, none of them attributable to "enemy" action.

A newspaper called *Kitty Litter* circulated below decks on the *Kitty Hawk*. Its August issue singled out the new commanding officer, Marland W. Townsend, a veteran of twenty-seven years' naval service, for critical assessment: "He may not be an 'Arnheiter' but instead of cheering the *Kitty Hawk*'s disregard for life"—a reference to Townsend's practice of regularly informing the crew of combat activity—"he should be racking his brains to find ways of making life a little better on the *Hawk*." Actually, in keeping with reforms and innovations ushered in by Rear Adm. Elmo Zumwalt, Jr., a progressive and controversial chief of naval operations, the *Kitty Hawk* had its minority affairs and "human relations" staffs in place, and as the carrier continued her patrols into the late summer months racial harmony on board showed signs of improvement. They were to prove deceptive.

The *Constellation,* meanwhile, following her extended combat tour, had returned to North Island Naval Air Station, San Diego, to face a disruptive period. Because of the war's quickened pace, she was needed back with the Seventh Fleet at an early date. A large package of repairs would be crowded into eight weeks, with prospects, in official parlance, of "seriously degraded living and working conditions." The ship became almost uninhabitable, with water often cut off, food and cleaning arrangements thereby impaired, and sleep ruined by the incessant din of drilling and hammering. And during these two late-summer months of intensive shipyard work there was a heavy turnover in the *Constellation*'s crew. But the most important reason for the increased risk of disciplinary problems was that of nine hundred new men reporting for duty on the *Constellation,* a larger percentage than ever before were from a ghetto environment, and they not only found themselves forced to live in conditions of extreme discomfort but were thrust into the dreariest, most menial, and most unpopular jobs on board.

The racial situation on large vessels was not helped by a perhaps unavoidable practice of treating minority affairs or "human relations" programs as a sideline for chief petty officers and others who already had their work officially cut out for them. Dealing with personnel numbering in the thousands, they could hardly have been expected to devote proper consideration, much less time, to grievances with whose social or ethnic origin many of them were utterly unfamiliar. In hindsight, Admiral Zumwalt concluded that if some of the programs he had initiated fell short of success it was because the commanding officers who implemented them were "more faithful to the letter than to the spirit." But critics were quick to blame the programs themselves as too radical and conducive to permissiveness.

Zumwalt's appointment in 1970 as chief of naval operations had itself raised eyebrows. Predecessors in the post thought the forty-nine-year-old admiral lacked such alleged prerequisites as fleet command experience and proven ability for working with the country's top defense planners. What Elmo Zumwalt undoubtedly possessed was, in his own words, a resolve to bring "the Navy's treatment of ethnic or racial minorities, especially blacks, into conformity with stated national policy, not to say common fairness and decency." No one, Zumwalt included, could have denied that the navy had moved forward. In 1948 President Truman had officially abolished racial segregation in the United States armed forces, and after another four years the naval academy had produced its first black graduate. But throughout the following two decades the navy dragged its feet, especially when compared with the progress made by the other services and on the domestic scene, and Zumwalt had determined that it should catch up.

He announced his innovations through a series of policy directives soon famed or notorious throughout the service as "Z-grams." An early one called for increased attention to providing equal opportunity for all minority groups. To this end, scores of programs were devised, some causing outcries from traditionalists who thought them designed to bypass the navy's hallowed "chain of command" system. Another Z-gram revised long-standing regulations about personal dress and appearance. There would be no restrictions on beards, mustaches, sideburns, and ethnic hairstyles. "We must learn," Zumwalt said, "to adapt to changing fashion." At the same time, recruiting standards were lowered and basic-training periods shortened to fill the navy's manpower needs more quickly and in fairer racial proportion. As much as anything, the new recruitment policies spelled trouble. Men lacking even an elementary education were entering an organization whose greatest demand was for personnel with high technical qualifications. Blacks were rushed "from street to fleet" in less than two months, only to find themselves performing the least attractive shipboard duties, usually under white supervision. It was a situation tailor-made for discontent and the recrudescence of old animosities.

Nineteen

⬛

THE TROUBLED CARRIERS

I n the first weeks of October 1972 the *Constellation* was at sea off San Diego, testing new equipment and conducting refresher-training exercises. The atmosphere below decks had not improved. When boiler-feed tanks were found contaminated and steam cata-pults on the flight deck tampered with, black crew members believing themselves under suspicion of sabotage demanded to see the captain. But Ward now seldom left the bridge. His voice was regularly heard over the ship's communications system, but he was an inaccessible figure to thousands of the men under his command. That his presence was required almost continuously on the bridge during these days of maxi-mum predeployment activity was an explanation unlikely to have satis-fied elements among his people primed by experience to detect discrimi-nation in even routine attitudes. The ship's closed-circuit color television system might have been used to some advantage in promoting better communications between command and the crew. But there was little time or opportunity. Racial polarization grew unchecked. Blacks took to meeting in the most secluded of the ship's three barbershops or in the "sidewalk cafe," a snug enclosure on the aft bomb assembly area used for relaxation, reading, and letter writing. Whites began to avoid this place, many of them forming conclaves of their own in the central electrical shop. And pretty soon, when sailors of different races met in the narrow passageways, some would make a show of refusing to turn sideways to let the others pass.

Far across the Pacific, whites and blacks among the crew of the *Kitty Hawk* had already come to blows. Of the carrier's 348 officers and 4,135

The trouble on the carrier *Kitty Hawk* sprang from an indefinite extension of her combat deployment. *(U.S. Naval Institute)*

enlisted men, 5 officers and 297 men were black. Ironically, what most inflamed emotions was a grievance common to all on board—an indefinite extension of the ship's deployment. Nobody, Capt. Marland Townsend included, had any sure idea about when they were going home. Comdr. Benjamin Cloud, Jr., recently appointed as the first black executive officer on a United States Navy aircarft carrier, could feel "the increasing tension and uncertainty." And because of the war pressures, the navy could not send any ships on furlough to Hong Kong or Japan. The *Kitty Hawk*'s only liberty port in almost a year had been Olongapo at Subic Bay in the Philippines, which the ship had visited in October and which was the main recreation center for American forces in Southeast Asia. With a reputation for unsavory night life it was itself something of a problem for the U.S. Navy.

Late on 11 October at the Sampaguita Club sailors of mixed races from the *Kitty Hawk* fought each other until a marine riot squad intervened. The next day the mood on board deteriorated when instead of making for home the carrier returned to the firing line. In the evening, while the flight deck bustled with aircraft takeoffs and landings, a young black apprentice seaman summoned to the ship's investigator's office for questioning about the Olongapo brawl brought nine companions with him and grew belligerent. The men stormed out of the office and on their way aft beat up a white mess cook who was stacking trays. About fifty black sailors had gathered on the after mess deck and were throwing furniture around. Unable to restore order, the chief master-at-arms summoned the marines. He apparently did this upon his own initiative. As subsequently noted in the navy's official report, "No officer was aware that the marines were responding until they were heard running through the passageway." Their involvement at this point was the first in what officialdom, with hindsight, would deem a series of mistakes.

At 9:37 P.M. Captain Townsend, informed of the unruliness, issued orders to intensify the white floodlight illumination of the flight deck for upgraded security. At the same time Capt. Nicholas Carlucci of the Marine Corps hurried to the after mess deck and sent the marines back to their living spaces. (The five blacks in the sixty-man detachment, it was later officially stated, "acted only as well disciplined Marines.") Some were roughed up as they withdrew. Commander Cloud was also on the scene, understandably convinced that he could appeal to the dissidents in brotherly fashion. What he should have done first, according to subsequent official review, was identify and arrest the original troublemakers. By instead adopting a question and answer approach he was "committing the command to a strategy of negotiation in lieu of firm discipline." Twice the executive officer's remarks prompted a clenched-fist salute from his audience, and he responded in kind. Perhaps it was at one such moment that Captain Townsend stepped unnoticed onto the after mess deck because "I did not like what I heard." He slipped back out, summoned Captain Carlucci to his stateroom, and told him to post special security details on the flight and hangar decks as a precaution against sabotage.

Commander Cloud left the after mess deck with fifteen sailors desiring further discussion with him in his quarters. The executive officer thought that the crisis was over. It was certainly localized. Most of the 60,000-ton carrier's complement knew nothing of what had so far occurred. But the trouble quickly flared up again. In compliance with Captain Townsend's security instructions, the marine commander had dispatched four patrols to the hangar deck with orders to break up groups of more than three men and to take any that objected to the ship's legal office, using force if necessary. The blacks whom Commander Cloud had addressed left the after mess deck unaware of these directions to the marines, and neither did Cloud know or he could have warned them to avoid returning to their berths by way of the hangar deck. When they reached this six-hundred-foot-long area, many in quite innocent groups of more than three, they were surprised to find that marines in line abreast, nightsticks at the ready, were blocking their path. Since the marines' withdrawal from the after mess deck and Commander Cloud's reassurances had only just pacified them, the fresh appearance of the marines struck many as a double cross. Too infuriated to disperse, they resisted. Scuffling began around and in between the F-4 Phantom jet fighters lined up to port and starboard.

Outnumbered, the marines found themselves forced back into the vicinity of the open doors between the forward and aft hangar bays. Many of the sailors wielded weapons, including tie-down chains from the parked aircraft. Someone hit the marine sergeant with a dogging wrench. At the height of the melee Captain Townsend and Commander Cloud arrived separately. A three-foot length of guardrail intended for the sergeant may have struck the captain, but his presence on the scene and the marines' departure (their second dismissal of the evening) had a subduing effect, or so it seemed to Commander Cloud, who, informed of another outbreak of violence in the medical spaces on the second deck, decided to head there and leave the hangar deck under the captain's control. On the way he met a trio of blacks out to get the marine sergeant: "Armed with weapons, chains and pipes, no two ways about it, they intended to kill." He ushered them into his stateroom with stern advice that they cool down.

Commander Cloud found the sick bay close to becoming a battleground. A marine corporal bled from wounds received on the hangar deck. While sprawled on an operating table awaiting attention, he came under a second attack and had to defend himself with an oxygen bottle. Upon the executive officer's arrival the commotion began to die down. But within minutes someone shouted that Captain Townsend was injured, perhaps killed, on the hangar deck. Commander Cloud would testify that he heard this dreadful news from two sources. Shaken by a vision of the bloodshed engulfing the aircraft carrier, he determined to separate black crew members from whites as distantly as possible. He raced down three levels to damage-control central and over the ship's loudspeaker system made what he would recall as a "very impassioned" announcement. Essentially, it identified himself, declared an emergency, and called on all "black brothers" to assemble on the after mess deck, where he would meet them. He also ordered, "All marines proceed on the double to the forecastle."

The announcement had the positive effect of making personnel on the bridge and at other key stations aware that something unusual was going on. But a relative handful knew its nature. When the *Kitty Hawk*'s operations officer telephoned the bridge, the ship's navigator replied that everything there was normal. As a safety precaution, however, he ordered the bridge doors locked. The officer of the deck, as stated in the report of a formal one-officer investigation of the trouble, was equally in the dark. "As a focal point for communications throughout the ship the bridge was omitted or bypassed." This was the inevitable result of the captain's and the executive officer's reacting to developments more often independently than in concert. It said much for their concern and compassion, but "by moving about the ship . . . both officers isolated themselves from bridge communication and left the ship without effective central direction." Those on the scene may not have appreciated such judgments arrived at with the benefit of hindsight, especially Captain Townsend, who happened to be safe and sound. He was conducting a more or less agreeable discussion with a dwindling number of sailors on the hangar deck when Commander Cloud's startling announcement issued from the loudspeakers.

Without any idea why "the X.O. was taking over the ship," he sped to damage-control central, brushed past his embarrassed while relieved second-in-command, and let his people know he was very much alive. He went on to sympathize with them in their dashed hopes for a return home. He shared their frustration, "but we have got to live with it." He would now adjourn to the forecastle and meet with whomever wished to see him: "But, for God's sake, the rest of you go back to your spaces."

The apparent conflict for command heard publicly throughout the ship emboldened those few men most disposed to violence. Some of the subsequent beatings at scattered locations were for settling old scores, others were mindless. Racial hostility was sadly manifest. At about 3:00 A.M. Commander Cloud confronted a large number of his fellow blacks on the forecastle. "They were chanting and hollering . . . shirts were off." To his pleas for restraint, several answered that he was no brother of theirs and should be thrown overboard. He invoked the names of Martin Luther King and Malcolm X, and in what was surely one of the most astonishing displays ever witnessed on an American ship of war, he tore off his own shirt, snatched a steel pipe from a sailor, and challenged any man who doubted his sincerity to take it and physically beat him. None did, and he was thereafter listened to with some respect. As would be officially acknowledged, the black executive officer, realizing the dissidents' "critical pitch," took needful and appropriate action: "[His] methods were unorthodox but the existing circumstances were extraordinary."

Captain Townsend also remonstrated with angry or confused knots of men in passageways and berthing compartments. He and his executive officer now acted in harmony, inviting all hands to the forecastle for a complete airing of grievances. The option of going to general quarters had occurred to the captain but did not impress him as expedient. Those of his superiors whose duty would be to review his conduct faulted him on this point, the failure to call general quarters being, in their judgment, one reason why the violence escalated. Missing from their conclusions was anything like an official avowal that had clear information regarding the length of the *Kitty Hawk*'s extended deployment been conveyed to Captain Townsend, enabling him to tell his people precisely when they could expect to go home, dulled hopes might never have turned into a riot in the first place.

To the captain, a gathering of blacks in the mess area, enjoying sandwiches and soul music from a record player, smacked uneasily of a victory celebration. It was primarily a sign of lowered tensions, or plain bodily tiredness, and he had little trouble clearing the decks so the cooks could prepare breakfast. Such are the size and intricacy of modern aircraft carriers that hundreds on board the *Kitty Hawk* still slept undisturbed. Many of the original rioters were also by this time under blankets. Townsend's meeting on the forecastle, attended by Commander Cloud, attracted only a few more than sixty black sailors (roughly equal to the number of that night's casualties in sick bay). But it lasted two hours. Halfway through the meeting a boatswain's mate emerged in his underwear from a berthing compartment where, he nervously whispered to the executive officer, scores of whites were plotting retaliation against their black shipmates. Cloud was quickly on the scene to talk them out of it. At 7:00 A.M., after fifteen hours of disorder, a sleepless Captain Townsend once more manned the bridge, to begin another day of scheduled flight operations. The *Kitty Hawk* remained on Yankee Station a further three weeks, conducting daily air strikes against North Vietnam, the whites and blacks of her crew working alongside one another in their customary billets, with no significant recurrence of trouble.

Less than a week after the disturbances on the *Kitty Hawk* black sailors demonstrated aboard the fleet oiler *Hassayampa* docked at Subic Bay. The same thing happened two days later on the aircraft carrier *Saratoga,* and only the captain's decision to sound general quarters averted a major riot. The growing threat of widespread racial turmoil in the armed services prompted the Defense Department's Race Relations Institute to unveil a program of annual guidance seminars for all generals

The *Constellation*'s "Sidewalk Cafe" was a snug enclosure for the airing of discontent. *(U.S. Navy)*

and admirals. Whether resulting from minority discontent or pacifist sentiment, the gathering crisis was impossible to ignore. In Norfolk on the last day of October 1972 the commander-in-chief of the Atlantic Fleet warned that "anti-military misfits" had become a "grave liability" in the navy. Admiral Zumwalt, at the officer's side just then, tended to contradict him, calling the problem still "minuscule." Two reports that reached Zumwalt's desk almost simultaneously a few days later might have persuaded him to think otherwise. One called the navy's classification, advancement, and placement systems "discriminatory. The recruiting slogan 'You can be black *and* Navy too' is false advertising. You can be black *or* Navy more truly represents the situation." Following on that came the findings of an assistant secretary of defense who had conducted a three weeks' overseas inspection concentrated on the aircraft carrier *Forrestal*, stationed in the eastern Mediterranean. The racial friction below decks disturbed him, and while "not prepared to predict mutinous conditions aboard the *Forrestal* or any other navy ship," he felt that without strong leadership and improved shipboard communications "human breakdowns are just bound to occur."

Such a breakdown was approaching on board the *Constellation*, back at sea in San Diego Bay to conduct refresher exercises. Black sailors still met in the barbershop or the sidewalk cafe, many of them now swearing an affinity with their beleaguered brothers on the *Kitty Hawk*. Captain Ward decided against interfering because "I did not want to drive these young men underground." Ward was a veteran naval aviator with an appreciation of shipboard conduct derived from the traditions of the old navy. When his executive officer, Comdr. John R. Schaub, suggested that an open forum be held, he gave his assent only because he believed that such a meeting might ease tensions. A date was set, 3 November. But events would not wait for that meeting. It had been ascertained that, counting the air-wing personnel yet to arrive for the return to South Vietnam, the ship would have 250 more men on board than it could properly accommodate. Rather than install chain bunks, thus lowering habitability standards, Captain Ward secured authority from Pacific Fleet command for the immediate release of men with less than ninety days left of service. And Ward intended that if this qualification applied to any of the fifteen that he had tabbed as troublemakers, they should be among the batch let go: "With redeployment ahead I had no desire for another *Kitty Hawk*." The *Constellation*'s personnel officer informed him that six of the fifteen could be among those "early outs" and, moreover, that they met the official criteria, which included poor efficiency ratings and disciplinary problems, for release through "general discharge," an ambiguous release with all the benefits of an honorable discharge but absent that designation. The six were notified of the impending action.

An anonymous telephone caller invited Commander Schaub to a meeting of black sailors on the after mess deck. With the captain's approval, Schaub accepted. The executive officer's attempts to deal in person with the complaints amounted to de facto recognition of the dissidents as a sort of "serviceman's union," something expressly prohibited. But as would be officially stated, Captain Ward's "priority objective, as a combat-experienced officer, was to achieve a safe environment for continued high-tempo training of the ship and air wing." In this connection, much would depend on Ward's own resourcefulness. Top-level directives regarding discipline were all very well, but they lacked guidance about how to proceed in critical situations. Supposing the small master-at-arms unit proved ineffective, the marine detachment, with its so-called rapid-reaction body, could not, strictly speaking, fill the breech as a shipboard police force. Untrained in modern riot control, the marines' considered role on board a navy ship is that of a security force to protect property. And as Captain Ward undoubtedly knew (and reference to the media's coverage of the problems on the *Kitty Hawk*

"I had no desire for another *Kitty Hawk*." The *Contellation*'s Capt. John D. Ward. *(U.S. Navy)*

could have reminded him), calling out the marines was far more likely to aggravate matters then defuse them.

The *Constellation*'s human relations council met on Thurday, 2 November, to plan the next day's open forum. In the meantime, however, the processing of the administrative discharges of the six troublemakers had gone awry. One of the records did not, upon closer examination, meet the required criteria. It was that of a popular young black who might have been the ship's barber had he not been relegated, allegedly through racial prejudice, to a job in the laundry. At the same time, with news of the discharges and of the plan for 250 "early outs" spreading among the *Constellation*'s more than 400 black sailors, a rumor grew that they would be especially targeted for release with "less than honorable" discharges. Commander Schaub quickly halted the processing of discharges, but his action did little to quiet emotions.

After finishing evening prayers over the ship's communications system, Comdr. Otto Schreider, one of the *Constellation*'s two chaplains, climbed to the bridge and told Captain Ward that events on the ship were proceeding as predicted in the findings of a Marine Corps study conducted at Camp Smedley Butler, Okinawa, the previous year. This report, which the chaplain had helped prepare, analyzed recent racial disturbances and said that they had certain identifiable phases in common. When trouble threatened, reference to this "predictive model" might help prevent escalation through a "catalytic" phase to the final turbulence. Because apparently no one else in the carrier had heard of the report, Chaplain Schreider, the following morning, had a copy made for the captain's use.

He had no sooner done this when he learned to his dismay that Commander Schaub intended to meet with two minority representatives after breakfast in the crew's lounge. "Of course," the chaplain later emphasized, "the Camp Butler report indicates this is one of the things you *don't* do. I pointed this out to the executive officer but the die was cast." The meeting lasted twenty minutes. One of the spokesmen read from a list of complaints that ranged from injustices at captain's mast to officers' use of racial expletives. From what he could hear of the conversation— "they met right outside my yeoman's office"—Chaplain Schreider figured that the demands being made of Schaub squared with the Camp Butler model, and he at once had a second copy of the report run off for the executive officer, drawing his attention to the very first of its guidelines: dealing with self-appointed leaders was a mistake, for it "tends to give command sanction to their unauthorized leadership." But it was not the command's concessionary attitude that determined the next "phase." Discontent was drawing sustenance from scuttlebutt about those less-than-honorable discharges. If a catalyst was needed, the would-be barber's erroneous discharge sufficed—it was later officially recorded as "providing the triggering mechanism for concerted action."

With the *Constellation* still in San Diego Bay and eight hours to go before the open forum that Captain Ward and his executive officer hoped would have a therapeutic effect on rising tempers, the two men were informed that more than sixty black sailors were staging a sit-down strike on the forward mess deck.

Captain Ward directed that division officers and leading petty officers see if any of their personnel were among the dissidents and get them back to their duties. At the same time the ship's chief master-at-arms took action to disperse the rest. These measures seemed at first effective, but as the captain was to say with an acerbity perhaps forgivable by that later date, "The group on the forward mess deck dissolved but lo! they reappeared on the after mess deck." Their number had increased to almost one hundred, many occupying chairs they denied to whites seeking a place to eat their noonday meal. In reponse to a telephone call from the executive officer, Comdr. James Yacabucci, the ship's dental officer, who was also the chairman of the human relations council, hastened to the men and tried to correct their erroneous impression about the discharges. But they also raised questions concerning social mistreatment in general, and, "of course, we couldn't answer those."

In the middle of that Friday afternoon Commander Schaub ordered the distribution of 3000 fliers explaining why it was necessary to reduce the ship's complement by 250 "early outs" and volunteers for discharge. The sit-in on the after mess deck continued. Adm. Bernard A. Clarey, then commander-in-chief of the Pacific Fleet, was among those to register an opinion that by this time Captain Ward should have sounded general quarters, calling the men to battle stations. But Ward felt that if they refused to move and he was compelled to mobilize his masters-at-arms and the thirty marines of the rapid-reaction force, injuries were bound to result. Yet while not willing to take the uncompromising step of calling GQ, he was at first uncertain of the alternatives: "Negotiations are new to my experience." His hopes were pinned on that open forum, for which Commander Yacabucci's council prepared by setting up a podium and two microphones in the dining area of the after mess deck. All that tense afternoon the captain manned the bridge, overseeing the constant shuttle of aircraft on and off the flight deck. Regarding the pockets of indiscipline on his ship, he felt determined that there would be no violence if he could help it, no bargaining with malcontents either. Shortly before 5 P.M. he radioed Pacific Fleet Air command that a cadre of his black personnel were trying to stir up trouble: "I intend to make every effort to avoid a confrontation while at sea . . . making plans for action as necessary upon returning to San Diego."

The open forum proved the opposite of therapeutic. In company with fourteen members of his human relations staff, eight of them black, Commander Yacabucci assured the men that all discharge proceedings had been stopped. But "the militants took full opportunity to turn [the meeting] into a fully-fledged tumult." Trying to explain the meaning of general discharge, Yacabucci was repeatedly interrupted by heckling and name-calling. Someone snatched the microphone from him and began a long-winded harangue peppered with curses and impossible demands.

The two spokesmen who had earlier met with the executive officer exerted a degree of crowd control. Chaplain Schreider's impression, gained through the lens of his Camp Butler report, was that "we had the charismatic leadership. I think we had the frustration level." Not that an attempted anatomy of mutiny engrossed anybody on the spot, least of all Commander Yacabucci, who could see his meeting slipping into pandemonium. The week-long course he had undertaken to prepare for council chairmanship, complete with encounter groups and sensitivity sessions, could hardly have equipped him for this kind of ordeal: "I took abuse that I as a naval officer would never take again."

By midnight a number of sailors were threatening a bloodbath unless the captain came down in person and listened to them. On the bridge he received unidentified phone calls. The ship would be "torn apart," his planes would not fly. Captain Ward had no intention of leaving the bridge, but still desirous of keeping hostilities in check, he thought some conciliatory approach over the loudspeaker system worth a try. "I assure all you gentlemen," he declared, "that I am readily available to discuss any and all problems and grievances. Would you individuals please come forward and I am certain we can resolve them to your satisfaction."

His words were received in the mess area with catcalls and obscenities. But the two group representatives had left the meeting and were soon on the bridge themselves. The captain recognized one of them as foremost on his private list of "agitators." They told him his physical appearance before the men was necessary to dispel their conviction that "you don't give a damn about them," also because "we didn't want another *Kitty Hawk.*" Ward's response was that flight operations kept him on the bridge, that meeting a truculent group would achieve nothing, and that anyone with a grievance could see him, using the "chain of command." The two spokesmen returned below with what was officially called "an incomplete and inaccurate report." They told their shipmates that they had got nowhere with the captain, that "he's messing with the windshield wipers, looking out the window at the planes, his mind and eye on the flight deck."

That was true enough. Afterward, a captain on the staff of Air Forces, Pacific Fleet (AIRPAC) openly opined that Ward should have left the bridge and talked personally with the dissidents. Traditional notions, this officer believed, needed drastic revision in the light of modern realities. Even the commander of AIRPAC thought that Ward's refusal to meet the men on the mess deck, combined with his decision against using force, "created a virtual impasse." This was also true, and equally so Admiral Zumwalt's portayal of Ward as "squarely on the hottest spot in the Navy, with very little in either his personal experience or the

Navy's corporate wisdom to guide him." But J. D. Ward was by no means at a loss, and preferable to possible bloody violence on the one hand and a humiliating confrontation on the other, "a virtual impasse" precisely suited the captain's plans.

His resolve to avoid "another *Kitty Hawk*" had doubtless weighed in the decision against calling the ship to general quarters. For the same reason marines were not summoned. Somebody on one of the *Constellation*'s 2,076 telephones did in fact call marines to the after mess deck, and Commander Yacabucci and his human relations people averted an immediate riot by inducing them to leave. The executive officer, meanwhile, functioned as sort of a conduit for information flowing between the bridge and after mess deck. For thus "[choosing] not to observe significant events taking place a hundred feet from his cabin" Commander Schaub would be formally criticized. He should, said a superior, have actively involved himself as "the authority figure." But on the mess deck, the executive officer, like the captain himself, would only have come in for the same disrespect and abuse already suffered by Commander Yacabucci. Besides, acceding to rebellious demands would have run counter to the Pentagon's own rules (not to mention those Camp Butler recommendations) against dealing with malcontents. Also, while the Defense Department's directive "Guidelines For Handling Dissident Protest Activities Among Members Of The Armed Forces" conceded a serviceman's right of free expression, there were limits. That right was to be allowed if "consistent with good order and discipline and the national security." The commander could not permit conduct inimical to the effectiveness of his command. And his alone was the power to decide, a salutary outcome depending on his "calm and prudent judgment."

On this occasion the captain's course of action suggests that he was both traditionalist and realist. Making deals with "agitators" would have been abhorrent to any officer of Ward's nature, but above all he deemed their presence on board a distraction, if not indeed detrimental to the proper enactment of the *Constellation*'s readiness program. He felt, therefore, that the sooner the ship was rid of them the better. Sometime in the night he had decided to suspend operations and return to North Island Naval Air Station. There the troublemakers would be put ashore "in a non-disciplinary status" to await disciplinary action. The ship, meanwhile, would continue its exercises. Ward had, in any case, legitimate reasons for going back into port. The ship's distilling plant had malfunctioned: "We would have to put in for fresh water. But I would have come back anyway, to offload these young men."

Thus determined, Ward conceived his only necessity regarding the situation on the after mess deck as keeping it under control for the few hours the ship remained at sea. When Commander Yacabucci told him in the early Saturday morning hours that things were getting out of hand, he was ready with a series of instructions. The ship was awakened, all below-deck lights turned on, security watches set up on the hangar deck, and senior personnel assigned to patrol berthing areas and passage-ways. Most importantly, to "envelop this group with a blanket of calm mature people," Ward gave orders for as many coolheaded officers and petty officers as possible to quietly enter the after mess deck and surround the dissidents in a passive show of strength. It was effective. A diehard group still demanded to see the captain. But others just bedded down for the night, played cards, or listened to a record player. A number drifted away. More than a hundred white personnel stood watching until their wordless intimidation seemed no longer required, and they too dispersed.

Twenty

◪

BEACH DETACHMENT

*N*aval history offers no parallel for what took place at San Diego during the first two weeks of November 1972. Command rooted in tradition faltered before a contumacy born of social flux and racial discontent. That may be putting it too glibly. Elements such as media exploitation of the sailors' protest, also their own enjoyment of securing an upper hand and receiving public notice, contributed to the conflict. The imminence of a national election injected political concerns. Higher authority felt itself able to maintain some degree of control over a novel situation only through hasty compromise and a confused progressivism, during the whole course of which conventional discipline and a captain's dignity got short shrift.

The *Constellation* docked at North Island on Saturday the fourth at 7:45 A.M. Her executive officer had earlier told the two chief spokesmen for the dissident group that a petition to the captain would be honored. One was forthwith drafted, "from the oppressed people of this command who, after constant attempts to resolve our problems, request an immediate conference with the commanding officer." It bore eighty-two signatures. A bevy of shore-based officers, including "human resources" and minority affairs specialists, met the ship, quickly making clear to Captain Ward their preference that he not form a beach detachment but settle his disciplinary problems on board, and that he remain in port to do so, notwithstanding the ship's tight turnaround schedule. At their persuasion Ward did finally go to the mess deck, where a spokesman for the dissidents (in the captain's opinion a leading troublemaker) thought him bored and uncommunicative. At 11:30, while Ward and various staff officers continued their discussion about whether to form a beach detachment, a black lieutenant given the luckless task of watching the protesters marched them ashore, 144 in all, including 8 whites. Apparently, word had passed that any who wished to join the beach detachment could do so. The captain's intention was to off-load only genuine agitators, and he attributed the unexpectedly large exodus to "some distortion of my guidance at a level unknown to me." On the USS *Ranger* moored nearby, Vice Adm. Thomas J. Walker, commanding the navy's Pacific Air Forces, decided that since so many dissidents were now off-loaded, returning them to their ship was "not a good option."

While Ward shared the general surprise at the number of men who had left the *Constellation,* uppermost in his mind was the desire to resume the training exercises without "a cadre of agitators" on board. What he could not have anticipated was the effort that grew on sundry levels to keep him involved with them under their formal designation as a beach detachment. The men were taken by bus to a naval air station barracks, where Ward addressed them in the afternoon, again without significant result. Having fresh water on board, the *Constellation* got back under way at eight the next morning. But in the evening an A-7 Corsair II aircraft practicing night landings veered after catching the flight deck's arresting gear, and at 7:15 on Monday morning the carrier returned to North Island with a damaged plane hanging over its port side.

An hour later the beach detachment gathered in the naval air station's auditorium and elected an eleven-man committee to present their views. Admiral Walker, meanwhile, had radioed a report of the *Constellation*'s troubles to Adm. Bernard Clarey, in overall command of the Pacific Fleet at Pearl Harbor, who in turn contacted Admiral Zumwalt. The consensus among these three, endorsed by Secretary of the Navy John Warner, was that the beached protesters should be returned to the *Constellation* where they belonged, even though, as Zumwalt was to phrase it, this meant "overruling Captain Ward."

During Monday forenoon a new and influential element was introduced, the commander and staff officers from the navy's Human Resources Development Center, San Diego. HRDC had been set up to study personnel problems, especially those of a racial or ethnic nature, and to conduct appropriate seminars and training programs. Admiral Walker's human relations and minority affairs officer, Capt. William Cross, had summoned this HRDC team because he had been schooled at the center and believed that in the settlement of human difficulties "it never hurts any of us to eat a little humble pie." Perhaps sensing that Captain Ward might find such fare unpalatable, Cross and his HRDC colleagues began racking their brains to find the most satisfactory means of getting the dissidents back on board. Obliged to conform with the wishes of his superiors but still hoping to keep his ship purged of malcontents, Captain Ward telephoned the lieutenant in charge of the beach detachment and explained that any who professed a wish to return on board should be personally interviewed "to evaluate their motivation and predict if they were possible troublemakers." Ward considered it his right as captain to decide who would be permitted to return to his ship. With that done, and relieved of the damaged jet plane, he took the *Constellation* to sea again—with perhaps too much alacrity to suit higher authority, for before sundown he was ordered to bring her back into port.

Captain Ward's predicament during the all-night sit-in on the *Constellation* may well have been what Elmo Zumwalt termed "the hottest spot in the Navy." But the chief of naval operations had himself now to act with considerable circumspection. Secretary Warner, while favoring racial fairness in the navy, was in the admiral's opinion too influenced by lawmakers who disapproved of his reforms and charged that his Z-grams were a formula for permissiveness. Such political opponents would have a field day if the situation so deteriorated as to become front-page news. Despite needed coverage of the presidential election, the media still found space and air time for fresh stories about the disorders on the *Kitty Hawk*. Rightly apprehensive lest this sort of publicity set back the progress made in the navy's racial policies under his impetus, Admiral Zumwalt wanted ways found to get the dissident sailors back on the aircraft carrier without delay.

Early on Tuesday, as polling booths opened across the land, the *Constellation* suspended redeployment exercises for the third time in as many days. The human relations team awaited her return with plans for educating the captain for his role in "the proposed dialogue with the Beach Detachment." He would be informed as to "words and/or phrases that experience has shown tend to 'turn off' members of a predominantly minority group and inhibit meaningful communication." Also in the planning stage were follow-on seminars for the ship's officers. As for the other side, the HRDC team met with its eleven representatives and heard the dissidents' conditions for returning to the *Constellation*. No one should be forced to return. The administrative discharges must all be reviewed, also nonjudicial (captain's mast) procedures. And there must be no disciplinary action taken against any member of the beach detachment.

Some of the protesters might have wished as an additional condition a change in the commander's attitude. According to Captain Cross, present at the "give and take" around the table, complaints were raised about Ward's "stand-offish manner, looking down on people . . . a mannerism. These are important in coming across to people. And this was explained to the group." The digression upon Captain Ward's personality made little if any impression, and after further speechifying the protest group arose, said they were tired of all the talk, and walked out of the meeting.

At noon the HRDC people advised Admiral Walker that the beach detachment might turn violent if given no immediate outlet for its frustrations. The men were thereupon told to consider themselves at liberty until the next morning. Meanwhile, Captain Ward was informed of their conditions for returning to the ship, and he gave a reluctant assent. These attempts to entice the protest group back to duty with assurances of "a general amnesty" would strike an investigative board as "not in the Navy's best interest . . . a regrettable scenario." Ward, also at a future date, recalled caustically how "we tenderly negotiated with these gentlemen." He had reserved the right to approve of those who would elect to come back on the ship, and Captain Cross considered this "a hitch," doubting that the disaffected sailors would go along. Intervention by higher authority produced another meeting, this time in Admiral Walkers' office, where the captain was persuaded to abandon the "right" he had clung to. And while all this was proceeding, members of the furloughed protest group aired their grievances before San Diego's television cameras.

With little time to spare for reading of Richard M. Nixon's landslide victory at the polls, Admiral Zumwalt kept in constant touch with the situation in San Diego, working out a plan to "break the deadlock" without having to arrest any of the protesters. The idea now was for Captain Ward to talk to them once more, declare their conditions agreed to, and grant them further liberty until 8:00 A.M. the following day, when they would be expected back on the *Constellation*. In preparation for the commander's address Captain Cross and the human relations staffers descended upon him in his cabin yet again, with suggestions on "how you can come across to the men . . . 'smile if it kills you,' that sort of thing." Ward had to endure such advice while he was sleepless, obviously under strain, and afflicted with a cold. Even Captain Cross later sympathized, "I'm certain this probably went against Captain Ward's grain. It would have mine."

A lack of unity at the highest level subverted this latest plan. Having

An officer from the *Constellation* advises the dissidents to reboard their ship or consider themselves unauthorized absentees. *(U.S. Navy)*

decided that "the time had come to take decisive action," Admiral Zumwalt wanted the dissident sailors told directly to get back on board or face disciplinary action. But the secretary of the navy was "not yet ready" to approve such an order. When Captain Ward went before the men at 10:15 on Wednesday morning in the auditorium, he could only ask them to return to the fold, promising a discussion of grievances on board and no punitive action. Captain Cross and his "human relations" colleagues thought Ward's performance excellent, a tribute to their coaching, and were accordingly surprised when the entire dissident gathering signaled their refusal to return on board with loud cries and clenched-fist salutes.

There followed more telephone calls between San Diego and Pearl Harbor and Washington, D.C. With emotions best imagined, Captain Ward was sent back before the men in the afternoon to tell them that they were no longer a beach detachment and could consider themselves at liberty until eight o'clock on Thursday morning. When that hour came and passed, more than a hundred men had been bused to the pier alongside the *Constellation,* but none ascended the accommodation ladder. Ward sent an officer to inform them that their liberty had expired and that they should immediately report on board or be regarded as unauthorized absentees. Some who showed a willingness to obey were

With clenched fists raised, the beach detachment expresses defiance and solidarity. *(San Diego Historical Society, Union-Tribune Collection)*

circled threateningly by others. News media were on the scene, also five civilian attorneys from the Black Servicemen's Caucus who boarded the ship, identified themselves as representatives for the dissidents, and sought to "negotiate" with the captain. Ward would not oblige, saying that the men must first return to the ship. In due course a few did, including the sailor Captain Ward remained convinced was the group's leading agitator.

Numbering more than 120 (including perhaps a dozen whites), those who stayed on shore were bused back to the barracks. All were then formally separated from the USS *Constellation*. For being "absent without leave" for six hours they received trifling punishments such as fines and extra work duties. By the middle of the following month, after personal counseling and discussion of their complaints, roughly two-thirds of their number were at new assignments in the navy. Others were given honorable or general discharges from the service. At about this time the *Kitty Hawk* returned from South Vietnam. A one-man fain investigation could find no fault with that ship's minority-affairs program, and there appeared, "after careful analysis, no logical or rational explanation for the outbreak." But the "agitators" held responsible had exploited a legitimate discontent: "Having been assured the Navy is committed to equal opportunity for all its members, [minorities] are understandably confused and angered when the better jobs and advancements are earned by those better qualified." Nine of the *Kitty Hawk*'s sailors were convicted of assault and punished with fines, imprisonment, and reductions in rank.

As his political foes fulminated about how permissiveness was destroying the navy, Zumwalt met the challenge head-on. On 10 November in a Pentagon auditorium he lectured ninety admirals and Marine Corps generals on the significance of his programs for improving racial relations and charged that the lukewarm manner in which commands had responded was "essentially obstructionism." Reported by the news media in such terms as "admirals on the carpet" and "a public dressing-down," his action incensed not only naval officers but Richard M. Nixon, whose national security adviser, Henry Kissinger, at the newly elected president's side in Florida, telephoned Zumwalt and "all but shrieked at me." Zumwalt learned later that what had especially upset the chief executive was a televised scene of some *Constellation* sailors giving a clenched-fist salute, and "he interpreted my speech as an expression of support for mutineers."

Was it a mutiny? The question inevitably arose at hearings before a subpanel of the Senate Armed Services Committee. The Library of Congress, which helped educate the senators on the subject, while unable to discover "any cases directly analagous" to the carrier troubles, listed past instances containing "some similarities." Among them were the *Somers* affair, the *Ewing* mutiny, and the mass work refusals by munitions loaders at Port Chicago. The hearings, conducted at San Diego, included the following exchanges:

Chairman Floyd Hicks (Washington): Would you characterize the [*Constellation*] incident as mutiny?

Admiral Zumwalt: Until I have seen the results of the [naval] board of investigation, I would not want to make a judgement as to that.

Hicks: What would be the definition of mutiny?

Zumwalt: The definition of mutiny? I will throw that one to my lawyer, if I may. In essence, it means an intent to take over the command of the ship from constituted authorities.

Hicks: The Caine Mutiny is about the only mutiny that I am familiar with, the novel, that was a true mutiny.

Zumwalt: I would think the mutiny on the *Bounty* is a similar one, sir.

The naval investigation to which Zumwalt referred stated finally that what happened on the *Constellation* was not mutiny. Likewise, the public affairs officer at fleet headquarters in San Diego contended that "essentially, mutiny is an announced threat to take over the ship and then a step in that direction. So [the *Constellation* incident] was not a mutiny." A career naval officer with degrees in history and international relations considered the dissidents "technically, guilty of mutiny" and felt that they got off with unusually light punishments. A future secretary of the navy, John F. Lehman, would describe both the *Constellation* and *Kitty Hawk* troubles as "real mutinies," and Captain Ward had apparently little doubt at all. Asked by the congressmen in secret session to define mutiny, he replied, "Simply a refusal to obey orders or a refusal to perform duty, either by a group or an individual. Simply a refusal to carry out your duties . . . or orders with regard to the operation of the ship." At this point, portions of what the Uniform Code of Military Justice and the *Manual for Courts Martial* had to say on mutiny were read into the record. Ward was then asked,

> "In view of those quotes, do you consider the incident on the
>   *Constellation* the night of November the third and fourth to
>   have been an act of mutiny?"
> "It certainly could be construed as mutiny."
> "Is it mutiny in your opinion?"
> "Yes, sir."

A captain may have the last word on his ship, but not ashore. In its final report the congressional panel did not mention mutiny but concluded that what had occurred on the *Constellation* was "a carefully orchestrated demonstration of passive resistance."

In happier circumstances, two weeks after the "mutiny" on the *Constellation* one of her officers married. The rites were conducted on the forecastle, Chaplain Schreider officiating, and Captain Ward gave the bride away. On the eve of the carrier's return to the West Pacific in early January the navy announced that Ward would receive the Legion of Merit for his service during the previous deployment. Two months later he was reassigned to Europe as chief of staff for operations and plans for American forces. The balance of Ward's career continued on a high level of distinction and, it is probably safe to say, never were his patience and judgment so acutely tested as during those November days and nights when his 60,000-ton aircraft carrier steamed in and out of San Diego because a portion of her crew, at least in the commander's opinion, had resorted to mutiny.

"We must learn to adapt to changing fashion." Admiral Zumwalt talking with a ship's human relations council. *(U. S. Navy)*

The Navy Department tacitly admitted that a mutinous element had indeed crept into the American fleet when it announced early in 1973 the discharge of more than three thousand men, by no means all of them black, considered a burden to command. Newspapers reported that the navy was "quietly ridding itself of what it considers misfits and malcontents." Recruiting standards were stiffened and "sensitivity sessions" made mandatory for officers and petty officers. Perhaps Admiral Zumwalt issued these latest directives without the zealous optimism that had characterized the earlier "Z-grams." Their necessity denoted in some degree the failure of his ambitious programs for hauling a tradition-bound service into the era of civil rights. But the work Zumwalt had begun continued long after his retirement. Not for the first time in naval history mutiny, real or alleged, had far-reaching consequences. Still experimenting throughout the 1980s with programs to secure racial harmony, the United States Navy paused at the close of that decade to take stock of the results. According to the study group's report, they were not all encouraging. Certainly, by the advent of the

1990s, black discontent on the scale manifest twenty years earlier was all but unthinkable. Even so, as the report conceded, "serious shortfalls continue for minorities in accessions, promotions, advancements and distribution." Racial prejudice persisted, and if instances of it were not readily reported to activate the machinery in place for stamping it out, it was because—and here, surely, was an echo from history—of "the lack of confidence in the grievance process with a widespread fear of reprisal if a grievance is submitted."

Twenty-One

❡

MUTINY AND MORALE

*I*f mutiny is a word that carries its own exclamation point, it also seldom lacks an invisible question mark or at least implicit quotes. A fundamental definition of the offense agreeable to all has proved elusive since the first British admiralty instructions of medieval times, when men who freely applied the adjective tended to balk at using the noun. All varieties of recalcitrance might be labeled "mutinous," but sailors had to try to seize their own ship before their deed was unarguably mutiny. What George II's Naval Articles of War prescribed a mandatory death sentence for was not mutiny per se but "mutinous assembly." The framers of the articles no doubt had mutiny in mind, and perhaps their choice of words was intended to convey that mutiny requires an "assembly" and cannot be committed by one person. But if this was the intention, it was as far as authority of that day ventured toward defining mutiny.

Subsequent rules and rumination upon mutiny reflected either a distaste for the effort required to establish a flat definition or resort to arbitrary if not capricious personal belief. Thus by the middle of the nineteenth century one sage could contemplate mutiny as having a quite legitimate purpose, the offense dwelling solely in the mutineers' attempt to achieve it "by their own means." This was the British legist, Hickman, who in 1851 had cited a court-martial opinion implying mutiny as conceivably originating with "a murmuring and a muttering . . . [having] a tendency to raise ill-humor or passions." He might have deemed such conduct more technically the *incitement* to mutiny but instead had argued therefrom that mutiny could begin (and end) with one person.

In the United States the first naval Articles of War, or the "Act for the Government of the Navy," had borrowed the British phraseology and displayed the same easy preference for "mutinous"—as applied to "assembly," "words," or "practices"—over "mutiny." But as understood by a succession of American legal interpreters toward the end of the 1800s, the law departed from the official British view of mutiny as an aggregate offense and leaned toward the somewhat heretical opinion of the aforementioned British officer, holding that an individual could commit mutiny. Beyond that, though, the definition was elaborated no further than to include resistance, active or passive, to lawful military authority. Among the published textbooks or treatises that sought to guide or interpret the Articles of War for the benefit of officers who might have to serve on courts, Winthrop's *Military Law* in 1886 directly faulted existing descriptions of mutiny as deficient in terms. Disobedience or disrespect toward a superior officer was not enough, nor yet threatening or actually doing him bodily harm. Likewise, such so-called mutinous conduct as muttering, demonstrating, or protesting: "When such disorders . . . are not characterized by deliberate intent to overthrow military authority [they] do not constitute in general the legal offense of mutiny."

As far as the United States Navy was concerned, the first official statement of anything like a detailed definition of mutiny appeared with the publication in 1923 of *Naval Courts and Boards,* its Section 46 describing the offense in Winthropean terms, asserting the necessity of "a deliberate purpose to subvert or override. . . ." This was not the only "essential element," for the overt act had to be completed before mutiny could be said to have occurred. A "mutinous assembly" was not enough. There things stood until the adoption of the Uniform Code of Military Justice, which, with its attendant *Manual for Courts Martial,* established that the "essential element" of preconceived intent applied to a one-person mutiny, another essential element of this form henceforth being the creation of violence or disturbance. In the other form of mutiny, that of "collective insubordination," no concert of intent was to be presupposed nor was required. And thus was the Winthropean conspiratorial basis for the military's legal view of mutiny restructured, if not abandoned.

This latest asseveration on the subject had not satisfied everyone. During the Port Chicago affair American naval legists wondered if through successive codifications the lengthening list of separate offenses of a "mutinous" character had not shorn naval mutiny of all identity other than solely that of subordinates taking over a ship or shore installation. There is still some relevance to their puzzlement. After generations of effort to nail down a permanent definition of naval mutiny, the one presently in use with the American defense establishment does seem somewhat attenuated and is thereby prone to conflicting interpretations. The same might be said of the British approach, and at least on the question of whether mutiny requires one or more individuals to commit it the two nations differ.

Officers in command may feel themselves secure against planned revolt or even simple and momentary disobedience by virtue of stern service rules and regulations, which, it is confidently assumed, inferiors must be aware that they violate at their own dire peril. Past history shows that this assumption, when nursed by temperamental or despotic commanders, can have unholy consequences. But even in more recent and enlightened times such dependence on the prohibitive power of bureaucratic precepts may prove treacherous indeed. For one thing, a commander cannot be sure that there is adequate comprehension of such orders among the lower ranks. When deciding what course to adopt should it become necessary to voice displeasure or air grievances, seamen are apt to rely more on instinct than on any clear understanding of formal disciplinary injunction. This is especially true in cases of mutiny, the most ambiguously defined yet gravest of all military or naval offenses.

It goes without saying that in our time naval mutinies are rarities—or at least are rarely reported. We should not feel too complacent on this point. Perhaps equally rare would be the captain who has not wondered, more than once and very likely far from home port, how he might handle a mutiny should one erupt from below his own decks. So much would hinge upon his personal judgment. He would have fewer officially ordained choices of action at his disposal than the hypothetical mutineers. No matter how inscrutably worded, regulations abound with the purpose of governing the conduct of enlisted men, but disproportionate attention has been paid to how the commander might best respond if those regulations are unexpectedly flouted. He can count on little in past experience or training to help him, no handy textbook on his cabin bookshelf to supply clear-cut guidance. And despite all the advanced communication systems that link modern sea commanders with headquarters ashore, he might well feel himself to be as essentially on his own in confrontation with an unruly crew as any captain in the age of sail and wooden hulls.

In such crises of discipline, how shall a commander act? Shall he negotiate with the ringleaders of the malcontents, discuss their grievances? To do so might feed their sense of autonomy and encourage further demands. Summon a show of force? This might invite counterforce, with the possibility of violence, even bloodshed. On the other hand, either course of action might indeed have the desired effect of quieting emotions and restoring good order. Whatever the commander does is a gamble— and in any case, the nature of events will determine the form any action takes. Does the situation merely threaten mutiny or has mutiny already flowered? No officers' manual explains how precisely to decide when that critical line is crossed. Above all, decisions must not be postponed. Any sign of hesitation, of uncertainty, carries its own hazard, for it is likely to impress the subordinates as weak-willed or vacillating or perhaps to be exploited by the craftier troublemakers as the sort of indifference to be expected from officers caring little for the legitimate needs of the lower deck.

To the extent that confusion continues to blur the meaning of mutiny, explanation might be found in high command's continuing abhorrence for the word and preference for euphemisms like "collective insubordination," "combat refusal," and "disciplinary problem" (not to mention the choice of the disaffected themselves for such as "strike," "work stoppage," and "demonstration of grievance"). All of which might well promote a fanciful longing for the unequivocal attitude toward naval mutiny expressed in motion pictures. In the first *Bounty* film ever made, an Australian production, Fletcher Christian (Errol Flynn) has an eve-of-mutiny confrontation with Bligh. "Mr. Christian, do you dare———?" "Yes, sir, I dare!" The dialogue in later versions is no less direct. When told by Midshipman George Stewart that the men are ready for anything, Christian (Mel Gibson) responds without hesitation: "What are you saying, are you inciting me to mutiny?" Bligh (Anthony Hopkins) condemns his mutinous former friend who is about to put him overboard. "You are a dead man, Fletcher!" And in another production, after casting his commander adrift, Christian (Clark Gable) prophesies, "From now on, they'll spell mutiny with my name." Dramatized mutiny on-screen is stark and unambiguous. "Comrades, the ship is in our hands," cries a sailor on the *Potemkin,* defying Captain Golikov's threat, in the same silent subtitles, to "shoot you down like dogs." Motivation is not overlooked in the cinema's fictional mutinies either, although Lieutenant Keefer (Fred MacMurray), while preaching dissension in the wardroom, is obviously overstating the case with his "There is no escape from the *Caine* save death. We're all doing penance, sentenced to an outcast ship."

It may be another reflection of the uncertainty surrounding the meaning of mutiny that, notwithstanding the popular novel's eye-catching title, no mutiny on the *Caine* was proven or even formally charged. *Naval Courts and Boards* during the Second World War (also in the postwar years when Herman Wouk wrote his story) provided neither charge nor specification for the drastic step that the *Caine*'s executive officer, citing Article 184 of the "Act for the Government of the Navy," took on the bridge that tempestuous Pacific night. His having wrested control of the ship from its lawful but allegedly sick commander presented the navy's legal pundits with what the novelist called "the queerest sort of twilight situation," a dilemma met by trying the officer on the "catchall charge" of conduct to the prejudice of good order and discipline. Had Wouk decided that the navy did have grounds for proceeding with a mutiny charge, good courtroom drama might still have resulted because mutiny's definition was such a source of dispute. And had the Uniform Code of Military Justice been in vogue at the time, a mutiny charge against the executive officer might even have led to conviction, for what occurred on the bridge was arguably "collective insubordination" on the part of the executive officer and the officer of the deck, their shared intent to "usurp or override" being demonstrable and it not being necessary to show "this concert of insubordination [as] preconceived."

The protagonists of the fictive *Caine* were commissioned officers. And questions of mutiny or conspiracy to one side, it was essentially a matter of officer versus officer in the real-life episodes of the *Vance,* *Somers,* and *Bounty.* Probably the rarest form of naval mutiny also features officers, but in revolt against their national regimes. An abortive mutiny of the Greek destroyer *Velos* in the spring of 1973 has the additional element of irony, for its underlying cause was less alienation than allegiance, the traditional loyalty of Hellenic sailors to their kings. After a military junta dethroned Constantine XIII in 1967 and forced him into Italian exile, a number of naval officers, both active and retired, secretly agreed to try to restore him to power should the opportunity arise. None did for six years, throughout which period the Greek navy went about its tasks within the NATO alliance, whose other members had no idea that half its admirals plotted mutiny against their government in Athens.

The plan was bold and sweeping. Ships would rendezvous off Syros Island in the Aegean Sea, where their insurgent commanders would rally the support of the army by radio and then demand the government's resignation. If enough ships had joined the mutiny, they would back their ultimatum with a blockade of the ports of Piraeus and Salonika. At the same time an underground youth movement ashore would engage in sabotage and political assassination. Perhaps that was the plot's fatal element. Royalist admirals and the revolutionary young make for mismatched co-conspirators. The government got wind of what was afoot. Several captains and two retired admirals with hopes of seizing warships at the Salamis naval arsenal were rounded up before they could leave Athens. Other arrests followed, and the grandiose rebellion shrank to a single madcap effort by Capt. Nicholas Pappas of the *Velos* and a handful of his officers.

The ship was taking part in NATO maneuvers off Sardinia. Early on 25 May, to the astonishment of British, American, Italian, and other naval commanders, the *Velos* abandoned the exercises, her radio messages affirming continued fidelity to the western bloc but also vowing to "restore democracy to Greece." There was no violence on the ship. The lower deck had little if any role in this "mutiny," the sailors perhaps curious or apathetic and at all times obedient to their superiors. The destroyer made for the fishing port of Fiumicino, Italy, where two officers went ashore in a launch and tried to telephone their exiled king, who was living on the outskirts of Rome. Italian authorities intervened and surrounded the *Velos* with police boats. NATO representatives were also on the scene. The question was what to do with Captain Pappas and the *Velos*. Athens wanted the officers returned to face trial. Mutiny is an extraditable offense. But their political motivation was taken into account. Italy sent the ship back to Greece and granted the officers asylum with their king. Soon enough, the Greek military regime's own excesses brought about its overthrow, and while the monarchy was not restored, as Captain Pappas and his brother officers might have preferred, events led to a return of the democracy for which they had claimed to make their forlorn bid.

Two and a half years after the *Velos* incident another naval officer with a passionate grudge against his country's rulers took the same bold and equally foredoomed action. The thirty-six-year-old son of a Red Army colonel, Lt. Comdr. Valery Mikhaylovich Sablin had dutifully absorbed communist teachings in his youth but was possessed of an independent streak perhaps bound to have dramatically shown itself sooner or later. It had, in fact, slowed his early advancement in the Soviet navy, but following studies at the Lenin Military Political Academy he was regarded as a loyal party member and appointed *zampolit,* or political commissar, on the missile frigate *Storozhevoy* in the Baltic Fleet.

The Soviet missile frigate *Storozhevoy.* "Love of life" drove her political officer to mutiny. *(U.S. Navy)*

Although subordinate to the vessel's commander, a *zampolit* enjoyed exclusive privileges, also private means of communication with not only bureaucratic officials ashore but lower-deck personnel, with whom he maintained a special and more or less confidential relationship because his principal function was to keep them toeing the party line. From the viewpoint of the rank and file, a *zampolit* was sort of a politicizing welfare officer who was in a unique position to secure the sailors' trust. Valery Sablin had done this by showing a humanitarian sympathy for their grievances, which were probably many. The 38,000-ton *Storozhevoy* was one of the sleek and powerfully armed *Krivak* class and had lately distinguished herself during coordinated sea exercises with aircraft and submarines. But despondency flickered below decks, as was implied by an article in the Soviet military journal *Red Star,* which complained of a decline in party zeal among the *Storozhevoy*'s officers.

The writer had not mentioned that sustaining morale, much less political homage, was no easy task on Russian warships, where comfort was too often sacrificed to increased weaponry. With poor pay and frugal meals added to the overcrowding, and relief habitually sought in alcohol, Soviet crews could hardly have remained fertile material for their twice-weekly sessions of Marxist-Leninist indoctrination. And although generations of totalitarian rule had virtually quenched the rebellious spirit so manifest among Russian sailors in 1905 and 1917, there had almost certainly occurred insubordinate outbreaks well into the post-Stalinist era. Reports of an attempted mutiny on a nuclear submarine in 1969 were followed in 1972 by rumors of another on a diesel submarine in a Norwegian fjord. Details were, of course, difficult to verify. But not even the most rigid censorship could have concealed forever a mutiny with the familiar characteristics of boldness and desperation and with a brand-new element as well, that of the ringleader's being an officer whose shipboard function uniquely affirmed his presumed devotion to the political regime.

On 7 November 1975 the *Storozhevoy* was moored on the eastern bank of the Daugava River at the Latvian town of Riga. Because the date marked the fifty-eighth anniversary of the Bolshevik Revolution, about half of her 250-man complement had gone ashore to celebrate. By nightfall, many of the officers and crew were still ashore, and of those back on board a goodly number were sleeping off the effects of their merrymaking. The situation was probably as favorable as it could have gotten for mutiny, which was precisely what Valery Sablin had in mind. During his usual political seminar that afternoon he had won over to his thinking perhaps a dozen officers and petty officers—he must have gradually worked on them and some of the people in previous weeks. His plan was to lock up the others, their captain included, and take the ship from the Gulf of Riga north into the Gulf of Finland and to Leningrad, from where he would, by radio and television, recount the sins and hypocrisies of the Soviet system and demand reforms. Sablin was a conscientious patriot who believed the Marxist cause betrayed by those who had come to rule. To judge from his own words, Sablin's instincts were more suggestive of an idealistic reformer than bellicose rebel or even everyday defector: "What spurred me to this thing? Love of life . . . a radiant honest life that causes sincere joy among all honest people."

Of the actual seizure of the *Storozhevoy*, her captain would recall how the missile ship's *zampolit* went about it: "At 8 P.M. Sablin entered my cabin without knocking. He was agitated, pale. 'Comrade, comrade,' he said, 'there is an emergency.'" The two rushed down ladders. "I had just run into the bow room when the steel lid slammed shut." The captain was a prisoner. Likewise others who had offered resistance. Most of the crew remaining on board while their shipmates enjoyed shore leave were very young conscripts who evidently gave no trouble when Sablin and his supporting officers ordered them to their stations. In the early morning hours, her gas-turbine engines whining, the *Storozhevoy* descended the Daugava River and headed into the Gulf of Riga.

A warrant officer who had refused to cooperate with Sablin escaped confinement somehow and leapt overboard. He swam ashore and attempted to reach, by telephone, the nearby naval base of Balderia. Bureaucratic skepticism prevented his getting through, and in disgust he began to hitchhike. But on the runaway vessel another nonconspirator had freed himself, or one of Sablin's men had had second thoughts. Accounts differ. At any rate, this man succeeded in getting to the ship's communications room undetected. His radio messages told of mutiny on board the *Storozhevoy*. Naval authorities in Riga and Moscow were aroused from sleep, and the Soviet Defense Council issued urgent orders. Shortly before dawn, when the *Storozhevoy* cleared the mouth of the Gulf of Riga at a steady thirty-three knots, she did so with ten bombing and reconnaissance aircraft and nine warships in pursuit.

If Sablin's original purpose had indeed been the implausible one of making directly for Leningrad and there generating a counterrevolution, he had changed his mind. His destination now was Gotland, a Swedish island in the middle of the Baltic Sea, where he might secure asylum. The *Storozhevoy* was more than halfway there when overtaken by the first aircraft. Sablin ignored their radioed instructions to "lie dead in the water" and kept on course. The aircrews were under orders not to sink the ship, and according to Swedish listeners monitoring their dialogue, some would have disobeyed if directed to destroy her. Their bomb bursts encircled her. Approaching ships fired shots across her bow. The *Storozhevoy* carried twin guns fore and aft and torpedo-launchers amidships, but either her incomplete crew, jittery by this time, were unable to work these weapons or, more likely, Sablin realized the futility of resistance. Also, it is fair to say that he would not have welcomed bloodshed. Whatever the reason, the *Storozhevoy* did not return fire, and a damaged rudder finally halted her evasive maneuvering. Not for the first time, air power or the threat of it had quelled a naval mutiny.

At daybreak the 400-foot-long ship lay inert thirty miles east of Gotland. Boarding parties were unopposed. Some were formally saluted. The *Storozhevoy*'s boatswain had freed her commander, whose hands were bloodied from his attempts to escape. Sablin was placed under arrest. The Soviet government ordered a total blackout on news of the mutiny, and within a few months the *Storozhevoy*, manned by a new crew, had sailed from the Baltic, via the Mediterranean, Suez Canal, Indian Ocean, and Pacific, to a remote anchorage off Siberia.

In May 1976 Sablin and fourteen others were tried before a military court in Moscow. The fourteen were sent to labor camps. Sablin received the death sentence. He took all the guilt upon himself, even writing cheerful letters to his parents. On 3 August he was executed by a firing squad. A new commander of the Baltic Fleet, whose predecessor had been relieved of duty within three weeks of the mutiny, denied that there ever was one. During the next five years, however, word of it leaked to the West. It was the subject of a master's thesis written by a student at the U.S. Naval Postgraduate School in Monterey, California. This in turn inspired a best-selling novel about a Soviet submarine's defection to the West. Infinitely less publicized but prophetic indeed were the words of Valery Sablin in a farewell letter to his parents: "I am convinced that a revolutionary consciousness will catch fire among our people."

Mutiny caused by tyrannical or neurotic officers can safely be considered a thing of the past. In modern warships there are too many areas of command, too many divisional interrelationships for any localized pockets of cruelty or insensitivity to develop. Officers' mutinies against the state are also an unlikely phenomenon in our day. But there is not a navy afloat (or an army on land) able to exist or successfully function without the maintenance of an unwavering morale, and truism though that may be it explains the mystery of mutiny, or at least the apprehension of it. The chance of any naval commander's confronting mutiny in our time is extremely remote. It was a regimental sergeant major in a British film about life on a colonial army post who said to a colleague when the troops disobeyed, "Mutiny, Ben. Like the Loch Ness Monster. Heard of it but never actually run across it." All commanders have "heard of it" and routinely disregard its possibility, and it may not even stir an unspoken fear. But the dutiful commander is concerned with morale, and to the extent that mutiny is the ultimate antithesis of sound morale, mutiny *is* within his or her thoughts, no matter how deeply buried.

"Morale is the greatest single factor in successful war," declared Dwight D. Eisenhower, and another American president repeated this observation more than forty years later when the soldiers he had ordered into a desert environment needed protection against such potential morale destroyers as boredom, impatience, and homesickness. Winston Churchill thought that a key factor in sustaining morale was that "the men be fully employed at useful and interesting work." Douglas MacArthur, even before his fame in the Second World War, firmly linked sound morale with competent and considerate leadership. Morale would "quickly wither and die if soldiers came to believe themselves the victims of indifference or injustice." In this connection there is a certain wisdom in the words of a British admiral: "We can none of us feel any complacency about the state of discipline in our ships and establishments unless we (admirals, captains and all officers) constantly and consciously take the utmost pains to get to know our men." But this was said in 1958, when that ideal of shipboard confraternity was already becoming ever more difficult to achieve.

In its absence, however, the confident assumption of lower-deck personnel that discontents will be promptly recognized and dealt with may be all that is needed to keep morale at a satisfactory level. But there is enduring disagreement over how this is best achieved. For the airing and redress of grievances, not all navies rely solely on the traditional "chain of command." As we have seen, the process may be supplemented with such innovations as human-relations councils and minority-affairs programs. And unionism has been proposed as an option, in some cases adopted, but not in America, where opposition to the idea has scarcely altered since the years when Ray Shepherd's *Our Navy* was advocating sailors' representation along labor-union lines.

During the Vietnam War a former soldier discharged for alleged subversive activities ran an organization called the American Servicemen's Union from a small office on lower Fifth Avenue, New York. When its membership was found to embrace at least thirty military bases, the First Army Command at Fort Meade, Maryland, issued a private memorandum warning commanding officers not to recognize "any organization that purports to be a collective bargaining unit representing members of the Army." But less than a decade later four officers of the United States Navy with operational experience and specialized training in manpower and management psychology discussed publicly whether military unionization was not an idea "whose time has come," while the U.S. Defense Manpower Commission took testimony from spokesmen for federal unions seeking to include servicemen on their membership rosters. Foreign examples were cited. A "soldiers union" formed at a Netherlands army post in 1966 by draftees anxious that the rights they enjoyed as civilians be protected in military life caught on so vigorously that the Dutch armed forces soon boasted the most powerful military-conscript union in Western Europe. With membership fees automatically deducted from military pay and representatives who meet periodically with officials of the Defense Ministry, the union enjoys the same bargaining powers of labor unions—but has no right to strike.

Members of Sweden's armed forces are permitted to join civilian labor unions. At the same time, intraservice unions exist on all levels of rank and may unite with civilian public employees' unions to secure improvements in pay and benefits. They cannot strike. A sort of noncompulsory quasi-union system grew within the forces of West Germany concomitant with their postwar emergence within the NATO framework. Personnel of all ranks are allowed to join, and elected representatives lobby, albeit with a limited agenda, before the Defense Ministry and the national legislature. With the arrival of German reunification these entitlements were extended to military personnel of what was formerly the German Democratic Republic. Spain's conscripted army has nothing like a union. Radical draftees in Italy's armed forces periodically agitate for one through which to secure better pay, food, and living conditions but have so far gained no success.

France has generally considered movements to create military unions as subversive. Serious efforts to "unionize" American services have long ceased. A secretary of defense, Donald Rumsfeld, declared military unionization "incompatible with the mission of the U.S. armed forces." According to Gen. George Brown, speaking as chairman of the Joint Chiefs of Staff, "military personnel cannot live up to the oath of service and still work under a union contract." A retired admiral thought a system of collective bargaining in the United States Navy likely to "erode military command authority, good order and discipline." The chief of naval operations, Adm. James L. Holloway III, foresaw "collective bargaining to determine whether or not certain operations would be undertaken" and that, of couse, was "unthinkable." Military unionization has made even less headway in Great Britain, where a secretary of defense in a conservative government, warning that it might come to pass should the opposition Labor Party regain power, resorted to derision: "Over the top, lads—just wait for the tea break. . . . If you want to turn that thin red line into just some sordid demarcation dispute, then I tell you, let the unions loose in the armed services. Services on strike. Licensed mutiny."

That politician's very use of the word can serve as a reminder that it is not out of date, that however undeniably rare mutiny (legally defined or not) may be in our present age of complicated "high-tech" battle fleets, naval commanders have still to contend with problems of morale, discipline, and the human condition. And since naval leadership manuals have been updated to cover problems of drug and alcohol abuse, less space than ever is devoted to instructions about how to deal with mass noncompliance. But mutiny retains its unique hold upon the imagination, and even in our time it challenges the attention of scholars and theoreticians. In 1966 a paper on the subject was read before the Sixth World Congress of Sociology in France. In 1981 "The Anatomy of Mutiny" was discussed at an American interuniversity seminar on the armed forces and society. Nine years later a prestigious British naval journal published an article that told how to identify a mutiny in the making and prevent its maturation.

Participants in these learned events made reference to some of history's earlier mutinies. When recalled at all, Fletcher Christian, Richard Parker, the violent men of HMS *Hermione,* and the cabinet minister's wayward son on the USS *Somers* are but odd phantoms of a distant past. In our century, the *Potemkin* affair has become hardly more than a footnote to Russia's turbulent story, perhaps was only vaguely remembered even by the last known survivor of that warship's crew, who died in Dublin, Ireland, in 1987 at the age of 104. But such bygone episodes together with those of more recent times serve to remind us that whether complex as in Christian's case or more clearly defined as in that of the Port Chicago fifty and that of the *Storozhevoy*'s *zampolit,* the pressures that compelled resistance to authority should not be presumed as peculiar to any one class, race, region—or era. In one form or another, and however seemingly remote or insignificant, they can be expected to last as long as there are national fleets and seeds for human discontent. "Mutiny. . . . Heard of it, but never run across it." Which is not to say that one never will.

References

◢

Introduction

The fracas on the *Robert M. Thompson,* the Great Lakes Training School incident, and the "mutiny" off Piney Point are detailed in court-martial reports, Records of the Office of the Navy Judge Advocate General, Naval Historical Center, Washington, D.C.

Chapter One

For additional material on how Magellan and Anson dealt with their shipboard rebellions, see Irving Anthony, *Revolt at Sea* (New York, 1937), and George Anson, *A Voyage Around the World* (London, 1899). Kempenfelt's recipe for good discipline is in Naval Records Society, XXXII (London), quoted by G. J. Marcus, *A Naval History of England: The Formative Centuries* (London, 1961). For an insightful account of life below decks in the eighteenth-century Royal Navy, see N. A. M. Rodger, *The Wooden World* (Annapolis, 1986). The example of flogging on the installment plan is from Naval Records Society, CXX (London), and for what flogging did to the torso see R. Hendrickson, *The Ocean Almanac* (New York, 1984). Mutinies on the *Egmont* and *Santa Monica* are recounted in Tom Wintringham, *Mutiny* (London, 1936), and for the *Chesterfield* affair see Rodger, *Wooden World* and C. Field, *Old Times Afloat* (London, 1932).

Chapter Two

Few if any other single episodes in naval history have inspired a greater volume of literature than the *Bounty* affair—witness the intimidating bibliography in Gavin Kennedy, *Bligh* (London, 1978). The following titles (abbreviated) strike me as forming an essential library of *Bounty*ana and reflect my principal sources for this and the next chapter, also those later where they touch on Bligh's and Christian's final years. Published personal writings of Bligh and others of the *Bounty*'s company: Bligh's *A Narrative of the Mutiny* (London, 1790), *A Voyage To The South Sea* (London, 1792), *An Answer to Certain Assertions* (London,

1794), *The Bligh Notebook* (transcript of his journal in the open boat published in 1986 by the National Library of Australia, Canberra); *Log of HMS Bounty 1787–1789* (facsimile edition, London, 1976); *Journal of James Morrison,* Boatswain's Mate, ed. Owen Rutter (London, 1935); *The Voyage of the Bounty's Launch, Bligh's Despatch to the Admiralty,* and the *Journal of John Fryer,* ed. Owen Rutter (London, 1934); *A Book of the Bounty by William Bligh and Others,* ed. George Mackaness (London, 1938). Also *The Court Martial of the Bounty Mutineers,* ed. Owen Rutter (London, 1931); George Mackaness, *The Life of Vice Admiral William Bligh, R.N.* (revised edition, London, 1951); Gavin Kennedy, *Bligh;* Charles Nordhoff, *The Bounty Trilogy* (Boston, 1930); Alexander McKee, *HMS Bounty* (New York, 1962); John Barrow, *The Eventful History of the Mutiny on HMS Bounty* (London, 1831; Boston, 1980); Richard Hough, *Captain Bligh and Mr. Christian* (New York, 1973).

Chapter Three

By virtue of their scholarship and liveliness, if not scrupulous objectivity, such contributions to the field as those of Rolf Du Reitz in successive volumes of *Studia Bountyana,* vols. 1 and 2 (Upsalla, Sweden, 1966) and Madge Darby in *Who Caused the Mutiny on the Bounty?* (Sydney, 1965), compel attention. Barrow, *Eventful History,* first revealed Midshipman Heywood's letter with its curious reference to Christian's disclosure of "other circumstances connected with that unfortunate disaster." Darby, *Who Caused?* and Hough, *Captain Bligh,* propose the explanation of a homosexual contretemps. D. Bonner Smith, "Some Remarks About the Mutiny on the Bounty," *The Mariner's Mirror* (vol. 22, no. 2, April 1936), suggests Christian's venereal disease. (Also see Smith, "More Light on Bligh and the Bounty," *Mariner's Mirror* [vol. 23, no. 2, April 1937]). C. S. Wilkinson, *The Wake of the Bounty* (London, 1953), examines the evidence for Christian's escape from Pitcairn and secret survival in his homeland. The concentration of scholars upon the wealth of primary research material in Australia and the United Kingdom has produced a tendency to overlook American sources. Unpublished letters of or about Bligh rest within more than one of the scattered hoards of Sir Joseph Banks's papers in the United States and Canada. The more than seven thousand Banks documents at Sutro Library, San Francisco (microcopy at the American Philosophical Society, Philadelphia), contain much new information on the breadfruit project, and a letter to the botanist from James Wiles, gardening superintendent at Jamaica, 3 June 1796, refers to "plants . . . lost by [Bligh's] obstinacy." A letter from Bligh to Banks, submitting a draft of his response to Edwin Christian's pamphlet, is found in the Gratz Collection, Historical Society of Pennsylvania, Philadelphia. The same group contains a letter Bligh wrote to Banks immediately after the Battle of Copenhagen, which, among other things, attests to his solicitude for the wounded under his command. Also in this collection is the torn fragment establishing that from the *Bounty's* halt at the Cape of Good Hope in June 1788, if not earlier, Fletcher Christian was not considered "acting lieutenant" on the *Bounty.*

Chapter Four

For accounts of the mutinies both at Spithead and The Nore, the following were consulted: Conrad Gill, *The Naval Mutinies of 1797* (Manchester, 1913); Anthony, *Revolt at Sea;* William J. Neale, *History of the Mutiny at Spithead and the Nore* (London, 1842); John Barrow, *Life of Howe* (London, 1888); Earl of Camperdown, *Life of Admiral Duncan* (London, 1898); Lawrence James, *Mutiny in the British and Commonwealth Forces, 1797–1956* (London, 1987); and James Dugan, *The Great Mutiny* (New York, 1965), the latter two drawing usefully on Admiralty documents found in the Public Records Office, London. The lower-deck letter complaining of "the tiriant of a captain" is in G. E. Manwaring and B. Dobrée, *The Floating Republic* (London, 1935). Records and correspondence of the naval nobility—Bridport, Howe, Spencer, et al.—and seamen's petitions were published in *Mariner's Mirror* (vol. 21, 1935).

Chapter Five

"The Age of Reason was at last resolved" is in Gill, *Naval Mutinies,* and for U.S. envoy Rufus King's assertion that British sailors had "heard so much of the Equality and Rights of Man" see his 20 May and 5 June 1797 letters, Diplomatic Dispatches, State Department Records, National Archives, Washington, D.C. Earl Howe's own views on the disorders at Spithead and The Nore are expressed in nine letters to Sir Roger Curtis, May–August 1797, at the Huntington Library, San Marino, California. Military reaction ashore to the Nore mutiny is described in the diary of Col. William Gore, National Maritime Museum, London. Also see D. Bonner Smith, "The Mutiny at the Nore, 1797," *Mariner's Mirror* (vol. 33, 1947). Master's Mate Hardy's letters from HMS *Nassau* appear in Christopher Lloyd, "New Light on the Mutiny at the Nore," *Mariner's Mirror* (vol. 54).

Chapter Six

Nelson's observations to Jervis, Earl St. Vincent, on the propriety of Sunday hangings are in *Letters and Despatches of Horatio, Lord Nelson,* ed. Sir N. H. Nicolas (London, 1846). Jervis's problems with mutineers are related in G. J. Marcus, *The Age of Nelson* (London, 1971). The fullest account of the *Hermione* mutiny is Dudley Pope, *The Black Ship* (London, 1963). Also see Rodger, *Wooden World,* and James, *Mutiny.* How Boatswain's Mate Thomas Nash figured in American political affairs is told in Edgar Thompson, "Saga of a Mutineer," *Mariner's Mirror* (vol. 53), and there is more on John Watson, another ex-*Hermione* seeking refuge under American colors, in Leonard F. Guttridge and Jay D. Smith, *The Commodores* (Annapolis, 1984). For the *Temeraire* see *All The Year Round,* ed. Charles Dickens, 23 November 1867.

Salt pickle was "applied to lacerated shoulders" of the men on HMS *Nereide,* according to C. Lloyd, *The British Seaman* (London, 1968).

Chapter Seven

For Commodore Truxtun and occurrences on the *Congress,* see James E. Valle, *Rocks and Shoals* (Annapolis, 1980), and Records of Naval Court Martials, National Archives, Washington, D.C. The case of Seaman Quinn, branded and flogged, is detailed in *Naval Documents Related to the United States Wars With The Barbary Powers* (Washington, 1939–45, vol. IV). Christopher McKee, "Fantasies of Mutiny and Murder," *Armed Forces Society* (vol. 4, no. 2, February 1978), cites the incident while speculating upon "the fascination that [the *Hermione* mutiny] held for seamen in the U.S. Navy." Valle, *Rocks and Shoals,* offers a review of early attempts to legislate "the Better Government of the Navy." For David Porter in the Marquesas and the *Serangapatam* mutiny see Guttridge and Smith, *The Commodores.* Alexander Slidell [Mackenzie's] unsuccessful effort to secure a place on the South Seas Exploring Expedition was traced through his and Thomas Ap Catesby Jones's correspondence with the secretary of the navy, Navy Department Records, National Archives, Washington, D.C. See Howard Chapelle, *The History of the American Sailing Navy* (New York, 1949), for details on the USS *Somers.* For Mackenzie as travel writer see his *A Year in Spain* and *Spain Revisited,* and as critic of the naval status quo see his *Popular Essays on Naval Subjects* and contributions to *Quarterly Review* (1836) and *Naval Magazine* (January 1837, vol. II, no. 6). The portrait of Mackenzie as commander and disciplinarian is drawn from his letter to the secretary of the navy and the log of the *Somers,* Navy Department Records, National Archives, Washington, D.C. Also see Solomon H. Sanborn's pamphlet, "An Exposition of Official Tyranny" in the Navy Department Library, Naval Historical Center, Washington, D.C. There is also a small collection there of papers donated by Spencer Murray that detail the release of the seamen Mackenzie had arrested as alleged mutineers.

Chapter Eight

For this account of what is sometimes misrepresented as the American navy's "only mutiny" I consulted Frederic F. Van de Water, *The Captain Called It Mutiny* (New York, 1954); Philip McFarland, *Sea Dangers, The Affair Of The Somers* (New York, 1985); Hanson W. Baldwin, *Sea Fights and Shipwrecks* (New York, 1954); Samuel Eliot Morison, *Old Bruin* (Boston, 1967); Edward L. Beach, *The United States Navy, 200 Years* (New York, 1986); *Proceedings of the Court of Inquiry into the Intended Mutiny on the Somers* (New York, 1843); Harrison Hayford, *The Somers Mutiny Affair* (Englewood Cliffs, New Jersey, 1959); Herman Melville, *Whitejacket* (Boston, 1950); Herman Melville, *Billy Budd, Foretopman* (New York, 1962); "Reminiscences of Philip Spencer,"

United Services Magazine (Ser. 2, IV, July 1890); J. Fenimore Cooper, *The Cruise of the Somers, Despotism on the Quarterdeck* (New York, 1944); Charles Sumner, "Mutiny on the Somers," *North American Review* (LVII, July 1843); "The Murder of Philip Spencer," *Cosmopolitan Magazine* (June–August 1889); Livingston Hunt, "The Alleged Mutiny on the U.S. Brig Somers," *U.S. Naval Institute Proceedings* (November 1925); A. J. Liebling, "The Navy's Only Mutiny," *New Yorker* (18 February 1939); and Proceedings of the Court Martial [of] Alexander Slidell Mackenzie, original transcript in National Archives. Unpublished materials seen include Mackenzie's correspondence with Bullus, Duer, and Gallatin in the New York Historical Society and with the secretary of the navy in National Archives; also the letters of Henry Rodgers, midshipman on the *Somers,* in John Rodgers papers, Historical Society of Pennsylvania, Philadelphia. Portions of the logs of the *Dolphin* while under Mackenzie's command, June–October 1838, and of the *Somers,* 14 September–19 November, are in the same Rodgers Collection.

Chapter Nine

For charting the ponderous controversy that accompanied and followed Mackenzie's court-martial, Hayford, *The Somers Mutiny Affair,* proved a most useful guide. Simon Cameron to John C. Spencer, 29 January 1843, on Mackenzie's "cowardly butchery" is at the Historical Society of Pennsylvania, and Mackenzie's correspondence with Francis Lieber is at The Huntington Library, San Marino, California. For the *Warren* mutiny see Valle, *Rocks and Shoals,* and that on the *Ewing* is detailed in *Army and Navy Journal* (7 March 1878); George Davidson, "Mutiny on the Ewing," *California Historical Society Quarterly* (vol. 30, no. 1, March 1951); and Emmans and Votaw, "The Ewing Mutiny," U.S. Naval Institute *Proceedings* (January 1956). The dispute between Lieutenant Prentiss and Captain Smoot is described in Valle, *Rocks and Shoals,* and is fully traceable in naval court-martial records and Navy Department correspondence, National Archives. For the trouble on the *Ocean Queen* see Charles Dana Gibson, "Ocean Queen," *Sea Classics* (vol. 20, no. 3, May 1987); *Official Records of the Union and Confederate Navies* (Ser. 1, vol. 3); and the proceedings of Commander Ammen's trial, naval court-martial records, National Archives. Lionel Yexley's career and the Royal Navy's lower-deck societies are detailed in E. Rasor, *Reform in the Royal Navy: Social History of the Lower Deck* (London, 1976); Stanley Bennett, *The Price of Admiralty* (London, 1968); and Anthony B. Carew, *Lower Deck of the Royal Navy, 1900–39* (Manchester, 1981).

Chapter Ten

The following were studied: Wintringham, *Mutiny;* Richard A. Hough, *The Potemkin Mutiny* (London, 1981); F. T. Jane, *The Imperial Russian Navy* (London, 1899); Anthony, *Revolt at Sea;* Constantin Feldman, *The Revolt of the*

Potemkin (London, 1908); A. Kamatchikov, *Revolt on the Armoured Cruiser Potemkin* (London, 1932); and U.S. consul dispatches from Odessa, 1905, State Department Records, National Archives. Also see Elihu Rose, "Mutiny on the Potemkin," *Military History Quarterly* (vol. 1, no. 1, Autumn 1988). For the Eisenstein motion picture see Herbert Marshall, ed., *The Battleship Potemkin* (New York, 1978); D. Mayer, *Sergei Eisenstein's Potemkin* (New York, 1972); and Daniel Gerould, "The Political Mutiny: Historical Simulation," *The Dramatic Review* (Summer, 1980).

Chapter Eleven

The earliest volumes of Ray Shepherd's *Our Navy* may be seen at the Library of Congress, Washington, D.C. For the unrest on HMS *Zealandia,* see Carew, *Lower Deck,* also the *Times* (London, 27 March 1914), and that same newspaper (25–26 May 1914) for the libel case against Yexley. His memorandum portraying the British navy's lower deck as "one great combustible mass" is in A. J. Marder, *From the Dreadnought to Scapa Flow,* vol. 5 (New York, 1970). "A match would have touched off an explosion," according to G. Lambert, M. P., Parliamentary Debates, *Hansard* (12 March 1919). The naval role in Russia's upheaval is well described in Normal Saul, *Sailors in Revolt: The Russian Baltic Fleet in 1917* (Lawrence, Kansas, 1978); Evan Mawdsley, *The Russian Revolution and the Baltic Fleet* (New York, 1978); and James Mavor, *Russian Revolution* (London, 1928). Also see J. D. Hayes, "Three Modern Naval Mutinies," U.S. Naval Institute *Proceedings* (September 1939), and Wintringham, *Mutiny.* For the two German naval mutinies that hastened the end of the First World War see David Woodward, *The Collapse of Power* (London, 1979); A. J. Ryder, *The German Revolution of 1918* (Cambridge, England, 1967); Daniel Horn, *The German Naval Mutinies of World War One* (Brunswick, New Jersey, 1969); Wintringham, *Mutiny;* H. H. Herwig, *Luxury Fleet: The Imperial German Navy 1888–1918* (London, 1980); Reinhard Scheer, *Germany's High Seas Fleet in the World War* (New York, 1934); Charles Vidil, *Les Mutineries de la Marine Allemande* (Paris, 1931); and Hayes, "Three Modern Naval Mutinies." W. H. Maehl, *German Militarism and Socialism,* and G. Roth, *The Social Democrats in Imperial Germany* (New York, 1963), were valuable for etching in the political background.

Chapter Twelve

P. G. Plaschka, *Cattaro-Prag* (Graz, Austria, 1963) details the mutiny in Adriatic waters. For the final days of Germany's High Seas Fleet see Anthony, *Revolt at Sea;* Hayes, "Three Modern Naval Mutinies"; Schubert and Gibson, *Death of a Fleet 1917–1919* (New York, 1932); G. Frederich Ruge, *Scapa Flow 1918* (London, 1973); and Dan Van der Vat, *The Grand Scuttle* (Annapolis, 1985). The matelots' rebellion against involvement in Russia's fratricide is detailed in

Wintringham, *Mutiny;* André Marty, *La Révolte de la Mer Noire* (Paris, 1932); and J. Le Ramey, *Mutins de la Mer Noire* (Paris, 1973). For reaction in Paris see *The New York Times* (14–15 June 1919). D. Lloyd George, *War Memoirs* vol. 2 (London, 1938), summarizes the Allies' rationale for intervening. British naval discontent at this period is described in Stanley Bennett, *The Price of Admiralty* (London, 1968), and Geoffrey Bennett, *Cowan's War* (London, 1964). Also see Edmund Ironside, *Archangel 1918–1919* (London, 1953) and B. D. Rhodes, *The Anglo-American Winter War with Russia, 1918–1919* (New York, 1988). That American lower ranks were by no means free of a near-mutinous resentment against immersion in Russia's internal affairs is indicated by War Department Military Intelligence Division memoranda of 19 June 1919 and 13 December 1919 on the subject "Mutiny Among the American Troops of the N.R.E.F.," Records of the War Department General and Special Staffs, National Archives, Washington, D.C. Also see *New York Call*, 17 April 1919. For the Kronstadt fighting see Alexander Berkman, *The Kronstadt Rebellion* (Berlin, 1922); Paul Avrich, *Kronstadt 1921* (Princeton, 1970); the London *Times* (30 March 1921); and *The New York Times* (27 and 31 March 1921).

Chapter Thirteen

For the warning that low pay scales threatened "disaster" to the U.S. Navy, see *The New York Times* (9 April 1920). Successive editorials in *Our Navy* show the consistency of that journal's theme that the navy was riddled with discontent. Note in particular its April and May 1921 issues. Data on Capt. Daniel Stearns is in the biography files, Naval Operational Archives, Naval Historical Center, Washington, D.C., and on Edwin Denby in P. E. Coletta, ed., *American Secretaries of the Navy* vol. 2 (Annapolis, 1980). Documents on Captain Stearns's controversial practices on the *Roanoke* and *Michigan* are in Records of the Secretary of the Navy and of the Office of Naval Intelligence, National Archives. See *The New York Times* (23 June 1921) for ex-Secretary Daniel's views. *Army and Navy Register* (16 April 1921) and *The New York Times* (24–25 June 1921) discourse upon the dangers of "sovietism" in the navy. Secretary Denby's circular of 5 April 1922 "to the Naval Service," warning of a "sinister propaganda," was prompted by a copy, sent him via military intelligence, of a "special report" dated 17 February 1922 that Walter J. Burns, head of the Justice Department, had placed before his chief aide, J. Edgar Hoover. It purported to quote from a secret letter signed by Grigori Zinoviev, chairman of the Communist party in Moscow, exhorting agents in capitalist countries to devote particular attention to navies because it was common knowledge that "sailors are least of all subject to subordination and are very much inclined to insubordination and disorders." See Records of the War Department, Military Intelligence Division, National Archives. My account of the Brazilian mutinies is derived from *The New York Times* (22–28 November and 13 December 1910 and 7 January 1911) and from Records of the Department of State, Diplomatic and Consular Dispatches,

Rio de Janeiro, 1910 and 1924. See in particular the report of the U.S. naval attaché in Brazil of 12 November 1924. The mutiny on HMS *Lucia* has served British naval historians as sort of a prelude to Invergordon, and for further reading on this event, also the economic factors leading to trouble in the Atlantic Fleet, see the titles listed in the notes for the following chapter. The Chilean naval uprising was reported in *The New York Times* (6–9 September 1931) and in a critical tone by the U.S. military attaché in his confidential reports from Santiago of 2, 3, and 11 September 1931. For a detailed account see William F. Sater, "Chilean Naval Mutiny of 1931," *Hispanic-American Historical Review* (May 1980).

Chapter Fourteen

The first significant account of the Royal Navy's most serious internal crisis since Spithead and The Nore was Comdr. Kenneth Edwards, *The Mutiny at Invergordon* (London, 1937). Post–Second World War studies have tended to adopt more of a lower-deck perspective and profit from the unlocking of private and official documentation. Len Wincott, *Invergordon Mutineer* (London, 1974) is a bold elaboration of his *Spirit of Invergordon* (London, 1931). Carew, *Lower Deck,* is sufficiently detailed and important to be nearly definitive on the subject, but for a thorough picture of what went on both in Cromarty Firth and the halls of the Admiralty the following should also be consulted: A. D. Divine, *Mutiny at Invergordon* (London, 1970); Barry Duncan, *Invergordon '31* (London, 1976); and Alan Ereire, *The Invergordon Mutiny* (London, 1981). There is significant light on Tomkinson and the attitudes of his fellow admirals in *Naval Record Society Roger Keyes Correspondence 1919–1938* vol. 2 (London, 1979). For the attention paid Invergordon and other instances of naval unrest by British Intelligence, see Nigel West, *MI5: British Secret Service Operations 1909–1945* (London, 1981). Also see Fred Copeman, *Reason in Revolt* (London, 1948); James, *Mutiny;* Hayes, "Three Naval Mutinies"; Charles Petrie, *The Life and Letters of Sir Austen Chamberlain* (London, 1940); S. W. Roskill, *Naval Policy between the Wars,* vol. 2 (London, 1976); and letters to the *Times* (October–November 1971) from S. W. Roskill, Len Wincott, and Comdr. Harry Pursey.

Chapter Fifteen

British high-level opinion that "grousing" had become "fashionable" with "too much talk of privileges" among British seamen is noted in Carew, *Lower Deck,* and the footless effort to subvert them reported in the London *Times* (17 October and 27 November 1931). The *De Zeven Provincien* episode is drawn from contemporary newspapers; Anthony, *Sailors in Revolt;* and Javanicus, "Mutiny in the South Seas," *The Living Age* (July 1934). For American concern over alleged subversion in the U.S. Navy, see Hearings, House Committee on Un-American Activities, and especially testimony before the House Committee on Naval Affairs in consideration of a *Bill to Punish For Exerting Mutinous Influence Upon the Army and the Navy*, July 1935. Churchill's recommended therapy for fatigued destroyermen is in a letter to his naval staff, 12 December 1939, *The Second World War: The Gathering Storm* (London, 1948). Material on the American navy's developing racial policies and problems is drawn from Dennis Nelson, *The Integration of the Negro into the U.S. Navy* (New York, 1951), and L. D. Reddick, "The Negro in the United States Navy During World War Two," *Journal of Negro History* vol. XXXII, no. 2 (April 1947). Causes of the Port Chicago explosion are discussed in chief, Bureau of Ordinance to secretary of the navy, 14 November 1945; Bureau of Ordinance Circular, March 1945; and proceedings of the Court of Inquiry, with findings, opinions, and recommendations, Records of the Judge Advocate General of the Navy, all at Naval Historical Center, Washington, D.C., at which location should also be seen the Port Chicago Naval Magazine, *War Diary*, Naval Operational Archives.

Chapter Sixteen

The proceedings of the Port Chicago court-martial are in Records of the Judge Advocate General of the Navy and contain both the judge's trial brief on the law concerning mutiny and Thurgood Marshall's statement to the Judge Advocate General of 3 April 1945. Letters on the case from Marshall, Admiral Wright of the Twelfth Naval District, and Eleanor Roosevelt to the secretary of the navy are in James Forrestal Papers, Naval Operational Archives, Naval Historical Center, Washington, D.C. Also see Robert L. Allen, *The Port Chicago Mutiny* (New York, 1989), and Charles Wollenberg, "The Mare Island 'Mutiny,'" *San Francisco Examiner and Chronicle* (22 July 1979). The mystery and beauty of "a ship on the bosom of the sea" is recalled by Edward L. Beach, *The United States Navy, 200 Years* (New York, 1986), and the reference to pride as a bulwark against mutiny is from C. A. Piggot, "Mutiny—Prevention Better Than Cure," *Naval Review* no. 62 (1974). For the account of a self-confessed mutineer on HMS *Lothian*, see Bill Glenton, *Mutiny in Force X* (London, 1986). The Royal Marines war diary Glenton quotes from is in Public Records Office, London. Additional material on the sad fortunes of Force X is found in the papers of U.S. Seventh Fleet commander Adm. Thomas Kinkaid and commander of the Seventh Amphibious Force Adm. Daniel Barbey, Naval Operational Archives, Naval Historical Center, Washington, D.C. See also John Winton, *Forgotten Fleet* (London, 1969); *Command History, Seventh Amphibious Force* (1945); Daniel Barbey, *MacArthur's Amphibious Navy* (Annapolis, 1969); Admiral of the Fleet Viscount Cunningham, *A Sailor's Odyssey* (New York, 1951); and Office of Naval Intelligence, *Allied Landing Craft of World War Two* (Washington, 1944).

Chapter Seventeen

Correspondence about the morale aboard the USS *Kilty* and elsewhere in the U.S. Navy's Pacific force is found in Admiral Barbey's papers at the Naval

Historical Center. The discontent among U.S. troops awaiting demobilization was widely reported in the press in January 1946. Also see R. Alton Lee, "The Army 'Mutiny' of 1946," *Journal of American History* (December 1966). A reference to the *Javelin* mutiny dated 26 December 1945 appears in Records of the Chief of Naval Operations, Naval Intelligence Reports, National Archives, which collection also contains the Ottawa-based envoy's dire listing of naval types "susceptible to subversive influence." For the troubles on Canadian warships see *Maclean's Magazine* (5 March 1985); *The New York Times* (27 March 1949); and Department of National Defense, *Report on Certain Incidents Which Occurred on HMC Ships,* etc. (Ottawa, 1949). For the brief digression on the continuing absence of a uniformly acceptable definition of mutiny, the following were consulted: Stephen T. Banning, *Military Law* (London, 1952); Edward M. Byrne, *Military Law* (Annapolis, 1981); *United States Courts of Military Appeals* vols. 4 (1953) and 12 (1960); *Court Martial Reports* vols. 30 and 42; and *Manual for Courts Martial,* United States, 1951 and 1984 editions.

Chapter Eighteen

While Neil Sheehan, *The Arnheiter Affair* (New York, 1971) affords a detailed coverage of this sad episode, anyone left unconvinced of its balance and objectivity might wish to examine the captain's earnest presentation of his own case, the letter (unpublished) to Secretary of the Navy Ignatius, 1 September 1967, original in Records of the Office of the Chief of Naval Operations, Naval Historical Center, Washington, D.C. *The New York Times* ran Sheehan's stories on the Resnick hearings on 9, 10, 12 (titled "Shades of the Caine Mutiny"), and 14 May 1968, with a fuller article, "The 99 Days of Captain Arnheiter" (containing the operations officer's "I'm not proud of what I did"), on 11 August 1968. Resnick sharply responded in *The New York Times* on 15 September 1968. Thoughts on the "Nuremberg principle" were in part prompted by James S. May, professor of law, University of Baltimore, letter in the *Washington Post* (6 February 1991). The development of the UCMJ is described in William T. Generous, Jr., *Swords and Scales* (New York, 1973). For the war protesters' campaign to keep the *Constellation* at home see *San Diego Union* (19–21 September 1971); Annual Command Histories, *USS Constellation,* Ships' History Division, Naval Historical Center, Washington, D.C.; and testimony of Adm. Bernard A. Clarey, *Hearings Before the Special Subcommittee on Disciplinary Problems in the United States Navy of the Committee on Armed Services, House of Representatives, Ninety-second Congress, Second Session.* There is more on the underground antimilitary press in Len Guttridge, "Mass Mutiny in the Military," *Saga* (October 1969). For Asian combat background see Mersky and Polmar, *Naval Air War in Vietnam* (Annapolis, 1981). The warning of "depersonalization of the fleet" appears in Rear Adm. Arleigh Burke, "Discipline in the United States Navy," *Naval Officers Manual* (Harrisburg, 1955). The figures on sabotage incidents in the Pacific fleet are in *Hearings,* pp. 912–914. Also see *The New York Times* (6

November 1972). "Kitty Litter" is quoted in *Hearings,* p. 529. For the Z-grams, their nature and purpose, see Elmo Zumwalt, *On Watch* (New York, 1978), and the controversy over Zumwalt's appointment is partly detailed in Lt. Comdr. Robert M. Ancell, USNR, "The Path to Four Stars," U.S. Naval Institute *Proceedings* (January 1981).

Chapter Nineteen

Media coverage was appropriately ominous. Drew Middleton, "Disciplinary Crisis Feared In Navy" and "Severe Storm Warnings," *The New York Times* (22 and 26 November 1972) were quickly followed by "Storm Warnings," *Time* (11 December 1972). The official sources most frequently consulted for my reconstruction of events aboard the *Kitty Hawk* and *Constellation* are *Hearings,* with the Subcommittee's *Report; Findings of Fact, Formal One-Officer Investigation Into Racial Violence on the Kitty Hawk,* 18 November 1972; and *Report, Informal Investigation of Group Protest aboard the USS Constellation, 7 January 1973,* the latter two documents among Records of the Judge Advocate General of the Navy, National Archives, Suitland, Maryland. The dental officer's "I took abuse" is in his testimony, *Hearings.* The *Constellation Report* questions the wisdom of Captain Ward's permitting an open forum but commends his decision not to appear before the dissidents on the mess deck. For Ward's strategy to contain the trouble, and Chaplain Schneider on mutiny's "development levels," see their testimony, *Hearings.* Growing tensions on the *Forrestal* are described in Zumwalt, *On Watch,* and testimony of Roger T. Kelley, *Hearings.*

Chapter Twenty

The *San Diego Union* (7–9 November 1972) reported events at North Island. The dilemma posed by the *Constellation*'s beach detachment is impossible to miss in Zumwalt, *On Watch; Constellation Report;* and relevant testimony, *Hearings.* For comment on Ward's "mannerisms" see Capt. William E. Cross, testimony, *Hearings.* Also consulted were H. P. Leiferman, "A Sort of Mutiny," *The New York Times Magazine* (18 February 1973); Capt. Paul B. Bryan, "The Constellation Flare-up, Was It Mutiny?" U.S. Naval Institute *Proceedings* (January 1976). That a secretary of the navy would consider the carrier disturbances as "real mutinies" is in John F. Lehman, *Command of the Seas* (New York, 1988). Zumwalt's "dressing down" of allegedly foot-dragging admirals was reported in most newspapers and detailed in *Hearings.* That Henry Kissinger "all but shrieked" at the chief of naval operations is recalled in Zumwalt, *On Watch.* For the U.S. Navy's subsequent programs to secure fairness and racial harmony see *Study Group Report on Equal Opportunity in the Navy,* Office of the Chief of Naval Operations, United States Navy, 1988.

Chapter Twenty-One

The *Velos* mutiny was reported in *The New York Times* (27–29 May 1973). Valery Sablin's foredoomed attempt to make off with the *Storozhevoy* was researched by Lt. Comdr. Gregory Young, USN, for the thesis *Mutiny on Storozhevoy: A Case Study in the Soviet Navy,* which earned him his master's degree from the Naval Postgraduate School, Monterey, California. Also see *People* magazine (16 September 1985); Thomas B. Allen and Norman Polmar, "The Hunt for the *Storozhevoy*: Red October Almost Happened," *Sea Power* vol. 28 no. 1 (January 1985); and "The Real 'Red October,'" *World Press Review* (May 1990), based on an article in *Komsomolskaya Pravda,* Moscow. The screen sergeant major who so succinctly conveyed the elusive near-mythic character of mutiny—"Like the Loch Ness Monster. Heard of it but. . . ."—was Richard Attenborough in *Guns at Batasi* (1964). General MacArthur's observation on morale was in *Annual Report: Chief of Staff,* U.S. Army, 1933. The warning against complacency about discipline came from Adm. Sir Richard Onslow, R.N., Plymouth, U.K., 1958, quoted in C. A. Piggot, "Mutiny—Prevention Better Than Cure," *Naval Review* no. 62 (1974). The unionizing of armies and navies was discussed in Lieutenants Kane, et al., "Is Military Unionization An Idea Whose Time Has Come?" U.S. Naval Institute *Proceedings* (November and December 1976). Additional information is in Clyde Weber, testimony before the Defense Manpower Commission on "Organizing the Military into a Union," Washington, D.C., 18 April 1975, and telephone conversation with Military Attaché, Embassy of Germany, May 1991. The caustic view of unionized armed forces as "licensed mutiny" comes from British Tory politician Michael Heseltine, as reported in the *Washington Post* (November 1990), and the British magazine feature on how to identify and deal with an incipient mutiny is Piggot, "Mutiny—Prevention Better Than Cure."

Index

ABOUT THE AUTHOR

A native of Cardiff, Wales, Leonard F. Guttridge served throughout the Second World War in Britain's Royal Air Force. Long resident in the United States, he has written short stories and articles on topics as diverse as jazz music and labor history. Both Time-Life's Giants of Jazz record series and the Smithsonian Institution's Big Band Jazz albums feature his essays. He wrote *The Great Coalfield War* with George S. McGovern, and with Jay D. Smith, *The Commodores*. This last book, credited with having great general appeal as well as scholarly influence, has been reprinted in the Naval Institute's Classics of Naval Literature collection. Guttridge is also the author of *Icebound: The Jeannette Expedition's Quest for the North Pole* (NIP, 1986), which was received with widespread and enthusiastic acclaim.

THE NAVAL INSTITUTE PRESS is the book-publishing arm of the U.S. Naval Institute, a private, nonprofit, membership society for sea service professionals and others who share an interest in naval and maritime affairs. Established in 1873 at the U.S. Naval Academy in Annapolis, Maryland, where its offices remain today, the Naval Institute has members worldwide.

Members of the Naval Institute support the education programs of the society and receive the influential monthly magazine *Proceedings* and discounts on fine nautical prints and on ship and aircraft photos. They also have access to the transcripts of the Institute's Oral History Program and get discounted admission to any of the Institute-sponsored seminars offered around the country. Discounts are also available to the colorful bimonthly magazine *Naval History*.

The Naval Institute's book-publishing program, begun in 1898 with basic guides to naval practices, has broadened its scope to include books of more general interest. Now the Naval Institute Press publishes about seventy titles each year, ranging from how-to books on boating and navigation to battle histories, biographies, ship and aircraft guides, and novels. Institute members receive significant discounts on the Press's more than eight hundred books in print.

Full-time students are eligible for special half-price membership rates. Life memberships are also available.

For a free catalog describing Naval Institute Press books currently available, and for further information about subscribing to *Naval History* magazine or about joining the U.S. Naval Institute, please write to:

Member Services
U.S. NAVAL INSTITUTE
291 Wood Road
Annapolis, MD 21402-5034
Telephone: (800) 233-8764
Fax: (410) 571-1703
Web address: *www.navalinstitute.org*

THE NAVAL INSTITUTE PRESS
MUTINY
A History of Naval Insurrection
Designed by Pamela Lewis Schnitter

Set in Galliard and Ragtime
by TCSystems, Inc.,
Shippensburg, Pennsylvania

Printed on 60-lb. S.D. Warren Sebago eggshell cream
and bound in Holliston Kingston Natural
by The Maple-Vail Book Manufacturing Group
York, Pennsylvania